CHAUCER AND MEDIEVAL ESTATES SATIRE

CHAUCER AND MEDIEVAL ESTATES SATIRE

The Literature of Social Classes and
the *General Prologue* to the *Canterbury Tales*

JILL MANN

CAMBRIDGE

AT THE UNIVERSITY PRESS

1973

Published by the Syndics of the Cambridge University Press
Bentley House, 200 Euston Road, London NW1 2DB
American Branch: 32 East 57th Street, New York, N.Y. 10022

Library of Congress Catalogue Card Number: 72–90490

ISBNS: 0 521 20058 X hard covers
0 521 09795 9 paperback

Printed in Great Britain
by The Anchor Press Ltd
Tiptree, Essex

TO MY PARENTS
EDWARD WILLIAM AND KATHLEEN DITCHBURN

Quha wait if all that Chaucer wrait was trew?
Henryson

Contents

CONTENTS

x

Preface

This book is an attempt to discover the origins and significance of the *General Prologue* to the *Canterbury Tales*. The interest of such an inquiry, as I hope will become clear, is many-sided. On the one hand, it throws light on the question of whether 'life' or 'literature' was Chaucer's model in this work, on the relationship between Chaucer's twenty-odd pilgrims and the structure of medieval society, and on the role of their 'estate' in determining the elements of which Chaucer composes their portraits. On the other hand, it makes suggestions about the ways in which Chaucer convinces us of the individuality of his pilgrims, about the nature of his irony, and the kind of moral standards implicit in the *Prologue*. This leads me to suggest that Chaucer is ironically substituting for the traditional moral view of social structure a vision of a world where morality becomes as specialised to the individual as his work-life.

Although my work is not a source-study in the straightforward sense of the term, my procedure is to examine medieval satire on the 'estates' or classes of society written in Latin, French and English within the period 1100–1400. The earlier date means that I can give full prominence to the rich abundance of twelfth-century Latin satire; the latter date is set by the date of the *Prologue* itself, which is usually taken to be 1387. I have, however, included works written before 1100 if they threw light on Chaucer or estates satire, and also a few early fifteenth-century works which give an idea of the unabated continuance of this satiric tradition. A few works in medieval Italian, German and Spanish have also been used for purposes of comparison. My method is comparative, but its aim is not to use other writers merely as a foil for Chaucer, as examples of 'convention' which contrast with his individual genius. Other writers had their own aims, which shaped their selection and use of material – and I hope that it may emerge from what follows that their aims and accomplishments are much more sophisticated than is often believed. But in order to build up a general impression of the traits associated with different medieval estates, and the range of satiric methods by which they are presented, I have had to deal with other writers in piecemeal fashion, and am fully conscious of not having done justice to writers of the stature of Jean de Meun or Langland. My main purpose in examining other satirists is to gain a clearer idea of Chaucer's distinctive use of estates satire, and this must stand as my excuse. If I have stimulated interest in this neglected area of medieval literature, what is inadequate here may be supplied by others.

There are many whom it is appropriate to thank here for their help and encouragement. My longest-standing debt is to those who taught me medieval literature as an undergraduate at St Anne's College, Oxford – Mrs D. Bednarowska, Miss E. Griffiths and Mrs P. Ingham. I have to thank Miss Pamela Gradon, my supervisor while I was registered as an Oxford research student, not only for suggesting the subject of this study to me, but also for her patience and helpfulness during the years that I was working with her, and for reading parts of the manuscript after our formal relationship had ceased. The last eighteen months of my work on this book were done in Cambridge under the supervision of Peter Dronke, to whom I am indebted for unfailing interest, stimulating comment, and great generosity with books, advice and time. In these warm thanks Ursula Dronke must also share. I am also grateful to Dr D. S. Brewer for reading and commenting on parts of this study, and for his prompt invitation, when I arrived in Cambridge, to the medieval graduate seminar, to which, as to the Cambridge Medieval Society, I read a paper on this subject, and received helpful comments. In slightly different form, this study was submitted for a Cambridge Ph.D., and I must also thank its examiners, D. A. Pearsall and A. C. Spearing, for stimulating comment. Clare Hall, Cambridge, awarded me a Research Fellowship in 1968, and gave me welcome financial support.

Finally, I should like to thank my husband, to whom I owe not only intellectual debts, but also the recognition that my work was as important as his.

J.M.

List of Abbreviations

AH	*Analecta Hymnica*, ed. G. M. Dreves, C. Blume, H. M. Bannister
Am. Journ. Phil.	
	American Journal of Philology
Anglo-Latin Satirical Poets	
	The Anglo-Latin Satirical Poets and Epigrammatists of the Twelfth Century, ed. T. Wright
BM	British Museum
BN	Bibliothèque Nationale
Bowden, *Commentary*	
	M. Bowden, *A Commentary on the General Prologue to the Canterbury Tales*
CB	*Carmina Burana*, ed. A. Hilka and O. Schumann
CFMA	Classiques Français du Moyen Âge
Chaucer Concordance	
	J. S. P. Tatlock and A. G. Kennedy, *A Concordance to the Complete Works of Geoffrey Chaucer and to the Romaunt of the Rose*
CT	*Canterbury Tales*
DA	*Dissertation Abstracts (formerly Microfilm Abstracts): A Guide to Dissertations and Monographs Available in Microfilm*, Ann Arbor, Michigan, 1938–
Du Cange	
	Glossarium Mediae et Infimae Latinitatis, 10 vols., Niort and London, 1884–7
EETS o.s.	
	Early English Text Society, original series
EETS e.s.	
	Early English Text Society, extra series
EHR	*English Historical Review*
ELN	*English Language Notes*
Godefroy	
	Dictionnaire de l'Ancienne Française ... du IXe au XVe Siècle, F. Godefroy, Paris, 1881–1902
GP	*General Prologue*

Hauréau, *NE*

> B. Hauréau, *Notices et Extraits de Quelques Manuscrits Latins de la Bibliothèque Nationale*

Hist. litt. de la France

> *Histoire littéraire de la France par les religieux bénédictins de la congrégation de Saint-Maur*

JEGP   *Journal of English and Germanic Philology*

Latin Stories

> *A Selection of Latin Stories from Manuscripts of the Thirteenth and Fourteenth Centuries*, ed. T. Wright

Lit. and Pulp.

> G. R. Owst, *Literature and Pulpit in Medieval England*, 2nd edition

Map Poems

> *The Latin Poems Commonly Attributed to Walter Mapes*, ed. T. Wright

MED   *Middle English Dictionary*, ed. H. Kurath and S. M. Kuhn, Ann Arbor, Michigan, 1954–(in progress)

MLN   *Modern Language Notes*

MLR   *Modern Language Review*

MO   *Mirour de l'Omme*, ed. G. C. Macaulay, *John Gower: The French Works*, Oxford, 1899

MP   *Modern Philology*

NE   *Notices et Extraits des manuscrits de la Bibliothèque Nationale, et autres bibliothèques*

Niermeyer

> *Mediae Latinitatis Lexicon Minus*, Leiden, 1954–

NQ   *Notes and Queries*

NR   *Nouveau Recueil de Contes, Dits, Fabliaux et Autres Pièces Inédites des XIIIᵉ, XIVᵉ, et XVᵉ Siècles . . . d'Après les MSS. de la Bibliothèque du Roi*, ed. A. Jubinal

OED   *The Oxford English Dictionary . . . a corrected re-issue of A New English Dictionary on Historical Principles*, ed. J. A. H. Murray, H. Bradley, W. A. Craigie, C. T. Onions, Oxford, 1933

PL   *Patrologiae Cursus Completus*, series latina, ed. J. P. Migne

PMLA   *Publications of the Modern Language Association of America*

Poésies Pop. Lat.

> *Poésies Populaires Latines du Moyen Âge*, ed. E. du Méril

PPl   *Piers Plowman*, ed. W. W. Skeat

PPl Crede *Pierce the Ploughmans Crede*, ed. W. W. Skeat

PPS   *Political Poems and Songs*, ed. T. Wright

PQ   *Philological Quarterly*

PSE   *The Political Songs of England From the Reign of John to that of Edward II*, ed. T. Wright

Religious Orders
     D. Knowles, *The Religious Orders in England*, vol. I
RES   *Review of English Studies*
RR   *Le Roman de la Rose*, ed. F. Lecoy
SA   W. F. Bryan and G. Dempster, *Sources and Analogues of Chaucer's Canterbury Tales*
SATF Société des Anciens Textes Français
SP   *Studies in Philology*
SS   *Nigel de Longchamps: Speculum Stultorum*, ed. J. H. Mozley and R. R. Raymo
TLS   *Times Literary Supplement*
Tobler–Lommatzsch
     Altfranzösisches Wörterbuch, A. Tobler and E. Lommatzsch, Berlin, 1925–
Trans. Am. Phil. Assoc.
     Transactions of the American Philological Association
UTQ   *University of Toronto Quarterly*
VC   *Vox Clamantis*, ed. G. C. Macaulay, *John Gower: The Latin Works*
Wagenknecht
     Chaucer: Modern Essays in Criticism, ed. E. Wagenknecht
Wells, *Manual*
     J. E. Wells, *A Manual of the Writings in Middle English 1050–1400*
ZfDA *Zeitschrift für Deutsches Alterthum*

Note on References

Major works (or a manuscript collection such as the *Carmina Burana*) are cited by title; details such as their date, diffusion, author and editor can be found by referring to the discursive section of Part I of the Bibliography, under the name of the language in which they are written, and fuller details of the editions in which they are to be found are given in Part II of the Bibliography. Short poems are referred to by their title or incipit (where the title is a vague one) and editor, and are listed alphabetically in Part I of the Bibliography, with a short reference to the work in which they are printed; the latter is to be found in Part II of the Bibliography under the name of the editor. If a primary source is used only once, or only within one section of a chapter, details of its date and diffusion are given in the footnotes, in which case it will not appear in Part I of the Bibliography. Part III of the Bibliography lists secondary works cited more than once in discussion. For abbreviated references, see the List of Abbreviations. References to page or column are preceded by 'p.' or 'col.'; numbers not so prefaced are line references.

I

Introduction

How are we to describe the *General Prologue* to the *Canterbury Tales*? What does it tell us about the society it represents? It seems rather late in the day to ask these questions. For no one could claim that the *Prologue* has suffered from a lack of critical attention; on the contrary, it has long been praised as the consummate achievement of Chaucer's art.

The enthusiasm ostensibly generated for the whole of the *Prologue* often proves, however, to be excited by the few characters who provide a focus for a critic's particular interest, whether this is in their comic aspects, their psychological complexity, or the moral significance attached to them. Study of the *Prologue* has too often meant a series of partial approaches, based on the figures who most conveniently offer themselves for character analysis,[1] or for investigation of possible historical prototypes,[2] or for interpretation according to the conventional iconography of medieval art or science.[3] So it does not seem redundant to attempt to analyse the character and meaning of the *Prologue* as a whole.

In the pages that follow, I shall be claiming that the *Prologue* is an example of a neglected medieval genre – that both its form and its content proclaim it to be part of the literature dealing with the 'estates' of society. This claim needs special justification, since it is usually assumed that the *Prologue* has no source and only shadowy analogues, an assumption which probably arises from an over-limited conception of its basic form as 'a collection of portraits'. This aspect of the *Prologue* clearly cannot be ignored, and I shall discuss the portrait tradition briefly at a later stage in this book. But the *Prologue*'s form can equally well be defined as 'a satiric representation of all classes of society' – the form of an estates satire. This aspect of the *Prologue* has not escaped notice, but its recognition has never instigated close and thorough investigation of estates satire in relation to Chaucer's work.[4] When estates satire has been used, it has been as supplementary evidence in a historically-oriented examination of fourteenth-century society.

[1] The notes appear between pages 213 and 294.

That is, the relationship between Chaucer and other estates satirists has most often been taken to be their common source of material in life itself.[5]

The 'real-life' basis of the *Prologue* was propounded most strongly in J. M. Manly's influential book, *Some New Light on Chaucer*.[6] In attempting to identify some of the Canterbury pilgrims with real fourteenth-century persons, Manly emphasised Chaucer's direct experience of the world around him as the source of his creation, and expressed his dislike of the 'abhorrent doctrine that [Chaucer] built up his matchless pictures of human life entirely by piecing together scraps from old books, horoscopes, astrological and physiological generalizations' (p. 263). But a literature–life antithesis would be misleading, as I shall try to show later, and though my approach differs from that of Manly, it is not inevitably opposed to it. Meanwhile, we may note that Manly's description of Chaucer's method of character-drawing – 'From the experiences and observations of his life, his imagination derived the material for its creative processes' – can bear elaboration. Even if the basis for the Canterbury pilgrims *was* Chaucer's observation of real people, we should still have to discuss and analyse the literary techniques by which he re-created them for his readers. And we should still need to consider the literary aim which animates this re-creation.

Manly's own approach to the *Prologue* was confessedly partial; he thought it likely that many of the characters were not meant to be identifiable.[7] He also concluded his study by remarking that in any case, Chaucer's character-drawing was never undertaken for its own sake, but always 'with strict reference to the requirements of his art' (p. 292). Manly did not specify more precisely how he thought these requirements determined the character-drawing of the pilgrims;[8] in fact this comment seems inconsistent with his earlier suggestion that Chaucer's selection of classes for inclusion in the *Prologue* was made on the basis of his own 'interests and prejudices' (p. 73). What Manly did show was the relevance of the *Prologue* to its contemporary social life rather than to a world of eternal human types. It is this aspect of his work that I want to pursue, by studying the relationship between the *Prologue* and estates satire, a medieval literary genre which is closely concerned with the life of society. In the course of this investigation, the way in which Chaucer's artistic requirements affected the presentation of the *Prologue* figures will also become clearer.

ESTATES AND ESTATES LITERATURE

The meanings of the word 'estate' which concern us are thus defined by the *Middle English Dictionary*: 'A class of persons, especially a social or political class or group; also a member of a particular class or rank', and 'A person's position in society...social class'. To these definitions I think it necessary to add a particular reference to the role played by a person's work in determining the estate to which he belongs. It is true that the estates included in estates literature are not classified only in terms of what we would now recognise as their occupation; they can, for example, be distinguished according to clerical or marital status. But clerical and marital status inevitably include some notion of the particular duties and temptations of the work that accompanies them.

Estates literature has been defined by Ruth Mohl, who has written the only book entirely devoted to the genre, in terms of four characteristics. First, an enumeration of the 'estates' or social and occupational classes, whose aim seems to be completeness. Secondly, a lament over the shortcomings of the estates; each fails in its duty to the rest. Thirdly, the philosophy of the divine ordination of the three principal estates, the dependence of the state on all three, and the necessity of being content with one's station. And last, an attempt to find remedies, religious or political, for the defects of estates.[9] However, these characteristics are by no means to be found in every piece of estates writing, and estates material is clearly recognisable in works not strictly belonging to the genre, such as *Piers Plowman*. My working definition of estates satire is therefore less rigid; it comprises any literary treatments of social classes which allow or encourage a generalised application. Thus the works I shall discuss in relation to Chaucer range in scope from brief poems dealing with one class only, to encyclopedic attempts to span all sections of society. In form they include not only works which satisfy the more rigid definition of estates literature – which deal with a fairly large number of social classes in sequence, and expound their duties or criticise their failings in a relatively direct way – but also works in such literary forms as debate, narrative, or drama, in which estates satire can play a more or less dominant role. (Some idea of the scope and form of individual works can be gained from consulting the first part of the Bibliography, and the first appendix, which outlines the estates lists of the more regularly-organised estates works.) The justification for making no

3

discrimination, within the main body of my discussion, between works differing in literary form, is the empirical observation that the estates material they draw on is of the same type and very often identical.

THE ESTATES FORM

For one important purpose, however, it is necessary to distinguish works which have an estates form from those which simply contain estates material. For the form of the estates genre and the form of the *Prologue* are one and the same. The framework of the *Prologue* is a list of estates. Chaucer specifically says at the end of the *Prologue* that he has described the 'estaat' of all the pilgrims (716).[10] The *Prologue* is also a collection of portraits, but this is a secondary consideration; if we had been presented with portraits of the Seven Deadly Sins, for example, we should quickly have recognised that the portrait series was merely a vehicle, while the conceptual framework belonged to the Sins tradition.

It is important to stress this relationship between the form of the *Prologue* and estates literature because of the assumption mentioned earlier that society itself, rather than a literary genre, would have been Chaucer's model. This assumption applies both to the question of the comprehensiveness of the *Prologue*, and to the order in which the characters are placed. On the first point, Manly, for example, questioned 'whether Chaucer really intended to present an exhaustive survey of fourteenth century society', because of his apparently arbitrary inclusion or omission of certain social classes (*New Light*, pp. 71–2). The assumption that the *Prologue* must be matched with fourteenth-century society if the pilgrims are to be taken as representative figures has characterised both the critics who think they are representative, and those who think they are not. Thus J. R. Hulbert, who thought that they were, commented, 'No one ever supposed it chance that there are *one* knight, *one* lawyer, *one* monk, etc.', but concluded from this that the *Prologue* was a 'conspectus of medieval English society'.[11] Manly's criticism of this kind of comment was surely right, for there are many aspects of fourteenth-century society which the *Prologue* does not cover. But it does cover the elements of social anatomisation made familiar by estates literature. Thus Bronson remarked on the 'relative scarcity of women in the company', and attributed this to the fact that their presence on a pilgrimage was 'realistically' unlikely.[12]

It can equally well be attributed to the fact that estates literature rarely listed more than two estates of women – religious and secular.[13]

The list of estates included in individual estates works given in Appendix A shows that some estates – especially monk, friar, priest, lawyer, doctor, knight – appear with great regularity, but that each author exercises considerable freedom in his selection. The estates included in the *Prologue* correspond well enough to this rather vague norm. Chaucer makes no serious omissions. The higher echelons of both clergy and laity are unrepresented, but in other works much of the material applied to them is identical with that assigned to their less exalted counterparts. Bishops and priests, kings and knights, are on the whole admonished in the same way. On the other hand, the third estate is represented in the *Prologue* with an unusual richness.

It can only have been with the aim of providing a full version of an estates list that Chaucer chose to introduce as many as thirty pilgrims in the *Prologue*. Thirty is an unwieldy number for description (and Chaucer evades describing all of them), for dramatic interplay, or for tale-telling – is there any other collection of tales with so large a number of narrators? Chaucer was concerned to impose an estates form on the *Prologue* in order to suggest society as a whole by way of his representative company of individuals – rather than to use estates material in the same incidental fashion as that which he may have culled from physiognomies, allegorisations of the sins, romances and so on. To adapt a phrase of Muscatine's to a different purpose, the estates framework provides 'a formal, *a priori* ideal ordering of experience, without which the naturalistic detail would have only the barest sociological significance'.[14]

On the second question, that of the order in which the estates are presented, two misconceptions seem to prevail. The first is that estates literature always proceeds, in an orderly way, from the top to the bottom of the social scale, in contrast to the fairly haphazard method of the *Prologue*.[15] Support for this view has been found in Chaucer's apparent admission, at the end of the *Prologue*, that he is unusual in ignoring social ranking:

> Also I prey yow to foryeve it me,
> Al have I nat set folk in hir degree
> Here in this tale, as that they sholde stonde. (743–5)

This may indeed mean that he is thinking of the more tightly-organised works of estates literature, and pointing out the vagaries of his own scheme. But tight organisation is not a *sine qua non* of an estates work, as the appended list shows, and Chaucer's apology cannot therefore be read as a statement that he is writing something else.

The second misconception is about the exact nature of the order which is being neglected in the *Prologue*. Modern writers have tended to assume that medieval perceptions of the class-hierarchy were the same as our own. Tatlock, for example, found the characters 'mostly middle-class': 'none is beneath the rather prosperous Plowman'.[16] On these grounds it is usually assumed, for example, that it is correct for Chaucer to begin with the Knight, that the Prioress is of high status, and that the Wife of Bath is middle-class.[17] The estates lists show that it would be more 'correct' for the clerical figures to precede the Knight, and that despite the high rank achieved by some women, their estate is placed lower in the list than *all* those of the men. The estates framework is more concerned to distinguish 'qualitatively', to separate clergy from laity, men from women, than to arrange an exact hierarchy of rank cutting across these divisions. The estates habit of distinguishing by function rather than by rank determines, for example, the treatment of women according to their marital, rather than their social, status, the undifferentiated treatment of *burgenses*, and the presentation of the lowest ranks of the clergy before the secular emperor. Clearly this literary order did not reflect the actual status of each class in society, and it is possible that social actualities affected the order which Chaucer developed for the *Prologue*. But if we say that the *Prologue* neglects a proper order, we must make clear whether we mean a literary order, or actual social ranking. And we must provide empirical evidence for the way in which both were perceived in the fourteenth century.[18]

As for Chaucer's apology for not setting his figures 'in hir degree', it may just as well refer to a literary as to a social order, since it occurs at the end of a discussion of literary propriety.[19] He apologises for the apparent lack of literary decorum that he is about to demonstrate in reporting the ribald tales of some pilgrims, and defends himself with a literary principle: 'The wordes moote be cosyn to the dede' (742). He continues this line of thought – '*Also* I prey yow to foryeve it me' – with an apology for another apparent violation of literary decorum; he has not proceeded in the 'right' order. The literary context of this apology strongly encourages the belief that the standard of correctness to which Chaucer is referring is provided by estates literature. Chaucer is consciously producing an example of this genre, and just as consciously refusing to adhere to the one principle of order that usually characterises it, the separate treatment of clergy and laity.

Chaucer's reasons for imitating the least regular, rather than the most regular estates pieces are not immediately obvious; the attempts that have been made to find conceptual schemes in the order of the portraits are forced, and depend on the development of external concepts as the 'key' to each portrait.[20] The likelihood that an order which is haphazard and casual as far as significance is concerned is operating, is surely strengthened by the fact that exactly this casualness of procedure operates *within* the portraits. They have indeed been praised for the 'lack of regular order' which was 'deliberately planned to produce the effect of spontaneity that creates a sense of intimate acquaintance with each pilgrim'.[21] Just as the haphazard order within the portraits does not prevent us from recognising the form of the *descriptio*, so the vagaries on a larger scale are not sufficient to destroy the recognisable estates form of the *Prologue*.

However, if we cannot find an abstract significance determining a particular order in the *Prologue* portraits, perhaps there is an abstract significance in their disorder. The strict order of estates literature is governed by the notion of function, of hierarchy in a model whose working is divinely established. It is precisely this notion of function that, as we shall see, Chaucer discards. He shows us a world in which our view of hierarchy depends on our own position in the world, not on an absolute standpoint. For some the Knight is at the apex of 'respectability' (in both its modern and etymological senses), for some the Ploughman, for others the 'gentil' Pardoner. More than once, Chaucer uses the estates concept against itself: the notion of specialised duties, when taken to its limit, destroys the idea of a total society in which all have their allotted place and relation to each other. Chaucer's use of the estates form, that is to say, is not the traditional one of criticising (even in a less heavy-handed, more amusing way) the failures of social classes in the light of a social ideal. What exactly happens to the estates form in the *Prologue* is a subject that will occupy us to the end of the book.

THE ESTATES CONTENT AND SOCIAL STEREOTYPES

The form of the *Prologue* is a reason for looking in estates literature, rather than any other literary genre, for its source. But as regards its content – the features attributed to each of the Canterbury pilgrims –

I have still to show why we should look to literature at all, rather than to Chaucer's own experience of life. If estates satire criticises the failings of social classes, could not Chaucer have observed and recorded these failings for himself?

Underlying this question is an assumption that literary works reflect life in a simple way – to make it over-explicit for a moment, that satirists observing their society are independently forced to the same conclusions on the sensuality of women or the greed of lawyers. It is, of course, generally recognised that satire practises both selection and distortion, and that its relationship with 'historical reality' is therefore impossible to define with exactness. But it is also necessary to go beyond this, and say that satire takes on a historical life of its own, perpetuating both specific ways of observing reality and conceptual frameworks within which it can be organised. It is the conceptual frameworks, rather than the historical reality, which are of interest to us here. These frameworks are not indeed peculiar to satirists; they are a condition of all kinds of perception. Estates literature depends on and exploits the frameworks known as 'social stereotypes' – the traditional images that make us eager to observe inscrutability in a particular Chinese or astuteness in a particular Jew, because we believe that the Chinese are inscrutable and the Jews astute.[22] And estates literature does not merely reflect, but can also create, or contribute to, stereotypes; the way in which an individual author writes about monks or women can well influence the way in which his audience henceforth perceives monks or women in real life. Stereotypes of this sort are transmitted by a variety of means, of differing degrees of formality, ranging from proverbs and anecdotes to learned treatises. It would be a hard task for anyone today to say precisely whence he derived his stereotypes of a country policeman or a civil servant; similarly, medieval stereotypes must have received constant reinforcement and embellishment from a multitude of daily experiences.

The social stereotype provides a common ground for estates treatments in literary works of the most diverse kinds. There are certain differences in the literary origins of the traditional material underlying the *Prologue* portraits, as will appear. The clerical figures are heavily dependent on Latin estates satire, in which the clergy figures very prominently and the laity are classified by a few 'blanket' terms such as *cives* and *rustici*. The treatment of secular trades is mainly developed in vernacular satire, and some figures derive from a more popular tradition reflected at times in Langland, sermons and the more detailed confessional manuals, but at other times only to be conjectured from proverbs and occasional indirect hints. These differences in source material, however, do not imply disruption in the texture of the *Prologue*. The popular stereotypes of the clerical orders must have been nourished and influenced by the commonplaces of Latin estates litera-ture, while vernacular estates literature must have drawn on popular prejudices and ideas when it wished to extend its range to new classes of the laity. The process must always have operated in both directions – from 'high' to popular culture, and *vice versa* – especially at a time when there was little distinction between formal and informal know-ledge, when a learned author would write 'Men say that...', and his readers would avow 'A learned authority says...'[23] Literature and popular prejudice supported each other,[24] and the social stereotypes became a means whereby estates satire could be smoothly and neatly expanded, as they were its original basis.

The estates stereotypes also afford an explanation for Chaucer's ability to conceive of his estates representatives in topical situations; they are not fixed types whose features are determined *solely* by their existence in a literary tradition, and must be consciously brought up to date. What is traditional about their features reflects not just literary tradition, but also what is traditional about their work and the experiences it gives rise to; what is topical and of the moment reflects the contemporary role of the social stereotype. This is not just true of Chaucer; each satirist re-creates the estates stereotypes afresh, 'seeing' for himself the vanity of women or the corruption of the clergy. But while his vision is conditioned by what is traditional, it will also reflect something of the immediate situation which he is analysing in terms of the old formulae.

The social stereotype thus allows us a wider scope than is found in conventional source-study. We can, that is, use estates literature in three different ways:

1. As a possible source of a direct kind for the form, the content, and the satiric techniques of the *Prologue*. Chaucer's use of such sources can be detected through similarities in language and technique.

2. As evidence for the medieval tradition of stereotypes for those estates that are featured in the *Prologue*. Because these stereotypes could have been conveyed to Chaucer by informal means such as conversation and anecdote as well as through literature, we can, and should, extend our own knowledge of them by using works of which

Chaucer was ignorant, but which illustrate commonplace notions. And on the same principle, we can also glean evidence of commonplaces from literary sources other than estates works.

3. As evidence of the kind of conceptual frameworks within which Chaucer would have organised his observation of individuals he knew, if or when he was drawing a portrait from life. The third approach is less important here, since it seems clear that the 'estates' features of the Canterbury pilgrims are not just the result of the frameworks within which Chaucer observed individuals belonging to certain social groups, but were deliberately used by Chaucer for the basis of his portraits.

The reason for thinking this is the large proportion of the *Prologue* devoted to the details of the pilgrims' occupations, which can have no other function than to ensure our sense of the estate.

THE ROLE OF WORK IN THE 'PROLOGUE' PORTRAITS

A long, cool look at the *Prologue* reveals to us an extraordinary amount of unadulterated information about the careers and occupations of the characters. Let us take, for example, this passage in the Knight's portrait:

> At Alisaundre he was whan it was wonne.
> Ful ofte tyme he hadde the bord bigonne
> Aboven alle nacions in Pruce;
> In Lettow hadde he reysed and in Ruce,
> No Cristen man so ofte of his degree.
> In Gernade at the seege eek hadde he be
> Of Algezir, and riden in Belmarye,
> At Lyeys was he and at Satalye,
> Whan they were wonne; and in the Grete See
> At many a noble armee hadde he be.
> At mortal batailles hadde he been fiftene,
> And foughten for oure feith at Tramyssene
> In lystes thries, and ay slayn his foo.
> This ilke worthy knyght hadde been also
> Somtyme with the lord of Palatye
> Agayn another hethen in Turkye. (51–66)[25]

This passage has traditionally been interpreted as if it were only designed to tell us certain things about the Knight's character: he has wide experience of campaigning; he is motivated by religious feelings;[26] he is 'worthy' in that he has attained distinction by honourable means. But from this point of view the style can hardly be called economical; is it really necessary to name every campaign? There is also a strain of casualness running through the passage – 'ful ofte tyme', 'many a noble armee', 'No Cristen man so ofte of his degree' – which counteracts the accuracy suggested by the geographical references; the information is not really as precise as its volume leads us to believe. Moreover, there is little attempt to vary the method of presentation. Chaucer alters the word-order slightly, but each sentence has the same basic repetitive structure: 'he was', 'he hadde bigonne', 'hadde he reysed', 'hadde he be', 'was he', 'hadde he be', 'hadde he been', 'hadde been also'. The laxity of this paratactic style contrasts strikingly with the hypotactic opening sentence of the Prologue, which builds up a series of evocations of spring-time, reaching a climax only at the end of a dozen lines. We suspect that the shift to a loose style is deliberate, but it is strange that it should occur in the first portrait of all, where one would have expected an attempt at a clear, incisive effect.

Muriel Bowden supplies a clue to an alternative explanation of this passage in the Knight's portrait when she tries to explain it 'historically': 'to many of Chaucer's contemporaries, this list was no mere catalogue as it is to us today, but a chapter of romance' (*Commentary*, p. 51). If we substitute for the last words, 'a chapter of religious chivalry', we shall be nearer the truth. The passage presents the Knight's qualifications as representative of his profession, and suggests, by a wide range of examples, a 'professional mystique'. The campaigns illustrate the idealistic, religious role of knighthood, and also a certain amount of the glamour and excitement of such a role, in the names of far-off places and the reference to such a dramatic event as the fall of Alexandria. The campaigns are so numerous because fewer names would suggest a narrower, individual experience, whereas the impression wanted is that of someone who epitomises the whole knightly profession in its aspect of religious chivalry. The information is casually presented because the aim is not to impart knowledge of a particular career, but rather to introduce references to as many campaigns and battles as possible so that the accumulation of examples may suggest a whole professional world. Viewed in this way, the passage is remarkable not for its laxity, but for its economy; in sixteen lines Chaucer not only tells us that the pilgrimage knight is 'worthy' and experienced, but suggests the whole texture and background of a professional way of life.

This passage has numerous parallels in the *Prologue* – simple references to the everyday activities and the special qualifications demanded by the profession or 'estate' of each pilgrim. We hear of the Squire riding and singing, jousting, dancing, drawing and writing poetry. We hear of the Wife's cloth-making, of the Merchant's bargains and dealings in exchange. We hear of the Franklin's public offices as sheriff, 'contour', knight of the shire, Justice of the Peace. We hear of the Cook roasting, simmering, broiling and frying, of chicken and marrow-bones, 'poudre-marchant tart and galyngale', 'mortreux' and 'blankmanger'. We are reminded of the knowledge and skill that each profession calls for, whether it is the Yeoman's skill in woodcraft, the close watch kept by the Reeve on the weather, the farm-animals and the tricks of his underlings, the Sergeant of Law's memorising of every statute and all the law-suits since the Conquest, or the Doctor's grounding in astronomy, the humours, and an astonishing number of medical authorities. We have a sense of professional jargon – whether it is the 'fee simple' and 'termes' of the lawyer, the Shipman's 'lodemenage', or the Merchant's 'chevyssaunce'.[27] All of this contributes relatively little to our sense of the individual psychology of the pilgrims, but it contributes a great deal to our sense of their working lives.

Chaucer's ostensible purpose in introducing this material is to assure the reader that each pilgrim is superlatively skilled in his trade; its presentation is marked by the casual use of hyperbole which we saw in the Knight's portrait. This hyperbole is a natural part of Chaucer's 'romance style'[28] and so we accept it as part and parcel of the Chaucerian idiom. Some critics have tried to account for it more precisely, as one of the conversational elements in Chaucer's style,[29] or as a characteristic of Chaucer the impressionable pilgrim,[30] as part of Chaucer's enthusiastic appreciation of people, or of the literary convention of magnifying character.[31] It is clear that the hyperbole cannot be taken at face value; even an author's manipulation of coincidence could hardly account for a random assembly of people all of whom are the best exponents of their craft in the country or out of it. In my view, the apparently redundant eulogies of professional skills are simply a means of enumerating professional duties and qualifications. The naturalness of this sort of expression in a romance style, and its conversational tone, enable us to accept it, but its motivation is to direct our attention to the social and occupational functions, habits and qualities of the *Prologue* figures.

Chaucer keeps reminding us of 'all trades, their gear and tackle and trim' – the world of work in which each character is involved, the special knowledge which he commands and towards which we can adopt only a layman's attitude. Chaucer often underlines such an attitude himself by using the word 'his' when referring to professional terms: 'his bargaynes...his chevyssaunce'; 'His stremes, ... his daungers...His herberwe, and his moone, his lodemenage'; 'his apothecaries...his letuaries'. Surely it is this attitude which is provoked in us by the Merchant's obsession with keeping open the sea between Middleborough and Orwell – recognisably a bee in a professional bonnet. Far from expecting us to probe the matter more carefully for information about the Merchant,[32] Chaucer wants us to react as laymen – with amusement at, and at the same time fascination with, the specialised viewpoint; how funny it is that this *is* the kind of thing merchants are interested in!

The range of professional characteristics introduced into the portraits is, however, far wider than this. They can include, for example, abstract and personal qualities. Thus, to return to the Knight, the virtues which he honours and embodies – 'chivalrie, | Trouthe and honour, fredom and curteisie', and even the phrases in which he is described – 'worthy', 'wys', 'verray', 'gentil' – are appropriate to an ideal type of religious chivalry.

The same is true of the 'personalities' of pilgrims who are not idealised in this way; the pompousness of the Merchant and Sergeant of Law, the Friar's winning charm, the Shipman's ruthlessness, suggest a professional manner as much as an individual personality.

The Squire's portrait shows us how the estate can also determine the physical appearance of the characters: his 'lokkes crulle', his fashionably short clothing embroidered with 'fresshe floures whyte and reede' which recall the conventional romance spring-time, are appropriate for his role as a figure of romantic chivalry, contrasted with the more sober religious aspects of chivalry represented by his father. The Clerk's lean and threadbare look has obvious connections with his calling, for in it we recognise the inseparable nature of poverty and scholarship; more important, so does Chaucer, who writes that the Friar was 'nat lyk a cloysterer | With a thredbare cope, *as is a povre scoler*' (259–60). We can therefore refer temperament and physical appearance to estates concepts just as well as to the concept of an individual or an 'eternal human type'.

It is also worth noting how often in the *Prologue* we have to do with professional rogues and scoundrels: Friar, Merchant, Manciple,

Miller, Reeve, Summoner, Pardoner, all take advantage of the opportunities for chicanery offered by their profession. We frequently find a sort of parody of the testimonies to professional skill, asserting the character's proficiency in the 'tricks of the trade' rather than the trade itself. The mark of this parody is usually the employment of the phrases 'wel koude he', 'wel knew he' which elsewhere characterise the straightforward testimonies of professional skill.

> Wel koude he stelen corn and tollen thries. (562)
>
> His lord wel koude he plesen subtilly,
> To yeve and lene hym of his owene good,
> And have a thank, and yet a cote and hood. (610–12)

The same phrases are used to give the character of 'professional skills to yet other types of behaviour.

> Wel koude she carie a morsel and wel kepe
> That no drope ne fille upon hir brest. (130–1)
>
> In felaweshipe wel koude she laughe and carpe.
> Of remedies of love she knew per chaunce,
> For she koude of that art the olde daunce. (474–6)

Those sleights-of-hand and verbal dexterities, those frauds and deceptions, those self-interested ambitions and habits of thought and speech which the practice of a profession permits or even encourages, can thus become linked with the concept of the estate.

An estate can be typified in two ways: Chaucer can evoke the qualities that should go with the profession, the 'idealised version'; alternatively, he can evoke the malpractices and frauds which usually go with it in actuality, the 'normal version'. Despite their differences in character, both the Knight and the Merchant, for example, are 'types' of their estate; each corresponds to a certain mental stereotype of the characteristics of their social class.[33] These two versions can be played off against each other; the information that the Clerk would rather spend money on books than on 'robes riche, or fithele, or gay sautrie' (296), implies that it is these that would be the normal preference of other clerks. Whether it is the 'good' or 'bad' version of an estate we are being given, the other is kept in our minds, so that the estate itself, rather than the individual, is the root idea. And it has been noted before that the profession often determines what we regard as sinful in a character. The Monk's love of hunting and good living would take on a totally different significance in the person of a lord of the manor; it is his estate which makes them out of place, and so is basic to our appreciation of the portrait.[34] Thus where a critic like Hulbert sees the socially representative features of the pilgrims as parallel with features belonging to universal human types – 'typical traits of temperament, appearance and manners' – I would see the estate as fundamental to most of these features as well.[35]

The chapters which follow will document the claim that the features of the Canterbury pilgrims are overwhelmingly those which were traditionally associated with their estates. The content of the *Prologue* therefore proclaims it to be an estates satire as much as the form. But we must note one paradoxical aspect of the *Prologue*'s estates content. The neutral and detailed enumeration of the daily duties of each occupation increases our awareness of the estate, rather than the individual – but this sort of enumeration is rarely found in estates literature itself. Where the satirists use concrete detail, it is not neutral, but illustrative of failings; where they are not criticising failings, they offer generalised moral advice rather than instruction in a trade. We do gain some acquaintance with the daily activities of some estates, in the development (on the whole late) of satire on different classes of artisans; the outlining of the various ways in which they can default in their craftsmanship or selling techniques gives us some idea of the details of their trades.[36] But there is nothing like Chaucer's continued insistence on the assembly of skills, duties and jargon that characterises an estate. This type of information is given only in the *Prologue*; elsewhere in the *Canterbury Tales* we find plentiful use of estates satire of the traditional sort, but nothing of this sense of daily work. Chaucer's introduction of this apparently 'colourless' material points to his intentions. It does not work against the assumption that the *Prologue* figures are estates types, since the new material helps to realise them in precisely this way. But it shows how Chaucer is concerned to develop certain implications of the estates form – its stress on specialisation, on the skills, duties and habits which separate one class of society from another – rather than to remain content with its traditional aims of moral criticism, whether humorous or solemn. The implications of this for the kind of society presented in the *Prologue* will emerge later.

To this paradox we can add another. In contrast to the usual view that Chaucer took typical figures as a point of departure and added new details which transformed them into individuals, I have suggested that Chaucer deliberately invented new material which reinforced the impression of the type.[37] Yet I do not wish to dissent from the general critical consensus that the Canterbury pilgrims give us an extraordinarily vivid *impression* of their existence as individuals. While examining what they have in common with their estates counterparts, I shall also examine the means by which Chaucer persuades us that they are individuals. Both lines of inquiry seem to me to lead to an increased understanding of, and admiration for, Chaucer's art in the *Prologue*.

2

The Anti-Clerical Tradition in Estates Satire

A traditional estates content is most easily recognisable in the portraits of the Monk and the Friar, both of them figures with a long literary history.[1] The different ranks of the clergy are the estates most frequently and fully treated by satirists, and it is therefore significant that the clerical figures are also among the most fully described of the Canterbury pilgrims. Far from drawing new inspiration from real life, Chaucer seems to have been most stimulated by the possibility of exploiting a rich literary tradition.

The estates treatments of monks and friars will conveniently illustrate the diverse features of character and behaviour associated with these classes, and also the way in which these diverse details are coherently linked with a unified stereotype, sometimes presented as a personification or typical figure ('Religioun', 'monachus', 'frater') which could be animated as an individual person. They also illustrate the variety of style in estates literature, the sophisticated handling of raillery, irony and word-play whose relationship with Chaucer is not one of simple inferiority.

THE MONK

The Monk's portrait suggests examination of the following features of the monastic stereotype: a love of good food, luxurious clothing, a love of horses and hunting, contempt for patristic and monastic authority, laziness, a refusal to stay within cloister walls, the temptations of holding various monastic offices. All of these are traditional topics in estates satire on monks, but a comparison of Chaucer's style with that of other writers will show that we are not given as much information about his pilgrims as critics have sometimes assumed. The preliminary listing of these features must therefore be taken only as a convenient basis for organising comparison, not as a final analysis of the Monk's 'character'.

If Chaucer wanted to produce a monk who was representative of his estate, he would inevitably be associated with gluttony. Despite wide differences in date and place of origin, a whole succession of writers attribute to monks the enjoyment of good food and drink. In the twelfth-century *Speculum Stultorum* of Nigel of Longchamps, for example, it is already so much taken for granted as to be revealed in an aside; the monk Fromundus comes to answer a knock slowly, as when he is called to prayer,

> Non tamen accelerans, nisi cum pulsatur ad ollam,
>   Ut solet, ad mensam ventre docente viam . . .[2]

> He went not hastily as was his wont
>   When called to meals, his stomach leading him. (trans. Regenos, p. 105)

When the topic is directly broached, a wide variety of literary styles and forms is in evidence. Gluttony can be presented through comic narrative – as in the story of the visitation of an abbot, who disqualified himself from enforcing his own rule against meat-eating by accepting the forbidden delicacies which a daughter cell pressed on him.[3] It can become the basis of a vividly dramatised scene, such as the sordid picture of the refectory table in the famous Latin poem, the *Apocalipsis Goliae*.[4] A debate between individuals can point to the guilt of all monks on this score; one monk attacks another for gluttony and is finally discomfited when his own indulgence in good food is inferred from his corpulent figure.[5] More direct in comment, and bitter in tone, are the contrasts made between the well-nourished body and the starving soul, or between the fat monk lugging about the burden of his stomach, and his peasant father who bears another kind of burden.[6] We seem nearer to Chaucer when gluttony is revealed through ironic approval of it: Nigel's Burnellus the Ass, seeking the 'best' features of existing monastic orders for inclusion in an 'ideal' one, enthusiastically seizes on the gluttonous self-indulgence of one order after another.[7] The same is true of the Order of Fair-Ease, the creation of an Anglo-Norman poet, whose members, for example, copy the Black Monks in being drunk every day –

> Mes il le fount pur compagnie
> E ne mie pur glotonie.[8]

> But they do it for companionship and not in the least out of gluttony.
>   (trans. Aspin, p. 139)

Irony also characterises a tradition of 'explaining' monastic customs or rules by reference to an indulgence in eating and drinking: the monk's head is shaved so that his hair doesn't interfere with his drinking; silence is enjoined at meals lest there be any interruption to eating; the monk's ample robe is designed to cover his paunch.[9] A writer can convey an impression of monastic gluttony by describing elaborate cooking methods,[10] or listing the luxurious foods in use.[11] Game and poultry often figure in these lists, because of the sophistical argument that it is only quadrupeds that monks are forbidden to eat.[12] The Middle English 'Land of Cokaygne' makes the greatest use of the technique of listing food, in describing the 'wel fair abbei | Of white monkes and of grei' which is made of 'pasteiis', 'fluren cakes' and 'fat podinges', and where the 'gees irostid on þe spitte' fly indoors crying 'Gees, al hote, al hot!' while the larks –

> Liȝtiþ adun to manis muþ
> Idiȝt in stu ful swiþe wel,
> Pudrid wiþ gilofre and canel.[13]

One more favourite method is to describe the fat, red-cheeked appearance of the monk, in implicit or explicit contrast to the lean, pale-cheeked figure envisaged in the ascetic ideal.[14] The author of the fourteenth-century English poem 'The Simonie' vividly describes such a representative of monastic ease:

> Religioun was first founded duresce for to drie;
> And nu is the moste del i-went to eise and glotonie.
> Where shal men nu finde fattere or raddere of leres?
> Or betre farende folke than monekes, chanons, and freres?
> > In uch toun
> I wot non eysiere lyf than is religioun.
>
> Religioun wot red I uch day what he shal don?
> He ne carez to muche for his mete at non;
> For hous-hire ne for clothes he ne carez noht;
> But whan he cometh to the mete, he maketh his mawe touht
> > off the beste;
> And anon therafter he fondeth to kacche reste.[15]

The last two methods have clearly influenced Chaucer's portrait of the Monk. Chaucer builds up our impression of the Monk's love of good food through the description of his physique, and the mention of his favourite food, which is, significantly, poultry:

His heed was balled, that shoon as any glas,
And eek his face, as he hadde been enoynt.
He was a lord ful fat and in good poynt;
His eyen stepe, and rollynge in his heed,
That stemed as a forneys of a leed; ...
Now certeinly he was a fair prelaat;
He was nat pale as a forpyned goost.
A fat swan loved he best of any roost. (198–206)

At first reading it seems obvious that Chaucer simply took over the well-established methods of indirect satire. But if we look longer at the passage, we see that Chaucer has increased the obliqueness with which the Monk's gluttony is suggested, to the extent of giving us only circumstantial evidence for it. We are not told that the Monk ate roast meat – a remark that suggests critical comment – but that swan was his favourite roast – a statement that innocently begs the question whether he should be eating roast meat at all.[16] Similarly, the physical description is partly given in negative terms; we are not told that the Monk was red-cheeked, but only that he was not pale, like a wasted ghost. Not only is it left doubtful whether gluttony is responsible for this, but the comparison also stresses how *unpleasant* is the appearance of the pale-cheeked ascetic approved by other satirists. Even more oblique as means of suggesting a love of good food are the comparison between the Monk's gleaming eyes and the fire beneath a cauldron – as if kitchen terms spontaneously came to mind when Chaucer thought of him – and the Monk's own references to items of food: 'a pulled hen' and 'an oystre'.[17] Certainly Chaucer expects us to interpret these details as pointing to the Monk's love of good food, but the obliqueness with which this is done also tells us something. It is not just a way of hiding moral comment so that we shall enjoy supplying it ourselves. For the passage cannot be read as entirely ironic; the Monk's undoubted attractiveness, and the innocuous imagery which reinforces our impression of it – 'that shoon as any glas' – establish one sort of reality for the author's claim that this is a 'fair prelaat'. We don't have reality played off against illusion, but two sorts of reality against each other. Like all the other satirists before him, Chaucer is giving his own slant to the traditional topic, but his originality lies, not in adding a bald head and gleaming eyes to the physical description of the greedy monk – although those features are indeed novel[18] – but in making our attitude to the whole description uncertain. The 'new' features, whose importance lies in the fact that they cannot be interpreted through traditional associations, and do not reveal any shortcomings of the Monk, play a subsidiary role in this process; but they do not set it in motion.

To suggest features which are traditionally satiric targets while making us uncertain whether their existence is firmer than that of a suggestion; to stress the attractiveness of the very features which we suspect reveal moral weakness – Chaucer uses one or both of these methods throughout his description of the Monk. Thus although the evidence for the Monk's weakness for fine clothing is beyond doubt, Chaucer's emphasises the attractive results of this weakness in a way that makes it difficult to respond with simple moral disapproval.

> I seigh his sleves purfiled at the hond
> With grys, and that the fyneste of a lond;
> And, for to festne his hood under his chyn,
> He hadde of gold ywroght a ful curious pyn;
> A love-knotte in the gretter ende ther was . . .
> His bootes souple, his hors in greet estaat. (193–203)

The Monk's fine clothes are as typical of his estate as gluttony. Fur, jewellery, fine horses, splendid footwear – all are among the illustrative details of other descriptions of the luxurious clothing of monks. Nigel of Longchamps writes of the Black Monks:

> Pellicias portant et plura recondita servant
> Quae non sunt sociis omnia nota suis.[19]

> They wear skin shirts and many things conceal
> Which they keep hidden from their fellow monks.
>
> (trans. Regenos, p. 105)

In a Latin debate-poem, one monk attacks another for the layers of fur covering his bed and himself:

> Quid ad te tuniculi, quid catinae pelles?
> Lateris et lectuli pellea supelles . . .[20]

> What have you to do with tunics, with cat skins?
> Fur covering on your back and bed . . .

In Gower's *Mirour de l'Omme* 'pelliçouns' which ward off the cold are also part of the luxurious dress of monks.[21] One description of monastic dress in this poem comes very close to that of the *Prologue* Monk, and it is difficult not to see a direct link with the Monk's 'purfil' of 'grys', and his 'ful curious pyn...for to festne his hood'.

nostre moigne au present jour
Quiert en sa guise bell atour
Au corps, et l'alme desfigure:
Combien q'il porte de dolour
La frocque, il ad du vein honour
La cote fourré de pellure.

Ne quiert la haire ainz quiert le say
Tout le plus fin a son essay,
Ove la fourrure vair et gris,
Car il desdeigne le berbis;
L'aimal d'argent n'ert pas oubliz,
Ainz fait le moustre et pent tout gay
Au chaperon devant le pis:
C'est la simplesce en noz paiis
Des moignes et de leur array. (20,995–1000, 21,016–24)

Nowadays our monk seeks for fine adornment for the body in his get-up, and disfigures his soul. Although he wears the gown of hardship, he has a tunic trimmed with vain-glorious fur.

He does not look for haircloth, but for wool, the finest he can find, with squirrel fur, for he scorns lamb. The silver ornament won't be forgotten, but makes a show, hanging gaily on the hood on his breast. This is the 'simplicity' of monks and their clothing in our country.

The closeness of the similarity stimulates us to ask whether the *Mirour de l'Omme* alone can have been responsible for Chaucer's description of his monk.[22] The Monk's 'souple' boots give us the answer, for they are not found in Gower, but like the fur, are a specific detail which has become an integrated feature of the tradition as it appears in other texts. The sybaritic abbot of a Goliardic prose satire, among a large supply of clothing, is especially well provided with footwear:

Tibiis quidem ipsius subveniunt femoralia linea, caligae laneae, ocreae, non tamen ferreae, immo ferinae, et tandem epicaligae. Pedilium vero certus non est numerus, crescit enim et decrescit secundum vicissitudines caloris et frigoris. Botas habet aestivales, hyemales, crepitas, filto triplicato ypoteticatas.[23]

Linen stockings cosset his shanks, woollen shoes, leggings, not of iron, but or leather, and overshoes as well. The number of his footwear is not fixed, for it waxes and wanes according to the alterations of heat and cold. He has summer boots, winter boots, sandals, underlaid with three layers of felt.

The author of the late twelfth-century *Roman de Carité* uses footwear of different types to symbolise the easy worldly existence of contemporary monks. The monk should have a wide boot to protect him from the mire of the world through which he must pass. But too many monks prefer 'l'estroit cauchier' – the fashionable tight shoes, which witness to the monk's 'pensée confuse'. Along with the fine shoes is mentioned the 'grys' that Chaucer puts into his portrait of the Monk:

> Cloistriers, ki tes dras et ton pié
> Dou point del ordre as despointié
> Et au point dou siecle apointié,
> Ki te kerra dou vair, dou gris,
> Ke tu n'en aies covoitié?[24]

Cloisterer, who have made your clothing and footwear out of harmony with your order, and have adapted them to the world, who will believe that you haven't coveted fur of squirrel?

'The Simonie' also uses footwear and fur together, as details illustrative of monastic comfort.

> This is the penaunce that monekes don for ure lordes love:
> Hii weren sockes in here shon, and felted botes above;
> He hath forsake for Godes love bothe hunger and cold;
> But if he have hod and cappe fured, he nis noht i-told
>   in covent;
> Ac certes wlaunknesse of wele hem hath al ablent.[25]

The strongest evidence that the detail was a familiar part of the monastic stereotype is its incidental occurrence in a poem which is a pedlar's recital of his wares:

> Si ai bottes de mostier maintes
> Netes, polies, et bien paintes.[26]

I have also boots for monasteries, very neat, polished and well stitched.

There is nothing strikingly individual, therefore, about the Monk's 'purfil' of 'grys', about his 'ful curious pyn' of gold or his supple boots.[27]

Nor is Chaucer original in giving his Monk a taste for fine horses.

> Ful many a deyntee hors hadde he in stable.
>   . . . his hors in greet estaat.
> His palfrey was as broun as is a berye. (168, 203, 207)

Such a taste was associated with monks and clerics in general; we think of Langland's criticism of 'bisschopes baiardes' (IV 124), and the passage (quoted later in this chapter) about 'Religion' being 'A priker on a palfray' (x 292ff.) – a phrase which finds an echo in Chaucer's vocabulary (189, 191). Already in the mid-fourteenth-century Belgian writer, Gilles li Muisis, we have an association between monks and fine horses, and in particular, the repeated mention of 'palefrois'. The topic arises in a context of the luxurious food and clothing of present-day monks: he asks,

> Sains Benois avoit-il dras les plus précieus,
> Palefrois sur lesquels gent fussent envieus?
> Avoit-il cescun jour des mais delicieus? . . .
>
> Ches abbés et ces moines rewardés cevauchant,
> Che samble qu'anemy les voisent encauchant.
> Compagnies gras mainent, se s'en vont exauchant.
>
> Palefrois et sommiers mainent ès compagnies;
> Cevalier et bourgois en ont grandes envies.[28]

Did St Benedict have such fine clothes, or palfreys of which people were jealous? Did he have delicious meals every day? . . . Look at these abbots and monks riding about – it seems that devils spur them on. They lead great retinues to raise their status. They lead troops of palfreys and pack-horses which knights and burgesses covet.

What is individual in Chaucer is the way that he stresses 'mere' observation as the reason for describing the Monk's appearance – 'I seigh his sleves' – offering the description for our approval, not for condemnation. We are not invited to notice that fur edging is contrary to monastic rules, but only that it is the 'fyneste of a lond'. Sensuous appreciation runs counter to moral disapproval.

The fine horses of Chaucer's Monk lead us to his love of hunting. As with his love of fine clothing, there is little doubt about this. We are told that he 'lovede venerie' (166) and scorned the text 'That seith that hunters been not holy men' (177–8).

> Grehoundes he hadde as swift as fowel in flight;
> Of prikyng and of huntyng for the hare
> Was al his lust, for no cost wolde he spare. (190–2)

The hunting monk is not as well-known a figure in other satiric works as the hunting parson, but the particular stereotype of the monk derives this feature from the general stereotype of the cleric. The hunting cleric can equally well be prelate, rector, parson, or clerk.[29] The particular elements of Chaucer's portrait can be seen in other works. Several other writers specifically mention 'huntyng for the hare', as Chaucer does.[30] And a passage on a typical monk from the *Mirour de*

l'Omme closely parallels the many horses 'in stable' and 'Grehoundes...
swift as fowel in flight' of the *Prologue* Monk:

> Et pour delit tient plus avant
> A la rivere oiseals volant,
> La faulcon et l'ostour mué,
> Les leverers auci courant
> Et les grantz chivals sojournant,
> Ne falt que femme mariée. (21,043–8)

And for his pleasure he has as well birds flying to hunt at the water's edge,
falcon and goshawk in coops, [swift-] running dogs and great horses kicking
their heels – all he lacks is a wife.

Chaucer's portrait may also be hinting at a double motive for the
Monk's hunting, if we read the words 'venerie' and 'prikyng' in the
light of the 'love-knotte' on the Monk's pin, and see in them a *double
entendre*.[31] In this the Monk would not be unusual;[32] other texts link
hunting with the cleric's opportunities for seducing women,[33] and
we can also find elsewhere the punning technique which links the two
activities. In a Latin poem beginning 'In vere virencia', young clerics
greet their approaching holiday with enthusiasm and propose to enjoy
the love of their girls after all their labour. The last stanza suddenly
introduces the prospect of hunting:

> In agris appetimus leporem venari.[34]

We long to hunt the hare in the fields. (trans. Dronke, p. 401)

There is a clear pun on 'lepos' (charm, attractiveness) and 'lepus'
(hare); their hunt for an animal will turn into a hunt for Beauty. Yet,
like the suggestion of gluttony, Chaucer's pun is characterised by an
obliqueness which is greater in degree and different in kind. The Latin
pun follows a clear reference to sexual behaviour, and can confidently
be related to it. Chaucer's puns are the *only* indication we have of the
Monk's sexual licence. That is, this characteristic of the Monk exists
only (as far as we are concerned) in the language with which the
narrator describes him; it is transferred from a factual status to a
linguistic one.

Chaucer's consistency in transferring estates features from factual
to linguistic status encourages the belief that the distinction is no mere
quibble, but is significant for both his establishment of the pilgrims as
individuals, and his larger purpose in the *Prologue*. The consistency
can be illustrated by his reduction of the 'oiseals volant' of Gower's

hunting monk to the level of a simile describing the Monk's grey-hounds – 'swift as fowel in flight'. It is equally evident in Chaucer's description of the Monk's jingling harness:

> And whan he rood, men myghte his brydel heere
> Gynglen in a whistlynge wynd as cleere
> And eek as loude as dooth the chapel belle. (169–71)

The implication seems to be that the Monk hears the chapel bell while he is out riding, so that the simile serves to point to a possible distaste for church services. This would be to play off a surface similarity (between the sound of the two bells) against a real disparity (between church services and hunting), in exactly the manner of a Latin satiric pun such as Nigel of Longchamps makes in a similar context:

> Silvarum sancta plusquam loca sancta frequentat,
> Latratusque canum canonis pluris habet. (SS 2795–6)

> He [the bishop] spends more time in woods than sacred place,
> And values dogma less than sound of dogs. (trans. Regenos, p. 128)

The linguistic similarity between 'canis' and 'canon' implies that *in the mind of the cleric* there is little to choose between them – can a change of two letters mean damnation? The obliteration of the real distinction between the two, by means of the pun, mirrors the fact that the distinction is not consciously felt by the cleric satirised. Gower and Langland both use metaphor to produce a similar effect. Gower says of the hunting curate:

> Clamor in ore canum, dum vociferantur in vnum,
> Est sibi campana, psallitur vnde deo.
> Stat sibi missa breuis, deuocio longaque campis,
> Quo sibi cantores deputat esse canes. (VC III 1507–10)

The belling from his dogs' mouths, as they clamour together, is to him a church bell whence God is hymned. Mass is short for him, but lengthy is his devotion in the fields, where hounds are appointed his cantors.

And Langland's figure of Sloth confesses:

> I haue be prest and parsoun · passynge thretti wynter,
> Ȝete can I neither solfe ne synge · ne seyntes lyues rede,
> But I can fynde in a felde · or in a fourlonge an hare,
> Better than in *beatus vir* · or in *beati omnes*
> Construe oon clause wel · and kenne it to my parochienes. (PPl v 422–6)

26

– it is as if the one skill will serve instead of the other. Chaucer's lines at first seem like this – the preference of one bell over the other becomes a matter of taste, not of conscience, and thus suggests that the real disparity between the two is not felt by the Monk. But then we realise that the lines are no more than a suggestion. Gower or Langland leave us in no doubt that hunting is a *substitute* for church services or parochial activity; in Chaucer the comparison which suggests this has nevertheless only the factual basis of a simile – the two activities are associated in language, not necessarily in actuality, and the language is the narrator's, not the Monk's. The narrator is made prominent because the emphasis is not on the *facts* about the Monk, but on *the way we get to know him*, working on hints and suspicions of a reality different from the superficial one, whose existence is obscured by the Monk's very unconsciousness of it.

We might say that whereas other satirists play off the cleric's view of a certain piece of behaviour against their own views as orthodox moralists, Chaucer in this instance unites his point of view with the Monk's to the extent that we lose the opportunity for any other standpoint. To say this is not the same as to claim that Chaucer (or the 'naive narrator') takes the Monk at face value. But it is to suggest that Chaucer's method is frequently to remind us of traditional satire while discouraging or circumventing the moral judgements it aimed to elicit. And one way in which Chaucer circumvents moral judgement is to show us the Monk from his own point of view. This is implicit in much of the description; we might well feel that the admiration for the Monk's appearance, and the contempt for the ghost-like pallor of others, reflects his own self-approval. Such a feeling would be 'carried over' from the long central passage of the description in which we see the Monk's viewpoint on his life.

> Ther as this lord was kepere of the celle,
> The reule of seint Maure or of seint Beneit,
> By cause that it was old and somdel streit
> This ilke Monke leet olde thynges pace,
> And heeld after the newe world the space.
> He yaf nat of that text a pulled hen,
> That seith that hunters ben nat hooly men,
> Ne that a monk, whan he is recchelees,
> Is likned til a fissh that is waterlees, –
> This is to seyn, a monk out of his cloystre.
> But thilke text heeld he nat worth an oystre;

27

> And I seyde his opinion was good.
> What sholde he studie and make hymselven wood,
> Upon a book in cloystre alwey to poure,
> Or swynken with his handes, and laboure,
> As Austyn bit? How shal the world be served?
> Lat Austyn have his swynk to him reserved! (172–88)

The characteristics suggested by these lines – contempt for monastic authorities and for the cloistered life, physical laziness, neglect of study, dislike of the old strict rules – were traditionally associated with monks. Chaucer himself probably translated these lines from the *Roman de la Rose*:

> Sek the book of seynt Austyn
> Be it in papir or perchemyn,
> There as he writ of these worchynges,
> Thou shalt seen that *noon excusynges*
> A parfit man ne shulde seke
> Bi wordis ne bi dedis eke,
> Although he be religious,
> And God to serven curious,
> That he ne shal, so mote I go,
> With propre hondis and body also,
> Gete his fode in laboryng,
> If he ne have proprete of thing.[35]

Laziness is also linked with ignoring sacred texts in the *Vox Clamantis* (IV 71–2), and contempt for the rule 'of seint Maure or of seint Beneit' is also described:

> Nil modo Bernardi sancti vel regula Mauri
>   Confert commonachis, displicet immo, nouis:
> Obstat avarus eis que superbus et invidus alter,
>   Ordinis exemplum qui modo ferre negant.
> Expulit a claustris maledictus sic Benedictum. (IV 337–41)

The rule of St Bernard or Maurus is no longer of use to new monks, who reject it. One through avarice sets himself against them, another through pride and envy, and refuse to tolerate the model of the Order. Thus a cursed monk has cast the blessed Benedict out of the cloister.

In the *Mirour de l'Omme*, Gower describes the monk's contempt for St Augustine, in connection with indulgence in gluttony.

> Et dist que c'est la reule jouste:
> Ne croi point de Saint Augustin,
> Ainz est la reule du Robyn,

> Qui meyne vie de corbyn,
> Qui quiert primer ce q'il engouste
> Pour soi emplir.[36]

And he says this is the right rule; I don't believe it's St Augustine's, but jolly Robin's, who leads a raven's life, spying out what he can gobble up to stuff himself with.

Gilles li Muisis repeatedly stresses the need for the monk to honour 'li rieule saint Benoit',[37] and on one occasion links the saint with his follower St Maurus and exhorts the monk to follow both.[38]

Distaste for work, whether manual or intellectual, and neglect of church services are also part of the monastic stereotype.

> Monachi sunt nigri
> et in regula sunt pigri.

There are black monks, who are lazy at fulfilling their Rule.

says one of the *Carmina Burana*,[39] and in another Latin poem, one monk taunts another with neglect of labour.[40] Gilles li Muisis speaks of the dominance of 'Preiche', especially in studying, and in singing services.[41] The *Mirour de l'Omme* criticises monks for 'Peresce' which makes them gossip and neglect their church services (5561–6, 21,170–2).

The monk out of his cloister is also a familiar figure in anti-monastic satire. In the *Speculum Stultorum*, Burnellus the Ass, insulted by the Cistercians, vindictively proposes as a punishment that they should not leave their cloisters – 'claustra nex exibunt'.[42] Another Latin satirist, who protests that he is only repeating commonplaces about monks, alleges:

> Tam deum quam loca dimittunt leviter
> in quibus voverunt stare stabiliter.[43]

They abandon at once God, and the place in which they vowed steadfastly to remain.

The proverb about the fish out of water is, as Robinson notes, a commonplace of ancient origin in this context, and it appears, for example, in the *Roman de Carité*:

> Ki gete posson de vivier
> Mort l'a, et le moine cloistrier
> Ki li done dou cloistre issue. (CIV 7–9)

He who throws a fish out of a pond, kills him, and so does he who gives a cloister-monk leave of his cloister.

Gilles li Muisis twice uses the proverb to give weight to his frequent complaints about monks leaving their cloisters.[44] Nearer home, for Chaucer, is Gower's use of the proverb in the *Vox Clamantis*:

> Non foris a claustris monachus, nec aqua fore piscis
> 　Debet, tu nisi sis, ordo, reuersus eis.
> Si fuerit piscis, qui postpositis maris undis
> 　Pascua de terra querat habere sua,
> Est nimis improprium piscis sibi ponere nomen,
> 　Debeo set monstri ponere nomen ei.
> Sic ego claustrali dicam, qui gaudia mundi
> 　Appetit et claustrum deserit inde suum.[45]

A monk ought not to be out of the cloister, as a fish ought not to be out of water, unless the order of things is turned upside down for them. If there were a fish who, abandoning the sea-waves, sought to obtain its food on land – it's wrong to give it the name of fish; I ought rather to give it the name of monster! I shall say as much to the monk who longs for the joys of the world and therefore leaves his cloister.

He expresses the same idea, this time giving it the authority of 'Austyn', in the *Mirour de l'Omme*:

> Saint Augustin en sa lecoun
> Dist, tout ensi comme le piscoun
> En l'eaue vit tantsoulement,
> Tout autrecy Religioun
> Prendra sa conversacioun
> Solonc la reule du covent
> El cloistre tout obedient. (20,845-7)

St Augustine says in his teaching, that just as a fish lives only in water, just so Religion must live his life according to convent rule, submissive in the cloister.

Langland endows Gower's rather colourless personification of 'Religioun' with vivid life:

> Gregorie the grete clerke · and the goed pope
> Of religioun the reule · reherseth in his morales,
> And seyth it in ensaumple · for thei schulde do there-after,
> 'Whenne fissches failen the flode · or the fresche water,
> Thei deyen for drouthe · whanne thei drie ligge;
> Eiȝt so, quod Gregorie · religioun roileth
> Sterueth and stynketh · and steleth lordes almesses,
> That oute of couent and cloystre · coueyten to libbe.' . . .

30

Ac now is Religioun a ryder ˙ a rowmer bi stretes,
A leder of louedayes ˙ and a londe-bugger,
A priker on a palfray ˙ fro manere to manere,
An heep of houndes at his ers ˙ as he a lorde were.[46]

These passages from Langland and Gower show how Chaucer uses our sense of the Monk's point of view to make convincing the shift from a personification ('Religioun') or type-figure ('monachus') to his own creation of an individual person. Gower approaches the 'fish-out-of-water' image by way of definition; with a parade of logic he 'proves' that a cloisterless monk is a monster. It is typical of Langland that he stresses the implications of disgust in the image; a cloisterless monk rots and stinks like a dead fish. In Chaucer, on the other hand, instead of the proverb condemning the Monk, we find the Monk condemning the proverb. For the first time, we get the *monk's* attitude to this old saw. Contempt for the cloister, and for those authorities who think it the only place for a monk, is only what we might expect to be expressed by the kind of monk satirised by Nigel of Longchamps or Gilles li Muisis; it is not *what* the Monk says that is important for our sense of his existence, but rather that Chaucer imagines him saying it. By the simple device of adopting *his* viewpoint rather than that of the moralist Chaucer both avoids an explicit or final interpretation of the Monk, and convinces us that the Monk has reactions – in short, that he exists.

As with the passage on the bridle, Chaucer seems here to be taking one stage further the satiric technique which traditionally identifies the sinner's viewpoint in order to contrast its specious plausibility with moral truth.[47] We can compare the Chaucer's endorsement of the Monk's opinion on 'the newe world' with the ironic approval of new monastic fashions in the *Roman de Carité*:

> Jou por mal pas ne lor repruef;
> Por lor cortoisie le suerf.
> Mout ont establi beles lois
> Beneoit, Augustin li neuf.
> Uns des nouviaus vaut des viés neuf.
> Viés Augustins et Beneois
> Ne doivent as nues avoir vois.[48]

I don't reprove them for wickedness – I attribute this to their refinement. They have established very fine rules, the new Benedicts and Augustines – one of the new ones is worth nine of the old. The old Augustine and Benedict mustn't have a say against the new ones.

This comment occurs in the context of monastic gluttony – 'li novel, come courtois' stuff themselves with delicacies – but the similarities with Chaucer's Monk are obvious. And although the self-defence is not so vivid, the notion that monks see themselves as following the 'new fashion' (in this case, too, by eating well) is also used satirically by Gower.

> Le vice auci dont nous lison [Gluttony]
> S'est mis ore en religion,
> Et donne novelle observance,
> En lieu de contemplacioun
> A prendre recreacioun.[49]

The vice we're reading about has now been introduced into the religious orders, and creates a new observance of taking recreation instead of contemplation.

Chaucer is clearly working in the same tradition, but develops it to the point where he presents *only* the Monk's point of view – and typically this point of view makes us aware of the 'unattractiveness' of the strictly religious life.

We may perhaps feel that Chaucer is doing the same as the other satirists, only more subtly, by expecting us to supply the orthodox view for ourselves. But apart from the dangerousness of such an expectation – Chaucer seems to leave it open to us to feel that the fact that monks are recommended to labour and study 'As Austyn *bit*', not 'As Austyn *did*', deserves the comment that he can keep his labour to himself – such an assumption runs into difficulty in the cases where we are left puzzled as to what an orthodox view might be. For example, Chaucer presents the Monk as a holder of one monastic office – 'kepere of the celle' (172) – and as apparently capable of a higher one still:

A manly man, to been an abbot able. (167)

A traditional type of comment on these lines might relate them to satire on the ambition to become an abbot and the pride and self-indulgence of the successful candidate. Thus, one Latin poem describes how the affability of monks quickly turns into aloofness when the position is won: the new abbot keeps his room and feasts with his cronies.[50] The same change from affability to arrogance is described in another Latin poem, which also shows how the new 'kepere of the celle' uses his power to ignore the 'reule of seint Beneit':

'Tacete, miseri', dicunt claustralibus;-
'Vos nihil sapitis, nos domum regimus.'
Si quid interrogant quidam claustralium,
ridentes revocant illud in irritum,
et soli retinent res quae sunt omnium,
quas sibi reputant ut patrimonium.
Illud despiciunt quod jubet regula.[51]

'Be quiet, wretches,' they say to the monks, 'you know nothing; we govern the house.' If any of the monks question them about anything, laughing they render inquiry futile, and keep for themselves what belongs to everybody, thinking of it as their own property. They despise what the rule orders.

Vernacular writers pick out the officers of the convent as having special opportunities for self-indulgence. Gilles li Muisis describes the progress of the worldly monk, and his growing self-importance:

En brief temps il sera dans abbés ou prieus
Ou grans officyers; si fait le prescieus
Par quoy tous li couvens li soit plus gratieus.[52]

In a short time he will be Master Abbot or prior or important officer; so he plays the big man, and all the convent is more obsequious to him.

But if we were to relate these passages to Chaucer's text, we realise how heavy a burden of meaning we should be imposing on the simple statement that the Monk was 'A manly man, to been an abbot able'. And what exactly does this line mean? Is the narrator saying that manly authority is desirable for anyone in a position of superiority? Or that the Monk was capable of being an abbot because in these degenerate days worldliness is a better qualification than holiness? Is he even, perhaps, implying only that it is the Monk's own opinion that he is fit to be an abbot, as it is later clearly the Guildsmen's own opinion that they are fit to be aldermen? We find that we cannot pinpoint with exactness the target of Chaucer's satire. Previous tradition raises the expectation that we shall be called on to make a moral judgement on the holder of, or aspirant to monastic office, but we are not, in this case, given enough information to do so.[53]

A similar ambivalance characterises Chaucer's use of the word 'manly' in this line. We can compare it with a sermon comment on one notion of 'manliness':

He that is a ffracer, a grete bragger, a grete swerer or a grete fyȝtter, soche men ben callyd 'manly men'.[54]

33

But while Chaucer makes us aware that the word is susceptible of both favourable and unfavourable interpretations, he gives us no help in deciding which to choose. Ambivalence also characterises Chaucer's handling of another strain of ironic vocabulary – that which deals with monastic 'lordliness'. We have already seen how this aspect of the Monk emerges in his hunting activities: all his equipment is of the best, his horse is 'in great estaat', and he shows a lordly disregard for expenditure – 'for no cost wolde he spare' (192). This aspect of the hunting cleric is also prominent in other writers. The French version of Matheolus' *Lamentations* comments that the hunting parson imitates squires ('Ressembler veut aux damoiseaux').[55] 'The Simonie' complains:

> And thise abbotes and prioures don aȝein here rihtes;
> Hii riden wid hauk and hound, and *contrefeten knihtes*,
> Hii sholde leve swich pride, and ben religious.[56]

Handlyng Synne points out that hunting is improper for clerics, and appropriate only to the aristocracy,[57] and we have seen how Langland's figure of Religioun rides about with his dogs 'as he a lorde were';

> And but if his knaue knele · that shal his cuppe brynge,
> He loureth on hym and axeth hym · who tauȝte hym curteisye.
>
> (*PPl* x 310–11)

Gower's picture of a monk who is, like Chaucer's, a greedy 'outridere' who enjoys his horseback rides over the countryside, also stresses a lordly open-handedness with money and a 'seignoral' attitude to the world.

> Cil moigne n'est pas bon claustral
> Q'est fait gardein ou seneschal
> D'ascun office q'est forein;
> Car lors luy falt selle et chival
> Pour courre les païs aval,
> Si fait despense au large mein;
> Il prent vers soy le meulx de grein,
> Et laist as autres comme vilein
> La paille, et ensi seignoral
> Devient le moygne nyce et vein:
> De vuide grange et ventre plein
> N'ert pas l'acompte bien egal.
> Du charité q'est inparfit,
> 'Tout est nostre', ly moignes dist,
> Qant il est gardein du manoir:
> En part dist voir, mais c'est petit. (*MO* 20,953–68)

That monk is not a good cloisterer who is made keeper or steward of any outside post. For then he needs saddle and horse, to ride through the countryside, and he spends open-handedly. He takes for himself the best of the crop, and leaves the chaff for others, as peasants, and so the silly vain monk acts like a lord. With an empty barn on one side and a full belly on the other, the scores aren't exactly equal. With impaired charity the monk says 'All is ours!', when he is guardian of the manor; there is some truth in what he says, but not much.

General aristocratic pretensions on the part of monks are the butt of a satiric tradition which also exploits for ironic effect semantic ambivalence similar to Chaucer's – that is, the tensions existing between the uses of the same word in circles of different social or moral status. We have seen how the *Roman de Carité* ironically pays tribute to the 'courtoisie' of modern monks, and it goes on to describe how they live like 'castelains'.[58] 'L'Ordre de Bel Ayse' praises the members of the order for virtues which are not obviously religious ones:

> Quar en l'Ordre est meint prodoume
> E meinte bele e bonne dame.[59]

For in the Order is many a worthy man and many a fair and good lady. (trans. Aspin, p. 138)

The word 'preudhomme' is not inappropriate to monks – Gilles li Muisis constantly insists that monks should be 'preudhommes'– [60] but it is a word which is also frequently applied to secular lords,[61] and it is therefore tempting to think that the author of the Anglo-Norman poem is ironically playing off two appropriate contexts for the word. This semantic irony is not of course applied solely to monks; Gilles uses it when discussing gluttons:

> Et qui plus en poet boire, c'est grans chevalerie:
> Tout chou ne tiènent mie que che soit gloutenie. (II, p. 92)

And whoever can drink the most of it – that is great prowess! They don't think of it as gluttony at all.

This strain of irony has obviously influenced Chaucer's presentation of his Monk as 'manly', 'a lord' and 'a fair prelaat' (172, 200, 204). Yet Chaucer's irony works in a different way from all the others. Gower, for example, tells us firmly how we are to interpret his monk's words ('En part dist voir') and points up the fact that 'despense au large mein' is not the same as 'charité'. And in the other portraits too, although we glimpse a worldly view of 'courtoisie' or nobility or manliness, our perception is firmly governed by the indications that it is a *false* conception of the word. With Chaucer, we cannot be so confident about what is truth and what is illusion. It would not be easy to agree in what sense the Monk is 'manly' or how far this quality is to be admired in him, while the judgement that he is 'to been an abbot able' ostensibly belongs to the narrator, not to him. As in the earlier instances, we have to distinguish between what is presented as fact, and what is merely suggested by the narrator's choice of vocabulary. Thus, Chaucer doesn't say that the Monk imitates a lord, but simply refers to him as a lord; his lordliness, like his unchastity, has linguistic rather than actual status.

The parallels with other estates writers show that the characteristics of Chaucer's Monk were readily associated with his estate over a long period of time, and in several countries, and that the details used to illustrate them are not peculiar to Chaucer's 'individual' portraits, but were equally common in generalised accusations.[62] But the parallels also serve to define Chaucer's style more clearly. We have seen that most estates satirists are not humourless sermonisers. The tradition boasts sophisticated literary techniques – debate, dramatic presentation, paradox, irony – which Chaucer develops. What is distinctive about his satire, however, is the way that he uses the 'facts' made familiar by other satirists to suggest their application to his Monk, while he himself does not give us as many as has been thought. Does the Monk neglect services? Is he sexually licentious? Do we correctly infer his gluttony from his appearance and his fondness for swan? We realise slowly that much of the 'information' that we have been led to derive from the portrait rests on very shaky evidence. Even where the Monk's behaviour is clear to us – his love of hunting and his contempt for the cloister – ambiguity is introduced by giving us the Monk's defence of his activities, in such a way as to perplex us again. Is his rebellion against 'texts' and 'rules' genuine, or a hollow pretence meant only to allow him to do as he pleases? We may well *suspect* the latter – my point is only that we cannot *know* whether he even believes his own opinion; even less can we know what final judgement lies behind the narrator's hearty endorsement of it. Our reactions are also complicated by the narrator's enthusiasm for the Monk's clothing, horses and dogs, for we are obliged to admit that this enthusiasm is relevant to the same degree that his moral disapproval would have been. It *is* very pleasant to imagine the company of such a sleek, gleaming lordly prelate – above all, he is 'fair'.[63] The language of the portrait thus stimulates us to condemn (in so far as it evokes tradition) and approve at the same time.

This appeal for approbation goes further than the use of ironic praise in other writers, because at the same time as they ironically commend, they clearly describe behaviour of which they disapprove, or they use images which repel us. The thirteenth-century satirist Guiot de Provins, for example, 'explains' the frequent change of priors in convents of the Black Monks by saying it is feared that they might stink too much if left long in one place.[64] In Chaucer's portrait, the images are sensuously attractive, and faulty behaviour is presented from the point of view of its perpetrator, or can only be inferred from hints. And thus we have a sense of depth, of contradictory responses to the Monk, of not knowing him fully, of his having views of his own which make him step out of the frame of 'observation'. We become convinced that he does not exist simply on the level of theoretical moralising ('what he ought to be' set against 'what he is') but on the plane of real existence.

THE FRIAR[65]

The Monk is 'fair'; the Friar is 'merye', 'swete', 'plesaunt' and 'worthy'. Once again, the epithets cannot be read as entirely ironical. It is a suggestion that, on one plane, these qualities really exist in the Friar that Chaucer brings to the traditional material of anti-mendicant satire.

This can be shown from the way Chaucer treats a traditional feature of the mendicant stereotype – his persuasive tongue. Chaucer repeatedly stresses the winning nature of his Friar's speech and manner; he is pre-eminently skilled in 'daliaunce' and 'fair langage' (211), his absolution and his *In principio* are intoned pleasantly (222, 254), and as a final touch,

> Somwhat he lipsed, for his wantownesse,
> To make his Englissh sweete upon his tonge. (264–5)

A similar 'gift of the gab' is one of the most prominent features of the mendicant stereotype. Often it is seen as an instrument of outright deception;[66] at other times, the friar is not deceiving his client, but acting as his accomplice in the aim of keeping life 'pleasant'. There is in Chaucer no hint of more bitter satiric comments on the friars' lies and hypocrisy, such as one writer's pointed reference to the similarity between 'mendicant' and 'mendacious'.[67] But many other writers lay equal stress on the blandness and pleasantness of friars' talk; in Gower's *Mirour de l'Omme* the friars 'Ipocresie' and 'Flaterie' are hand in glove (21,249ff.). Mendicant flattery appears in Latin in the 'Viri fratres, servi Dei', where friars 'titillate the ears of the great',[68] and the *Vox Clamantis* describes those friars

> qui verba colorant,
> Qui pascunt aures, aurea verba sonant,
> Verbis frondescunt, set non est fructus in actu,
> Simplicium mentes dulce loquendo mouent.[69]

who colour their words, and stuff our ears with the sound of their golden phrases. They blossom forth in words, but there is no fruit in their actions; they sway the minds of the naive by their sweet speaking.

In the *Roman de la Rose*, Amis refers to the mendicants who are 'strong in body' ('poissanz de cors') – as Chaucer's Friar is 'strong ... as a champioun' – and yet

> se vont par tout enbatant,
> par douces paroles flatant. (1 8070–2)

go thrusting their noses into everything, flattering with their soft speech.

Faus Semblant likewise cloaks deception with 'softe ... and plesaunt' words.[70] Similarly, Gilles li Muisis sees the friars' success as founded on their 'bielles paroles':[71] 'Les gens par biel parler sèvent enollyer'.[72] ('They know how to butter people up with their fine talk.') In the *Mirour de l'Omme*, besides the two accomplices 'Ipocresie' and 'Flaterie' who go about to cajole and flatter ('Pour blandir et pour losenger'), and who also grant a pleasant confession and absolution,[73] we have a denunciation of the ready tongue ('langue liberal') and the fine and elaborate speech ('parole belle et queinte') of the friars, and an echo of the biblical warning against people whose speech is too gentle ('debonnaire'), and whose hand is too ready to give blessing.[74]

Other writers stress the 'queinte' rather than the 'belle' aspect of the friar's speech: 'Ful wysely can thai preche and say.'[75] For Langland, mendicant eloquence most often takes the form of 'hiegh clergye shewynge',[76] over-subtle preaching and 'glosing',[77] although it is with the picture of one 'frere Flaterere' throwing the church into confusion that *Piers Plowman* comes to an end (xx 311ff.). For the author of *Pierce the Ploughmans Crede*, the 'glauerynge wordes' of the friars are primarily a tool in their seduction of women.[78]

There is both unity and variety in the development of this feature of the mendicant stereotype. The descriptions of lying, flattering, 'glosing' and simple 'blarney' are inseparable from the central notion of the friar as fine talker, and yet they provide later satirists with a stock of detailed accounts of mendicant behaviour and the possibility of provoking a wide range of reactions, from disgust to amusement. Chaucer is thus drawing on tradition in giving his Friar skill in 'daliaunce' and 'fair language', and yet it is significant that it is this blandness that he has chosen to stress and develop. More than other satirists, Chaucer emphasises the façade rather than the deceptive intent behind it. The ambiguity in the word 'daliaunce' prevents us from being sure that the Friar's eloquence has a sexual aim.[79] Chaucer does not comment directly on the hollowness of the Friar's 'swete' confession and 'pleasaunt' absolution, and the lisp – while it is an addition clearly in line with, and stimulated by, the tradition – is a feature as yet innocent of any associations with deception and self-interest. As with the Monk, Chaucer seems to have more ends in view than moral criticism of the character he is describing.

This also becomes clear as we see how Chaucer again reduces traditional satiric topics to a series of brief hints. The friars' facility in 'glosing', for instance, is linked by satirists with their pride,[80] and one way in which this was traditionally conveyed was through use of the biblical strictures on the scribes and the pharisees, who love to be called 'Rabbi, Rabbi' and are admonished 'Neither be ye called masters.'[81] The biblical passage had long afforded material for satire on intellectual arrogance: Jerome applied it to heretics,[82] and later satirists to scholars in general.[83] In the latter context, 'Master' signifies 'M.A.' The hint for its application to friars comes from St Francis himself, who exhorted his followers that they should not be called masters.[84] Soon afterwards, the Roman de la Rose is complaining that friars

> willen that folk hem loute and grete
> Whanne that they passen thurgh the strete,
> And wolen be cleped 'maister' also.[85]

And thereafter both English and Continental writers use the biblical passage, and the desire to be called 'master', to illustrate the friars' pride in learning.[86] We know that Chaucer was well aware of this tradition, not only because of his reading of the Roman de la Rose, but because the Host twice addresses the Friar as 'maister deere',[87] and because the friar of the Summoner's Tale, although he accepts

being called 'deere maister' by the sick Thomas, protests to the lord of
the village that he is

> 'No maister . . . but servitour,
> Thogh I have had in scole that honour.
> God liketh nat that "Raby" men us calle,
> Neither in market ne in your large halle.'[88]

All this seems to lay a large burden of significance on Chaucer's simple
statement that Huberd was 'lyk a maister' (261). But the allusion is of
the briefest, and this feature too has linguistic rather than factual status.
As in the Monk's portrait, we are given no firm basis for moral
judgement.[89]

The satire on the friar's ready tongue also leads the satirist, in another
direction, to the stereotyped notion of the friar as womaniser. It is a
small step from descriptions of the blandishment of women to descriptions of their seduction. Not only, as Arnold Williams has noted,[90]
can charges of spiritual seduction readily become charges of bodily
seduction, but also it is easy to see how a class enjoying freedom to
travel about and to have secret conferences with women would quickly
take on the role assigned to the commercial traveller in modern anecdote. There are several different approaches to this topic. Some writers
make lechery the prime motivation;[91] others see women simply as
more gullible victims for friars than men, as they are for Boccaccio:

Costoro colle fimbrie ampissime avvolgendosi, molte pinzochere, molte
vedove, molte altre sciocche femine e uomini d'avviluparvi sotto s'ingegnano,
ed é lor maggior sollicitudine che d'altro esercizio.[92]

They enlarge widely the borders of their garments, and strive to entangle in
them many beghines, many widows, and many other foolish women and men,
and this, more than any other activity, is their greatest endeavour.

Gower describes the friar practising his persuasion on women, in a
passage whose influence on Chaucer is obvious:

> Maisque la dame ait poy ou nient,
> Ja meinz pour ce ne s'en abstient
> Clamer, prier et conjurer;
> La maile prent s'il n'ait denier,
> Voir un soul oef pour le souper,
> Ascune chose avoir covient. (MO 21,376–81)

Even if the lady has little or nothing, not for that does he cease to cry, beg and
conjure. He takes a ha'penny if there isn't a penny – even a single egg for his
supper – he must have something.

Yet Chaucer's Friar is given a softer, more wheedling technique; he does not need to 'Clamer, prier et conjurer':

> He was the beste beggere in his hous; . . .
> For thogh a wydwe hadde noght a sho,
> So plesaunt was his '*In principio*',
> Yet wolde he have a ferthyng, er he wente. (251-5)

Gower evokes a similar impression of cajolery, in a passage which also shows how the friar's professional meddling gives him the opportunity for seducing women:

> Spiritus vt domini, sic frater spirat vbique,
>   Et venit ad lectum quando maritus abest . . .
> Hic est confessor domini non, set dominarum,
>   Qui magis est blandus quam Titiuillus eis.[93]

Like the spirit of the Lord, the friar bloweth where he listeth, and comes to the bed when the husband is absent . . . He is a confessor not of the Lord, but of ladies, and is smoother than the devil with them.

At the close of *Piers Plowman*, Peace refuses a friar entry to Unity (the Church) with the indigant words:

> I knewe such one ones · nouȝte eighte wynter passed,
> Come in thus ycoped · at a courte ther I dwelt,
> And was my lordes leche · and my ladyes bothe.
> And at the last this limitour · tho my lorde was out,
> He salued so owre wommen · til somme were with childe! (xx 351-5)

The apparent inevitability of this consequence of the friar's professional activities leads us to suspect the same implications in Chaucer's portrait, and indeed, we hear repeatedly of the Friar's connections with 'yonge wommen', 'worthy wommen of the toun', 'faire wyves', 'tappesteres' and 'wydwes'. We have noted the ambiguity in the word 'daliaunce', and can go on to note a similar ambivalence in the statement that the Friar could 'rage' like a puppy. Does this refer to harmless entertainment or to love-making?[94] The way in which it follows the reference to the widow might seem to imply the second – and we remember Chaucer's ambiguous description of the Friar as 'wantowne'.[95] Yet the *evidence* for our impression of Huberd's licentiousness is slender; it is no more than a series of linguistic suggestions, which the traditional view of the friar attunes us to pick up, but which do not allow a definite conclusion.

With literary economy, Chaucer links one more hint of the Friar's

lechery with the presentation of his role as 'businessman'. The picture
of the friar as business adviser, controlling the lord's family and drawing
up his will (to the friar's own advantage) can be found in Latin satire,[96]
but the major influence on the treatment of this topic is the portrait of
Faus Semblant, who boasts:

> Si m'entremet de corretages,
> je faz pes, je joig mariages,
> seur moi preign execucions
> et vois en procuracions.
> Messagiers sui et faz enquestes.[97]

Also I busy myself with broking, I arbitrate quarrels, I marry people. I act as
executor and procurator. I am a messenger and conduct inquiries.

Most of the many later treatments of this topic model themselves on
this passage,[98] so that we are not surprised to find that Chaucer's Friar
likewise arranges marriages and settles disputes:

> He hadde maad ful many a marriage
> Of yonge women at his owene cost . . .
> In love-dayes ther koude he muchel help. (212-3, 258)

But we *are* surprised to find that, so far from making a profit out of the
marriages he arranges, the Friar actually pays for them himself; as
with the love-knot on the Monk's pin, Chaucer uses one feature of the
stereotype to suggest another. Are they not women he has seduced
whom he is anxious to marry off well?[99] Is there not, perhaps, even a
double entendre in the mention of the 'love-days' following on the claim
that the Friar can 'rage' so successfully? Playful high spirits are not
what one would most enthusiastically recommend in an arbitrator
of quarrels, but in another sort of 'love-day' their relevance would be
clear.

Apart from a possible wish to use the opportunity for a double
meaning, Chaucer's specific reference to 'love-days' (official days for
legal reconciliation)[100] seems due to Langland's contempt for them and
those who arrange them,[101] although Langland associates them with
'Religion' in general rather than friars in particular. It is also Langland
who talks of 'charite' turning 'chapman and chief to shryue lordes',[102]
and this may be a reference to the friar as pedlar – another of his 'business activities'. A Middle English poem describes this aspect of mendi-
cant life in detail; like Chaucer, it mentions 'knyves | And pynnes'
and links the feature with an appeal to 'faire wyves':

Thai dele with purses, pynnes and knyves,
With girdels, gloves, for wenches and wyves.

Some frers beren pelure aboute,
For grete ladys and wenches stoute,
To reverce with thair clothes withoute;
Al after that thai ere ...
    Al that for women is plesand
    Ful redy certes have thai;
    Bot lytel gyfe thai the husband,
    That for al shal pay.

If a friar gives a woman a knife, he will have its value ten times over
before he leaves.[103]

Chaucer's reference to mendicant lechery is thus reduced to a series
of hints, arising during his presentation of other aspects of the Friar.
Other mendicant features are treated with parallel obliqueness. Thus
although Chaucer describes without ambiguity the Friar's splendid
clothing – the 'semycope' of 'double worsted' – his ostensible purpose
in doing so is a documentary interest in the Friar's appearance, and the
expression of his admiration for the way it 'rounded as a belle out of the
presse' (262–3). Whereas the Monk's clothing impresses us mainly
with its attractiveness, the Friar's cope conveys to us an impression of
his status, and is thus linked naturally with the suggestion of the Friar's
desire to be called 'master':

For ther he was nat lyk a cloysterer
With a thredbare cope, as is a povre scoler.
But he was lyk a maister or a pope. (259–61)

Not only is fine clothing traditionally associated with friars, but this
aspect of it is emphasised by other writers; Burnellus the Ass rejoices
that as a Jacobin

trabee regis equalis erit mea uestis,
Ut me magnificet talia quisque uidens.[104]

My habit will be like a king's state-robe, so that anyone seeing it will honour
me.

Another poet contrasts the clothing of friars with that of 'possessioners'
just as Chaucer contrasts it with that of 'a cloysterer'.[105] In Boccaccio
the figure of the splendidly-coped friar recurs constantly, and the intent
to impress is emphasised:

dove dagl' inventori de' frati [le cappe] furono ordinate strette e misere e di

43

grossi panni ... essi oggi le fanno largho e doppie e lucide e di finissimi panni, e quelle in forme hanno recate leggiadra e pontificale intanto che paoneggiar con esse nelle chiese e nelle piazze.[106]

... né San Domenico né San Francesco, senza aver quattor cappe per uno, non di tintillani né d'altri panni gentili ma di lana grossa fatti e di natural colore, a cacciare il freddo e non ad apparere si vestissero.[107]

Whereas their copes were ordained by the friars' founders to be narrow, poor, and of coarse cloth ... nowadays they make them wide, of double thickness, resplendent and of the finest materials, and they are made in a stylish and pontifical cut, so that they flaunt them like peacocks in churches and squares.

Neither St Dominic nor St Francis, without having four copes instead of one, not dyed in grain or of other fine cloth, but of coarse undyed wool, dressed for show, but to keep out the cold.

For Langland too, the friar is inseparable from his 'coueitise of copis', to gain which he believes they will follow Antichrist.[108] He too implies that fine clothing matches the friars' self-importance:

> Many of this *maistres freris* · mowe clothen hem at lyking,
> For here money and marchandise · marchen togideres. (*PPl* Prol. 62–3)

Langland has obviously influenced the anti-mendicant satire of *Pierce the Ploughmans Crede,* which complains that there is more cloth in a Minorite's cope than was in St Francis' tunic (292–7). But the *Crede* also seems to show the influence of Chaucer, in the description of a corpulent Dominican:

> His cope þat bi-clypped him · wel clene was it folden,
> Of *double worstede* y-dyȝt · doun to the hele;
> His kyrtel of clene whijt · clenlyche y-sewed;
> Hyt was good y-now of ground · greyn for to beren.[109]

Whether or not the author has taken the detail from Chaucer, this passage shows very clearly that it can help to realise a type just as well as to suggest a particular individual.

One feature of Chaucer's portrait which does *not* figure prominently in the satiric stereotype of the friar is his musical ability, on which Chaucer lays stress. A great deal of Huberd's attractiveness lies in the description of his 'murye note':

Wel koude he synge and pleyen on a rote;
Of yeddynges he baar outrely the pris . . .
And in his harpyng, whan that he hadde songe,
His eyen twynkled in his heed aryght,
As doon the sterres in the frosty nyght. (236–7, 266–9)

There is only one satiric parallel to this passage, in the *Decameron*, where a friar turns lover, and begins to compose songs, sonnets and ballads, and to sing them ('a fare delle canzoni e de'sonetti e delle ballate, e a cantare').[110] Are we then to assume that Chaucer was describing a particular friar who was musically accomplished? That this trait is invented in order to individualise the Friar? Or that Chaucer had observed such friars as Wycliff describes:

þei studien on þe holy day aboute experymentis or wiche craft or veyn songis and knackynge and harpynge, gyternynge & daunsynge & oþere veyn triflis to geten þe stynkyng loue of damyselis.[111]

This passage may well point to an association of friars with musical entertainment in the popular, as opposed to literary, stereotype. But whatever the particular stimulus for including this feature, the reason for stressing it is surely that this is a parody of an aspect of the friar's *profession*.[112] St Francis called his followers 'joculatores Domini' – 'God's minstrels' – and in moments of spiritual ecstasy, he would mimic the playing of a viol, and sing in front of the faithful. Exactly the same desire for popular appeal that led St Francis to this symbolic, spiritual entertainment, would have encouraged his followers to revert to more worldly amusement. Thus Chaucer's Friar, so far from being a 'viellator Dei', is a worldly jongleur.[113] It is through verbal and literary analysis, rather than through an appeal to real life – whether in terms of particular individuals or historical generalisations – that we can best understand this passage.

So far we have followed Chaucer in stressing the attractiveness of the Friar; his music, his pleasant speech, his twinkling eyes and white neck, his muscular physique, seem intended to seduce us as well as the women he converses with. Yet sinister overtones may be felt throughout the portrait; the Friar's cunning manipulation of the world to his own advantage, the possibility that he is a 'fixer', and a blackmailer of the rich friends whose secrets are confessed to him, lurk just out of the range of our vision. His pleasantness is strictly dependent on the reaping of financial gain:

> And over al, *ther as profit sholde arise,*
> Curteis he was and lowely of seruyse.
> Ther nas no man nowher so vertuous. (249–51)

The narrator's modification in the first of these lines suddenly alters the meaning of what he is reporting and the angle from which we view it, so that the comment becomes a direct parody of the description of the 'Curteis ... lowely and servysable' Squire. The same sort of shift occurs in an earlier reference to the Friar's avarice:

> He was an esy man to yeve penaunce,
> Ther as he wiste to have a good pitaunce. (223–4)

The shifts in Chaucer's lines effect shifts in our attitude to the Friar, from complaisance to cynicism, and back again. But most other writers adopt a consistently cynical attitude to the traditional mercenariness of friars –

> Quos mendicandi uexat tantummodo feruor,
> Spirituum cura nulla molestat eos.[114]

Whom the passion for begging harasses while the care of souls doesn't trouble them at all.

The author of 'Le Dit des Patenostres' is equally blunt: 'they know how to spy out their own profit on all sides' ('bien scevent partout leur profit espier'),[115] while Faus Semblant boasts openly

> En aquerre est toute m'entente,
> mieuz vaut mes porchaz que ma rente.[116]

My whole aim is to make a profit – my earnings are more than my stipend.

– a proverbial expression which becomes a mark of other clerical villains besides Huberd.[117] Gilles li Muisis, on the other hand, has a pair of lines denouncing mendicant avarice which, like Chaucer's, give with one hand what they take away with the other.

> De donner as ouvrages, c'est bien leur volentés,
> Mais qu'il aient pitances avoecque chou plentés.[118]

They are very willing to provide funds for good works, so long as they meanwhile have abundant provisions.

But Chaucer may well have learned the effectiveness of this satiric technique from Boccaccio. The story of Fra Alberto da Immola in the *Decameron* describes how this new-made friar cominciò a far per sembianti una aspra vita e a commendar molto la penitenzia e l'astinenzia, né mai carne mangiava né bevea vino, *quando non n'avea che gli piacesse.*[119]

began to adopt the appearance of a harsh life, and to praise highly penance and abstinence; nor did he eat meat or drink wine – when there wasn't any he liked.

Yet, when set in its context, Chaucer's alteration of the angle from which we view the Friar's conduct does not 'explode' his genial manner with the same finality that characterises the deflation of the mendicants in Boccaccio and Gilles le Muisis. It is with the Friar's 'harpynge' and twinkling eyes that the portrait closes. Whether the sinister or the pleasant aspects of the Friar predominate in our final impression of him will obviously be influenced by subjective matters; our attitude will depend on whether we would prefer villainy to be frankly, if brutally, practised, and on whether we are more amused or shocked by the cunning invitation to ignore such unpleasant matters as sin and sickness. But however this is decided, I think it is mistaken to assume that the pleasantness of the Friar's façade is stressed *merely* as a contrast with the unpleasant reality; the pointer to some other purpose is contained in the observation that Chaucer so often renders our grasp of 'reality' uncertain.

The same complexity characterises Chaucer's presentation of the Friar's eagerness to make money from hearing confessions. This also is traditional. The 'debonnaire' confessor 'Flaterie' provides a 'plesaunt' absolution which, like the Friar's, is dependent on the amount of money given him rather than any signs of contrition:

> Ipocresie tielement
> Du dame et seignour ensement
> Quiert avoir la confessioun;
> Mais Flaterie nequedent
> Par l'ordinance du covent
> En dorra l'absolucioun,
> Car il ad despensacioun
> Solonc recompensacioun,
> Que vient du bource du riche gent,
> Qu'il puet donner remissioun
> Sanz paine et sanz punicioun,
> Pour plus gaigner de leur argent.[120]

Thus Hypocrisy seeks to become confessor to both lord and lady, but nevertheless it is Flattery who, according to the rule of the convent, will give absolution.

For he has a dispensation, depending on the reward which proceeds from the purses of the rich, to grant remission of sins without penance or punishment, with the aim of gaining more of their money.

Other writers emphasise the contemptible nature of the bribes for which the friars will excuse the most enormous sins. 'Lesse then a payre of shone' will absolve a man for having slain all his kin,[121] for 'sixe pens' you can 'sle thi fadre, and jape thi modre',[122] and for a 'seme of whete' a friar offers to absolve Lady Meed for the falseness and lechery of fifty years.[123] Langland's dreamer is advised:

> have no conscience · how thow come to gode;
> Go confesse the to sum frere · and shewe hym thi synnes
> For whiles Fortune is thi frende · freres wil the louye. (*PPl* XI 52–4)

and in the final Passus, 'Frere Flaterere' removes the plasters which the parson had laid on Contrition, and offers absolution 'for a litel syluer';

> Thus he goth and gadereth · and gloseth there he shryueth,
> Tyl Contricioun hadde clene forȝeten · to crye and to wepe.[124]

This passage reminds us of the quarrel with the secular clergy to which the friars' eagerness for the lucrative work of confession is supposed to have contributed. Friars are consistently presented in literature as hating and being hated by the clergy.

> Oves alienas tondunt
> Et parochias confundunt.[125]

They shear the flock of others, and throw the parishes into confusion.

'Thai travele ȝerne and bysily, . . . | To brynge doun the clergye', says another writer,[126] and Langland's figure of Wrath describes how he has so successfully grafted lies on to 'limitoures' that now people confess to them rather than to their parsons –

> And now persones han parceyued · that freres parte with hem,
> Thise possessioneres preche · and depraue freres,
> And freres fyndeth hem in defaute · as folke bereth witnes.[127]

Chaucer incorporates these traditional features into the portrait of his Friar, but he presents them from the Friar's own viewpoint:

> For he hadde power of confessioun,
> As seyde hymself, moore than a curat,
> For of his ordre he was licentiat.
> Ful swetely herde he confessioun,

And plesaunt was his absolucioun:
He was an esy man to yeve penaunce,
Ther as he wiste to have a good pitaunce.
For unto a povre ordre for to yive
Is signe that a man is wel yshrive;
For if he yaf, he dorste make avaunt,
He wiste that a man was repentaunt;
For many a man so hard is of his herte,
He may nat wepe, althogh hym soore smerte.
Therfore in stede of wepyng and preyeres
Men moote yeve silver to the povre freres. (221–32)

Part of the stimulus for the irony in lines 229–32 may have come from such a text as 'L'Ordre de Bel Ayse', which describes how sinners' hearts are so hard that only a great deal of wine can move them to repentance.[128] Even greater is the debt to the speech of Faus Semblant, who boasts of his superiority to the secular clergy as Chaucer's Friar does:

> je sui d'ordre et si sui prestres,
> de confessier li plus hauz mestres
> qui soit, tant con li mondes dure.
> J'ai de tout le monde la cure,
> ce n'ot onques prestres curez,
> tant fust a s'iglise jurez,
> et si ai, par la haute dame!
> .c. tanz plus pitié de vostre ame
> que voz prestres parrochiaus,
> ja tant n'iert vostre especiaus.
> Si rai un mout grant avantage:
> prelat ne sunt mie si sage
> ne si letré de trop con gié.[129]

I am in orders and a priest as well, fit for confessing the highest master who may exist until the end of the world. I have all the world in my charge – which no parish priest ever had, however much he might have received charge of his church by oath, and also I have, by our Lady! a hundred times more pity on your soul than your parish priest, however friendly with you he is. Also I have a very great advantage – even prelates are not as wise and learned as I am.

The claim to 'power of confessioun...moore than a curat', the 'plesaunt' absolution given out of pity for the sinner's unfortunate situation, are here presented in the half-boasting, half-wheedling tones which we seem to hear in Chaucer's lines. But a significant difference is that Jean de Meun retires completely behind the figure of Faus

Semblant, who happily acquiesces in Amors' comments on the nature of his villainy. Whatever our surface enjoyment of this rogue, we are all the time simultaneously aware of two viewpoints – the 'false' one of the sinner and the 'true' one of the moralist.[130] Chaucer enters his own poem as narrator to make the sudden qualification – 'As seyde hymself' – which creates an abrupt *shift* of viewpoint. Again it is Gilles li Muisis who uses such a transition in a similar context:

> Boin clerc sont et soutil, se sèvent besongnier,
> Se les croit-on de chou qu'il voellent tesmoignier. (II, p. 41)

They are good and subtle scholars and know how to do their work – if their testimony is to be believed.

But Gilles leaves the two viewpoints in revealing opposition. Chaucer reverts to a third-person description which leaves us in doubt as to whose opinions are being recorded. Whose are the 'For's and the 'Therfore' which triumphantly conclude the defence of the Friar? The viewpoints of Friar and narrator are no sooner distinguished than they are fused again. Chaucer could well have learned from earlier writers the possibility of satiric exploitation of different points of view, but his own shifts are Protean compared with theirs.

In describing the company the Friar keeps, Chaucer withdraws the narrator's direct comments, and we are once again in a world of hints and ambiguities. It is impossible to be sure that the Friar's fondness for the company of 'selleres of vitaille' (248) derives from the well-documented tradition of the friars' gluttony, although this is inevitably brought to mind.[131] There is less doubt about the Friar's tavern-haunting:

> He knew the tavernes wel in every toun
> And every hostiler and tappestere
> Bet than a lazar or a beggestere. (240-2)

This habit is not peculiar to Chaucer's Friar; Burnellus says of the Carmelites:

> His magis interne mulieres atque taberne
> Et mendicare quam sacra uerba dare.[132]

They are more intimate with women and taverns and begging than with spreading the gospel.

And when the narrator of *Pierce the Ploughmans Crede* tracks down the Carmelites, sure enough they are in a tavern 'wiþ a full cuppe' (340).

But the reasons given for the Friar's preference of the company of inn-
keepers are not related to the demands of his stomach:

> For unto such a worthy man as he
> Accorded nat, as by his facultee,
> To have with sike lazars aqueyntaunce.
> It is nat honest, it may nat avaunce,
> For to delen with no swich poraille,
> But al with riche and selleres of vitaille. (243–8)

The sudden modification of 'It is nat honest' into 'it may nat avaunce'
parallels the shift in the reader's response between the first and second
line of an earlier reference to the company the Friar keeps:

> Ful well biloved and famulier was he
> With frankeleyns over al in his contree,
> And eek with worthy wommen of the toun. (215–17)

Such a preference for the rich over the poor was traditionally attributed to friars, and the motive is often seen as profit – 'it may nat
avaunce'.

> Dantibus adplaudunt care,
> Sed, qui nihil possunt dare
> Vel replere eis manum,
> Illos mittunt ad plebanum . . .
> Per verborum apparatum
> Aures pruriunt magnatum.
> Valde diligenter notant,
> Ubi divites aegrotant,
> Ibi currunt nec cessabunt,
> Donec ipsos tumulabunt,
> Sed ad casas miserorum
> Nullus ire vult eorum.[133]

They praise highly those who give to them, but those who cannot give them
anything or fill their hands, they send to the parish priest . . . They titillate
the ears of the rich through their fine array of words. They note with great
assiduity where the rich fall sick, and run there, not stopping their visits
until they have buried them. But none of them will go to the houses of the
poor.

The profit that friars make from associating with rich people is
frequently visualised as funeral fees or legacies,[134] but just as often the
rich man's home is desirable as the place 'where they see most smoke
from the kitchen' ('où il verront plus fumer la cuisine'),[135] and the

Franklin's portrait leads us to suspect that this may be the cause of the
Friar's cultivation of franklins. This is the motive assumed by Langland,
who urges the nobility

> Nou3t to fare as a fitheler or a frere ˙ for to seke festes
> Homelich at other mennes houses ˙ and hatyen her owne. (*PPl* x 92–3)

'L'Ordre de Bel Ayse' ironically approves of this behaviour; 'I will
tell you', says the author, 'in what way the Minorites practise the
poverty in which they are founded' –

> Quant il vont par le pays
> Al chief baroun ou chivaler
> Se lerrount il herberger,
> Ou a chief personne ou prestre,
> La ou il purrount a oese estre.
> Mes par Seint Piere de Roume,
> Ne se herbigerount ov povre houme!
> Taunt come plus riches serrount
> Ostiel plustost demanderount.
> Ne ne deyvent nos freres [of the Order of Fair-Ease] fere
> Ostiel en autre lyu quere
> Fors la ou il sevent plenté.
> E la deyvent en charité
> Char mangier e ce qu'il ount
> Auxi come les menours fount.[136]

When they travel about the land they will let the chief baron or knight put
them up, or the principal parson or priest, where they can take their ease. But
by St Peter of Rome, they will not take shelter with a poor man! The richer the
persons, the more readily will they ask lodging [from them]. Nor must our
brothers go and seek hospitality in any place except where they know there is
abundance. And there they must eat meat and whatever they have by charity,
as the Minorites do. (trans. after Aspin, p. 140)

The ironic pretence that 'char' has something to do with 'charité'
is matched by Chaucer's pretence that the 'facultee' of a friar prevents
him from associating with poor people. For profit is not Huberd's
only reason for choosing his company carefully; he is conscious that
he is 'worthy' and has a 'facultee' whose status must be preserved
from contamination by people whose company is not 'honest' or
respectable. This aspect of mendicant motivation had not been
overlooked: Faus Semblant boasts that he seeks to confess the
aristocracy,

Mes des povres genz est ce hontes,
je n'aim pas tel confession.
Se n'est por autre occasion,
je n'ai cure de povre gent:
leur estat n'est bel ne gent.[137]

But with respect to poor people this is shameful – I don't like that sort of confession. If there isn't some special reason, I don't have poor people in my charge, for their position is neither pleasing nor respectable.

The complexity of Chaucer's portrait therefore reflects the complexity of the tradition, in the various motives it attributes to friars, and the ironic presentation of these motives. Yet we must not fail to see that while seeming to attribute two motives – avarice and snobbery – to his Friar, Chaucer is actually making it more difficult to see what the 'real' motive is. Concrete evidence of the profit that the Friar derives from rich people is lacking; there is only a hint that one form it may take is good dinners. The comment that 'it may nat avaunce' the Friar to associate with poor people may not even refer to material profit, but to social ambition; at any rate, we cannot dismiss the excuse that 'it is not honest' as a mere 'cover-up' for material greed. And when we examine the Friar's conception of his social calling, we find it not completely illusory. The adjective 'worthy' can be applied without irony to a man who has a certain social standing, irrespective of his moral qualities.[138] This semantic ambiguity in the everyday use of a word leads us to see that a friar's 'facultee' exists in two spheres. In the religious sphere it would demand that the friar associate with the poor and the sick; in the worldly sphere it implies that the person exercising it has a level of education and spiritual authority which gives him a social ranking in worldly terms. The ethical and the social implications of words like 'worthy' and 'honest' are at odds with each other, and at no time more so than they are applied to a friar. The paradox involved in the absorption of the followers of an unworldly ideal into established society lies at the basis of the Friar's portrait.

We are now, I think, in a position to appreciate the 'estates' basis of Chaucer's Friar, which is responsible not only for general outlines, but for specific details such as the 'semicope'.[139] The traditional picture is a complex unity, seeing dual motives of lechery and avarice in mendicant activities, and producing a convincing image of a class that flatters and wheedles and yet at the same time is inspired by pride and a strong sense of status. Moreover, this image had already been given literary expression in representative figures such as Faus Semblant, Ipocresie, Flaterie and Frere Flaterere. The *coherence* of the Friar's character is therefore something already developed for Chaucer by the tradition of estates satire.

What Chaucer brings to this tradition is not merely 'redundant' detail.[140] It is the constant use of ambivalent words which make it hard to subject the Friar to moral analysis. Characteristic of Chaucer also is the frequent identification of the observer's viewpoint with that of the Friar – although in this portrait there is much more switching back and forth between the viewpoints of the Friar and the narrator than in the Monk's portrait. Yet in all this shifting back and forth, the narrator still does not dictate a moral attitude to us; he simply supplies another item of information – 'He was better qualified – as he said himself', 'He was well-beloved – by franklins' – which gives us another view of what has gone before. And finally, what is new in the portrait is the growing realisation that there is much in common between the approval of this 'worthy' and 'merye' Friar, and everyday social standards of judgement. It is we (and Chaucer's original audience) who prefer real music to spiritual entertainment, and who set up a notion of respectability which rates inn-keepers higher than lepers and beggars. We may suspect that the Friar's portrait is so long and complex because his estate reveals more clearly than any other the gulf between the standards of an ordered society and of Christianity. What emerges from the portrait is not just that the Friar does not live up to his ideals; it is that were he to do so, he would come into conflict with the audience's equally 'ideal' notions of social hierarchy.[141] Looking back to the Monk's portrait, we can see the same tension between the spiritual and the social. An orthodox moralist might well blame the Monk for his 'lordly' aspect – but while monasteries are supported by manors, how can monks avoid acting like lords of them? We shall see that the *Prologue* shows us that the question 'How shal the world be served?' cannot be put aside as easily as it might seem.

3

Estates Ideals

In the portraits of the Parson and the Ploughman, Chaucer gives a positive expression to two medieval estates ideals – those of the clergy and the peasantry. The Clerk and the Knight are also presented as individuals who live up to an ideal of their estate, but Chaucer's attitude to the particular ideals that they embody is an elusive one. The ideal of chivalry underlying the Knight's portrait is treated in a later chapter where it can be usefully contrasted with that of the Squire; here I should like to discuss the Parson, the Ploughman and the Clerk.

Although most of the Canterbury pilgrims have failings or vices, Chaucer portrays idealised representatives of the three estates which form the skeletal structure of medieval society – Knight, Parson, Ploughman. From this observation it has been deduced that although Chaucer wished to criticise individuals for failing in their social and moral duties, he did not wish to attack the social ideology of medieval society, or the view that social cohesion depends on the interchange of specialised services provided by each class.[1] Certainly it is striking that Chaucer not only presents the Parson and the Ploughman as ideal members of their respective classes, but also indicates how each benefits the other. Yet the isolated position of this sense of 'common profit' in the *Prologue* is also significant, and examination of the Clerk's portrait will modify the view that this is the social ethic implicit in the *Prologue*.

THE PARSON

The Parson's portrait, in comparison with those of the Monk and Friar, is like a drink of cold water after being excited and fuddled by wine; satiric ambiguities and ironic tones vanish in favour of a simple purity. The narrator's comments do not disturb our impression of the Parson's character, but confirm it; the values on which his praise, and the Parson's life, are founded, are clear and absolute in their demands. The pace of the verse is slow and measured, removing even the expectation of the sudden shift in attitude which so often complicates our reaction to other characters. Simple, unambiguous adjectives and adverbs are clustered thickly near the opening in order to make clear to us the narrator's attitude and to encourage us to share it: 'a good man...riche of hooly thoght and werk...trewely...devoutly ...Benygne...diligent...pacient'.

To form this idealistic estates portrait, Chaucer could draw on two aspects of preceding tradition.[2] He could invert the satiric criticisms of the clergy – as we can see him doing in the presentation of the Parson's virtues in terms of what he did *not* do: 'He sette *nat* his benefice to hyre' (507; cf. 492, 514, 516, 525–6). Chaucer could equally well base his description of the Parson on accounts of what a priest should do, or what priests in the good old days used to do. I noted earlier how the simultaneous existence of the 'ideal' and the 'normal' versions of an estates stereotype provided alternative possibilities for describing its representatives. When Chaucer describes an 'ideal' representative, he takes care to indicate also what is the 'normal'; the account of the Parson's virtues inevitably suggests the sins of the average priest, and his portrait thus becomes representative of the estate in both its good and its bad aspects.

Prominent in treatments of the clergy, in whatever aspect, is the biblical imagery of the shepherd and his sheep.[3] Such imagery occurs throughout Chaucer's portrait, reaching a climax in the lines:

> [He] dwelte at hoom, and kepte wel his folde,
> So that the wolf ne made it nat myscarie;
> He was a shepherde and noght a mercenarie. (512–14)[4]

This image is a *sine qua non* of any treatment of the priest's estate, especially in Latin and French, where a pun on 'pastor' is possible, and it is, by the same token, an inevitable feature of Chaucer's description. It is so commonplace elsewhere that it seems superfluous to provide examples, but a few which include comment on 'mercenaries' and the 'wolf' will illustrate the convention. The *Speculum Stultorum* lists the three sorts of creature who are found near the parochial sheepfold:

> Primus enim pastor est, mercenarius alter,
> Tertius insidians dicitur esse lupus.[5]

> The shepherd, who is first, the hireling next,
> And then the lurking wolf, which makes the third.
>
> (trans. Regenos, p. 125)

56

The comments of 'Ecce dolet Anglia' are typical of the use of the image:

> Pastorum pigritia greges disperguntur . . .
> Christi grex dispergitur, lupus insanivit;
> Pestisque diffunditur, agnos deglutivit . . .
> Heu! nunc mercenarii, nec veri pastores,
> Rectores vicarii mutaverunt mores.[6]

Through the shepherds' laziness the flocks are scattered . . . Christ's flock is scattered, the wolf makes his ravages; disease is rife, the lambs are devoured. . . . Alas! now mercenaries, no longer true shepherds, rector-vicars have changed their ways.

Chaucer's imagery resembles these conventional exploitations of the biblical passage in its easy, unexplained reference to the Parson's 'sheep', to the 'wolf' and to the 'mercenary'. His use of the pastoral image to discuss absenteeism is anticipated in a Goliardic Latin poem, although here the priests go off not to 'chaunteries' but to the court.

> Nam cum regum curias pastores sequuntur,
> pastorale regimen et jus postponuntur;
> pastoris absentia greges disperguntur,
> morsuque laetifero dispersi laeduntur.[7]

For when pastors run after kings' courts, their pastoral guidance and duty are abandoned. The flocks are scattered by the shepherd's absence, and once scattered, are wounded with a fatal bite.

Gower also uses the metaphor for absenteeism in the *Mirour de l'Omme*, although, for the sake of rhyme, the 'wolf' becomes a bear (20,302–4).

In Chaucer's use of the image, the concrete and realistic aspects of the metaphor are brought out by his insistence on the shit-covered sheep, and the flock 'encombred in the myre'; conventional phraseology is transformed into vivid and down-to-earth expressions. Some writers had already explored other realistic aspects of the image for similarly vivid effects. The *Roman de Carité* stresses the physical sickness of the flock:

> Pastre garde se berbis saine,
> Et s'ele enferme, il le resaine.
> Mais mercheniers dit: 'Assés tousse;
> Cui caut se muert ou lous l'en maine?'[8]

The shepherd keeps his sheep healthy, and if one falls sick, he cures it. But the hireling says 'He's coughing a lot – who cares if he dies or is dragged away by the wolf?'

Gilles li Muisis also develops the everyday aspect of the metaphor when he, like Chaucer, uses it to condemn absenteeism:

> Comment bien les brebis paistres connistera,
> Qui pau ou nient toudis il les compaignera?
> Pour siervir les signeurs en ce point laiscera;
> Qui ne set *a* ne *b* tel y commetera.[9]

How shall a shepherd know his sheep well if he accompanies them little or not at all? He will neglect this in order to serve lords, and will set over them someone who doesn't know *a* from *b*.

The satire on absenteeism is not, however, inseparable from this traditional pastoral imagery; explicit condemnation is just as frequent. The attraction which lures priests from their parishes is not always paid mass-singing; the *Apocalipsis Goliae* criticises their absence without assigning any particular reason,[10] Matheolus' *Lamentations* trace the parson's absence to pluralism, while Gower, like the author of 'Cum plures ordines', focusses on the court as the main lure.[11] It is Langland who, like Chaucer, presents absentee priests making for a 'chaunterie' in London:

> Persones and parisch prestes · pleyned hem to the bishop
> That here parisshes were pore · sith the pestilence tyme,
> To haue a lycence and a leue · at London to dwelle,
> And syngen there for symonye · for siluer is swete.[12]

In Chaucer's lines, therefore, we can see the union of scattered elements of a tradition.

The history of different elements in the lines describing the Parson's generosity can be traced in a similar way.

> Ful looth were hym to cursen for his tithes,
> But rather wolde he yeven, oute of doute,
> Unto his povre parisshens aboute
> Of his offryng and eek of his substaunce.
> He koude in litel thyng have suffisaunce. (486–90)

This passage can be seen as the inversion of a complaint such as that made by 'Totum regit saeculum' on the use to which priests put their 'offryngs':

> Emunt sibi praedia pauperum de bonis,
> non videntur memores dandae rationis.[13]

They buy themselves manors with the goods of the poor; they don't seem to be mindful of giving.

The parson's avarice is often described in general terms, and as such it is part of a wider discussion of the financial corruption of the clergy, which includes simony, taking tithes from dishonest profits, and extortion.[14] But even in general complaints, a reference to tithes often seems clear:

> He taketh al that he may, and maketh the churche pore.
> . . . he hath the silver of wolle and of lambe . . .[15]

Chaucer's phrasing in line 486 may well come from Wycliff, who twice, in his frequent condemnation of 'cursynge for tithes', uses these actual words,[16] although Robert Mannyng too had earlier criticised the priest 'þat for lytyl, curseþ hys parysshenes'.[17] But this aspect of the priest's behaviour does not seem to figure largely in estates treatments,[18] and it is therefore significant that Chaucer should take it on himself to stress the very matter which caused so much ill-feeling between the priest and his flock. In examining the Plough-man's portrait, we shall see that tithing cheerfully and honestly was a traditional part of the labourer's duties; it seems likely therefore that Chaucer has 'retrospectively' attached to the Parson a reluctance to excommunicate for non-payment of tithes, precisely in order to emphasise the ideally harmonious relationship between these two estates.

The effects of the Parson's generosity are felt not only by those whom he refuses to curse, but also by the 'povre parisshens' to whom he makes donations. In this he corresponds to part of the 'ideal' stereotype of the priest. 'Non te lusisse pudeat' calls the priest a 'compassionate protector of the poor' ('Pius protector pauperum') and counsels him to give to all who ask ('omni petenti tribue').[19] Feeding beggars ('mendicantes pascere') is listed as a priestly duty in 'Totum regit saeculum',[20] and one version of 'Sacerdotes mementote', after criticising 'despisers of the wretched' ('Miserorum contemptores') concludes

> Sit sacerdos benedictus
> per quem potus vel amictus
> datur illi qui constrictus
> est algore, fame victus.[21]

May that priest be blessed by whom drink or clothing is given to the man oppressed by cold or overcome with hunger.

Perhaps nearer to Chaucer's more prosaic depiction of alleviating distress among one's flock is Gower's recollection of the old days

when priests used to give a third of their income to the beggars of
their parish ('De leur paroche les mendis' *MO* 20,437–48).

Chaucer's description of the Parson's parish-visiting is also
prosaically realistic.

> *Wyd* was his parisshe, and houses *fer asonder*,
> But he ne lefte nat, *for reyn ne thonder*,
> In siknesse nor in meschief to visite
> The ferreste in his parisshe, muche and lite,
> *Upon his feet, and in his hand a staf.* (491–5) [22]

Again, emphasis is being thrown on an aspect of the priest to which
there are only brief references in estates satire. 'Totum regit saeculum'
mentions the priest's duty to visit often the sick and feeble ('infirmos
et debiles saepe visitare'), [23] while Gower complains that this is a task
neglected by the hunting parson (*VC* III 1491–2). 'Le Dit des
Patenostres' takes it for granted that – when practised with virtuous
intentions – this is a priest's duty, in its ironic praise of 'prestres curez'

> qui ne se faignent mie
> De leurs parrochianes par jor et par nuitie
> Visiter, si qu'il aient ouverte la crevace. [24]

who are not at all reluctant to visit their female parishioners by day and by
night, so long as there is a crack through which they can penetrate.

While these instances show that there is nothing odd about including
visiting in the portrait of an ideal priest, what strikes us about Chaucer's
treatment is its suggestion of long-established habit – the repetition of
the task, day in, day out, in varying conditions. Line 495 also gives
us a sense of the habitual appearance of the Parson as he goes on his
rounds; we seem to see him picking up his staff and setting out time
after time. This sense of daily routine as part of a person's past is a
recurring characteristic of Chaucer's portraits, and is one more element
which contributes to our sense of the reality of his pilgrims; unlike
the subjects of estates satire or of rhetorical description, they are em-
bedded in a historical and geographical context. But this 'realistic'
aspect of the pilgrims is a development of the estates concept, since it
is evoked *through* our sense of the duties of an estate, the daily round
of tasks in one's work-life.

The estate also underlies several features of the Parson's portrait
which we might at first attribute to this individual personality – for
example, the statement that

> He was to synful men nat despitous
> Ne of his speche daungerous ne digne,
> But in his techyng discreet and benygne . . .
> But it were any persone obstinat,
> What so he were, of heigh or lough estat,
> Hym wolde he snybben sharply for the nones. (516–18, 521–3)

The stereotype of the ideal cleric includes just such a combination of gentleness and severity. 'Non te lusisse pudeat' in addressing priests, balances counsels of charity with the exhortation that they should 'vigorously rebuke the wicked' ('malos potenter argue').[25] The poem 'Viri venerabiles, sacerdotes Dei' also stresses the duality of the priest's role,

> Consolantes miseros, pravos corrigentes.[26]

Consoling the wretched, correcting the wicked.

And in Gower the pastoral ideal is similarly balanced:

> Non nimis ex duro presul nos iure fatiget,
> Nec nimis ex molli simplicitate sinat.[27]

The bishop shouldn't harass us with too strict a rule, nor be too permissive out of a gentle meekness.

Robert Mannyng's expression of this idea comes very close to Chaucer's; priests should address sinners with 'feyre techyng, and gode spelles', and then 'stoutly, whan they wyl nat elles'[28] – as the Parson's 'discreet and benygne' speech rapidly turns into a sharp retort when met with obstinacy. Many writers stress that priests have a duty to rebuke, without mentioning the softer qualities that should accompany this,[29] and these passages, as well as the others, ultimately derive from a verse in Timothy whose influence on the priestly ideal is now easy to see:

praedica verbum, insta opportune, importune: argue, obsecra, increpa in omni patientia, et doctrina.[30]

Preach the word, be instant in season, out of season; reprove, rebuke, exhort with all longsuffering and doctrine.

The statement that Chaucer's Parson will speak sharply to any sinner 'whether of high or low degree', is not merely padding, but a response to the association of the clergy with a failure to attack the vices of the rich and powerful: 'ces seignours tu laisses coy' ('lords you leave in peace').[31] The Parson's behaviour is, then, less an expression of his individual personality than careful performance of his duty.

We might also think that the Parson's individual character is indicated in the series of adjectives applied to him: 'Benygne...wonder diligent...ful pacient...hooly...vertuous...nat despitous...Ne... daungerous ne digne...discreet and benygne'. Yet these too seem to be linked with a tradition which includes in the stereotype of the priest a similar list of adjectives indicating ideal moral qualities. 'Non te lusisse pudeat' exhorts the priest:

> Sis pius, iustus, sobrius,
> prudens, pudicus, humilis,
> in lege Dei docilis.[32]

Be merciful, just, sober, wise, chaste, humble, obedient in God's law.

The poem 'Viri venerabiles, sacerdotes Dei' has a similar list:

> Estote benevoli, sobrii, prudentes,
> Justi, casti, simplices, pii, patientes,
> Hospitales, humiles, subditos docentes.[33]

Be benevolent, sober, wise, just, chaste, honest, merciful, patient, hospitable, humble, teaching your flock.

These words have a biblical resonance, deriving from their use in the Epistles of St Paul. The central text is the advice given to bishops (1 Timothy 3: 2-4):

Oportet ergo episcopum irreprehensibilem esse . . . sobrium, prudentem, ornatum, pudicum, hospitalem, doctorem, . . . modestum . . . filios habentem subditos cum omni castitate.

A bishop then must be blameless . . . vigilant, sober, of good behaviour, given to hospitality, apt to teach; . . . patient . . . having his children in subjection with all gravity.

These adjectives, and others in the Latin poems quoted, echo throughout the Epistles,[34] in such a way that it is easy to understand how the compiling of a list of virtues could be half-subconsciously influenced by them. Chaucer's portrait seems to have a similar relationship with 1 Cor. 13: 4:

Charitas patiens est, benigna est . . . non agit perperam, non inflatur, non est ambitiosa . . . non irritatur.

Charity suffereth long, and is kind; . . . charity vaunteth not itself, is not puffed up, doth not behave itself unseemly, . . . is not easily provoked.

Also biblical in resonance is Chaucer's opening paradox: 'a povre

Persoun of a toun, | But riche he was of hooly thoght and work'
(478–9). The contrast of material and spiritual riches runs right through
the New Testament, but we may take as an illustrative example James
2: 5: 'nonne Deus elegit pauperes in hoc mundo, divites in fide?'
('Hath not God chosen the poor of this world rich in faith?').[35] This
contrast is used by Gower, in the opposite way to Chaucer; he says of a
bad priest

> Sic viget in curis diues, set moribus expers
> Indiget, et vano more gubernat opes. (*VC* III 1395–6)

Thus he flourishes in business as a rich man, but is destitute and a beggar in
virtues, and governs his wealth according to a sterile practice.

Thus the language in which Chaucer describes his Parson does not
animate him as an individual personality; it links him with ideals of
virtue formulated and popularised by the Bible and medieval satirists.

Finally, we come to an important set of features which loom large
in the traditional conception of the priest. The first of these appears in
the stress Chaucer lays on the Parson's example:

> This noble ensaumple to his sheep he yaf,
> That first he wroghte, and afterward he taughte.
> Out of the gospel he tho wordes caughte,
> And this figure he added eek therto,
> That if gold ruste, what shal iren do?
> For if a preest be foul, on whom we truste,
> No wonder is a lewed man to ruste;
> And shame it is, if a preest take keep,
> A shiten shepherde and a clene sheep.
> Wel oghte a preest ensaumple for to yive,
> By his clennesse, how that his sheep sholde lyve . . .
> To drawen folk to hevene by fairnesse,
> By good ensaumple, this was his bisynesse. (496–506, 519–20)

The notion that it was a priest's duty to set an example is given great
prominence in estates satire, and a large number of images are used to
express it with vividness. Walter of Châtillon discusses the effects of
example in terms of light:

> Ubi sunt ecclesiam   in Christo regentes,
> qui velint existere   benefacientes,
> exemplorum lumine   tantum relucentes,
> ut letentur pariter   et exultent gentes?[36]

Where are those who should rule the church in Christ, who should wish to exist in doing good, shining with the light of example so that the nations should rejoice and exult together?

or a mirror – 'Christi sacerdotes...mundo sunt pro speculo' ('the priests of Christ are a mirror for the world').[37] Such images are repeated in later writers,[38] as are the biblical tags on the blind leading the blind, or 'like priest, like people'.[39] Chaucer chooses two metaphors which are different from all these: the image of rust, and the image of the 'shiten shepherde'. A slightly less vivid version of the latter – as a spreading stain – occurs in Walter of Châtillon,[40] and in Gower:

> Sic ouis ex maculis pastoris fit maculosa. (*VC* III 1063)

Thus the sheep is dirtied from the shepherd's stains.

But a much more striking parallel with Chaucer, as Kittredge long ago noted, is contained in the *Roman de Carité*:

> Se ors enrunge, queus ert fers?
>
> Quel merveille est, se merveille ai
> De fol pastour, de sage oeille?
> Chele est nete, chil se soeille.[41]

If gold rusts, what will iron do? What a marvel it is – if I stop to marvel at it – a foolish shepherd and wise sheep! The one is clean, the other filthies himself.

Yet if the *Roman* was the source of Chaucer's images, it could not have been his only source for the concept. Of all the other writers who stress the necessity of clerical example, we may quote only the attractive sermon story of a priest who walked through a puddle, observing to his parishioners that they followed his example no better than his precepts.[42]

In the Parson's portrait, setting a good example is combined with practising what he preaches: – 'first he wroghte, and afterward he taughte' – and Chaucer later repeats this statement on its own (527–8). This too is a commonplace of clerical satire.[43] The author of 'Le Dit des Patenostres' ironically begs the clergy not to practise the virtue they preach:

> Le dire leur souffist sans entrer en la trace. (*NR* I, p. 240)

Saying it is enough, without their entering into action.

In several writers this topic is, as in Chaucer, linked with the priest's example.

> Vos habent pro speculo legem ignorantes
> Laici, qui fragiles sunt et inconstantes.
>
> Quidquid vident laici vobis displicere
> Dicunt proculdubio sibi non licere;
> Sed quidquid vos opere vident adimplere,
> Credunt esse licitum et culpa carere.[44]

You are a mirror to those who are ignorant of the law, the weak and unstable laity. Whatever the laity see to displease you, they say is certainly forbidden to them, but whatever they see you perform, they believe to be lawful, and free from blame.

Langland says that if only priests would reform themselves,

> Lothe were lewed men · but thei ӡowre lore folwed,
> And amenden hem that mysdon · more for ӡowre ensamples
> Than for to prechen and preue it nouӡt · ypocrysie it semeth.[45]

So we not only find the same ideas and images in other writers as in Chaucer, but we find them linked together in similar ways. The *coherence* of Chaucer's Parson pre-dates his individual creation.

The links extend further, to embrace the priest's function as teacher. Again, this is a feature twice introduced by Chaucer – in the long passage already quoted, which describes how the Parson's teaching followed on his actions, and in another near the opening of the portrait:

> He was also a lerned man, a clerk,
> That Cristes gospel trewely wolde preche;
> His parisshenes devoutly wolde he teche. (480–2)

Learning is here subordinated to teaching, as it traditionally was in the conception of the priest; in fact several writers stress only the priest's duty to teach his flock without mentioning the need for him to be 'lerned',[46] while the opposite is almost never true.[47] A Latin poem fuses with ease the topics of learning, teaching and setting an example:

> Sacerdoti convenit
>   legem sacram scire,
> Plebem vita, moribus,
>   verbis erudire.[48]

It is fitting for a priest to know the holy law, to instruct the people by his life, morals and words.

The inverse of such an exhortation can be seen in the complaints about clerical ignorance [49] – in these too it is taken for granted that the purpose of the priest's ability to 'construe oon clause wel' is to 'kenne it to his parochienes'.[50] This is dramatically illustrated by the Latin debate poem 'Hora nona sabbati tempore florenti'; a parson is discovered sitting on the grass expounding the Bible to his parishioners, but a passing scholar contests his interpretations, which are marred by grammatical errors.[51]

The priestly stereotype, like those for the regular clergy, has coherent links between its features. Discussion of the example which the priest should set leads naturally to considering his education, his assiduity in teaching, the congruity between his precepts and his practice, the general morality of his life, and so on. It is not surprising to find Chaucer following along these well-worn paths.

Yet as we look at the long passage in which Chaucer describes these characteristics, we realise that once again, it is the *character himself* who is speaking. It is not the moralist commentator who quotes from the gospel and adds the 'figure' about rusting gold; it is the Parson himself. And in the lines following, Chaucer is playing a favourite trick; he has merged his own voice with that of the pilgrim, so that we are unsure if it is reported speech, or the narrator's own comment, that is contained in the lines which energetically point out the priest's duty to set an example (501–6). Envisaging the Parson as someone who, like the Monk, is *aware* of the criticism of his class suggests to us his response to the world around him, and thus his actual existence. But a further effect is a little disquieting. This narrator can so easily adopt 'false' values that his identification with the 'true' values of the Parson also seems to become a temporary thing – a matter of sympathy, although certainly stronger than usual, with a point of view adopted only during association with the person who holds to it. The suggestion is of the subtlest, and is not raised by the rest of the portrait, where the narrator describes the Parson from the 'outside'. But as we shall see later, it has important implications for the kind of moral statement which is made by the *Prologue* as a whole.

The Parson is representative of what the estate of priesthood should be like.[52] He possesses all the virtues which writers for centuries had associated with the pastoral ideal, and he is described in terminology which has an aura of biblical holiness. What is more, this is no abstract, timeless figure; Chaucer envisages him in a realistic spatial and temporal existence, and as not merely acting out a role, but expressing his consciousness of doing so. The way in which the Parson is praised, especially towards the close of the portrait, reflects obliquely on the other pilgrims. Unlike the Friar, he is not 'daungerous' to anyone, nor does he respect 'heigh estat'; unlike the Sergeant of Law, he does not receive 'reverence' from others, and his 'fairnesse' is of a different kind from the Monk's. And yet it must be said that the moral certainties of this portrait fail to upset the confident tone in which the skills of the *Prologue*'s rogues are presented. The equal enthusiasm which characterises *both* 'Unto his ordre he was a noble post', *and* 'A bettre preest I trowe that nowher noon ys', implies that each character is being accepted on his own terms. The absolute values of the Parson are temporarily made relative by being taken as absolute only *for him*. Their use as a basis for comment on the other pilgrims is only a possibility which we may wish to realise.

Yet the objection could be made that Chaucer not only presents his Parson as an isolated ideal figure but also as a blood-relative of the Ploughman. Aren't we here being forced to connect one social class with another and to use this ideal relationship as a basis for judging the self-limited worlds of the other pilgrims? It is to examine the implication of this relationship between the two brothers for the kind of social structure represented in the *Prologue*, that we shall now turn.

THE PLOUGHMAN

The first thing we learn about the Ploughman is that he is the Parson's brother. The relationship is not a clue to the background and social status of the Parson, but symbolic of a connection between their two estates. The estates of priest and peasant had already been particularly linked, both in their functional aspects, and in an emotional identification of their 'Christ-like' virtues. It is the perversion of the functional interchange of services that concerns Nigel of Longchamps, when, in the middle of an attack on clerical luxury, he directs our attention to the oppressed peasant, who

> Uritur alget eget sitit esurit ulcere plenus,
> Qui dedit, unde suam cuique levare famem. (*SS* 2715–16)

> He's hot, cold, needy, thirsty, hungry, bruised,
> Who gave whence each his hunger might relieve.
> > (trans. Regenos, p. 126)

The relationship between Chaucer's Parson and his Ploughman reverses this situation; the Parson's reluctance to exact his tithes is matched by the Ploughman's willingness to pay them, and the Parson's spiritual care of his parishioners is complemented by the Ploughman's unstinting labour for their material wants. But more important than Nigel's simple demonstration of interdependence is the fusion of the two ideals of priesthood and labour in the figure of Piers the Ploughman, who embodies Langland's belief that there are

> none sonner saued ' ne sadder of bileue,
> Than plowmen and pastoures ' and pore comune laboreres. (*PPl* x 458–9)

The close union between these two ideals of Christian virtue in the *Prologue* is surely inspired by the co-existence of the same ideals in the single figure of Piers, and the moral power with which Langland's poem invests him.

The natural consequence of this observation is to look for Piers' influence in the details of the Ploughman's portrait, and indeed Coghill has already noted resemblances between the two figures.[53] I shall discuss these parallels in turn in commenting on the features of Chaucer's portrait. But to show the *a priori* likelihood of Langland's influence, we may first ask a very simple question, which Coghill overlooked. Why did Chaucer choose to include a Ploughman rather than, say, a Labourer? The word 'ploughman' is by no means the inevitable one for the labouring class: other writers refer, in Latin, to 'rustici',[54] 'coloni',[55] 'agricolae',[56] in French to 'paisant',[57] 'vilain',[58] 'laborëor',[59] and in English at this time, 'vileyn' and 'laborere' were possible terms.[60] It must surely have been the powerful influence of Langland's major work, in which the plough, as in the Bible,[61] is important as both a religious and a secular symbol, which identified the representative of the labouring classes as a ploughman.

Coghill sees Langland's influence in the language in which the Ploughman is praised:

> A trewe swynkere and a good was he,
> Lyvynge in pees and parfit charitee. (531–2)

With these lines, Coghill compares Piers' list of the ladies who serve Treuthe, among whom are 'Charite', 'Pacience' and 'Pees',[62] and also Piers' advice that the road to Treuthe leads through 'Mekenesse' to fulfilling the commandments to love God and then one's neighbour,[63] as the Ploughman's 'pees and parfit charitee' is also expressed in the fulfilment of these commandments. Langland may well have been the immediate stimulus for Chaucer's attribution of these ideals to his

Ploughman, but they also occur together, and specifically applied to peasants (as Flügel has noted), in Wycliff:

If þou be a laborer lyve in mekenesse, and trewly and wylfully do þi labour . . . And ever kepe pacience and mekenesse and charite, boþe to God and man.[64]

But the similarities between Wycliff and Langland are even more striking than the similarities between Chaucer and either author; once again we seem to have a tradition which is wider than the influence of a single writer, and which is also reflected, for example, in the comment of 'Le Dit des Planètes' on 'laboureurs':

> S'il vousissent passiens estre
> Plutost qu'autres fussent savez. (NR I p. 379)

If only they were long-suffering, they would be saved more easily than any others.

This is also one of the few estates expressions of a belief in 'sancta rusticitas'[65] before Langland.[66]

Langland's stress on 'treuthe' and 'lewte' as secular Christian virtues may also have impressed Chaucer, but it is likewise traditional.[67] 'Let him love and keep faith' ('Servet ametque fidem')[68] is the advice of 'Debemus cunctis proponere' to 'villanus', and the Chessbook declares that the peasant must be loyal ('Legalem . . . oportet esse agricolam').[69] Étienne de Fougères urges that he keep his faith honestly ('leialment sa fei aquite')[70] and Jean de Condé exhorts him to be faithful in doing his work ('Soies loiaus en t'oeure faire').[71] The Roman de Fauvel indicates the failings of 'laboureurs' merely by saying that they are 'without honesty' ('sans leautei').[72]

In telling us that the Ploughman is a 'trewe swynkere', Chaucer emphasises his industriousness. Labour was the first, and often the only duty urged on the peasant by estates writers. One of the three tools which the Chessbook gives the figure symbolic of the labourer is a hoe with which to till the earth ('ligonem, quo terra foditur'), and he is exhorted to 'persevere in labour' ('labori insistere').[73] The Sermones nulli parcentes assure peasants that they are numbered with the blessed if they persevere in labour, and tell them not to rest on any day unless it is for divine worship (969–72). The author of 'Mult est diables curteis', after stating that God created the villein to win bread for others ('Pur gaainer as altres pain') goes so far as to assert that the harder he works, the happier and healthier he is ('Tant est plus halegre et sain').[74] A corresponding prominence is given to complaints that labourers are idle.[75]

It is also usual for writers to mention representative activities of the peasant in the course of exhorting him to labour, as Chaucer refers to dung-carrying, threshing, and 'dyking and delving' (530, 536). Étienne de Fougères lists the peasant's duties in some detail:

> Teres arer, norir aumaille,
> Sor le vilain est la bataille . . .
>
> Il seinme seigle, il here aveine,
> Il fauche prez, il tose leine . . .
>
> Il fet paliz, il fet meiseires,
> Il fet estanz par ces rivières,
> Primes corvées, peis preières
> Et peis cent choses costumières.[76]

Ploughing land, feeding cattle, is the peasant's burden (?) . . . He sows rye, he ploughs in oats, he reaps meadows, he shears wool. He makes fences and enclosures, he makes fish-ponds by the rivers; first at his forced labour, then at his prayers, and a hundred routine chores.

Is there any special significance in Chaucer's selection of the Plough-man's activities? Coghill has related them to *Piers Plowman*, where Reason says that if each man were to meet with his deserts,

> Lawe shal ben a laborere · and lede a-felde donge.[77]

and Piers says of himself,

> I dyke and I delue · I do that treuthe hoteth;
> Some tyme I sowe · and some tyme I thresche.[78]

The parallels are not striking in precisely the way that they at first appear to be: 'dyke and delve' was a common phrase meaning 'to work hard at manual labour',[79] and its appearance in both Langland and Chaucer could be coincidental. But to find this phrase linked in both writers with threshing does suggest a connection between the activities of the two ploughmen.

Some virtues which the peasant was traditionally supposed to strive for can be inferred from complaints about his failings. Thus the 'pees' in which Chaucer's Ploughman conducts his life may represent the reverse of the quarrelsomeness sometimes associated with the peasantry,[80] and his love of God, 'with al his hoole herte' (533), may be an inversion of the peasant's supposed hatred of the church and the clergy,[81] and his failure to observe Sundays and religious festivals.[82]

This characteristic is not represented only in negative terms, however, for the *Sermones nulli parcentes* command the peasant directly,

> fidem Christi conservatis, . . .
> sitis ergo in labore
> dei semper et timore. (p. 41, 946–50)

Keep the faith of Christ . . . so continue always, working for and fearing God.

The most important sign of the peasant's hatred of the church, in the estates writers' eyes, was his failure to tithe,[83] and Chaucer's Ploughman clearly conforms with the stereotype of the ideal peasant in paying his tithes 'ful faire and wel' (539). The *Chessbook* says that the peasant should thank God for his gifts by tithing: 'decimas rerum offerat, eligat meliora, ne velud alter Chaim respuatur' – 'let him offer tithes of his goods, choosing the best, lest he be rejected like another Cain' (col. 381–2). The *Sermones nulli parcentes* advise:

> censum decimasque detis
> et de reliquo vivetis. (p. 41, 954–5)

Pay your tax and tithes, and live on the remainder.

Like Jacobus de Cessolis, Étienne de Fougères uses the story of Cain and Abel to illustrate the importance of this duty,[84] and the early mystery plays may well have reinforced this as a popular notion.[85] Langland's Piers is, as we might expect, a faithful tither:

> The kirke shal haue my carogne · and kepe my bones;
> For of my corne and catel · he craued the tythe.
> I payed it hym prestly · for peril of my soule.[86]

So that in fulfilling this duty of his estate Chaucer's Ploughman again resembles Piers.[87]

After loving God, the Ploughman loves his neighbour, and thus obeys both Christ's 'new' commandments.[88] There is little association of the typical peasant with love of his neighbour, although a large number of complaints about his avarice may indicate that charity was a feature in the ideal of his estate.[89] The Ploughman's labour

> For Cristes sake, for every povre wight,
> Withouten hire, if it lay in his myght. (537–8)

may well have been inspired by Piers' intention to be Treuthe's 'pilgryme atte plow · for pore mennes sake'[90] – and even more probably, by Hunger's advice to Piers to 'comforte' the unfortunate 'with thi catel'.[91] Certainly Langland inspired the ideal ploughman of *Pierce the Ploughmans Crede*, who offers to share his food with the poem's narrator (444–6). But again the notion is not confined to texts influenced by Langland;[92] well before he wrote, the *Sermones nulli parcentes* had advised the peasant:

> cum bonis ambuletis
> et cum his participetis
> de labore acquisitis,
> si necesse fore scitis,
> ut evadere possitis
> iram dei, quam nescitis,
> quia fratrem non pavistis
> pascere cum potuistis. (pp. 41–2, 959–66)

Walk with the righteous, and share with them the winnings of your labour, if you know it to be necessary, so that you may escape the wrath of God (with which you are unacquainted) because you did not feed your brother when you could.

The final item in the Ploughman's portrait is the description of his clothing:

> In a tabard he rood upon a mere. (541)

These details are in accordance with the Ploughman's humility: the mare is an inferior mount,[93] and the tabard is a humble dress,[94] which had already been used as an example of simplicity of attire by Gilles li Muisis (1 p. 362). The effect of the description is once more that of an inversion of complaints on the fine clothes now worn by peasants.[95] The details are not individualising ones any more than those selected by other satirists; they make concrete the abstract outlines of the Ploughman's portrait, which are those of a type.

This increase in the concrete realisation of a conventional outline is also evident at other moments in the portrait – most obviously in the blunt reference to the piles of dung with which the Ploughman works, but also in the qualifiers (he loved God 'thogh him gamed or smerte', he would work for the poor without pay 'if it lay in his myght') which show idealised virtues operating under the restrictions of real life. In this concrete visualisation of an ideal Chaucer may have been following Langland as much as in formulating the ideal itself.

But one aspect of Langland's picture of the peasant is significantly absent from Chaucer, and that is his suffering. Not only Langland, but many other estates writers are united on the subject of the peasant's subjection to the demands of knights and clergy, and his miserable dependence on the vagaries of weather and harvest.[96] Sympathy for the hardships of the poor is the basis on which Langland builds our sense of their moral strength, for Christianity itself links suffering and persecution with virtue.[97] If Chaucer had wished for 'realism' alone, he might well have described the actualities of the Ploughman's existence with greater vividness; as it is, the concreteness of the portrait serves merely to reinforce the outlines of an ideal. Moreover, compared with Langland, Chaucer's interest in the ploughman seems perfunctory; the portrait in the *Prologue* mentions enough traditional characteristics to ensure our recognition of an ideal stereotype, but shows little feeling for his position. Why does Chaucer give us this relatively colourless ideal instead of Langland's detailed reality, as if, despite re-creating a suggestion of the link between Parson and Ploughman as representatives of a social ideal of mutual benefit, he was uninterested in the social context in which his Ploughman lived?

I do not think that Chaucer's aim in these two portraits can have been solely to endorse the idea that society coheres through the mutual benefits arising from the interchange of services. The Parson and the Ploughman indeed correspond to the ideal of the estates writer, but Chaucer seems to be showing us that this ideal is inadequate to account for the workings of society. This is the basis on which society *should* be organised; but the isolation of these two figures in the *Prologue* shows us that the actuality is something different. The Parson does not seem to impinge on the other pilgrims, nor does the Ploughman. They exist in a separate sphere which is as exclusive and specialised as those inhabited by the other pilgrims. Their blood-relationship here takes on another significance; their connection is not solely due to the interaction of their estates, but also to the accident of birth. In the realistic narrative setting in which the pilgrims are introduced, the 'brotherhood' of these two has *more* than a symbolic suggestion; on its 'real' level, it suggests the transformation of functional social relationships into individual relationships between families or friends.

We shall see this transformation working again in the other groupings of the Canterbury pilgrims, but meanwhile it can serve to illustrate the existence of other principles besides 'common profit' that make for social cohesion. Indeed, it is an obvious response to other estates writers too that if society coheres, it cannot be by the estates ideal of 'common profit', for as the estates writers themselves stress, selfishness is now the order of the day. Chaucer has his own view of the cohesion of society, which I shall try to describe later. In order to understand it, we must first examine the ideal of the Clerk's estate, and the operations of irony in the rest of the *Prologue*.

THE CLERK

The Clerk is an ideal representative of the life of study. Yet the phrase 'the eternal student' aptly sums up our impression, not only of his willingness to go to learning and edifying others, but also of his slight remoteness from the world of social ends – an impression which is not completely effaced by the picture of him readily edifying his acquaintances. His conformity with the ideal is faultless, but it was an ideal even more likely in medieval than in modern times to be associated with an 'ivory tower'.

Such an impression does not affect our admiration for the way in which the Clerk performs the role of the ideal scholar. He is no novice in study; Chaucer assures us that it is 'longe ygo' since he entered on 'logyk' (286) – an assurance that may be an inversion of satiric complaints that mere beginners now boast themselves learned.[98] Study dominates the Clerk's life; he takes 'moost cure and moost heede' of it (304), and spends all his meagre income on 'bookes and on lernynge' (299–300):

> For hym was levere have at his beddes heed
> Twenty bookes, clad in blak or reed,
> Of Aristotle and his philosophie,
> Than robes riche, or fithele, or gay sautrie. (293–5)

The clerk in 'Hora nona sabbati' is another who apparently spends a great deal on books, and with whom Aristotle is a favourite author; the servant who accompanies him is weighed down,

> Dorso ferens sarcinam ventre tensam lato,
> Est hic Aristoteles, Socrates et Plato.[99]

carrying on his back a bundle, with its capacious belly at full stretch; here is Aristotle, Socrates and Plato.

This is the ideal; the 'normal' is given in the complaint of 'Le Dit des Mais', of which Chaucer's lines are an almost exact reversal:

> A Paris viegnent clerc et lai por estudier,
> ... plusieur leur loez miex aimment oublier
> Et bouclers ot motez, et les gens plaidier,

Sans livre vont souvent itel clerc a l'escole,
Et ceulz qui prestre sont et qui portent estole,
Mais pis leur concubine tiennent il en geole
Et les dez la taverne souvent qui mains afole.[100]

To Paris come clergy and laity to study . . . Several like better to forget their dues to their relatives in favour of goblets with songs, and people gossiping. Such clerks often go to the schools without books – both priests and deacons. But worse, they keep their concubines safely locked away, and the dice of the tavern, which drive many mad.

Tavern-haunting, drinking and gambling,[101] whoring,[102] playgoing[103] and aimless wandering[104] are the activities associated with students by other estates writers. 'Robes riche, or fithele or gay sautrie' are not used by them as illustrations of student dissipation, but these are clearly the props of the goliard-clerk,[105] and they reappear in connection with Nicholas and Absalon, the clerks of the Miller's Tale.[106]

The stress on 'bookes and on lernynge' is what we might expect in the portrait of a scholar. More surprising, at first, is the emphasis on the 'moral vertu' which is the content of the Clerk's conversation, and which seems to determine the tone of his character. Estates writers, however, give as much attention to the moral as to the intellectual qualities of clerks. The *Sermones nulli parcentes* advise scholars, if they wish for advancement,

toto nisu studeatis
in virtutibus pollere,
iam doceri, iam docere,
semper qualiter sincere
possitis domino placere. (p. 29, 500–4)

Strive with all your might to excel in virtues. Constantly be now learning, now teaching, how you can truly please God.

Gower also presents study as a moral discipline, the expression of other-worldly values:

Nuper erant mundi qui contempsere beati
Pompas, et summum concupiere bonum;
Et quia scire scolas acuit mentes fore sanctas,
Scripture studiis se tribuere piis.
Non hos ambicio, non hos amor urget habendi,
Set studio mores conuenienter eunt: . . .
Moribus experti dederant exempla futuris,
Que sibi discipulus debet habere scolis.

(*VC* III 2121–6, 2133–4)

Once there were saintly men who despised the trappings of the world, and yearned for the highest good. And since acquaintance with the schools stimulated their minds to holiness, they gave themselves over to the devout study of scripture. It was not ambition, nor the love of possession that urged them; virtue aptly went hand in hand with study: . . . 'Qualified' in virtue they gave examples to posterity of what a student in the schools ought to possess.

He complains that nowadays the scholar reads about virtue, but his own actions are vicious (2139–40). The criterion by which Gower judges a good teacher is his degree of virtue, rather than his degree of learning (2057–8). And in the *Mirour de l'Omme* his criteria for a good clerk are also moral rather than academic.[107] So the Clerk's 'moral vertu' is quite in keeping with his professional role.

But closer comparison between these writers reveals that Chaucer, significantly, stresses the Clerk's skill rather than the functions of that skill. The *Sermones* anticipate Chaucer's balanced phrase, 'And gladly wolde he lerne, and gladly teche' (308), in their exhortation 'iam doceri, iam docere',[108] but they go on to specify the subject of the learning and teaching, which is how to please God. Gower stresses study as a means of attaining the end, which is the 'summum bonum',[109] whereas in Chaucer's portrait study itself has become the end: 'Of studie took he moost cure and moost heede'. Of the ultimate purpose of his study we do not hear. What is the specific content, the 'hy sentence', of his edifying conversation? It hardly seems to matter. Chaucer's admiration is directed towards the Clerk's proficiency in his professional functions, not towards the purpose of those functions. We are taken into a specialised world, where 'estates' values are the important ones.

I had better say again that I do not think Chaucer's aim in this is moral criticism of the Clerk. His devotion to the fulfilment of his estates role is beyond question. It is borne out by our impression of his earnestness – a quality itself appropriate for his estate, as may now be shown. Our impression largely arises from Chaucer's statement that the Clerk 'looked holwe, and therto sobrely' (289). Latin estates writers variously define the manner which befits the scholar: it can be 'gravitas'[110] ('seriousness'), or 'rigiditas'[111] ('severity'), or the gentler ideal of 'Totum regit saeculum':

Clericos simplicitas decet puellaris.[112]

A maidenly innocence is fitting for clerks.

And Gower praises students of old for their patient spirit ('animus paciens'; *VC* III 2067). The word that Chaucer uses occurs in 'Hora nona sabbati', where the clerk boasts that though poor, he lives 'soberly' ('Pauper vivo sobrie'),[113] and in Langland, whose Dame Study gives 'Sobrete' as a stage on the way to Clergye (*PPl* x 165). Yet Chaucer transforms this virtue by a touch of gentle comedy, in making 'sobrely' follow on 'holwe', and both succeed the description of the painful thinness of the Clerk and his horse. The clerk's sobriety thus becomes a feature of the other-worldly scholar, remote alike from material concerns and worldly distractions. The affectionate amusement which this type evokes in us effectively 'distances' him from us: we admire and are amused by him precisely because his values are not ours. The 'distancing' thinness of the Clerk and his horse is the reverse of the attractively rounded Monk with his sleek palfreys; the emotional effect urges us *towards* the character who shows moral failings, and distances us *from* the character presented as an ideal. What is constant in both, and partly as a result of this, is our sense of what is special in their different existences, of their own preferences, habits, and points of view. This is the end to which, as we have frequently noticed, the 'estates' concept contributes.

To return to the influence of the estates concept on the portrait – it determines, for example, Chaucer's stress on the brevity and pointed-ness of the Clerk's speech:

> Noght o word spak he moore than was neede,
> And that was seyd in forme and reverence,
> And short and quyk and ful of hy sentence. (304-6)

These lines reverse a tradition of satirising intellectual pride,[114] several of whose features we have already seen in their borrowed role as part of anti-mendicant satire. The scholar's garrulous tongue ('garrula lingua')[115] is taken for granted by the poets of the school of Walter of Châtillon, and the picture of a grandiloquent scholar which provides the best contrast with Chaucer's portrait may be by Walter himself:

> Loquitur sublimia,   se prebet acerbum,
> mox dilatat fimbrias,   manifestat limbum
> subiectis, set audiat   sapientis verbum:
> desine grande loqui, frangit deus omne superbum.
>
> Velut alter igitur   Censorinus Cato
> eructat parabolas   sermone cribrato,
> de corde sententias   nimium elato
> eliquat ac tenero subplantat verba palato.

Stultus et scientie   cultu destitutus,
quibusdam panniculis   verborum indutus
videri pre ceteris   conatur astutus,
rancidulum quiddam balba de nare loqutus.

Exultans scematibus   diversis ornari
se credit pre omnibus   mira cornicari,
set auctorum noverit   ista sibi fari:
metiri se quemque decet propriisque iuvari.[116]

He utters great thoughts, he shows himself rigorous, he enlarges the borders of his garments, parades his fringe before his inferiors – but let him hear the word of the wise: 'Cease to speak grandly, God crushes all pride.'

Like Cato the Censor all over again, he gulps out proverbs in refined speech; from a heart too conceited he pours forth opinions and distorts his words with his dainty palate.

Foolish, and destitute of the civilising influence of knowledge, fitted out with a few rags of words, he tries to seem more shrewd than others, stammering out some stinking trash through his nose.

Triumphing in being tricked out with different figures of speech, he thinks he is cawing out marvels before everyone else – but he shall soon learn that this dictum of writers is said of him: everyone should take stock of himself and be content with his own abilities.

Both Gower and Langland describe the corresponding ideal in passages that provide parallels for the simplicity and didactic qualities of the Clerk's conversation; Langland's dreamer is told he will find Clergye by proceeding until he comes to a court called

Kepe-wel-thi-tonge-
Fro-lesynges-and-lyther-speche ' and-likerouse-drynkes.
Thanne shaltow se Sobrete ' and Symplete-of-speche,
That eche wiȝte be in wille ' his witte the to shewe,
And thus shaltow come to Clergye ' that can many thinges.

(*PPl* x 163–7)

Gower says:

Cil q'ad science du clergie,
Ne falt point q'il se glorefie
En beal parole noncier,
Aincois covient q'il sache et die
Dont soi et autres edefie
Au bien de l'alme. (*MO* 14665–70)

He who has a clerical education must not take pride in uttering fine words; rather it is fitting that he should know and repeat that by which he may edify himself and others, to the soul's benefit.

Like the windows which illumine the church, the clerk

> As autres doit donner aprise
> D'oneste conversacioun.[117]

must give a lesson to others in decent conversation.

Chaucer's stress on this characteristic of his Clerk therefore very obviously reflects an emphasis of estates satire.

The feature most firmly associated with the clerk's estate in medieval literature was his poverty, which is so much taken for granted that Alanus de Insulis can say simply

> Et qui dives fuerat iam philosophatur.[118]

He who was once rich is now a philosopher.

Chaucer takes pains to show us that his Clerk is no exception to this rule:

> But al be that he was a philosophre
> Yet hadde he but litel gold in cofre. (297-8)

Some writers see poverty as a necessary condition for scholarship:[119] Walter of Châtillon harks back to the past, when scholars supposedly embarked on study for its own sake, and knew that poverty is the only life free from anxiety ('quod sola pauperies vita sit secura').[120] The clerk of 'Hora nona sabbati' refutes the view of his priestly opponent that his poverty degrades him:

> Paupertas quam increpas felix est ruina.
> O beati pauperes! clamat vox divina.
> Pauper vivo sobrie, dives tu rapina.
> Dic, quaeso, quae magis est res Deo vicina?[121]

The poverty you censure is a blessed misfortune. Blessed are the poor! cries the divine voice. Poor, I live soberly; rich, you live off oppression. I ask you to tell me, which is nearer to God?

At other times the clerk's poverty is the subject of complaint or cynical rejection;[122] in such cases, it is usually contrasted with the prosperity of other educated groups. Some poems focus on the contrast between the poverty of the student and the wealth of the bene-ficed clergy,[123] but more striking to the satirists was the financial gulf between the 'philosophre' or Arts student, and the lawyer or doctor. Walter of Châtillon sums up the situation:

> Seminat gramatica,   semper tamen indiget,
> lex autem et phisica   manipulos colliget.[124]

Grammar sows seeds, but is always poor; law and medicine, on the other hand, rake in purses.

And his imitators take up the theme:

> Expedit pauperibus adhaerere legi;
> Insudare nimium artibus elegi.

The poor should stick to law; I have chosen to waste too much sweat on the arts.

A rich logician is rarer than a black swan, and anyone who wants his study to be profitable will turn to Galen or Justinian.[125] Gilles li Muisis carries this tradition into the vernacular; he too complains that 'lucrative sciences' are cultivated, and comments that so long as clerics can earn money by these means, they don't worry about their lack of a benefice.[126] This traditional contrast between the logician and the lawyer or doctor throws an interesting light on the relationship between the Clerk's portrait and the Sergeant of Law's, which immediately follows it in the *Prologue*. The self-important Sergeant, with his many 'fees and robes' (317) presents an obvious contrast with the poor and modest Clerk. The 'reverence' displayed in the Clerk's conversation (305) is a very different thing from the 'reverence' evident in the Sergeant's manner (312) – it has already been noted that this word suggests the same implicit contrast between the Parson and the Sergeant.[127] There is another implicit contrast between the Clerk and the Doctor of Physic in the import of the two 'professional' jokes about gold (297-8 and 443-4). These contrasts are no more than hints suggested by echoes in the vocabulary, or the contrasting impressions produced by each portrait, but they reflect and repeat the conventional contrast between the estates of these characters. The echoes in vocabulary are particularly interesting, since they share the characteristics of the ambivalent vocabulary in the portraits of the Monk and Friar; we are presented with a 'moral' sense for the word 'reverence' which can be quite at odds with its 'social' sense. The effect of the contrast is not to suggest that we use one sense as a standard by which to reject the other, but to show us how the concept has a different meaning according to our point of view; each pilgrim is presented in his own vocabulary. Though this is not typical of estates writing, it can again be seen as Chaucer's own refinement of the notion of specialised estates worlds.

The Clerk's appearance is obviously linked with the traditional poverty of his estate: he 'nas nat right fat' and

> Ful thredbare was his overeste courtepy. (288-90)

In contemplating a life of study, Burnellus the Ass bravely refuses to be deterred by living in thin clothing ('sub veste leui' *SS* 1185). 'Meum est propositum' indicates the poverty of 'logici' by saying that they live in want of clothes ('egentes…indumenti').[128] 'Hora nona sabbati' gives us a description of a poor clerk, with bare feet and striped cope; the priest who debates with him 'glosses' his appearance for us:

> Totus signas inopem quocumque me vergo.[129]

You indicate poverty wherever I turn my gaze.

The short rations which seem to be indicated by the Clerk's physique are also a traditional part of the scholar's life: writers describe his meagre diet ('tenuis diaeta') with its miserable pulse ('triste legumen'), and constant endurance of hunger and thirst.[130] The clerk is also traditionally visualised as too poor to afford a horse, unlike rich lawyers or priests.[131] Chaucer's Clerk must have a horse in order to join the pilgrimage, but it is fitting that it should be a wretched beast, 'as leene…as is a rake' (287).

Like the friar's ready tongue, the clerk's poverty is a general characteristic which integrates a number of diverse features of the estate stereotype. Its natural corollary, for example, is the dependence of the clerk on donations: thus Chaucer's Clerk has to live off what his 'freendes' give him (299). Estates writers include in their treatment of clerks advice on the right relationship between the student and his benefactors. The *Sermones nulli parcentes* divide clerks into those with, and those without benefices; the first group is warned not to succumb to complacency, while the second is admonished against living on alms and giving nothing in return (525–36). What the clerk should offer in return is prayer for the souls of his benefactors, whether they are alive or dead, as Jean de Condé makes clear.[132] The writer of 'Le Dit des Mais' envisages the burden of maintaining students as falling on their families (*NR* I, p. 184). 'God will provide', says Gilles li Muisis, grandly, to intending students, but in more realistic moments he too realises that it is the clerk's relatives who will have to pay, and so encourages the laity to give money to students:

> Vo parent, vo cousin en poront bien avoir,
> Mais que studyer voellent, et s'ayment le savoir,
> Et s'aiment les sciences asés plus que l'avoir.[133]

Your relatives may properly have it [i.e. your wealth] provided they wish to study, and love learning, and are fonder of knowledge than possessions.

And Robert Mannyng threatens divine punishment for the lazy student who lives off his father,

> But he ȝelde hym ȝyf þat he may,
> Or preye for hym boþe nyghte and day.[134]

So that in living off his friends, and busily praying 'for the soules... | Of hem that yaf hym wherwith to scoleye', Chaucer's Clerk conforms both with the traditional situation, and the traditional duty, of the scholar.[135]

Chaucer also comments on some of the immediate reasons for the Clerk's poverty; one is that he was not 'so worldly for to have office' (292). This comment reflects complaints such as that in 'Totum regit saeculum' that clerks carry on business which isn't theirs ('Clerici negocia gerunt aliena').[136] Gower says of the virtuous scholars of old that they did not involve themselves in state administration (*VC* III 2129). Langland's casual reference to the clerk as 'administrator' shows how familiar a figure he was:

> seruauntes that seruen lordes · selden falle in arrerage,
> But tho that kepen the lordes catel · clerkes and reues.[137]

Another reason for the Clerk's poverty is that 'he hadde geten hym yet no benefice' (291). A whole literature on the benefice question lies behind this statement; writer after writer expands on the clerk's desperate desire for a living, and the necessity for bribery and influence in gaining one.[138] Étienne de Fougères' comment is typical:

> Si bon clierc est de bon tesmoing
> Et n'a deniers plus de plein poig,
> N'aura mostier ne pres ne loig,
> Si einz la paume ne li oig.[139]

If he is a good clerk, of good reputation, and he has not more than a good fistful of money, he won't get a church anywhere without oiling his [the bishop's] palm.

Gilles li Muisis describes the good old days when

> En estude partout ensi clers aprendoient;
> Nature leur donnoit que savoir desiroient;
> Remunéret de Dieu yestre bien entendoient;
> Bénéfisces avoir tous les jours attendoient. (I p. 263)

Clerks everywhere learned by study; Nature gave them a desire for knowledge, they expected reward from God, and always could expect that they would get benefices.

Now studies are declining, he says, because there is a lack of benefices. We might therefore construe Chaucer's statement that his Clerk had no benefice as a comment on the iniquities of a system that failed to use the talents of such a man, merely because he was poor. To do so would not necessarily be wrong, but I want to point out that this is only one of several possible readings of Chaucer's line. First of all we must ask what kind of benefice the Clerk wanted. Was it a parish position, or was it an academic benefice, a scholarship at one of the rapidly multiplying Oxbridge colleges?[140] This is perhaps unlikely, for 'benefice' always seems to mean a parish job among the satirists, but we cannot be sure that his desire was to take on the parochial duties of the Parson; perhaps, as Flügel thinks,[141] the Clerk wanted to prolong his studies indefinitely – and this possibility is suggested not because of his failings but by his very excellence.[142] Wycliff vividly conveys the unattractiveness of a benefice for serious students; it will effectively put a stop to their intellectual activity,[143] and moreover,

þei dreden sore þat bi þis singuler cure ordeyned of synful men þei schulden be lettid fro betre occupacion & fro more profit of holi chirche . . . for þei han cure & charge at þe fulle of god to helpe here breþeren to heune ward, boþe bi techynge, preiynge & ensaumple ȝeuynge; & it semeth þat þei shullen most esily fulfille þis bi general cure of charite, as dide crist and his apostlis, þouȝe þei bynden hem not to o synguler place as a tey dogge.[144]

Chaucer, however, gives no hint *either way* to suggest what is the ultimate reason for the Clerk's lack of a benefice. Whether we accept Flügel's suggestion, or take the line to be a criticism of clerical simony, we are relying on our own interpretation rather than one that Chaucer gives us.

This recognition of the way in which Chaucer can be ambiguous by means of an apparently matter-of-fact statement – he hadn't got a benefice – draws our attention to another controversial area in Chaucer's portrait – a subject on which other satirists could adopt different positions, but on which Chaucer deliberately seems to adopt none. The Clerk's studies, in so far as we hear of them, are secular ones; we hear of 'logyk', of 'Aristotle and his philosophie', but nothing of theology, the queen of sciences. For some satirists, who stress that the other disciplines should be subordinate to divinity,[145] and that pagan authors are unworthy of study,[146] this omission might well indicate a failing on the Clerk's part. Guiot de Provins illustrates such a point of view, in discussing 'divinitei':

> C'est li ars sor toz honoreiz,
> [ce] est veraie letträure, . . .
> C'est li ars qui l'ome corone;
> qui sa vie et son cuer li done
> son tens ne puet mal enploïer . . .
> Teil soloient li devin estre
> que li boin clerc et [li] boin mestre
> lisoient por Deu purement,
> et en verai entendement
> tenoient escolles loaus.
> Or les vos ont si desloaus
> que ne beent mais qu'a l'avoir . . .
> Sil devin de ce qu'il ne font
> nos parollent si en parfont
> chascun semble Dyogenés,
> Aristote et Socratés.[147]

It is the art honoured above all, it is true scholarship . . . it is the art that crowns man; he who gives his life and his heart to it cannot misspend his time . . . Theologians used to be such that good students and teachers read for the sake of God alone, and in true understanding, they kept the schools faithful. Now their vows are so false that they have their eyes on nothing but possessions . . . These divines speak to us of what they don't practise, so profoundly that each one seems Diogenes, Aristotle or Socrates.

A passage like this certainly does not warrant our saying that Chaucer's Clerk is *criticised* for his secular studies,[148] but it is noteworthy that such dislike of the classical authors is based on a laymen's hostility for something the need for which he doesn't understand, while their defence is made in terms of 'professional necessity':

> Fructus ibi maximus est utilitatis;
> Ex his multa discimus quae vos ignoratis.[149]

There is the greatest profit of a useful sort in them; from them we learn many things of which you are ignorant.

This is a clerk's answer to the question of what he learns from a sinner like Socrates. Chaucer stresses the professional nature of the Clerk's studies, and does not look beyond their immediate object to their ultimate goal. The effect of Chaucer's presentation of professional skills,[150] here as well as in the portraits of less virtuous pilgrims, is to emphasise means rather than ends.

In these three portraits of medieval estates ideals, Chaucer may almost be said to use the concept of the estate against itself. Starting from the usual theory of the estates, he throws into prominence the concept of specialised services for each class, and subtly undermines the concept of the interchange of such services which leads to social harmony and the fulfilment of God's will. The portraits of the Parson and the Ploughman are unusual in the *Prologue* in indicating the effects of the actions of each on the other; they are like actors playing in a different style from the rest of a cast, and if we are to ask what makes the production hang together, it is evident that it cannot be the principles on which they, but nobody else, are working. In the Clerk's portrait it becomes clear that we can admire the way in which a character acts out an ideal, while remaining unclear about the social role of the ideal itself. What unites these portraits with those that are satirical in tone is the apparently consistent principle that each pilgrim is a splendid example of his estate; the *Prologue* acts on the assumption that *all* the portraits are of 'estates ideals', exploiting the ambiguity in the notion of an ideal form. In this sense, the relationship between the portraits of the Parson and the Ploughman and those of the other pilgrims operates in two directions: their portraits can be used to criticise the other pilgrims if we wish to identify our viewpoint with theirs, but at the same time we are made conscious that their values too are 'specialised' – appropriate to, and determined by, the work by which they live.

4

The Omission of the Victim

The concentration on means rather than ends in Chaucer's descriptions of the professional skills of the pilgrims is clearly illustrated by the portraits to be discussed in this chapter – Sergeant of Law, Doctor of Physic, Merchant, and Guildsmen. These pilgrims receive the narrator's enthusiastic admiration for their professional qualifications and capabilities, but the social effects of their sometimes dubious practices are left out of account. What I shall call the 'omission of the victim' is a common feature of their portraits, and explains their grouping in this chapter.[1] A concomitant feature is Chaucer's substitution of satire on pompousness and self-importance for the attacks on fraud and malpractice made by other writers. Another characteristic of three of these portraits is the attention paid to the details of professional work-life; Chaucer does not omit the conventional attacks on bribery and fraud in order to describe personal or individual features of the pilgrim, but in favour of presenting his daily occupation and the way in which it determines, and indeed constitutes, his character.

THE SERGEANT OF LAW

The laity are not given such detailed treatment as the clergy in estates satire, but lawyers and doctors were technically clerics, and therefore appear regularly in estates lists. They are not, however, described in much detail; thus the tradition for lawyers is full but remarkably unified.[2]

Before examining this tradition, we should observe how Chaucer, with typical hyperbole, stresses the Sergeant's qualifications as a representative of his estate. He starts in a low key; the Sergeant had 'often... been at the Parvys' (310) – where lawyers met their clients;[3] he is not only representative of sergeants (a superior order of barrister),[4] but also of judges:

> Justice he was ful often in assise,
> By patente and by pleyn commissioun. (314–15)

The technical distinction between the two types of authorisation in the last line might not be completely appreciated by Chaucer's audience,[5] but it sounds as impressive and 'professional' as the reference to 'fee symple'[6] in what follows:

> So greet a purchasour was nowher noon:
> Al was fee symple to hym in effect;
> His purchasyng myghte nat been infect. (318–20)

Warming to his subject, Chaucer moves on to the Sergeant's legal knowledge, and here too he stresses professional jargon or 'termes':[7]

> In termes hadde he caas and doomes alle
> That from the tyme of kyng William were falle.
> Therto he koude endite, and make a thyng,
> Ther koude no wight pynche at his writyng.
> And every statut koude he pleyn by rote. (323–7)

These testimonials to professional skill and experience take up most of the portrait, and are also the basis on which Chaucer introduces some of the usual features of the lawyer's stereotype. It is 'incidentally' suggested, for example, that the Sergeant is a buyer of land, since it is to this operation that the term 'fee symple' belongs. In buying land for himself, the Sergeant would conform to a recognised pattern. A Latin poem, 'Beati qui esuriunt',[8] devoted to satire of the processes of law, describes what happens when clerks become bailiffs:

> mox superbiunt
> et crescunt sibi dentes,
> collaque erigentes.
> Incipiunt perpropere
> Terras et domos emere,
> et redditus placentes;
> nummosque colligentes,
> Pauperes despiciunt,
> Et novas leges faciunt,
> vicinos opprimentes. (*PSE* p. 230)

Soon they become arrogant and 'grow teeth', holding their heads in the air. They immediately start buying lands and houses, and leasing rents, piling up money. They spurn the poor, and establish new laws which oppress their neighbours.

Gower also describes how the lawyer schemes to increase his estates at the expense of his neighbours, and addresses him:

> Agrorum fines longos extendere queris,
> Nec reputas vite tempora curta tue.[9]

You seek to extend the already long boundaries of your lands, and do not reckon on the short limits of your life.

And 'The Simonie' also claims that however poor are entrants to legal offices, in a short time

> Theih bien londes and ledes, ne may hem non astonde.[10]

For Chaucer to call the Sergeant a 'purchasour' is probably suspicious in itself,[11] for the word 'purchas' echoes, with distaste, through Gower's description of the lawyer's wealth in the *Mirour de l'Omme*:

> Ensi ly pledour orendroit
> Combien q'il povre au primer soit,
> Bien tost apres avera du quoy
> Si largement, que tout q'il voit
> Luy semble a estre trop estroit
> De pourchacer soulein a soy . . .
> O vous, dist dieus, je vous di vray,
> Les terres vous deserteray,
> Que vous tenetz du fals purchas.
>
>   qui voldroit au droit descrire
> Les pledours et les advocatz
> Dirroit mervailles en ce cas;
> Car quique vent, ils font purchas. (24,535–55, 24,809–12)

Thus the barrister nowadays, however poor he may be at first, will afterwards quickly have something substantial – so much so that everything that he sees seems too limited for him to get all for himself . . . 'Verily I say unto you', says God, 'I will lay waste your lands, which you possess through false acquisition.' . . . Whoever would correctly describe barristers and advocates, would speak marvels – for whoever sells, they are the buyers.

The connotations of the word 'purchasour' had already been established by Robert Mannyng (although not in connection with lawyers):

> ȝe ryche men, ȝe ryche purchasours,
> ȝe wene þat al þe worlde be ȝours.[12]

Chaucer presents the Sergeant's 'purchasyng' as evidence of professional skill, and so is able to leave it unclarified whether the land was bought for clients, or on his own behalf – whether it is truly evidence of business proficiency, or of personal pride. On moving back to discuss portraits that are satirical in tone, we recognise the same kind of ambiguity that circumvented moral criticism of the Monk and the Friar, and the same tendency to suggest rather than to state, to transfer a characteristic from factual to linguistic status.

The wealth of Chaucer's Sergeant is another feature suggested by way of a professional testimonial:

> For his science and for his heigh renoun,
> Of fees and robes hadde he many oon. (316–17)

The lawyer's riches were taken for granted,[13] and splendid robes were used by satirists to indicate it.[14] Moreover, in Langland, we find references to the lawyer receiving robes for payment; when Meed is banished,

> Shal no seriaunt for here seruyse ˙ were a silke howue,
> Ne no pelure in his cloke ˙ for pledyng atte barre.[15]

Yet despite his many robes, on pilgrimage the Sergeant

> rood but hoomly in a medlee cote
> Girt with a ceint of silk, with barres smale. (328–9)

– a dress which may well be the professional garb of a lawyer.[16] We may suspect that by following a professional stereotype Chaucer, like other satirists, was led into inconsistencies.

The most important observation to be made on the Sergeant's 'fees and robes', however, is that in any other satirist they would undoubtedly form part of an attack on the avarice and pride of the lawyer.[17] Muriel Bowden's comment suggests that this is how we are to read the lines in Chaucer:

Nothing explicit is stated about the Sergeant's acceptance of bribes, but we are led to believe that he has more 'fees and robes' than can be honestly explained. (*Commentary*, p. 171)

It is true that charges of corruption are the most frequent and most fully developed items in estates treatments of judges and lawyers,[18] and that 'sergeants du loy' or 'seriauntz' are specifically mentioned in this connection by Gower and Langland.[19] But although these sources may have influenced Chaucer in selecting a Sergeant for description, the fact that he has *not* taken over the complaints about bribery and corruption is the most striking feature of the Sergeant's portrait. Chaucer almost blatantly omits any reference to venality, and, by the same token, he avoids referring to the victims of legal manoeuvres and dishonesty. The *Sermones nulli parcentes*, for example, have a clear picture of the suffering caused by the lawyer:

> egenos semper spoliatis
> Antichristumque ditatis.
> Ad vos pauper si clamaret
> seque flendo laceraret,
> nisi munus apportaret,
> inconsultus remearet.[20]

You continually despoil the poor to enrich Antichrist. If the poor man were to cry to you, and weeping, rend himself, unless he brought a bribe, he would leave without a consultation.

Gower is likewise conscious of the poor victim whose misery is ignored by the lawyer:

> Deliciis fruitur de rebus pauperis iste,
> Dampna set alterius computat esse nichil.
> Si posset mundum lucrari, quis deus esset,
> Vlterius scire nollet in orbe deum. (*VC* vi 347–50)

He enjoys the delights acquired from the poor man's property, but he counts the losses of the other as nothing. If he could gain possession of the world, he would not wish to know who God might be, or whether there were God in the world.

For Gower, the victim does not exist in the lawyer's consciousness. It is from just such a viewpoint that Chaucer seems to write his account of the Sergeant; the possible existence of victims of the Sergeant's behaviour is left out of the portrait just as it is left out of the Sergeant's consciousness. The *effectiveness* of the Sergeant's professional actions becomes also irrelevant; the gifts of 'fees and robes' are given neither for the successful prosecution of justice, nor for its circumvention, but 'for his science and his heigh renoun'. To read the statement only as a way of saying that the Sergeant is corruptible is to destroy the ambiguity that Chaucer has carefully created, and to miss the point he makes by its means.

The reader's expectations of the traditional complaint may of course have been so strong that Chaucer's line suggested it. But Chaucer allows no support for such a suspicion. We are forced to take the Sergeant on the terms of his façade. It is, of course, a façade:

Nowher so bisy a man as he ther nas,
And yet he semed bisier than he was.[21] (321–2)

The point is that we do not know what lies behind it. To suggest a front without giving away the reality is a feat which Chaucer manages with dexterity. Estates satire provides a few hints for the pompousness and conscious wisdom of the lawyer; 'Beati qui esuriunt' concludes its description of the avarice of new-made judges by saying that they become 'wise' ('fiuntque sapientes' *PSE* p. 230). Langland implies that 'seriauntz' are the kind of people who take offence if they are not treated with servile respect.[22] Chaucer extends these and other hints to establish the key-note of his portrait:

A Sergeant of the Lawe, war and wys,[23]
. . . ful riche of excellence.
Discreet he was and of greet reverence –
He semed swich, his wordes weren so wise.
Nowher so bisy a man as he ther nas,
And yet he semed bisier than he was. (309–13, 321–2)

The stress is on the face that the Sergeant presents to the outside world; the narrator's modifications make sure that we know it is a face. This aspect of the Sergeant is made prominent not only because it has more comic potential than any reference to grinding the faces of the poor, but also to emphasise the basis of any social relationship between the Sergeant and his acquaintances. In associating with him, all we should know – and it is part of his professional expertise that it is all we should know – would be that he was an excellent lawyer – at least, 'he semed swich'.

THE DOCTOR OF PHYSIC

The doctor's link with the lawyer assures him a regular place in estates satire,[24] and descriptions of his chicanery and malpractice are frequent. Chaucer's portrait of the Doctor of Physic shows the same shift in emphasis as the Sergeant's; the victims of quackery and greed are removed to the periphery of our attention, and instead Chaucer enlarges on the technical details of the Doctor's daily activities. The irony of the portrait, and the complexity of our reactions, are produced by transforming the features which other writers attack into evidence of professional skill.

Of medieval complaints about the inefficiency, and indeed dangerousness of medical practice, there is no trace in Chaucer's portrait.[25] It is not the result of the Doctor's practice that we are interested in; the 'sike man' makes a brief appearance in line 423, and having received the prescribed 'boote', disappears. Chaucer's main concern is to show that the Doctor is superbly efficient in the required techniques of medieval medicine. His knowledge of his subject, like the Sergeant's, is encyclopaedic:

> Wel knew he the olde Esculapius,
> And Deyscorides, and eek Rufus,
> Olde Ypocras, Haly, and Galyen,
> Serapion, Razis, and Avycen,
> Averrois, Damascien, and Constantyn,
> Bernard, and Gatesden, and Gilbertyn.[26] (429–34)

Lists of famous doctors, who have all passed away, are used elsewhere to demonstrate the inevitability of death,[27] and the names cited in such lists partially coincide with Chaucer's selection. But the aura of specialist learning created by Chaucer's recital of these great names is closer to the use of similar lists to suggest medical expertise or 'mumbo-jumbo'. A short version is used as an indication of essential specialist knowledge in the *Chessbook*:

In eis [sc. medicis] debet esse . . . signorum egritudinis requirendorum in libris auctorum, maxime Ypocratis, Galieni, Avicenne et Rasis solicitudo omnimoda. (col. 593–4)

[Doctors] ought to take every care to search out the signs of illnesses in the books of authorities, especially of Hippocrates, Galen, Avicenna and Razis.

Matheolus' *Lamentations* dismiss such authorities, and the whole medical paraphernalia, with disgust:

> Le temps et les urines faillent,
> Le poulx et les signes qu'il baillent . . .
> Serapion et Galien,
> Ypocras, Ysaac, Rasis,
> Ne valent pas deux parisis,
> Ne leur art ne leur aliance.[28]

Their 'hours' and inspections of urines are unreliable, the pulse and the symptoms they give . . . Serapion and Galen, Hippocrates, Isaac, Razis, aren't worth twopence, neither their art nor their fraternity.

And when Renart the fox becomes a doctor, his greatest concern, like the Doctor of Physic's, is 'to *speke* of phisik and of surgerye' (413).

> alleguoie Galien
> Et si monstroie oeuvre ancienne
> Et de Rasis et d'Avicenne,
> Par Constantin, par Tholomé
> (Plusieurs fois les ay or nommé),
> Par Senecque, par Alixandre,
> Et a tous les faisoie entendre
> Qu'estoie drois phisiciens
> Et maistre des praticiens.[29]

I cited Galen, and expounded old works of Razis and Avicenna, Constantine and Ptolemy, (I named them several times), of Seneca and Alexander, and I gave every one to understand that I was a true doctor, and a master practitioner.

Is Chaucer, perhaps, hinting that the Doctor, like Renart, is more familiar with medical names than with medical works, by opening his list with the legendary figure of Aesculapius, whose authentic writings are non-existent?[30] Chaucer's list is also even longer than Renart's, or any of those other writers; as usual he goes one better than the tradition. The source of the extra names need not concern us;[31] wherever Chaucer derived them, their inclusion only re-inforces the impression of specialist learning which the list usually evokes.

Renart's professional 'front' is of further interest in illustrating the reason Chaucer gives for the Doctor's particular excellence.

> In al this world ne was ther noon hym lik,
> To speke of phisik and of surgerye,
> For he was grounded in astronomye.
> He kepte his pacient a ful greet deel
> In houres by his magyk natureel.
> Wel koude he fortunen the ascendent
> Of his ymages for his pacient.
> He knew the cause of everich maladye,
> Were it of hoot, or coold, or moyste, or drye,
> And where they engendred, and of what humour.[32] (412–21)

Not all the medical authorities that the Doctor knew so well would agree that a good doctor needed to be grounded in magic, even if it were 'natureel'.[33] But Renart is in no doubt that if one wants to speak about medicine in an impressive way, astrological knowledge has an important role to play:

> Et avec le phisicïen
> Faisoie l'astronomïen.
> Je nommoie signes et poins

Et des constellacions les poins,
Les planettes et les figures.
Celles sont moles, celles sont dures;
Tel planette va en croissant,
Et telle va en descroissant.
Jupiter est planette lie,
Et Herculès est courouchie,
La Lune, Mercure, Venus . . .
Comptoy d'herbes et carrateres
Les mouvemens et les esperes,
Comment les planettes gouvernent,
Comment les poins, les signes servent
Et si comment chascune estoille
A son gouvernent et voille,
Et comment trestout Nature
Est gouvernée par droiture,
Selon le cours des influences
Dont on poeult vëoir demonstrances,
Et si comment toute rien qu'on voit
A dessus lui qui le pourvoit.[34]

And together with the doctor, I played the astronomer. I named signs and points and the positions of the constellations, the planets and the figures – some mild, some harsh. One planet is favourable when it is in the ascendant, and another when it is in decline. Jupiter is a joyful planet, and Hercules is wrathful, [then there are] the Moon, Mercury, Venus . . .

I told of herbs and writings, the movements and the spheres, how the planets rule, what role is played by the points and signs, and also how each star has its rule and influence, and how all nature is lawfully governed, according to the course of the influences, of which one can see proofs, and also how everything one sees has above it that which causes it.

The complicated 'laituaires' which Renart boasts he can make (and which are not as effective as simple medicine)[35] are also introduced into the Doctor's portrait, prefaced by the 'his' that, in the *Prologue*, denotes professional paraphernalia (426). But we do not have to wait until the fourteenth century for satire on doctors' parade of science: Guiot de Provins is equally suspicious of 'lor laituaire',[36] and for him the humours are also among the terms to conjure with:

En chescun home truevent toche:
se il ait fievre ou toz soiche
lor dïent il qu'il est tesiques,
ou enfunduz, ou ydropiques,

> melancolious, ou fious,
> ou corpeus, ou palasimous.
> Qui les oroit de colerique
> despondrë, ou de fleumatique! (*Bible* 2565–72)

They find a defect in everyone; if he has a fever or a dry cough they say he is phthisic, or has glanders or dropsy, is melancholy or has the piles, is corpulent (?) or paralytic. If you were to hear them going on about choler, or phlegm!

None of these authors is necessarily attacking medical or astrological theories as such; they are protesting against the dubious uses to which a specialist knowledge can so easily and exasperatingly be put. Chaucer may wish to evoke such complaints about being blinded with science, but he does not himself repeat them; the Doctor's portrait claims the delighted admiration for this 'verray parfit praktisour' which Renart's gusto in fraud also, but subordinately, suggests.

We are also expected to admire the Doctor's arrangements with apothecaries:

> Ful redy hadde he his apothecaries
> To sende hym drogges and his letuaries,
> For ech of hem made oother for to wynne –
> Hir frendshipe nas nat newe to bigynne. (425–8)

What could be more sensible than this situation, in which 'mutual profit' is ensured? Other writers, however, would see this as a travesty of the ideal co-operation between estates. For Gilles li Muisis, doctor and apothecary are united in their interest in the patient's money; he says of the doctor,

> S' on li promet argent, il vos visitera,
> A l'apoticarie connoistre vous fera,
> Par sen varlet des boistes assés envoiera:
> Se bien ne li payés, de tout il cessera. (1 p. 112)

If he is promised money he will visit you, and will introduce you to the apothecary's medicine. He will send you by his boy many boxes of pills – but he will stop altogether if you don't pay him well.

Renart says that no-one had any joy of his medical practice except the apothecary, the priest, and the maker of shrouds.[37] Gower spells out in detail the whole process of collusion:

> Phisicien de son affaire
> En les Cités u q'il repaire
> Toutdis se trait a l'aquointance
> De l'espiecer ipotecaire;

> Et lors font tiele chose faire
> Dont mainte vie ert en balance:
> Car cil qui de leur ordinance
> User voldra d'acoustummance
> Le cirimp et le lettuaire,
> Trop puet languir en esperance
> D'amendement, car tiele usance
> Est a nature trop contraire. (*MO* 25,633–44)

The physician, for the sake of his business, in whatever city he goes to, always cultivates the acquaintance of the apothecary or spicer – and they have things made up from which many a life will hang in the balance. For whoever at their direction is willing to make a habit of taking syrup or electuary, may languish only too long in hope of improvement. For such a custom is too contrary to nature.

The doctor will purge your stomach, and the apothecary your purse.[38] Chaucer characteristically avoids a similar explicitness on the high cost of the drugs, or their ineffectiveness; his admiration is given to the smooth co-operation between these two branches of the same profession. The patient's benefit is not in question.

So far the Doctor's portrait has been devoted to the details of his profession; now Chaucer apparently moves on to his personal life – for what could be more personal than a man's eating habits?

> Of his diete mesurable was he,
> For it was of no superfluitee,
> But of greet norissyng and digestible. (435–7)

Yet a constant association between good health and a temperate diet in medieval writers suggests that the Doctor is merely obeying the theories of his profession. Guiot de Provins complains that doctors forbid the best foods ('les millors maingiers'), and he rejects their fancy medicines in favour of good clear wines and strong sauces ('boins clers vins et fors sauces').[39] Renart's practice as a doctor is obviously founded on this model:

> Bien disoie: 'Junez, junez,
> Et de la purée prenez,
> Et vous gardés de boire vin.'[40]

I said 'Fast, fast, and take only purée, and make sure not to drink wine.'

When Piers Plowman falls sick, Hunger lectures him on the same principles:

'I wote wel,' quod Hunger ˙ 'what syknesse ȝow eyleth,
ȝe han maunged ouer-moche ˙ and that maketh ȝow grone . . .
Lat nouȝt sire Surfait ˙ sitten at thi borde.
And ȝif thow diete the thus ˙ I dar legge myne eres,
That Phisik shal his furred hodes ˙ for his fode selle.' (*PPl* VI 259–71

This passage suggests that the Doctor's temperate diet is not only
what is recommended by his profession, but may be designed to render
the ministrations of his kind unnecessary.[41]

The Doctor's clothing looks as individual as his diet.

> In sangwyn and in pers he clad was al,
> Lyned with taffata and with sendel. (439–40)

But the individual details are used to evoke a very typical characteristic)
– the doctor's wealth[42] – for Chaucer goes on to say that *nevertheless*
he is not extravagant. *Piers Plowman* may serve as a simple example of
the traditional association of wealth with the doctor, and the luxurious
clothes which bear witness to it: the figure of Phisik conjured up by
Hunger has not only 'furred hodes', but also a 'cloke of Calabre' with
'knappes of golde'.[43] The description of fine clothing, separated from
that of the fraud through which it is acquired, means that in Chaucer's
portrait we can respond with pleasure to the gay colours and the
swish of taffeta and silk; our emotional response, as with the Monk,
runs counter to our incipient moral criticism.

In the last four lines of the Doctor's portrait we recognise another
familiar technique – the blending of the narrator's viewpoint with that
of the pilgrim.

> And yet he was but esy of dispence;
> He kepte that he wan in pestilence.
> For gold in phisik is a cordial,
> Therefore he lovede gold in special. (441–4)

Whose are the 'For' and the 'Therefore'? Is Chaucer explaining the
Doctor, or is the Doctor explaining himself? Whoever it is, is 'explaining away' a love of money which is traditionally assigned to doctors.[44]
Chaucer's 'esy of dispence' echoes the phrasing of Matheolus' satire on
medical avarice:

> Chascuns a paour qu'il ne perde,
> Et pour ce pleurent leur despense,
> Tristes, pensis et en offense;
> Car avarice les rebourse,
> Qui ne leur lait ouvrir leur bourse.[45]

Each is afraid of losing money, and therefore they grieve at their expenditure, sad, anxious and mortified, for avarice holds them back, and doesn't let them open their pursues.

So great is the doctor's avarice, says Gower, that

> Phisicien d'enfermeté,
> Ly mires de la gent blescé,
> Sont leez, q'ensi gaigner porront.[46]

The doctor is glad when people fall sick, the surgeon when they are wounded, for so they will be able to make a profit.

The macabre juxtaposition of the 'gent blescé' and the 'lée' doctor seems to lie like a shadow behind Chaucer's line – 'He kepte that he wan in pestilence.' But his reference to the disease, rather than to the diseased, preserves the poise of the portrait, and our attention is quickly diverted by the humorous 'excuse' for the Doctor's avarice. This is merely the latest version of a long line of jokes about gold. The father of them all may well be the one in the 'Gospel According to the Mark of Silver'; the pope, seeing that his subordinates have received bribes from a cleric, while he has none, falls 'sick, nigh unto death'.

Dives vero misit sibi electuarium aureum et argenteum, et statim sanatus est.[47]

The rich man however sent him medicine of gold and silver, and straightway he was made whole.

The bitter tone of the Latin satirist disappears in Chaucer's adaptation of the joke. We 'accept' the explanation because it saves us from having to think too hard about the less attractive aspects of the Doctor; we choose to concur in the surface amiability of the portrait.

For we have no *evidence* that the Doctor is a grasping charlatan, despite our suspicions. Similarly we may be tempted to link Chaucer's statement that the Doctor's study of the Bible was scanty (438) with the proverbial atheism of the medical profession.[48] Yet as Curry says,

he *may* be a pious man who has no time for reading the Bible or a rank materialist who contemns religion – we are not sure. In fact, we cannot be absolutely sure about anything in the Doctor's character. Chaucer has created him so. And it is this very uncertainty as to his honesty, his honour, his sincerity, and his learning which lends a certain life-like complexity to his character and actions; it is this human contradictoriness which the author . . . seizes upon and develops by suggestion. (*Chaucer and the Mediaeval Sciences*, p. 36)

What I want to add to this is that, just as the ambivalent vocabulary in the Friar's portrait showed us, the 'human contradictoriness' is something which belongs to Chaucer's audience as much as, if not more than to the Doctor. It is we who have mental frameworks which will admit admiration both for the 'verray parfit gentil knight', and for this 'verray parfit praktisour'.

THE MERCHANT

The Merchant represents one of the few secular estates regularly treated in estates satire, and as with the lawyer, the treatment varies little whatever his rank: the vices attributed to international traders are identical with those criticised in humble retailers. The important distinction for the estates writer was that which separated those involved in agricultural labour from those who worked in the towns, so that merchants are often implicitly included with craftsmen and retailers in descriptions of 'cives' or 'burgenses'.

The vices of merchants are very quickly enumerated. An overwhelming number of satirists associate them with fraud and dishonesty.[49]

> 'Londoniis natus Gila de matre parentis
>   Nomine Truffator nuncupor ipse mei.
> Gula mihi soror est, multis notissima regnis;
>   Est et Truffa mihi foedere juncta tori.' (SS 785–8)
>
> At London Gila gave me birth, and from
>   My father's name Truffator [Trickster] I am called.
> My sister Gula [Gluttony] is of great renown
>   And Truffa [Deceit] has become my wedded wife.
>
> (trans. after Regenos, p. 59)

This is how the merchant whom Burnellus the Ass meets introduces himself, and his spiritual lineage would suit many other merchants described in estates satire.[50] The image of a family of mercantile vices recurs elsewhere, and in Gower its head is Avarice, a trait often, and understandably, associated with merchants.[51] The final member of the family in the Vox Clamantis is Usury, who is Fraud's sister.[52] Satirists are conscious, once again, of the victims of greed and dishonesty:

> Insontes astutia mercantum falluntur,
> Fraus et avaritia sorores junguntur.[53]

Simple people are deceived by merchants' cunning; fraud and avarice unite as sisters.

Langland is similarly aware that those who 'rychen thorw regraterye' found their fortunes on 'that the pore people shulde put in here wombe' (*PPl* III 83–4).

It is against such a background that we have to see Chaucer's lines on the Merchant:

> Wel koude he in eschaunge sheeldes selle.
> . . . estatly was he of his governaunce
> With his bargaynes and with his chevyssaunce. (278, 281–2)

These statements look like innocent praise of the Merchant's success in business, but their phraseology is derived from the estates satire on fraudulent business practices. In the *Mirour de l'Omme*, it is 'Triche' or 'Trickery' who goes around snapping up bargains ('vait les bargaigns pourpernant' 25,353). Although money-exchange sounds an innocuous activity it was often connected with shady or illegal dealings,[54] and is one of the practices boasted of by Langland's Avarice.[55] But suspicion of money-changers is not confined to England; 'trestout change, si est usure' – 'all exchange of money is usury' says Renart the fox,[56] and Gilles li Muisis would agree with him.[57] The use of the word 'chevyssaunce' to suggest shady dealings is equally widespread, even when it seems to mean no more than 'profit':

> Il faut mentir et parjurer,
> Et le plus biau dehors monstrer
> Qui veult avoir sa chevisance.[58]

Whoever wants to get his profit must lie and perjure himself and show the best side outward.

Far more often the word is a simple euphemism for usury,[59] and so Gower introduces it into the *Mirour de l'Omme* under a description of the third daughter of Avarice, whose name is Usury ('la tierce file d'Avarice, la quelle ad noun Usure' 7212, 7234–6). Later he associates wool-merchants with

> Eschange, usure et chevisance. (25,417)

Money-changing, usury and chevisance.

We might see this line as the source of Chaucer's, were it not that Langland's Avarice confesses,

> Eschaunges and cheuesances with suche chaffare I dele,
> And lene folke that lese wol a lyppe at euery noble. (*PPl* V 249–50)

Chaucer's vocabulary is not derived from a single source: it recalls a tradition. What is remarkable is that he does not make more of it. The shadiness which might characterise the 'eschaunge' of money is ignored, and the 'bargaynes' and the 'chevyssaunce' are mentioned only incidentally, to give us an idea of the Merchant's importance. The words themselves take on the air of professional jargon; they emphasise our position as laymen *vis-à-vis* a specialist world. The general shift in emphasis parallels that made in the Sergeant's portrait. Instead of the Merchant's avarice and dishonesty, we hear of his 'estatly' manner and his 'worthy' qualities.[60] The 'innocent' or the 'poor', who are elsewhere mentioned as the inevitable sufferers from this avarice and dishonesty, are conspicuous by their absence. And once again we have to note that estates failings are suggested by the *language* which the narrator uses to describe the pilgrim, rather than being described as facts.

As with the Sergeant, Chaucer has some basis in other writers for describing the Merchant's carefully-preserved dignity, although its role elsewhere is comparatively slight.[61] There is even a satiric tradition behind such a detail as Chaucer's description of the Merchant's conversation:

> His resons he spak ful solempnely,
> Sownynge alwey th' encrees of his wynnyng. (274-5)

When 'Triche' is a wool-merchant, says Gower,

> de son encress
> Lors trete et parle asses du pres.[62]

Then he enlarges on his gains, and talks a lot about loans.

Thomas Wimbledon refers to this mercantile habit casually, as if it were well-known; priests, he says, nowadays speak 'vnhonestly as cherlis, oþer of wynnynge as marchaundis', and he is not the only sermon-writer who provides evidence of this stereotype.[63] Chaucer uses this feature to suggest the Merchant's façade, which is cultivated as carefully as the Sergeant's, and which is just as difficult to penetrate. He also uses it for the same kind of 'realism' that we have in the description of the Parson's parish-visiting: the 'alwey' adds a 'time-dimension' to the character by revealing the *habitual* channels of his thought and conversation.

But the reality of the Merchant's character, as of the other pilgrims, depends as much on what is hidden from us as on what is revealed. There is, first of all, the professed ignorance of his name (284), which suggests Chaucer's role as reporter rather than omniscient creator. Subtler is the process of concealment in lines 279–80:

> This worthy man ful wel his wit bisette:
> Ther wiste no wight that he was in dette.

The exact meaning of these lines has been disputed.[64] Do they mean that no-one could accuse the Merchant of being in debt because his prudence protected him from it? Or do they mean that although he *was* in debt, he was so circumspect that no-one knew of it? If he was in debt, he would be no more than typical: 'on voit moult de faus kétis et endetés' – 'one sees many dishonest rogues with debts owing' – is Gilles li Muisis' comment on merchants (II p. 58), and Gower describes how they

> font leur parlance
> De mainte Mill; et sanz doubtance
> Des tieus y ad que s'il paioiont
> Leurs debtes, lors sans chevisance
> Ils n'ont quoy propre a la montance
> D'un florin, dont paier porroiont.[65]

make mention of many thousands – and without doubt there are some such that if they were to pay their debts, without manipulation of credit they haven't the property, not so much as a florin, to do it with.

But such passages should help us to perceive the deliberate ambiguity of Chaucer's lines: '*if* he was in debt, no-one knew of it'. The professional façade is the basis of our knowledge of the Merchant.[66]

The rest of the portrait seems to have been invented by Chaucer; the basis of this invention is the estate. First, we have a professional obsession with the protection of trade:

> He wolde the see were kept for any thyng
> Bitwixe Middelburgh and Orewelle. (276–7)

We may relate the Merchant's interest in the wool staple to Gower's satire on wool-merchants,[67] but the detail is clearly Chaucer's. Significantly it belongs to a professional, not an individual consciousness. Yet it has another interesting aspect; Chaucer seems concerned to give a topical flavour to the estates stereotype, for it has been pointed out that these lines would have an immediate relevance between 1385 and 1386.[68] It is not the eternal human type that Chaucer seems to be interested in, but the consciousness aroused in each estate by the contemporary situation.

The details of the Merchant's appearance likewise give life to a professional stereotype:

> A Marchant was ther with a forked berd,
> In mottelee, and hye on horse he sat;
> Upon his heed a Flaundryssh bever hat,
> His bootes clasped faire and fetisly. (270–3)

These details are new with Chaucer, but their genesis in the Merchant's wealth and foreign travel is easy to guess at.[69] Without our sense of the Merchant's professional *persona*, of the enigmatic reality behind it, and of the past history which makes it possible to label a characteristic as a habit, they could not give us the sense we have of the Merchant as an individual.[70]

THE GUILDSMEN

In the Guildsmen also, Chaucer satirises self-importance rather than fraud. Their traditional background is at first hard to discern, for we may search in vain for evidence of the medieval stereotypes for 'An Haberdasshere and a Carpenter, A Webbe, a Dyere, and a Tapycer' (361–2).[71] But having added these five to the list of occupations in the *Prologue*, Chaucer makes no further use of them, classing the Guildsmen together as members of 'a solempne and greet fraternitee' and dealing with them as a group.[72] They wear the same clothing, the livery of their fraternity, and are given the same status, characteristics and ambitions. Their occupations seem to be arbitrarily chosen,[73] and to have assumed no particular significance in the *Canterbury Tales*; 200 lines later, Chaucer re-assigns the Carpenter's trade to the Reeve, and it is he who takes offence at the Miller's Tale of the Oxford carpenter (I (A) 3913–15).

It is as a group therefore that the Guildsmen belong to a recognisable estate. The clue lies in line 369 –

> Wel semed ech of hem a fair burgeys.

Whether labelled 'cives', 'burgenses' or 'ceaux qui vivont du mestier et d'artifice', the bourgeoisie makes a regular appearance in estates satire, often separately from merchants, although sharing their characteristics.[74] The innumerable occupations of secular city life defeat the satirist, and the most general failings are attributed to the urban middle-class:

> inter vos sunt deceptores
> fideique destructores
> atque haeresis auctores,
> paganis multo viliores.
> habetis malos detractores,
> proximorum traditores,
> substanciae devoratores,
> tabernarios et lusores,
> usurarios, foeneratores,
> malos et fornicatores. [75]

Among you are deceivers and destroyers of the faith, originators of heresy, much worse than pagans. You have evil slanderers, betrayers of their neighbours, wasters of wealth, tavern-haunters and gamblers, usurers and lenders for interest, and wicked fornicators.

At the same time, some writers give concreteness to their satire by specifying different crafts and trades, as Chaucer does. The *Chessbook* distinguishes several classes of craftsmen – notaries, tailors, dyers, weavers, barbers, pelterers, butchers, tanners – which it links as 'workers in cloth or skins' ('lanifices') and addresses with the same exhortation to honesty (col. 449–54). The long list of occupations in Gower's estates works forms a series of particular illustrations of the general theme of avarice. [76] Chaucer follows this practice in naming several different trades, but treating their exponents in a body.

Tradition is, however, disregarded in the features assigned to the Guildsmen, in a way that exactly parallels the treatment of the other estates discussed in this chapter. The corporate treatment of the bourgeoisie is most often based on the mercantile vices of fraud, usury and avarice. [77] Chaucer ignores these features completely. The possession of wealth is once again cut loose from its association with corrupt practices, and allied instead with self-importance and consciousness of status:

> Wel semed ech of hem a fair burgeys
> To sitten in a yeldehalle on a deys.
> Everich, for the wisdom that he kan,
> Was shaply for to been an alderman.
> For catel hadde they ynogh and rente. (369–72)

Does this testimonial originate with Chaucer, or the Guildsmen themselves? At first we assume that it is the narrator's voice we are hearing, but the way that the genial assurance of worth is quickly followed up by a statement of qualifications seems to suggest the

Guildsmen's eagerness for office as much as their fitness for it.[78] And what follows makes our feelings even more complex:

> And eek hir wyves wolde it wel assente;
> And elles certeyn were they to blame.
> It is ful fair to been ycleped 'madame',
> And goon to vigilies al bifore,
> And have a mantel roialliche ybore. (374–8)

The 'vigil' was traditionally the scene for more feminine weaknesses than a delight in precedence,[79] but what Chaucer gives us in these lines is more than traditional comedy at the expense of pride.[80] He brings into the open the 'hidden motive' for acquiring a public position, innocently pointing out the advantages of importance in a way that emphasises the basis of the social hierarchy in pride as well as order and service to the community. This portrait, like those of the other 'bourgeois' estates, illustrates the nature of social 'worthiness'. But we shall be missing Chaucer's point if we merely contrast it with moral 'worthiness' and criticise the pilgrims on this basis. The moral state of the Guildsmen is not something on which we're given evidence; what Chaucer suggests is that our own concept of 'wisdom' or of 'a solempne and greet fraternitee' might, if we examined it closely enough, be based on the same assumptions as this one. The narrator's hearty sympathy with the attitude of the wives is merely the explicit expression of an attitude that is present, if submerged, in our everyday views on society.

The demonstration is not made in any bitter or cynical mood, however. The Guildsmen's 'array' testifies to their sense of their own status:

> Ful fressh and newe hir geere apiked was;
> Hir knyves were chaped noght with bras
> But al with silver; wroght ful clene and weel
> Hire girdles and hir pouches everydeel. (365–8)

The details may be Chaucer's own,[81] but the technique in these lines clearly derives from satire on a hankering for fine knives and girdles.[82] But Chaucer is not disgusted by their 'fressh and newe geere' as Langland is by the 'pisseres longe knyves' of contemporary priests (xx 218). As in the Monk's portrait, there seems to be justice in Chaucer's choice of epithet when he assures us that each is a 'fair burgeys'.

5

Independent Traditions: Chivalry and Anti-Feminism

Estates satire is no more of a watertight compartment than any other literary genre. Although the enumerative estates form may be abandoned, the traditional satire on social classes is recognisable in such forms as fabliau or the drama, and it is exactly this pervasiveness which justifies the use of heterogeneous sources for evidence of estates stereotypes. The influence is not, however, one-way; something of the original contribution of independent traditions will be reflected in estates satire.

Behind the Knight and the Squire lies the rich tradition of chivalric literature, behind the Wife of Bath that of anti-feminist writing. It is impossible to deal with these genres in their entirety; even less is it possible to examine the social realities which are reflected in the differing ideals of knighthood.[1] I shall concentrate on the literary expression of chivalric ideals and of anti-feminism contained in the kind of sources used so far in this study. The independent traditions will be considered only in so far as they affect estates satire, and Chaucer's portraits.

THE KNIGHT

The Knight and the Squire are representatives of chivalry, but in different aspects. The Knight is a 'worthy man', the Squire a 'lovyere and a lusty bachelere'. The difference does not merely derive from their individual personalities, nor even from their difference in age; it reflects differing aspects of the ideal of chivalry itself.

Before pointing up the difference, however, we shall examine those characteristics of the Knight which are equally relevant to any chivalric ideal. First, his 'worthynesse', which Chaucer makes into the key-note of his portrait (43, 47, 50, 64, 68).[2] The repetition of this word is paralleled in Gower's insistence that the knight should be 'bonus' or a 'prodhomme'.[3] And the other virtues to which the Knight is devoted are, like this one, appropriate to his estate:

> he loved chivalrie,
> Trouthe and honour, fredom and curteisie. (45–6)

The particular elements in this list may well derive from Watriquet de Couvin's praise of his dead master, the constable Gautier de Châtillon.

> Prouesce faisoit esveillier,
> Courtoisie, honneur et largesce
> Et loiauté, qui de noblesce
> Toutes les autres vertus passe.[4]

He awoke from their sleep valour, courtesy, honour, generosity and loyalty, which surpasses in nobility all other virtues.

But it is doubtful whether this selection had any final or original significance even for Watriquet, who produces differing groups of knightly virtues even within the same poem.[5] For both writers, the aim is to suggest an ideal knight by associating him with several recognised chivalric virtues, and this aim is also responsible for similar lists or selections of virtues in estates satire and works on chivalry. The *Chessbook*, for example, lists 'Sapientia, fidelitas et liberalitas, fortitudo, misericordia' ('wisdom, loyalty and generosity, courage, pity'),[6] and Gower refers to knights as those

> en qui toute prouesce,
> Honour, valour, bonte, largesce
> Et loyalte duissent remeindre.[7]

in whom all prowess, honour, valour, excellence, generosity, and faithfulness should reside.

The Knight also conforms to an ideal in being 'wys' as well as 'worthy' (67).[8] For Geoffroi de Charny, writer on chivalry and a knight accorded the distinction of carrying the oriflamme at Poitiers, the 'vaillants' or 'worthy' knights are those who unite 'sens' and 'prouesce' while being 'preudhommes'.[9] Another feature of the Knight which belongs to his character as 'verray parfit gentil knyght' is his meekness, surprising though it may seem as part of a military ideal:

> And of his port as meeke as is a mayde.
> He nevere yet no vileynye ne sayde
> In al his lyf unto no maner wight. (69–71)

Meekness and courteous speech are also characteristics for which Watriquet praises the constable of France:

> Tant fust plains de courouz ne d'ire,
> Onques n'issi hors de sa bouche
> Vilains mos; maniere avoit douche,
> Plus que dame ne damoisele.[10]

However much he might be full of anger or wrath, there never issued from his mouth a boorish word; he had a manner gentler than that of lady or girl.

But in this the constable is no more individual than Chaucer's Knight, for the English poem 'The Simonie' refers to these ideal characteristics (and in Chaucer's order, not Watriquet's) in a complaint about the knightly class:

> So is mieknesse driven adoun, and pride is risen on heih.
> Thus is the ordre of kniht turned up-so-doun,
> Also wel can a kniht chide as any skolde of a toun.
> Hii sholde ben also hende as any levedi in londe,
> And for to speke alle vilanie nel no kniht wonde
>   for shame;
> And thus knihtshipe is acloied and waxen al fotlame.[11]

Thus far the Knight's portrait derives from a common chivalric ideal; it is the description of his 'array' at the end of the portrait which serves to indicate the particular aspect of the chivalric role with which he is identified.

> But, for to tellen yow of his array,
> His hors were goode, but he was nat gay.
> Of fustian he wered a gypon
> Al bismotered with his habergeon,
> For he was late ycome from his viage,
> And wente for to doon his pilgrymage. (73–8)

It is choice of outward 'array' by which St Bernard, in his address to the Templars, distinguishes two different conceptions of the knightly role. St Bernard sees the new order as representing a new role for the knight: the union of chivalry and monasticism. He scornfully describes the adornments of secular knights, the trappings of their horses and armour, the decoration of their shields and spears.[12] The Templars, on the other hand, like Chaucer's Knight, bear the marks of their service:

Nunquam compti, raro loti, magis autem neglecto crine hispidi, pulvere foedi: lorica et caumate fusci.

Never combed, rarely washed, but rather shaggy, with unkempt hair, black with dust, dirty with the heat and their corselets.

And like him also they have 'goode' horses, although they are 'nat gay':

Equos habere cupiunt fortes et veloces, non tamen coloratos aut phaleratos.[12]

They wish for strong and swift horses, not with gay colours or trappings.

In contrast to this ideal stands that of Ramón Lull, which, in the words of Caxton's translation, considers a knight to be 'oblyged and bounden ...to honoure his body in beyng well cladde and nobly',[14] although here too the importance of good horses for the knight is emphasised.[15] In general, the satirists concur with the preferences of St Bernard, without necessarily exhibiting his ascetic rigidity. Thus they criticise knights who plunder

propter superbiam,
ut equos habeant et vestem nobilem.[16]

out of pride, so that they may have horses and fine clothing.

'The Simonie' expresses the satirist's ideal:

Knihtes sholde weren weden in here manere,
After that the ordre asketh also wel as a frere;
Nu ben theih so degysed and diversliche i-diht,
Unnethe may men knowe a gleman from a kniht,
  wel neih.   (PSE, p. 335, 253-7)

The significance of the Knight's armour-stained tunic extends further than the indication of his ascetic dedication; it plays an important role in our 'realistic' impression of his existence. In this function it is partly anticipated by St Bernard's reading of hot and dusty campaigning from the knight's appearance. It is not the de-glamourising tendency of the description which is important – armour rusty with wear appears in such courtly works as the *Teseida* and *Gawain and the Green Knight*[17] – it is that Chaucer's statement again evokes a time-dimension, a past which not only leads up to but determines the reality 'observed' in the present. This time-dimension is present elsewhere in the portrait; Chaucer does not merely tell us that the Knight honoured chivalric virtues, he tells us that he has loved them 'fro the tyme that he first bigan | To riden out'. And again the past which is evoked, and which has left its mark on the individual pilgrim, is the daily routine of professional life; it is an 'estates' past.

We have seen that Chaucer's Knight shows certain affinities with the religious and ascetic role outlined for the crusading orders by St Bernard;[18] indeed, it is possible that Chaucer meant to suggest his association with such an order, that of the Teutonic Knights.[19] But Chaucer is not writing a tract on chivalry, and the influence of the crusading ideal does not imply its total dominance. Thus Chaucer's stress on the Knight's service to his lord seems to lie outside it.

> Ful worthy was he in his lordes werre,
> And therto hadde he riden, no man ferre,
> As wel in cristendom as in hethenesse. (47–9)

These lines reflect the stress by both chivalric and estates writers on a knight's duty to his earthly lord.[20]

Fideles debent esse milites principibus. Militis enim nomen amittit, qui servare fidem principi non novit.[21]

Knights must be loyal to their princes. For he forsakes the name of knight, who has not known how to keep faith to his prince.

Yet we hear no more of this earthly lord, or how his service requires the Knight's participation in a multitude of campaigns in foreign countries. Perhaps Chaucer is after all thinking of the Knight as a fighter for God, for all his battles are against the heathen.

> At Alisaundre he was whan it was wonne.
> Ful ofte tyme he hadde the bord bigonne
> Aboven alle nacions in Pruce;
> In Lettow hadde he reysed and in Ruce,
> No Cristen man so ofte of his degree.
> In Gernade at the seege eek hadde he be
> Of Algezir, and riden in Belmarye.
> At Lyeys was he and at Satalye,
> Whan they were wonne; and in the Grete See
> At many a noble armee hadde he be.
> At mortal batailles hadde he been fiftene,
> And foughten for oure feith at Tramyssene
> In lystes thries, and ay slayn his foo.
> This ilke worthy knyght hadde been also
> Somtyme with the lord of Palatye
> Agayn another hethen in Turkye. (51–66)

This list of campaigns has been the most important stimulus in the search for real-life originals of the Knight – a search unrewarded by any convincing success, not because of the impossibility of finding any real fourteenth-century knights whose careers are similar, but on the contrary because of the frequency with which suitable candidates present

themselves.[22] And if we look at the way in which the Knight's career
is presented, rather than the historical events involved in it, we shall
find that the fact that it takes the form of a list of places tells us something about the origins and connotations of the Knight's portrait.
Such lists, although not part of the estates treatment of the knight,
have an important role in the literary tradition of the *chansons de geste*.
Even a cursory examination of these poems shows that frequently a
knight's career is summarised, either by himself or by the narrator,
by a list of the important places where he has fought successfully. Thus
at the moment of his death, Roland speaks of his sword, Durendal,
and the countries he conquered with its aid:

> Jo l'en cunquis e Anjou e Bretaigne,
> Si l'en cunquis e Peitou e le Maine,
> Jo l'en cunquis Normendie la franche,
> Si l'en cunquis Provence e Equitaigne
> E Lombardie e trestute Romaine,
> Jo l'en cunquis Baiver' e tute Flandres
> E Burguigne e trustute Puillanie,
> Costentinnoble, dunt il out la fiance,
> E en Saisonie fait il ço qu'il demandet,
> Jo l'en cunquis e Escoce e Irlande
> E Engletere, que il teneit sa cambre.[23]

With this I won Anjou and Brittany, with this I conquered Poitou and Maine,
with this I won Normandy the free, Provence, Aquitaine, and Lombardy and
all Romagna. I conquered with it Bavaria and all Flanders, Burgundy and the
whole of Apulia, Constantinople, whose homage he [Charlemagne] had, and
in Saxony he does what he requires. I won with it Scotland, and Ireland and
England, which he held as his domain.

In the late thirteenth century, the achievements of Garin de Monglane
are similarly summarised by a list of places in *Doon de Maience*:

> tout chel Toulousan de paiens delivra,
> Et tout le Nerbonnois et Orenge combra,
> Venice sus la mer et Biaulande aquita,
> Puille et Calabre aussi et quanque il i a.[24]

he delivered all those of Toulouse from infidels, and seized all of Narbonne and
Orange, he delivered Venice on the sea and Beaulande, Apulia, Calabria, and
everywhere else.

The function of such a list is not only to 'prove' the knight's worth and
experience, but also to evoke the exotic aspects of foreign travel, the

romance of battle in far-off lands. This aspect is particularly evident in the use of similar lists in Machaut's *Dit dou Lion*, where courtly ladies excitedly discuss the exploits of their knights in 'Irlande' or 'Cornuaille', or in the Holy Land:

> 'il revient de Damas,
> D'Antioche, de Damiette,
> D'Acre, de Baruch, de Sajette,
> De Sardinay, de Siloë
> De la monteigne Gelboë,
> De Sion, dou mont de Liban,
> De Nazareth, de Taraban,
> De Josaphat, de Champ Flori,
> Et d'Escauvaire ou Dieu mori . . .'
> 'Aussi fu il en Alixandre,'
> Dit l'autre, 'et en mont Synai.'

'He is coming back from Damascus, from Antioch, from Tamiathis, from Acre, Beirut, Sidon, from Sardinia, the river of Shiloah and mount Gilboa, from Sion and the mount of Lebanon, Nazareth and Ceylon (?), the vale of Jehosaphat and Paradise, and Calvary where God died . . .' 'He was also in Alexandria,' says the other, 'and on mount Sinai.'

Such was the eagerness of knights to serve their ladies in olden times says Machaut,

> Car s'il sceüssent une armée
> Ou une guerre en Alemaigne,
> En Osteriche ou en Behaingne,
> En Hongrie ou en Danemarche
> Ou en aucun estrange marche,
> En Pruce, en Pouleinne, en Cracoe,
> En Tarterie ou en Letoe,
> En Lifflant ou en Lombardie,
> En Atenes ou en Rommenie,
> Ou en France ou en Angleterre,
> Il y alassent honneur querre,
> Puis s'en raoient en Grenade.[25]

For if they knew of an expedition or a war in Germany, in Austria or Bohemia, in Hungary or Denmark, or in some strange country, in Prussia, Poland, Cracovia, Tartary or Lithuania, Livonia or Lombardy, Athens or Romagna, in France or England, there they went to win honour, and then set off for Granada.

Some of the places in Chaucer's list were also used by Machaut to illustrate the brilliant career of 'le bon roy de Behaingne':

Qui en France et en Alemaingne,
En Savoie et en Lombardie,
En Dannemarche et en Hongrie,
En Pouleinne, en Russe, en Cracoe,
En Masouve, en Prusse, en Letoe,
Ala pris et honneur conquerre.[26]

Who went to France and Germany, Savoy and Lombardy, Denmark and
Hungary, Poland, Russia, Cracovia, Masovia, Prussia, Lithuania, to win fame
and honour.

The fact that this is a description of a real-life career might be taken to
indicate that Chaucer is also documenting the real experiences of a
contemporary – but it is possible to put the connection in another
light: Machaut is using the list of campaigns which summarises the
chanson de geste hero in order to idealise a real personage. Similarly,
despite the undoubted topicality of the campaigns in Chaucer's list,
its *framework* is a literary one, whose function is to place the Knight in
a line of heroes of chivalry.

But the tenor of the list of campaigns, its significance for the ideal of
chivalry that the Knight adheres to, has still to be established. Despite
the fact that foreign campaigning can be simply a means of making
money,[27] and that in Machaut, fighting in the Holy Land is a way of
impressing ladies, it seems clear that Chaucer wishes us to accept the
Knight's motivation as religious. Not only do the historians tell us that
all the campaigns named were against the heathen, but the vocabulary
of the portrait stresses the opposition between 'cristendom' and
'hethenesse' (49), that the Knight is a 'Cristen man' (55), who has
'foughten for oure feith' (62) and campaigned against the 'hethen' (66).[28]
This stress on the Knight as a crusading fighter is one of the roles
which the Church envisaged for chivalry, and defending the Church
against the barbarity of pagans and heretics ('contra saevitiam Pagano-
rum, atque Haereticorum') is one of the duties laid on the knight in the
dubbing ceremony.[29] Estates literature accordingly preaches this
knightly duty:

Aprés clers sunt chevalers
Pur [garder] terres et musters
De Sarazins et d'adversers,
Qui Deu ne ses sainz n'unt chers;
Que poesté
N'aient sur nus li mescreant ne li malfé.[30]

After the clerks come the knights to [protect] lands and churches from the

Saracens and the enemies who do not hold God nor His saints dear; that un-believers and evil-doers may not have power over us. (trans. Aspin, p. 124)

'Knights are not brave enough to go overseas' says 'Le Dit des Mais',

> Se ce n'est aprez boire, ou quant dite est complie. (*NR* I p. 188)

unless it's when they've been drinking, or when compline is over [and it's too late?].

This is the knightly role stressed by 'The Simonie':

> Hii sholde gon to the Holi Lond and maken there her res,
> And fihte for the croiz, and shewe the ordre of knihte,
> And awreke Jhesu Crist wid launce and speir to fihte
> and shel.[31]

Some passages of this sort mention places on Chaucer's list, such as 'Garnade' or 'Espruce'.[32]

Fighting the heathen was not the only sphere of duty assigned to the knight, even if we leave out of account his role as courtly lover. In the dubbing ceremony, his sword is given him not only that he may attack the heathen, but also that he may be the defender of churches, widows and orphans ('defensor Ecclesiarum, viduarum, orphanorum').[33] The difficulty of combining the two duties does not appear to have troubled the deviser of the ceremony, nor the satiric writers who urge both.[34] A similar conflict exists at least implicitly between the crusading ideal and that expressed in Passus VI of *Piers Plowman* where Piers describes the knight's task as preserving 'holikirke and my-selue' from evil-doers, as watching over the rights and duties of 'tenaunts', 'pore men' and 'bonde-men' (25–49). Such contradictions within or between different ideals of knighthood are by no means unique;[35] writers could at different moments reconcile different chivalric roles,[36] but as Daniel Rocher has pointed out, such reconciliations exist only within the bounds of each individual work, and must be established afresh by new writers or social theoreticians.[37] Of the two major roles envisaged for the *miles Christianus*, we have seen that Chaucer's Knight follows primarily the ascetic crusading ideal rather than that of the secular lord who stays at home and protects Piers Plowman. Yet if estates satire preaches the knight's duty to fight the heathen, it stresses even more strongly his duty to punish wrong-doers and protect the poor,[38] and complains about his rapine, injustice and oppression.[39]

Chaucer's choice of the crusading role for his ideal Knight is signifi-cant, and the nature of its significance is suggested, as so often, by a comparison with Langland. Despite the fact that he is a much more 'religious' writer than Chaucer, Langland does not put forward the knight's duty to campaign against the heathen, because he sees too clearly the demands of his role in a social structure at home. The absence of such a sense of social *structure* in the general ethic of the *Prologue* was commented on in the discussion of the other estates ideals. If we examine the Knight's portrait closely, we see that the immediate ends of his professional activities are undefined. Is their aim conversion of the heathen?[40] or their extermination, to make way for the permanent occupation of the Holy Land by Christians?[41] The Knight's role, as it is described in his portrait, is merely to fight, win, and move on. One might say that his campaigns have a religious *character*, but not a religious *aim*.[42]

Chaucer's Knight is a 'verray parfit gentil knyght', but, like the other pilgrims, he is a professional specialist, and the relevance of his profession to the lives of the rest is not made clear.[43]

THE SQUIRE

Accompanying the Knight is 'his sone, a yong Squier'. As with the Parson and the Ploughman, the blood-relationship between the individuals seems to derive from a connection between two estates. Not only are knights and squires often placed side by side in estates lists,[44] in *Lordre de Chevalerie* we find the assumption that the knight is the father of the squire:[45]

La science & lescole de chevalerie est que le chevalier face son filz aprendre a chevaucher en sa ieunesse . . . Et convient que le filz du chevalier pendant quil est escuyer se sache prendre garde de cheval. Et convient quil serve avant, & quil soit devant subgect que seigneur. . . . Et pour ce que tout chevalier doit son filz mettre en service dautre chevalier affin quil aprengne a taillier a table & a servir, & a armer & habilier chevallier en sa ieunesse. (p. 276)

The scyence and the scole of the ordre of Chyualrye / is that the knyght make his sone to lerne in his yongthe to ride . . . And it behoueth / that the sone of a knyght in the tyme that he is squyer can take kepynge of hors / And hym behoueth that he serue / and that he be first subgette or he be lord / . . . And therfor euery man that wylle come to knyghthode hym behoueth to lerne / in his yongthe to kerue at the table / to serue to arme / and to adoube a kny3t. (trans. Caxton, p. 21)

Chaucer's Squire conforms to this model:[46]

> Curteis he was, lowely, and servysable,
> And carf biforn his fader at the table. (99–100)

But the ideal of 'curteisie' which the Squire serves has different overtones from that admired by his father. This is emphasised at the
beginning of the portrait, when he is introduced as 'A lovyere and a
lusty bacheler' (80).[47] This is no incidental feature of his character, but
the motivation of his feats in arms:

> And he hadde been somtyme in chyvachie
> In Flaundres, in Artoys, and Pycardie,
> And born hym weel, as of so litel space,
> In hope to stonden in his lady grace. (85–8)[48]

The desire to win the favour of a lady is one important motivation
attributed to the knight in medieval literature.[49] It could, as I have
suggested, be combined with other aims, such as the service of God,
and an estates writer could say of knights, without impiety,

> arma frequentare, decet hos ardenter amare.[50]

The exercise of arms, and the ardent pursuit of love is incumbent upon them.

Gilles li Muisis, indeed, criticises those knights whose slogan is 'Love
to the ladies and death to horses!' ('l'amour à dames et le mort à
chevauls!' II p. 46), but the basis of his criticism seems to be that they
stay at home and tourney, rather than riding out to adventure like
Percival. Moreover, their devotion to women is not as selfless as it
should be; they are only interested in 'l'amour des dames', and don't
care whether they are ugly or beautiful so long as they are sexually
compliant. Such a complaint might suggest a very concrete meaning
for Chaucer's lines on the Squire:

> So hoote he lovede that by nyghtertale
> He sleep namoore than dooth a nyghtyngale. (97–8)

This suggestion seems to be reinforced by a comment on sleepless
gallants in a macaronic poem, 'Syngyn y wolde':

> Qwan men rest takyn,
>   noctis somno recreati,
> Swoch felawys wakyn,
>   ad damna patrata parati.
> Ful oftyn tyme iwys
>   gelido fervent in amore,
> Here specialis yf y kys,
>   distillat nasus in ore.[51]

Yet there is nothing of this writer's disgust in Chaucer's statement;

the image of 'hoote' love is immediately counteracted by the innocent and romantic comparison with the nightingale. The first line suggests sexual passion, the second romantic pining, and we are unable to read a clear reference to one or the other. The sexual passion itself may be aroused in the course of a lustful *affaire,* or a noble attachment. So Chaucer makes the Squire enigmatic to us, and our attitude to him, in the same way as with many of the other pilgrims, becomes complex.

Romantic chivalry can, however, be condemned even when the love is of an ideal nature. Gower explicitly rejects love as a motivation for the knight in both his estates poems:

> Dic michi nunc aliud: quid honoris victor habebit,
>   Si mulieris amor vincere possit eum? . . .
> Nil nisi stulticiam pariet sibi finis habendam,
>   Cui Venus inceptam ducit ad arma viam. (*VC* v 19–20, 25–6)

Now tell me something else: what glory will a conqueror have, if a woman's love can overcome him? . . . The end will produce nothing but folly for the man whom Venus leads to take up the way to arms.

And he demonstrates the folly of devoting one's service to women by a long digression composed of anti-feminist satire (Chapters II–VI). In the *Mirour,* where Gower defines serving God as the only good motive for fighting, he names two false motives – the knight desires fame ('loos'), or else he says

> 'c'est pour m'amye,
> Dont puiss avoir sa druerie,
> Et pour ce je travailleray.' (23,902–4)

'it's for my lady, so that I may have her love, and for this I shall labour.'

This is clearly the motivation which Chaucer assigns to the Squire, but it is characteristic of the *Prologue* that although Chaucer thus attributes to him aims of which Gower would disapprove, and attributes to the Knight aims which Gower would admire, he himself betrays no *system* of ethics which would lead us to prefer one to the other. The only criterion applied is the way in which each measures up to his chosen ideal.

The Squire's devotion to love and to his lady seems appropriate to his youth and 'lustiness' – it is part of his 'estate' in another of its aspects, and thus takes on a *relative* validity. This impression of the estate of the young knight is confirmed by Geoffroi de Charny's description of those who are especially fond of jousting:

Ce sont li aucun qui ont bon corps sain et appert, et qui se tienent nettement et joliement, ainsi comme il affiert bien à joeune gent dous et courtois et de bonne manière entre la gent.[52]

There are some who are healthy and agile of body, and dress themselves cleanly and gaily, as befits charming and well-bred young people, who have a good social manner.

The 'bon corps sain et appert' corresponds to Chaucer's description of the Squire's physique:

> Of his stature he was of evene lengthe,
> And wonderly delyvere, and of greet strengthe. (83–4)

And this physical fitness is also required by the chivalric ideal that *Lordre de Chevalerie* had outlined.[53] But the same work disapproves of a carefully-cultivated and fashionable appearance,[54] such as is associated particularly with squires in estates literature. Gilles li Muisis takes it for granted, when he complains that shepherds and carters now want to be dressed like squires ('ensi k'uns esquyers').[55] Usually, the estates writer is critical of the squire's fashionable appearance:

> And nu nis no squier of pris in this middel erd
> But if that he bere a babel and a longe berd . . .
>
> A newe taille of squierie is nu in everi toun;
> The raye is turned overthuert that shulde stonde adoun,
> Hii ben degised as turmentours that comen from clerkes plei.[56]

The details of the Squire's appearance can be linked with this satiric tradition:

> With lokkes crulle as they were leyd in presse . . .
> Embrouded was he, as it were a meede
> Al ful of fresshe floures, whyte and reede, . . .
> Short was his gowne, with sleves longe and wyde. (81, 89–90, 93)

In the knightly context, the tradition of satirising fashionable clothing is an old one: St Bernard uses it to distinguish the worldly knights he despises from the ascetic Templars. 'You decorate your horses and armour,' he says,

Vos . . . in oculorum gravamen femineo ritu comam nutritis, longis ac profusis camisiis propria vobis vestigia obvolvitis, delicatas ac teneras manus amplis et circumfluentibus manicis sepelitis.[57]

You make yourselves eye-sores, coaxing your hair in woman's fashion, enveloping your feet with long and ample shirts, burying your dainty soft hands in wide and flowing sleeves.

Already here we have the neat hair and the flowing sleeves which appear in the Squire's portrait, although St Bernard ridicules the ample robes of worldly knights, rather than the shortness of their gowns. Nicholas Bozon also associates carefully-arranged coiffures with dandyish squires, who are 'besotted with women' ('asoté...des femmes'), and, presumably in the desire to impress them, are always smoothing down their hair.[58] Other writers also use carefully-arranged hair as sign of foppishness in general,[59] and the 'sleves longe and wyde' are a symbol of aristocratic vanity for many satirists beside St Bernard.[60] Short gowns are satirised by writers who associate them with both lovers and knights.[61] Yet the 'lokkes' of the Squire curl only *as if* they were 'leyd in presse'.[62] It seems as if the Squire was born a dandy; we cannot be sure that we have a warrant to criticise him for crimping and combing his hair through personal vanity. Again, Chaucer puts the possible failing on to a linguistic level – this time an apparently innocent simile. And where we are in no doubt, as with the profuse embroidery, which Geoffroi de Charny tells us adorns a knight less than virtue,[63] our moral reaction is thwarted by a sensuous one; the embroidery is not presented critically, but enthusiastically, by means of a comparison that evokes the spring-time setting of romantic love.

The attitude to a gay appearance was not always negative, even in estates writings. 'Make yourself gay' ('Te maintien ioliement') is Jean de Condé's advice to squires.[64] And corresponding to a different aspect of the Squire's estate, the *Roman de la Rose* advises the lover:

> Mayntene thysilf aftir thi rent,
> Of robe and eke of garnement;
> For many sithe fair clothyng
> A man amendith in myche thyng.
> And loke alwey that they be shape,
> What garnement that thou shalt make,
> Of hym that kan best do,
> With all that perteyneth therto.
> Poyntis and sleves be well sittand,
> Right and streght on the hand ...
> And kembe thyn heed right jolily.[65]

Chaucer's Squire resembles not only the *Roman*'s Amant, but also the unmarried gallant who is described with enthusiasm in Matheolus' *Lamentations*:

> Il chante, il saute ou il chevauche,
> Assés plus grant qu'il n'est se hauce,

> Souvent fait ses cheveus laver,
> Recroquillier, pignier, graver;
> Il porte chauces semelées
> Et robes estroites ou lées.[66]

He sings, leaps or rides; he makes himself taller than he is. He has his hair often washed, curled, combed and parted. He wears well-soled shoes and gowns that are tight or flowing [lit: wide].

Chaucer's Squire, it will be noted, is fond of the same kind of activities as Matheolus' lover:

> Syngynge he was, or floytynge, al the day;
> He was as fressh as is the month of May . . .
> Wel koude he sitte on hors and faire ryde.
> He koude songes make and wel endite,
> Juste and eek daunce, and weel purtreye and write. (91–2, 94–6)

And both resemble in this the Lover of the *Roman de la Rose*, who is advised by Amour:

> Whereof that thou be vertuous,
> Ne be not straunge ne daungerous.
> For if that thou good ridere be,
> Prike gladly, that men may se.
> In armes also if thou konne,
> Pursue til thou a name hast wonne.
> And if thi voice be faire and cler,
> Thou shalt maken [no] gret daunger
> Whanne to synge they goodly preye;
> It is thi worship for t'obeye.
> Also to you it longith ay
> To harp and gitterne, daunce and play;
> For if he can wel foote and daunce,
> It may hym greetly do avaunce.
> Among eke, for thy lady sake,
> Songes and complayntes that thou make;
> For that wole meven in hir herte,
> Whanne they reden of thy smerte.[67]

Amour suggests to the Lover that he should cultivate *one* of these accomplishments; with the hyperbole that characterises his estates presentations, Chaucer endows his Squire with *all* of them. And he also takes over the *Roman*'s appreciation of the charm of youth, gaiety and love; admiration of the Knight's ascetic ideal of chivalry does not mean, within the *Prologue*'s terms, rejection of that of his son.[68]

THE WIFE OF BATH

Anti-feminism was a subject that stimulated medieval writers no less than the ideal of chivalry. As with the literature of chivalry I shall examine primarily the reflection of anti-feminist satire in estates literature.[69]

The first question that confronts us is what estate the Wife of Bath represents – and the answer is not far to seek, for women were recognised as a separate class in estates lists.[70] The *Sermones nulli parcentes*, for example, put 'mulieres' last in a list of lay classes, as they had put nuns at the bottom of the ecclesiastical hierarchy,[71] and Jean de Condé addresses 'Dames et pucielles' as an estate.[72]

The duties and failings of the estate of women are often seen from the standpoint of the male moralist. Woman's sexual role is of great importance; the whole of the chapter on women in the *Sermones* is occupied in defining the attitude men should adopt toward them. The classification of women, not by trade or social rank, but by marital status, also betrays this approach. Thus it is part of the hyperbole with which Chaucer presents the estates 'qualifications' of the pilgrims that the Wife's sexual role has been played to the full:

> She was a worthy womman al hir lyve:
> Housbondes at chirche dore she hadde fyve,
> Withouten oother compaignye in youthe, –
> But therof nedeth nat to speke as nowthe ...
> Of remedies of love she knew per chaunce,
> For she koude of that art the olde daunce. (459–62, 475–6)

What is more, the fact that two of these lines are taken directly from the *Roman de la Rose* shows that this sexual role corresponds to one established for women in traditional satire.[73]

Yet this is not the only evidence of the Wife's qualifications to be a representative of her profession. At the head of her portrait stands a testimony to her skill as a weaver:

> Of clooth-makyng she hadde swich an haunt,
> She passed hem of Ypres and of Gaunt. (447–8)

The Wife herself later reveals the appropriateness of cloth-making to her estates role:

> Deceite, wepyng, spynnyng, God hath yive
> To wommen kyndely, whil that they may lyve. (III (D) 401–2)

This proverb is also a favourite with Gilles li Muisis,[74] and the assumption that cloth-making is the duty of the feminine estate can also be seen in Gower's complaint, in the *Vox Clamantis*, that women neglect their spinning in order to entice knights away from their duties (v 349–50). Étienne de Fougères had already complained that the rich lady does not weave, spin or wind ('Ne teist, ne file, ne traoille').[75] In the division of labour supervised by Piers Plowman, this is the task assigned to women:

> And 3e, louely ladyes · with 3oure longe fyngres,
> That 3e han silke and sendel · to sowe, whan tyme is,
> Chesibles for chapelleynes · cherches to honoure.
> Wyues and wydwes · wolle and flex spynneth,
> Maken cloth, I conseille 3ow · and kenneth so 3owre dow3tres.[76]

The fact that we never hear again of the Wife's 'clooth-makyng' strongly suggests that the only reason for introducing it here is to emphasise her estate function.[77]

The Wife's estate also forms the basis of her character as it is presented in the *Prologue*. In the first instance, Chaucer describes a piece of behaviour which bears witness to her strong sense of her own status.

> In al the parisshe wif ne was ther noon
> That to the offrynge bifore hire sholde goon;
> And if ther dide, certeyn so wrooth was she,
> That she was out of alle charitee. (449–52)

Concern for precedence in making the offering is a trait described in the Parson's Tale as an example of Pride (x (I) 407) – a vice regularly associated with women.[78] And the church is traditionally a place for women to exhibit it: Gilles li Muisis describes how they examine and comment on each other's clothes as they go up in turn to offer, and how they fight for the best seats.[79] When the Emperor Pride in Nicholas Bozon's poem sends out his letters of command to women, he orders them to contest for their seats in church. The response is enthusiastic:

> 'Sire,' fount eles, 'ceo est resoun
> Ke femme honure soun baroun.
> Ataunt de tere ad la meen
> Come dit ma veisine que ad le seen;
> Pur quey donck mey dey retrere?'[80]

'Sire', they say, 'it's only right that a woman should respect her husband. Mine has as much land as my neighbour says hers has. Why then should I hang back?'

Matheolus' *Lamentations* describe similar quarrels:

> S'il a une coustumiere
> De seoir au moustier premiere
> Ou d'aler devant a l'offrande . . .
> Souvent grans batailles en sourdent;
> Celles qui d'envie se hourdent
> Ne veulent pas ainsi souffrir
> Que premiere deüst offrir.[81]

Also, there is a custom of sitting in the first seat in the church, or going first to the offering . . . often great battles arise from this; those who are characterised by envy don't want to allow that anyone should offer first in this way.

This episode likewise testifies to the irascibility of women, which is also a traditional part of their character.[82] The Wife is again typical of her estate in being so 'wrooth'.

But Chaucer complicates our reaction to the Wife's pride by making it difficult for us to see how far it is justified by her social position. As with the Guildsmen, he first assures us of the Wife's high social standing, and then leads us, by way of an amplification of his statement, to suspect (although not to be *sure*) that it exists mainly in her own imagination. Prompted in this way, we may go on to ask what kind of 'worthiness' is illustrated by having had five husbands (459–60). It seems rather like the 'wisdom' that is proved by having a large income. Satire on social façades in the *Prologue* is by no means reserved for the Merchant and the Guildsmen.

The Wife is also typical of women in her love of pilgrimages:

> And thries hadde she been at Jerusalem;
> She hadde passed many a straunge strem;
> At Rome she hadde been, and at Boloigne,
> In Galice at Seint-Jame, and at Coloigne.
> She koude muchel of wandrynge by the weye. (463–7)

Illicit purposes are assumed for such trips in the most well-known Goliardic satire on women:

> Petit licentiam uxor nefaria
> ut vadat peregre per monasteria,
> et tecta subiens prostibularia,
> plus illa celebrat quam sanctuaria.[83]

The wayward wife asks leave to tour the monasteries abroad, and, entering the brothels, she frequents them more than the shrines.

Chaucer's 'wandrynge by the weye' also seems to echo Matheolus' complaint that women choose distant goals of pilgrimage:

> Mieulx leur plaist le pelerinage,
> Quant la voye est un peu longnete,
> A saint Mor ou a Boulongnete,
> Et aucune fois au Lendit,
> Qui est en juin, si com l'en dit.[84]

A pilgrimage pleases them better when the journey is a longish one, to St-Maur or Boulogne, and at times to the Lendi, which is in June, so they say.

But yet again, we have to note that the object of moralising attack is only suggested by the language in which Chaucer describes something in itself quite innocent; it is only the possible double meaning in the phrase 'wandrynge by the weye' that suggests that the Wife may morally as well as geographically abandon the 'straight and narrow' path.[85]

The Wife's appearance is also – at least in part – related to the satire of her estate. This is particularly true of Chaucer's stress on her outrageous head-dresses:

> Hir coverchiefs ful fyne weren of ground;
> I dorste swere they weyeden ten pound
> That on a Sonday weren upon hir heed . . .
> Ywympled wel, and on hir heed an hat
> As brood as is a bokeler or a targe. (453–5, 470–1)

There has been some argument about whether the Wife is in or out of fashion with her 'coverchiefs';[86] the question seems academic when we realise that there was a healthy satiric tradition of attacking women's head-gear which went back at least 200 years.[87] Women's 'horns' provide a favourite target for attack,[88] but English writers in particular seem to have featured veils, kerchiefs and wimples;[89] Robert Mannyng refers contemptuously to 'wymples, kerchyues, saffrund betyde' as items of female finery, and sees women 'wyþ here kercheues' as baits of the devil.[90] Some writers stress the excessive cost of the head-gear; the jealous husband in the *Roman de la Rose* accuses his wife:

> vos . . . portez qui vaut .c. livres
> d'or et d'argent seur vostre teste.[91]

You wear on your head what is equivalent to £100's worth of gold and silver.

Could it be that the Wife has misread her fashion magazine? That

instead of a head-dress *worth* £100, she has acquired one that *weighs*
ten pounds? At least it can be observed that the effect of her head-dress
is not to make the Wife the seductive temptress of moralising anti-
feminist satire, but a comic caricature.

The same could be said of Chaucer's description of her stockings and
shoes:

> Hir hosen weren of fyn scarlet reed,
> Ful streite yteyd, and shoes ful moyste and newe. (456–7)

Jean de Meun's jealous husband likewise accuses his wife:

> Et tant estrait vos rechauciez
> que la robe sovent hauciez
> por moutrer voz piez aus ribauz.[92]

And you wear such tight shoes that you often raise your dress to show your feet
to debauchees.

In seizing on tight shoes as a symbol of vanity and fashion, Le Jaloux
is only making an association common among satirists.[93] Yet the
fashionable allurements are oddly misplaced; scarlet stockings on the
Wife's sturdy legs are in a sense attractive, but hardly make her a
femme fatale.

This reaction is reinforced by the rest of the details Chaucer gives
about the Wife's appearance and physique:

> she was somdel deef, and that was scathe . . .
> Boold was hir face, and fair, and reed of hewe . . .
> Gat-tothed was she, soothly for to seye.
> Upon an amblere esily she sat, . . .
> A foot-mantel aboute hir hipes large,
> And on hir feet a paire of spores sharpe. (446, 458, 468–9, 472–3)

For these details I have found no satiric tradition. Curry has interpreted
some of them from the manuals of physiognomy,[94] and it may be
that, as Curry suggests, they derive from this source, or else from
Chaucer's own imagination. But it is legitimate even here to ask what
stimulated Chaucer's search, or his invention, and to observe that the *significance* of the details, as Curry interprets them, fits into the traditional
character of woman, rather than that of an individual personality.[95]
However much we may be struck by the unexpected detail, by the
deafness or the wide teeth, the strength and vividness of the Wife's
personality cannot come from such a source alone.

In seeking to analyse the impression of originality which the Wife's portrait makes on us (although not so strongly as the Prologue to her Tale), aid may be sought in the *Roman de la Rose*. Jean de Meun's influence on the portrait at several points has been indicated, and the figure of La Vieille, the *vetula* or old woman with a lifetime's experience of the other sex, has deeply influenced Chaucer's conception of a middle-aged woman who 'has had her world in her time'. Yet in one important respect Chaucer's character differs from the presentations of woman in the *Roman de la Rose*. The *Roman* is traditional, and unlike Chaucer, in separating the beautiful young woman who is able to carry on love-affairs, and the ugly old woman who knows all the lore of love but cannot practise it. This dichotomy characterises the medieval satiric treatments of women.[96] When a satirist does describe the sexual life of an old woman, it is her *false* attractiveness he emphasises:

> Mais cestes vieves jolyettes,
> Vestant le vert ove les flourettes
> Des perles et d'enbreuderie,
> Pour les nouvelles amourettes
> Attraire vers leur camerettes,
> A turtre ne resemblent mye:
> Mais sur trestoutes je desfie
> La viele trote q'est jolie,
> Qant secches ad les mammellettes.[97]

But these merry widows, wearing fur with little flowers of pearls and embroidery, to lure new loves to their chambers, aren't like the [faithful] turtle-dove. More than all of them I scorn the old coquette who is flirtatious when her breasts are all withered up.

The uniqueness of the Wife of Bath is that, although she has certain traits in common with the *vetulae*, Chaucer presents her as attractive. Our impression of her complex personality arises from an inability to categorise her as temptress or as bawd. The estates presentation also plays a part here, for we are not asked to take up the usual standpoint which *judges* a woman's sexual behaviour. The Wife's sexual experience is ambiguously described as 'compaignye in youthe', 'wandrynge by the weye' or 'the olde daunce', and offered as evidence of her estate 'qualifications'. We can hardly accuse her of a contrived and tempting beauty, but neither are we disgusted by a withered, painted coquette, or a wrinkled bawd.

Our standards in this portrait, as in the others, are no longer moral but 'social' in the narrow sense – and a sign of this is Chaucer's transformation of the endless stream of words with which the satirists reproach womankind,[98] into the flowing talk of a lively companion:

In felaweshipe wel koude she laughe and carpe. (474)

In the social ethic of the *Prologue*, what ensures our admiration for the Wife is that she is fun to be with.

Although drawing on very different areas of literary tradition, the three portraits discussed in this chapter provide excellent illustrations of Chaucer's approach in the *Prologue*. We have an ideal figure – but one whose perfection is as little of 'our business' as the Merchant's fraud; we have a gay representative of youth who persuades us of the appropriateness of his characteristics *for him*; we have a typical woman whose feminine weaknesses are her strength as an estates representative. Although social considerations loom large in the portraits, they do not take the form of services offered by each pilgrim to the community, but the surface courtesy, gaiety or fellowship of a chance acquaintance.

6

Descriptive Traditions: Beauty and the Beast

The rhetorical *descriptio* does more than provide the form of the *Prologue* portraits; its conventional uses contribute something to their content. In this chapter, I shall discuss the portraits of the Prioress and the Summoner. The links between the Prioress' portrait and descriptions of romantic heroines have been fully recognised,[1] but it is not usually realised that the Summoner is linked in a similar way with conventional descriptions of ugliness. In what follows I shall not only discuss these links with the *descriptio* tradition, but shall try to show how Chaucer incorporates the descriptive material into his presentation of the estate.

THE PRIORESS

The traditional description of a romantic heroine accounts for almost all the *external* features included in the Prioress' portrait.

> Ful semyly hir wympul pynched was,
> Hir nose tretys, hir eyen greye as glas,
> Hir mouth ful smal, and therto softe and reed;
> But sikerly she hadde a fair forheed;
> It was almoost a spanne brood, I trowe;
> For, hardily, she was nat undergrowe. (151–6)

This description, in outline and detail, reproduces the appearance of a worldly beauty.[2] Moreover, the Prioress is called, romantically, 'madame Eglentyne' (121).[3] Her 'smylyng' Chaucer describes as 'symple and coy' (119) – a pair of adjectives that J. L. Lowes has shown are applied over and over again to the heroines of Old French romance.[4] Her behaviour is also consonant with the lady of a castle rather than the head of a nunnery:

> At mete wel ytaught was she with alle:
> She leet no morsel from hir lippes falle,
> Ne wette hir fyngres in hir sauce depe;

> Wel koude she carie a morsel and wel kepe
> That no drope ne fille upon hire brest.
> In curteisie was set ful muchel hir lest.
> Hir over-lippe wyped she so clene
> That in hir coppe ther was no ferthyng sene
> Of grece, whan she dronken hadde hir draughte.
> Ful semely after hir mete she raughte. (127–36)

This account of punctilious table manners is taken directly from the advice in the *Roman de la Rose* on how to make oneself charming to one's admirer when in company.[5]

The other aspect of the Prioress' life – that she is 'a Nonne, a Prioress', as we are reminded by the information that she sings divine service 'Ful weel',[6]

> Entuned in hir nose ful semely (123)

– seems to run directly counter to this attention to worldly attractiveness and refinement.[7] Our first question may therefore be to ask what suggested to Chaucer this conflation of the courtly lady and the nun.

One answer presents itself immediately, for, as has been pointed out by other writers, in anti-feminist satire the same characteristics are often attributed to nuns as to their secular sisters.[8] Boccaccio explicitly expresses his wonderment at those who are so foolish as to believe that a woman ceases to experience feminine desires as soon as she has assumed a religious habit.[9] For the medieval satirist, it would seem, 'the feminine' was not even imperfectly 'submerged in the ecclesiastical'.[10] In estates satire, the failings attributed to nuns are identical with those assigned to women in general; they are considered to be sensual,[11] quarrelsome or recalcitrant,[12] deceitful,[13] fond of luxury,[14] unable to keep a secret,[15] lacrimose,[16] and hungry for praise.[17]

Chaucer does not explicitly associate the Prioress with such failings, but his description of her does betray in her a fondness for nice clothes akin to that which characterises secular women.

> Ful fetys was hir cloke, as I was war.
> Of smal coral aboute hire arm she bar
> A peire of bedes, gauded al with grene,
> And theron heng a brooch of gold ful sheene,
> On which ther was first write a crowned A,
> And after *Amor vincit omnia*. (157–62)

In this the Prioress also resembles the streoetype of the worldly nun. As early as the eleventh century, we find a Latin song in which a nun laments the tediousness of singing divine office, and describes the luxuries she longs for.

> Fibula non perfruor,
> flammeum non capio,
> strophum assumerem,
> diadema cuperem,
>   heu misella! –
> monile arriperem
>   si valerem,
> pelles et herminie
>   libet ferre.[18]

I have no brooch to enjoy, can wear no bridal-veil; how I'd long to put on a ribbon or a coronet – woe is me! – I'd get a necklace if I could, and wearing ermine furs would be lovely.

The author of the Middle English *Ancrene Wisse* warns religious women against rings, brooches, girdles, gloves, and attention to their wimples.[19] Pleating or 'ipinchunge' of the wimple is specifically disapproved of.[20] In estates writing, we find Gilles li Muisis, for example, associating nuns with an elaborate manner of dress ill-fitted to their professions of humility.[21] The specific details of the Prioress' clothing – 'pynched' wimple, fine cloak and elaborate rosary with its gold brooch – fit easily into this tradition.

However, such resemblances are in a sense misleading, for in each case the context of these descriptions is concerned with sexual sins. The nun in the Latin song is dying for a young man to come and rescue her, and although the titivating nuns in the *Ancrene Wisse* illustrate the sin of Pride, it is clearly assumed that their efforts are designed to attract masculine admiration.[22] This emphasis also characterises much of the other literature featuring nuns, such as the twelfth-century Latin *Council of Remiremont* (in which nuns debate the respective merits of knights and clerks as lovers),[23] or Old French nuns' complaints.[24] And nuns' sensuality is also assumed in passages which parallel other features in Chaucer's portrait – such as the description of the nuns in the *Speculum Stultorum*, who, like the Prioress, sing divine office diligently – but 'so that you would think them sirens' (2377-8). As Lowes has noted, Chaucer carefully omits any suggestion of sexuality, and stresses instead the Prioress' reverence for 'curteisie'. The woman who is imperfectly submerged in the nun is not the greedy shrew or the sensual temptress of the anti-feminist's imagination, but the idealised heroine of the romance-writer.

Estates literature can show some ironic uses of the romance heroine in its treatment of nuns, but not on the same scale. Thus Nigel of Longchamps describes his nuns with the hints at 'the beauties beneath the gown' traditional in rhetorical descriptions.

> Hae caput abscondunt omnes sub tegmine nigro,
> Sub tunicis nigris candida membra latent.[25]

> Beneath black veils they all conceal their heads,
> Beneath black skirts they hide their lovely legs. (trans. Regenos, p. 115)

The Order of Fair-Ease contains 'meinte bele e bone dame' whose beauty is as irrelevant to their profession as that of the Prioress.[26] But we have to turn elsewhere to discover the background for the Prioress' refinement and the gentle treatment it elicits from Chaucer.

We find it, partially, in the *Sermones nulli parcentes*, which advise the friars not to attack nuns too harshly lest they break so fragile a vessel ('vas tantae fragilitatis').[27] Gower's attitude is also gentle; the frailty of nuns is more pardonable because they belong to the weaker sex (*VC* IV 555–62). The soft and sensitive nature which these writers seems to impute to nuns is explicitly described by Langland's Wrath:

> I haue an aunte to nonne · and an abbesse bothe,
> Hir were leuere swowe or swelte · than soeffre any peyne . . .
> I was the priouresses potagere · and other poure ladyes,
> And made hem ioutes of iangelynge · that dame Iohanne
>   was a bastard,
> And dame Clarice a kni3tes dou3ter · ac a kokewolde was
>   hir syre,
> And dame Peronelle a prestes file · priouresse worth
>   she neuere,
> For she had childe in chirityme · al owre chapitre it
>   wiste. (*PPl* V 153–61)

Wrath here attributes to the nuns a combination of snobbery and refined sensibility which corresponds more nearly than anything discussed so far to the aristocratic 'curteisie' of Chaucer's Prioress,[28] who speaks French, the aristocratic language, 'ful faire and fetisly' (although it is 'After the scole of Stratford atte Bowe'),[29] who

> peyned hire to countrefete cheere
> Of court, and to been estatlich of manere,
> And to been holden digne of reverence. (139–41)

and who is so tenderly affected by the sight of 'any peyne'. But the shrewishness of Langland's nuns is not to be found in the Prioress, who is 'of greet desport, | And ful plesaunt, and amyable of port' (138–9). Again, Chaucer stresses the *pleasantness* of a pilgrim, even (or especially) in her failings. We have one more piece to fit into the mosaic, but the pattern must be sought elsewhere.

First, however, the ambiguous nature of some of the pieces must be noted. We have already seen how fine clothes can be a sign of sensuality or of personal fastidiousness, while refined sensibility can be an excuse to queen it over one's sister nuns, or an attempt to attain an ideal (though a misconceived one) of the 'best' behaviour. A similar ambiguity attaches to the dogs of which the Prioress is so fond.

> But, for to speken of hire conscience,
> She was so charitable and so pitous
> She wolde wepe, if that she saugh a mous
> Kaught in a trappe, if it were deed or bledde.
> Of smale houndes hadde she that she fedde
> With rosted flessh, or milk and wastel-breed.
> But soore wepte she if oon of hem were deed,
> Or if men smoot it with a yerde smerte;
> And al was conscience and tendre herte. (142–50)[30]

The satirist traditionally contrasts excessive tenderness for animals with indifference to human suffering; in the *Speculum Stultorum* it is the cleric who has a passion for hunting who feels so strongly for his animals:

> Plus cane percusso dolet anxius aut ave laesa
> Quam si decedat clericus unus ei.[31]

> He's troubled more when dogs are struck or when
> A bird is hurt than when a cleric dies. (trans. after Regenos, p. 128)

Nicholas Bozon describes how the 'little dogs that ladies love so much' ('les petiz kenez ke dames unt si cher') are allowed to sleep on the trains of their dresses – where no poor man would be allowed to set his foot.[32] And the Knight of La Tour Landry has a story of the punishment of one such lady, who cared more for her dogs than for the poor.[33] But in the Prioress' portrait any suggestion of feeding the poor is omitted (the 'victim' being once again ignored), and the dogs, in the context of 'curteisie', become part of the trappings of a romantic heroine, like the 'twey whyte grehoundys' that accompany Sir Launfal's mistress Tryamour.[34] Chaucer's deliberate omission of any possibility of the moral judgement which is the usual point of describing the clergy's dogs, transforms the significance of the feature, and so preserves the harmonious self-consistency of the portrait.

The passage also brings out the ambivalence of the word 'conscience'; we assume from the important flourish with which Chaucer introduces the word, that he is going to comment on the Prioress' 'moral sense, awareness of right and wrong' (*MED* 2). But since the evidence for this 'conscience' is the Prioress' concern for small animals, it is clear, by the time that the word reappears in conjunction with 'tendre herte', that we are dealing with the less elevated (but not *im*moral) conception of 'solicitude, anxiety' (*MED* 4). The point that needs to be made here is not that Chaucer is stressing the Prioress' failing in exhibiting one kind of conscience rather than the other, but that he shows us how this 'value-word', like 'reverence' or 'worthy', can be differently defined from different standpoints. The narrator uses the word here with the meaning it has for the Prioress, just as, in the Parson's portrait, he uses it in the more serious sense that the Parson's moral frame of reference gives it (525–6), or in the Shipman's portrait, he is prepared to leave undefined whether it means excessive susceptibilities or a moral sense, since the definition is unimportant for the Shipman – the one sort of 'conscience' seems to him as 'nyce' as the other (398). But all the different uses of the word are linguistically valid; they show us something of the relativist nature of our language of values, and of our usual, everyday criteria for judgement.

The word 'curteisie' is subject to the same shifting definitions as 'conscience'.[35] For one thing, it has a special and quite correct application to a nun which throws a new light on her relationship to the courtly lady and the appropriateness of describing the one in terms of the other. For this was something that had already been done, in a completely serious context, by numerous writers before Chaucer. Religion and 'curteisie', as has been increasingly recognised since Lowes' day, are not mutually exclusive ideals. The poet of *Pearl* not only describes the Virgin Mary as 'Quen of cortaysye',[36] in *Cleanness* he takes out of context yet another piece of advice on pleasing one's lover from the *Roman de la Rose,* and gives it a religious application. As the worldly lover is advised to adapt himself to the moods of his mistress, the Christian is advised to adapt himself to Christ.

If þou wyl dele drwrye wyth dryʒtyn þenne,
& lelly louy þy lorde & his leef worþe,
þenne confourme þe to Kryst, & þe clene make,
þat euer is polyced als playn as þe perle seluen.[37]

This type of spiritual 'courtesy' was seized on as especially appropriate for the nun. The 'ladylike' aspect of the spiritual life had been emphasised by the *Ancrene Wisse*:

Noble men & gentile ne beored nanes packes. ne ne feared wid trussews ne wid purses. hit is beggilde riht to beore bagge on bac. burgeise to beore purs. nawt godes spuse þe is leafdi of heouene. (p. 87, fol. 45a, 19–23)

The Latin and Old French poems about nuns' lovers take on, in this light, a new significance; they may concentrate on the sexual longings of nuns, but they also envisage the favoured suitor as a *courtly* lover, and it is assumed that he must possess qualities of virtue, wealth and breeding.[38] Correspondingly, in the serious ideal, it is Christ, in his role as the nun's heavenly Bridegroom, who is discussed in terms appropriate to a courtly lover.[39] This was perhaps only natural when there were such convents as Remiremont, where a girl had to have four noble ancestors on both her father's and her mother's side to be able to enter.[40]

For such girls, presumably, arose the tradition of translating the role of the courtly heroine into a religious sphere. Two examples of this are particularly illuminating, since they describe estates ideals. First, in Latin, we may take one of the 'sermones ad status' (sermons to the estates) of Guibert of Tournai, a Franciscan who died in 1284,[41] and whose works were widely diffused.[42] His sermon 'Ad moniales et religiosas' is based largely on texts from the Song of Songs and the Book of Wisdom, and takes beauty ('pulchritudo') as its theme.[43] Christ, himself the fairest, wishes to find in the nun a beautiful bride. But we are not to think that this is physical beauty ('Non est pulchritudo corporalis de qua laudatur'): as painters overlay a rough colour wash with finer colouring, so we use physical beauty as a ground for the finer colours of spiritual beauty. A woman's beauty – and here Guibert significantly breaks into the more courtly language of French ('dame bele et auenant') – consists of three elements: 'bel corsaige', 'beau visage', 'beau langage' (beauty of body, face and speech). Each is divided into three further sections; for example, the beauty of the body lies in feet, hands and stature. And each of these features is spiritually 'glossed'; beauty of stature, for example, means not being too small through pusillanimity or carnality, nor too tall through presumption or boldness. The way in which Guibert thus proceeds through the items that make up physical beauty – feet, hands, stature, cheeks, eyes, nose – reflects the itemising rhetorical descriptions of romantic heroines, and the same criteria of beauty are applied, such as the rose-and-lily complexion, here signifying shame and purity.[44] One feature which illustrates the lady-like aspects of this feminine ideal is Guibert's treatment of the beauty of the feet. He begins with a text from the Song of Songs: 'How beautiful are thy slippered feet (AV 'feet with shoes'), O prince's daughter!'[45] The nun is to be 'corteis' or 'courtly', which Guibert glosses in Latin as 'liberum, notabile et urbanum' ('free, distinguished and elegant'). She should not walk peasant-fashion like a crone slopping her shoes as she goes to market ('non vadit rusticane sicut vetula ad forum torquendo sotulares'); the reason she slops her shoes is that they are too wide, and nuns likewise are too widely open to bodily delights, such as foods, drinks and sleep ('et nimis accipis large delectationes carnis vt cibi, potus et somni'). Guibert is here exploiting the fashionable ideals of secular literature, for tight shoes are, as we have seen in discussing the Wife of Bath, modish and seductive. The role that the nun is to act out in spiritual terms is that of the elegant courtly lady.

The second example of the importance of this metaphorical role in the ideal of the nun is a long poem addressed to nuns by Gautier de Coincy, *La Chastée as Nonnains.*[46] Gautier's theme is the nun's marriage with God, which he amplifies by giving spiritual significance to features of the courtly lady and her love. Again, it is as a courtly lover that God deserves the nun's devotion.

> Si biau baron ne si poli
> Com Diex est ne poez avoir.
> Ce doit chascune bien savoir
> Que nul amant tant amoreus,
> Tant vrai, tant dox, tant savoreus
> Com Diex est avoir ne poez. (p. 128, 90–5)

So handsome nor so gracious a lord as God is can you never have. Everyone ought to know this: that a lover so ardent, so true, so gentle, so pleasing as God is, you cannot have.

As the courtly lady adorns her body, the nun must adorn her soul; as the lady looks in her mirror, the nun must examine herself in the mirror of her conscience (248–89).

The imagery in which Gautier clothes his counsel is appropriately delicate and romantic. Of Virginity and Chastity he says

> Mout sont sobres, blanches et netes
> Et plus assez que violetes
> Defuient tai, fumier et fanc.
> Mout sont lor chainze bel et blanc
> Et bien ridé et bien lié
> Soëf flairant et delïé. (pp. 145–6, 400–6)

Very modest, white and clean are they, and more than violets do they shrink from dirt, filth and mud. Their linen is fair and white, well pleated and tied, sweet smelling and fine and delicate.

The pleated linen referred to here is probably the wimple, since 'liier' has a precise meaning 'to tie on the wimple'.[47] The parallel with the Prioress' 'pynched' wimple is striking. Flower-imagery runs through the whole poem; the nuns are told, for example, that their flesh is sweeter than violet, rose or 'eglentiers' – the eglantine whose name Chaucer has given his Prioress. Moreover they, like her, are 'simples' (785). (The application of this adjective to religious women is not confined to Gautier; Gilles li Muisis uses Chaucer's very phrase when he says that nuns used to be 'coyes, simples, estrinnes' – 'serene, innocent, withdrawn'.[48]) Gautier encourages the nun to sing a popular love-song, in which a girl thanks her mother for marrying her well ('hautement'); it is the woman wedded to an earthly lord who is the 'mal mariée' (1094ff). In this set of images, the devil plays the role of the old bawd; like La Vieille and Pandarus, he knows so much of 'la vieille dance' that he is quick to take advantage of any wavering (429). And Gautier seems to be trying to assuage the aristocratic nun's longing for the luxuries of her class as he itemises the details which must be translated into spiritual adornment:

> Voz indes fleurs, vous violetes,
> Qui les grans plices d'erminetes,
> Qui la soie, le vair, le gris
> Avez laissiez por les dras bis . . . (p. 180, 1059–64)

You purple flowers, you violets, who have abandoned long ermine cloaks, silk, squirrel and miniver, in favour of dun-coloured robes . . .

Both Guibert and Gautier see the nun not just as the bride of Christ, but as his *courtly* mistress. They attempt to turn aristocratic fastidiousness into spiritual scruple, and not to discourage a girl from romantic dreams, but to attach them to a new hero.

Chaucer's Prioress has returned the imagery of such writers as Guibert and Gautier to its original context. Her portrait operates as a kind of three-dimensional pun; the imagery has become reality, but the ambiguity about the omnipotent 'Love' commemorated on her brooch,[49] was already present in the tension between the ideal of the nun and the language in which it was recommended. The 'curteisie' which the Prioress venerates is worldly, not spiritual; instead of refinement of the soul, we have, not even the Knight's ideal of honour, but 'cheere of court'. Her role as the feminine counterpart of the Squire reveals the inapplicability of his type of 'curteisie' in a religious sphere.[50] Thus in understanding better the estates ideal of the nun, we also understand better the object of Chaucer's satire in the Prioress' portrait. And it is the use of the estates ideal which teaches us the relativist character of each pilgrim's values; 'curteisie' is not an absolute, but an ideal that each pilgrim defines for himself.

THE SUMMONER

The Prioress' beautiful and elegant appearance, her fastidious manners and tender concern for dumb animals, help us to 'forgive' her shortcomings as a nun (and once again, they are shortcomings which we must largely infer by 'reading in' knowledge external to the *Prologue*).[51] With the Summoner, the case is just the opposite: his revolting physical appearance convinces us of his unpleasantness *before* we know of his moral corruption. The connection between the moral status and the physical attractiveness of the pilgrims will be discussed more fully in the Conclusion; here I should like to show what the Summoner's portrait owes to the *descriptio* tradition and to the estates stereotype.

The most striking aspect of the portrait is the Summoner's ugly face – together with his liking for strong-smelling foods, probably the strongest factor in our aversion to him.

> A Somonour was ther with us in that place,
> That hadde a fyr-reed cherubynnes face,
> For saucefleem he was, with eyen narwe.
> As hoot he was and lecherous as a sparwe,
> With scalled browes blake and piled berd . . .
> Ther nas quyk-silver, lytarge, ne brymstoon,
> Boras, ceruce, ne oille of tartre noon;

Ne oynement that wolde clense and byte,
That hym myghte helpen of his whelkes white,
Ne of the knobbes sittynge on his chekes.
Wel loved he garleek, oynons, and eek lekes . . . (623–34)[52]

Commentators on this passage disagree on the exact malady with which the Summoner is afflicted, but most of them agree that it is consequent upon his lechery and his fondness for drink and that it is at least aggravated by his indulgence in onions, garlic and leeks.[53] Chaucer encourages our sense of the diseased nature of the Summoner by his use of the technical term 'saucefleem' for his condition, and by the list of medicines.

But this list of foods, and the Summoner's face, have more than a medical significance. Onions, garlic and leeks are also a biblical, and satiric, symbol of moral corruption,[54] and 'leprosy' is used as an image of sin in the tradition of moral satire.[55] Nor should we ignore the fact that these features also have a very powerful effect on an immediate level; the reek of garlic and onions, and the repulsiveness of the red, slit-eyed face, covered with 'whelkes white', produces strong disgust. Similarly, in a Middle English poem which satirises 'rybaudz' and 'harlotes', a scabby face seems to imply lechery, but is introduced primarily for its repulsive effect on the reader.

> þe rybaudz aryseþ
> er þe day rewe;
> he shrapeþ on is shabbes,
> ant draweþ huem to dewe.
> sene is on is browe,
> ant on is eȝe brewe,
> þat he louseþ a losynger,
> & shoyeþ a shrewe.[56]

Arousing disgust by these means is one of the main aims of the formal *descriptio*, and the set-piece describing extreme ugliness is a feature of twelfth-century Latin *comedia*.[57] In the *Alda* of William of Blois, a servant called Spurius is described in this way; he also suffers from scabs:

> Velleris instar erat scabie concreta tenaci
> Cesaries, unus tota capillus erat.
> Deturpant oculos frontis sub ualle sepultos
> Silua supercilii continuusque sopor.[58]

His hair, like an animal's pelt, is matted with clinging scabs – none of his hairs could be separated from the others (lit.: it formed only one single hair). The forest of his eyebrows, and his unalleviated stupidity, disfigure his eyes, which are buried in the hollow of his forehead.

And Matthew of Vendôme gives a model description of a strikingly ugly woman, who is similarly afflicted by a skin disease.

> Corpore terribilis, contactu foeda, quietas
> Cervicis scabies non sinit esse manus.
> Dum latitat scabies rigido servata galero,
> Debita deesse sibi pabula musca dolet.
> Pelle, pilis caput est nudum, ferrugo rigescit
> Fronte minax, turpis, lurida, sorde fluens . . .
> Non parcit scabies collo vicina, quod horret
> Nodis.[59]

Horrible in body, disgusting to the touch, her hand will not let the scurf on the nape of her neck rest in peace. When the scabs are kept hidden by her rigid [with dirt?] hat, the fly grieves at losing its due food. Her head is bare of skin or hair; the dirt stiffens; louring of visage, vile, filthy, dripping with pus . . . The encroaching scabs do not spare her neck, which bristles with knobs.

The 'harlot'-like aspect of the Summoner, which is conveyed by these conventional means, has clear connections with the stereotyped idea of his calling. For purposes of comparison, his estate can be defined in a general way as that of a consistory court official.[60] These officials are consistently seen as oppressors of the poor, who will wink at sexual misdemeanours only if bribed, but are themselves guilty of fornication.[61] The section devoted to archdeacons in the *Apocalipsis Goliae* describes how they too mercilessly persecute those who do not buy them off, and make priests' concubines their especial victims.[62] The oppression of the poor man who cannot afford to bribe the consistory court is emphasised in 'Crux est denarii'.[63] 'The archdeacon and dean are worse than pagans', says Étienne de Fougères; they should remove priests' concubines, but the acceptance of 'v sols' converts them to the view that

> 'Bon est l'ostel ou fame habite.'[64]

'The lodging with a woman in it is a good one.'

The victim of this dishonesty is given a voice in an English poem; he is a peasant accused of seducing a girl, and expresses his hatred for all the court officials, including the 'somenours syexe oþer seuene', of whom he says

> hyrdmen hem hatieþ, ant vch mones hyne.[65]

'The Simonie' describes the same pattern of corruption in archdeacons as does the *Apocalipsis Goliae*, and associates a similar venality with 'officials and denes'.

> Theih sholde chastise the folk, and theih maken hem bolde.
> Mak a present to the den ther thu thenkest to dwelle,
> And have leve longe i-nouh to serve the fend of helle
> to queme;
> For have he silver, of sinne taketh he nevere ʒeme.[66]

Such treatments show how Chaucer's Summoner conforms to expected behaviour:

> He wolde suffre for a quart of wyn
> A good felawe to have his concubyn
> A twelf month, and excuse hym atte fulle;
> Ful prively a fynch eek koude he pulle.
> And if he foond owher a good felawe,
> He wolde techen him to have noon awe
> In swich caas of the ercedekenes curs,
> But if a mannes soule were in his purs;
> For in his purs he sholde ypunysshed be. (649–57)

The Summoner is guilty of the lechery he should punish:

> As hoot he was and lecherous as a sparwe. (626)[67]

– and as well as taking bribes, he 'makes bold' the offenders he meets. As in Chaucer's treatment of several other pilgrims, the 'victims', here the poor who can't afford a bribe, are left out of account, and the relationship between the Summoner and his 'clients' is presented as one of cosy convenience.

But why is it a summoner, rather than an archdeacon or a commissary, whom Chaucer chooses to describe? Again, the stimulus seems to come from Langland, in whom scornful references to summoners are frequent. The sins that Langland associates with the summoner are those traditionally assigned to officials of the consistory courts; they are financially corrupt,[68] and are particularly lenient with sexual offenders.

> Ac thanne swore Symonye˙and Cyuile bothe,
> That sompnoures shulde be sadled˙and serue hem vchone . . .
> 'Denes and suddenes˙drawe ʒow togideres,
> Erchdekenes and officales˙and alle ʒowre regystreres,
> Lat sadel hem with siluer˙owre synne to suffre,
> As auoutrie and deuorses˙and derne vsurye,
> To bere bischopes aboute˙abrode in visytynge.'[69]

At one point, Langland sees summoners and their like as participating in a universal corruption; the illegal gains of the laity are promptly creamed off by an equally dishonest clergy –

> The whiche aren prestes inparfit ' and prechoures after syluer,
> Sectoures and sudenes ' somnoures and her lemmannes. (*PPl* xv 129–30)

Might this have suggested to Chaucer the situation in which the cleric and the lay offender share the same values, and accept a financial, rather than a moral, basis for their relationship?

Certainly Chaucer is concerned at some points in the portrait to stress the corrupt and corrupting nature of the Summoner. The most sinister touch in the description is the line

> Of his visage children were aferd. (628)[70]

And this juxtaposition of ugliness and corruption with youth and innocence is repeated towards the end of the portrait.

> In daunger hadde he at his owene gise
> The yonge girles of the diocise,
> And knew hir conseil, and was al hir reed. (663–5)

Here, at last, we have a strong sense of a 'victim'.[71] Yet it is significant that it appears in the description of a pilgrim who is also physically unpleasant; is it too cynical to suggest that our sympathy for the 'yonge girles', and our judgement of the Summoner's moral corruption, are affected by the same instinctive and irrational fear of ugliness as children feel?

This portrait also contains one of the relatively rare moments in the *Prologue* when the narrator dissociates himself entirely from the pilgrim.

> 'Purs is the ercedekenes helle,' seyde he.
> But wel I woot he lyed right in dede;
> Of cursyng oghte ech gilty man him drede,
> For curs wol slee right as assoillyng savith,
> And also war hym of a *Significavit*. (658–63)

The joke about being punished in one's purse is an old one; in a Latin satire, for example, the cardinals of Rome beg the Pope to forgive a group of sinners, for

> Se purgabunt, ut ius docet, post hec ab infamia,
> et dum bene purgabuntur ipsorum marsupia,
> erit horum a peccatis munda conscientia.[72]

They will afterwards purge themselves, as justice teaches, from their disgrace, and when their purses are well scoured, their conscience will be clean of sins.

The joke still flourishes in Chaucer's time, for Gower, among others, uses it in both his estates works.[73] While Chaucer equates the purse with hell (and may in this be thinking of Dante[74]), Gower, in another variation, identifies it with a man's soul.

> Ne sai ce que la loy requiert,
> Mais merveille est de ce q'il quiert
> Dedeinz ma bource m'alme avoir. (MO 20,197–202)

I don't know what the law requires, but it's a wonder that he [the dean] seeks to secure my soul in my purse.

Chaucer takes over the disgust of these writers for the lie perpetrated by the Summoner. And yet he increases our sense of the Summoner's viewpoint, even as he sharply distinguishes it from that of the narrator.[75] For once again, it is the pilgrim himself who is aware of, and repeats, the satire on his class. As the Monk knows his anti-monastic satire, and the Parson knows the estates writing on his calling, so the Summoner is aware of the satire on corrupt officials. And this convinces us of his reality as of theirs.

The same transformation of the material of traditional satire into the attributes of a realistic character can be observed in Chaucer's presentation of the Summoner's drunkenness. It is significant that the derisory bribe which will dissuade him from harassing lechers is a 'quart of wyn', for he loved

> to drynken strong wyn, reed as blood;
> Thanne wolde he speke and crie as he were wood.
> And whan that he wel dronken hadde the wyn,
> Thanne wolde he speke no word but Latyn.
> A few termes hadde he, two or thre,
> That he had lerned out of som decree –
> No wonder is, he herde it al the day;
> And eek ye knowen wel how that a jay
> Kan clepen 'Watte' as wel as kan the pope.
> But whoso koude in oother thyng hym grope,
> Thanne hadde he spent al his philosophie;
> Ay 'Questio quid iuris' wolde he crie. (635–46)

In this vivid picture the conflation of two traditional ideas can be discerned. The first is that of the talking bird who is trained to repeat material beyond his comprehension. This is a metaphor for which medieval, and earlier, writers automatically reached when they wanted to satirise, for example, the uncomprehending repetition of church services by ignorant clerics or layfolk,[76] or minstrels who recite the literary creations of others.[77] Chaucer encourages recognition of the proverbial nature of the comparison in his parenthesis: 'ye knowen wel'. A similar image of the empty garrulity of birds is linked in the *Apocalipsis Goliae* with the kind of eloquence achieved through drink that characterises the Summoner:

> Quisque de monacho fit demoniacus
> et cuique monacho congarrit monachus
> ut pica pice vel psittaco psittacus,
> cui dat ingenium magister stomachus.[78]

Each is turned from a monk to a demon, and each chatters to the other, like a magpie to a magpie or a parrot to a parrot, endowed with wit by their master the stomach.

The magical power of drink over the intellect is also recorded in satiric tradition,[79] and its special efficacy in the gift of tongues to the unlearned is 'noted' by Gower:

> Yveresce fait diverse chance,
> Latin fait parler et romance
> Au laie gent, et au clergoun
> Tolt de latin la remembrance.[80]

Drunkenness has diverse effects; it makes lay people talk Latin and French, and makes the clerk forget his Latin.

Drunkenness is not, as lechery is, tied firmly to the idea of the consistory official; it is therefore all the more striking that Chaucer firmly connects the Summoner's behaviour when drunk with his everyday working life. For the Latin that he is 'inspired' to quote is the 'termes' that he hears 'al the day', the legal jargon on which he prides himself, although he does not understand it.[81] Once again, Chaucer endows a character with a past, and a past which has *resulted in* the present, which has conditioned the actions and personality of the pilgrim in the present. And once again, it is specifically the past history of the pilgrim's work that has this shaping role.

In the Summoner's portrait we do not oscillate between liking and condemnation, but between disgust and amusement; it is on this (comparatively) gentler note that Chaucer closes the portrait.

> A gerland hadde he set upon his heed
> As greet as it were for an ale-stake.
> A bokeleer hadde he maad hym of a cake. (666–8)

And looking back on the rest of the portrait, we see that Chaucer has not *consistently* called forth in us an attitude of moral outrage, or even physical loathing. There is an extroverted gaiety, although of a very crude kind, about the Summoner's drunken behaviour that can arouse amused enjoyment as much as moral disapproval. Moreover, if Chaucer, in his capacity as narrator, dissociates himself from the Summoner at some moments in the portrait, at others he adopts the Summoner's viewpoint. The talk about 'pulling finches' is surely part of the idiom of a sexual boaster; a 'good felawe' is so defined by the Summoner's standards. And it is by the same standards that Chaucer presents the Summoner to us:

> He was a gentil harlot and a kynde;
> A bettre felawe sholde men noght fynde. (647–8)

If we see the Summoner through the eyes of the shocked narrator–pilgrim, and of the 'yonge girles' of the diocese, we also see him through the eyes of his drinking companions.[82] Even Chaucer's most sarcastic utterances provoke the recognition that for *some* people, or for some of us at some moments, they constitute truth.

7

'Scientific' Portraits

The portraits discussed in this chapter – Pardoner, Franklin, Miller, Reeve – represent an *ad hoc* selection rather than a group intimately related in material or treatment. But these four descriptions have all been interpreted in the light of medieval scientific lore, and they therefore form a convenient basis for considering to what extent there is a separate 'scientific' tradition which might modify our view of the stylistic origins of the *Prologue*. The question becomes an important one in connection with these pilgrims because their estates figure in satiric literature in only a minor way. We shall find, however, that Chaucer uses other aspects of this literature, and the estates stereotypes of popular culture, for the basis of his portraits.

THE PARDONER

The introduction of the Pardoner at once reveals that the 'lecherous' Summoner is also a homosexual.

> With hym ther rood a gentil Pardoner
> Of Rouncivale, his freend and his compeer,
> That streight was comen fro the court of Rome.
> Ful loude he soong 'Com hider, love, to me!'
> This Somonour bar to hym a stif burdoun;
> Was never trompe of half so greet a soun. (669–74)[1]

This is not our only evidence: Chaucer also gives a detailed account of the Pardoner's effeminate appearance, culminating in a statement of what is by now obvious:

> A voys he hadde as smal as hath a goot.
> No berd hadde he, ne nevere sholde have;
> As smothe it was as it were late shave.
> I trowe he were a geldyng or a mare. (688–91)

After this one wonders how the Pardoner's 'secret' could ever have been thought to be concealed;[2] the modern stereotype of the homosexual is identical in every respect. Yet Curry has done useful work in documenting the medieval picture of the homosexual, and in some details clarification is certainly needed. For example, the Pardoner's 'glarynge eyen' (684) would not now be recognised as a sign of shamelessness,[3] and the ironic point of the comparison with the hare, in ancient and medieval times thought to be hermaphroditic, has also become obscure.[4]

The homosexual is not a new figure in medieval satire; the topic of sodomy was already an old one when Walter of Châtillon handled it.[5] In 'Stulti cum prudentibus', Walter closes with a charge of general moral corruption, in which he uses the image of the 'mare':

> se mares effeminant   et equa fit equus,
> expectes ab homine   hoc usque ad pecus . . .
>
> virum viro turpiter   iungit novus hymen,
> exagitata procul non intrat femina limen.[6]

Males grow effeminate, and the horse becomes a mare – you can look for this from men right down to animals. . .

a new kind of marriage basely joins man to man; the reviled woman is not allowed near the threshold.

In 'A la feste sui venuz', we find the charge in the context of the anti-clerical satire of a Feast of Fools; the 'baculifer' is exhorted not to give gifts to lechers and those who 'refuse to do battle in the field of nature'.[7] In 'Fallax est et mobilis', Walter accuses rulers of the church of this vice:

> Ex hiis esse novimus   plures Sodomeos,
> deas non recipere,   set amare deos.[8]

Of these we have known many to be sodomites, not admitting goddesses, but giving their love to gods.

Yet the fact that this complaint occurs in the midst of a protest against the selling of offices and favours by ecclesiastics (also the context in 'Stulti cum prudentibus'), suggests that for Walter the literal nature of the charge is less important than its use as an image of the perverted nature of cash-basis relations.

It has been suggested that Chaucer is attacking the same target as Walter; that the Pardoner's relationship with the Summoner is intended to satirise the complicity of the church authorities in the abuse of selling pardons. The Summoner, in other words, should be arresting the Pardoner, not riding as his 'compeer'.[9] But the reverse seems equally likely to be true. The Pardoner's homosexuality was originally linked with estates such as his in a *metaphorical* presentation of institutional corruption, but in the *Prologue* it has become both real, and the attribute of an individual.

This can be said, not just of the homosexual relationship between the Summoner and the Pardoner, but of all the relationships between individual pilgrims. They nearly all exist between pilgrims whose *estates* were originally linked, but in almost every case they have become merely *individual* relationships, based on the chances of birth (as with Knight and Squire), personal friendship (as with Sergeant and Franklin), or paid service (as with Guildsmen and Cook). The haphazard nature of these connections is already foreshadowed in Chaucer's introduction of his company of 'sondry folk': they are '*by aventure* yfalle | In felaweshipe' (25–6). A first reaction to the observation of this feature of the *Prologue* might be that Chaucer is more 'modern' than other estates writers in placing a greater stress on 'individualism'. But the most intense relationship between two pilgrims, and the one which most expresses their 'individuality', is precisely that of the Summoner and Pardoner – that is (in Chaucer's world), a perverted relationship.

The haphazard groupings in the *Prologue* suggest, not the free expression and association of individuals, but a specialised, blinkered approach, in which an individual's relation to the rest of society does not extend beyond his immediate family or friends. The exception once again is the mutual social benefit between the estates of the Parson and the Plowman; yet even this, as I commented earlier, is a relationship between kindred – a hint that the limited exchange of services that characterises the rest of society is at work here too. If we are to read the Pardoner's homosexuality symbolically, I should prefer to define its meaning in accordance with this aspect of the *Prologue*, as a symbol of the perverted nature of merely individual relationships, in contrast to estates connections determined by the demands of society as a whole.

Within the portrait, the Pardoner's sexual make-up is more important at the immediate than at the symbolic level. As with the Summoner, Chaucer relies on our reacting strongly against the Pardoner's appearance *before* we learn of his fraudulent professional practices. Our reaction is ensured by the use of items of appearance familiar from the satiric tradition on foppery, already described in discussion of the Squire. The elements are the same, but they are differently handled. We are not left to wonder whether the Pardoner lavishes attention on his hair, as we are in the case of the Squire's curls.

> This Pardoner hadde heer as yelow as wex,
> But smothe it heeng as dooth a strike of flex;
> By ounces henge his lokkes that he hadde,
> And therwith he his shuldres overspradde;
> But thynne it lay, by colpons oon and oon.
> But hood, for jolitee, wered he noon,
> For it was trussed up in his walet.
> Hym thoughte he rood al of the newe jet;
> Dischevelee, save his cappe, he rood al bare. (675–83)

Not only the carefully-arranged hair, but also the Pardoner's smooth face come from satire on fops – as is appropriate, since it is effeminacy of which they are accused.[10] 'The Simonie' pictures the fashionable squire riding with hood off, like the Pardoner.

The hod hangeth on his brest, as he wolde spewe therinne. (*PSE* p. 336, 279)

And the Pardoner's reverence for the 'newe jet' also reveals his background in the texts where this, and allied phrases, are wielded with scorn.[11]

There is nothing unusual, therefore, about associating the details of the Pardoner's appearance with effeminacy, nor is it necessary to go to a specifically scientific tradition in order to explain them; scientific and satiric traditions go hand in hand. It remains to comment on the by now familiar techniques through which Chaucer presents these details – the apparent acceptance of the Pardoner's view of 'jolitee', counteracted by the fascinated disgust in the exact description of his thin, lifeless hair, and the careful ambivalence of the comment that *he thought* he was in the latest fashion.

The final item in the Pardoner's appearance – the 'vernycle' in his cap – leads us back to his profession, for, as Langland shows us,[12] it indicates a journey to Rome, whence the Pardoner has brought his wallet-full of pardons, 'al hoot' (686–7). A few lines later, Chaucer makes the shift of interest explicit, with another testimony to the superlative professional skill of a pilgrim.

> But of his craft, fro Berwyk into Ware,
> Ne was ther swich another pardoner. (692–3)

148

Chaucer's inclusion of a pardoner in his estates list seems once again to correspond to a stimulus from Langland.[13] Again and again in the early Passus of *Piers Plowman* pardoners feature as villains.[14] In his survey of the Field full of Folk, Langland focusses on one in particular.

> There preched a pardonere ˙ as he a prest were,
> Brouȝte forth a bulle ˙ with bishopes seles,
> And seide that hym-self myȝte ˙ assoilen hem alle
> Of falshed of fastyng ˙ of vowes ybroken.
> Lewed men leued hym wel ˙ and lyked his wordes,
> Comen vp knelyng ˙ to kissen his bulles;
> He bonched hem with his breuet ˙ and blered here eyes,
> And rauȝte with his ragman ˙ rynges and broches.
> Thus they geuen here golde ˙ glotones to kepe,
> And leueth such loseles ˙ that lecherye haunten. (Prol. 68–77)

Chaucer's Pardoner, like this one, is skilled in preaching, and resembles him too in having an eye on the silver.[15]

> But trewely to tellen atte laste,
> He was in chirche a noble ecclesiaste.
> Wel koude he rede a lessoun or a storie,
> But alderbest he song an offertorie;
> For wel he wiste, whan that song was songe,
> He moste preche and wel affile his tonge
> To wynne silver, as he ful wel koude;
> Therefore he song the murierly and loude. (707–14)

But Chaucer's pardoner is unlike Langland's in his deception of the parish priest:

> But with thise relikes, whan that he fond
> A povre person dwellynge upon lond,
> Upon a day he gat hym moore moneye
> Than that the person gat in monthes tweye;
> And thus, with feyned flaterye and japes,
> He made the person and the peple his apes. (701–6)

In Langland, the pardoner and the priest together cheat the 'poraille' of the parish (Prol. 80–2); in Chaucer, the Pardoner deceives both priest and people. As with his friend the Summoner, our consciousness of his victims reinforces our sense of his nastiness. The narrator abandons the Pardoner's viewpoint, as he had also, at one point, abandoned the Summoner's, and speaks with the parson's vocabulary of the 'feyned flatery and japes' that are used to trick him.

Yet the distinction between the two viewpoints is not maintained; before and after this outburst, we are seeing the world through the Pardoner's eyes. This is true of Chaucer's introduction of the relics used to deceive the country congregations. They are described in plain terms which leave us in no doubt as to their lack of authenticity – that is, we see them with the disenchantment of the Pardoner himself.

> in his male he hadde a pilwe-beer,
> Which that he seyde was Oure Lady veyl:
> He seyde he hadde a gobet of the seyl
> That Seint Peter hadde, whan that he wente
> Upon the see, til Jhesu Crist hym hente.
> He hadde a croys of latoun ful of stones,
> And in a glas he hadde pigges bones. (694–700)

The tradition of satirising false relics is an old one, and is not tied to any particular clerical group.[16] Already in the eleventh century, we have satire based on the miraculous powers of the bones of saints Albinus and Rufinus – silver and gold.[17] But these relics belong to the realm of parodic fantasy, and have little to do with real attempts at deception. These we find described by Guiot de Provins, in his satire on the members of St Anthony's hospital.[18] Not only do they fake 'miraculous' cures of sick people,[19] but they also tour the countryside with relics, and preach.

> Molt preochent a haute voix,
> et puez portent checes et croix . . .
> Il n'ait bon oraour en foire,
> n'en bone vile, c'est la voire,
> ou lor borce ne soit pandue . . .
> En mainte guise font deniers. (*Bible* 2031–44)

They preach a good deal in a loud voice, and then they carry reliquaries and crosses . . . There isn't any good chapel at a fair, or in a fine town, to tell the truth, where their purse isn't hung up [for contributions] . . . They make money in many ways.

Such satire on the financial gains to be made from relics seems to be assumed in Gautier de Coincy's re-telling of a miracle of Our Lady at Soissons.[20] A villein ridicules his companions for venerating Our Lady's shoe, and is punished by a horrible illness which only this shoe will relieve. In the original Latin story, the peasant's scepticism is based on common-sense; the Virgin's shoe would have rotted long ago. In Gautier's re-telling, his disbelief is based on a suspicion of the ecclesiastical exploitation of relics for profit.

> Ces nonains noz vont asotant
> Qui d'un soller font saintuaire
> Por nostre argent sachier et traire.
> Pour la gueule, pour la gargate
> D'un viez soller, d'une çavate
> Si faites ore si grant feste . . .
> Cele vieille, cele abeesse
> Tot l'avoir Dieu met en sa borse
> Et jor et nuit adés emborse. (40–52)

These nuns are making fools of us, when they make a relic of a shoe in order to rake in and get hold of our money. What you're making such a fuss about is the tongue, the throat, of an old shoe, a boot! . . . This old woman, this abbess, puts all God's money in her purse, and continually pockets it, day and night.

In this case, the suspicion of fraud is unfounded, but the relics touted around by a monk in Adam de la Halle's *Jeu de la Feuillée* are of more doubtful validity (322–37). We never learn what these relics of St Acaire are, but they conspicuously fail to cure the half-witted as the monk claims they will (544 ff.), and at the end of the play he disrespectfully leaves them with an inn-keeper as a pledge until he can pay his bill (1012–16). The inn-keeper also shows scant respect for them while they are in his possession, claiming 'Or puis preeschier' – 'now I am entitled to preach' (1018).

Such satire on the clerical use of false relics attains its most sophisticated development in the *Decameron*. Fra Cipolla, a brother of St Anthony, is sent to collect the annual dues for his convent from the town of Certaldo. He promises the townsfolk that he will show them a feather of the Angel Gabriel – in reality from a parrot. Two practical jokers substitute some coals for the feather; unabashed, Fra Cipolla declares them to have come from the fire which roasted St Lawrence. To gain time while he is thinking up this story, he makes an address to the people in which he lists the wonderful relics owned by the Patriarch of Jerusalem:

Egli primieramente mi mostrò il dito dello Spirito Santo così intero e saldo come fu mai, e il ciufetto del Serafino che apparve a San Francesco, e una dell'unghie de'Gherubini, e una delle coste del Verbum-caro-fatti-alle-finestre, e de'vestimenti della Santa Fé cattolica, e alquanti de'raggi della stella che apparve a'tre Magi in oriente, e una ampolla del sudore di San Michele quando combatté col diavolo, e la mascella della Morte di San Lazzaro e altre.[21]

He first showed me the finger of the Holy Spirit as whole and strong as it ever was, and the tuft of hair of the Seraph who appeared to St Francis, and one of the nails of the Cherubim, and one of the ribs of the Word-made-flash-to-the-window, and some vestments of the Holy Catholic Faith, and some of the rays of the star that appeared to the three Wise Men in the East, and a phial of St Michael's sweat when he fought with the devil, and the jaws of death of St Lazarus, and more.

The falsity of these relics goes further than mere deception on the part of the preacher. The Virgin Mary, to Chaucer's mind, undoubtedly once had a veil, although it is certainly not in the Pardoner's possession. In describing relics that never existed, Boccaccio seems to come near to satirising the whole nature of religious belief – the abandonment of a 'common-sense' basis for belief means also an inability to distinguish genuine mystery from fraudulent mystification.

Chaucer is so far removed from this satire of what the relics are meant to be, rather than what they are, that we do not even find out what the Pardoner's stones and pig-bones are passed off as. His satire depends on the contrast between the holy awe felt for the supposed relics, and the tawdry nature of their reality. We are taken behind the scenes, and shown the squalid and unromantic nature of the props which the Pardoner transforms, by his professional skill, into venerated objects. With Fra Cipolla, we are 'out front', watching the performance.

It is our knowledge of the Pardoner's skill in his tricks of the trade that enables us to understand the point of view from which he is a 'noble ecclesiaste'. Despite our physical disgust for the Pardoner, and the moral disgust which the narrator shows at one point, the poise of tone is recovered at the end of the portrait. Amusement, not disgust, is predominant in the final picture of the Pardoner singing enthusiastically in hope of good pickings; in more ways than his skill in selling absolution, the Pardoner has resemblances with the 'merye' Friar.[22]

THE FRANKLIN

Franklins as a class do not figure in estates literature.[23] The term itself is not a precise one,[24] and from his presentation of the Franklin, it seems that Chaucer is using it as a way of linking together several of the offices of county administration, and one important aspect of the life of the gentry – the conduct of their feasts. It therefore seems justifiable to look for separate stylistic backgrounds to three aspects of the Franklin's portrait: first, his character as gourmet and host; secondly, his sanguine complexion; thirdly, his tenure of various public posts.

The greater part of the Franklin's portrait is taken up with a description of his love of food. Chaucer begins with a specific example –

> Wel loved he by the morwe a sop in wyn.[25]

and this is speedily followed by the mention of many other partialities.

> His breed, his ale, was alweys after oon;
> A bettre envyned man was nowher noon.
> Withoute bake mete was nevere his hous
> Of fissh and flessh, and that so plentevous,
> It snewed in his hous of mete and drynke,
> Of alle deyntees that men koude thynke.
> After the sondry sesons of the yeer,
> So chaunged he his mete and his soper.
> Ful many a fat partrich hadde he in muwe,
> And many a breem and many a luce in stuwe.
> Wo was his cook but if his sauce were
> Poynaunt and sharp, and redy al his geere. (341–52)

The Franklin's preferences are not unusual; birds and fish are especially prized by the *bons viveurs* in satire on gluttony.[26] The 'luce' or pike in particular is mentioned by Alanus de Insulis as one of the fishes which pious modern prelates like to see martyred by various cooking processes, and baptised in a font of holy pepper, before being brought to table.[27] Pike and partridge also play a part in the reveries of the glutton in *Renart le Contrefait*:

> Glout ne poeut messe entiere oÿr,
> Bonne compagnie sieuir
> Qu'il ne pense qu'il mengera,
> En quel vin se delitera
> De Vianne ou de Soissonnois;
> Trop sont fesbles ces vins francois.
> N'a point de marée venue?
> Harens fres ou fresche molue,
> Ou saumon, ou quelque fillarde?
> Quant venra ce que il me tarde?
> Ou ung morseau de venoison,
> D'une pertris en la saison . . . (II 36,737–48)

The glutton can't hear a mass through or be in good company without thinking what he will eat, in what wine he will revel – of Vienne, or of Soissons. 'These French wines are too weak. Has no sea-food arrived? Fresh herrings or cod, salmon or pike? When will my delay be over? Or a piece of venison, or partridge in season . . .'

'Baken mete' is placed on the groaning table of Waster,[28] and the spicy sauces on which the Franklin is so insistent are a sign of good living in both Guiot de Provins and *Renart le Contrefait*.[29]

Most of these details also occur in Gower's satire on different forms of Gluttony, in which, as in *Renart*, the description of the sin shows signs of becoming the description of an individual sinner, whether its subject is 'Ingluvies' –

> Ne luy souffist un soul capoun,
> Aincois le boef ove le moltoun,
> La grosse luce et le salmoun,
> A son avis tout mangeroit. (*MO* 7746–9)

A single capon isn't enough for him – rather, in his own opinion, he could completely devour beef and mutton, a large pike and salmon.

or 'Delicacie' –

> Ne vuil les nouns del tout celer
> Des vins q'il ad deinz son celer . . .
> Si nous parlons de sa cuisine,
> . . . n'est domeste ne ferine
> Du bestial ne d'oiseline
> Qe n'est tout prest deinz cel office:
> La sont perdis, la sont perdice,
> La sont lamprey, la sont crevice . . .
> Ly delicat ne tient petit
> Pour exciter son appetit;
> Diverses salses quiert avoir
> Et a son rost et a son quit,
> Dont plus mangut a son delit.
> Selonc que change son voloir,
> Son parlement fait chascun soir,
> Et as ses Coecs fait assavoir,
> Qu'ils l'endemein soient soubgit
> Tieu chose a faire a leur povoir,
> Du quoy le corps pourra valoir. (*MO* 7813–47)

I have no wish to conceal the names of the wines in his cellar . . . If we speak of his kitchen . . . there is no bird or beast, wild or domesticated, which is not all ready in that workroom. There are partridges, male and female, there are lampreys and shellfish. The gourmet sets no little store by arousing his appetite; he seeks to procure different sauces for his roast and boiled meat, so that he can eat more pleasurably. According as his desires change, he has a consultation every evening and informs his cooks that they should be obedient next day in making such-and-such a thing from which his body will profit, as best they can.

The pike, the partridges, the sauces, the well-stocked cellar, the varia-tion of different foods,[30] re-appear in the Franklin's portrait – and the 'sop in wyn' of which he is so fond in the morning is enjoyed at the same hour by greedy town ladies:

> Et en gernache au matinez
> Font souppes de la tendre mie.[31]

And in the morning they make a sop of soft bread in Malmsey (vernage).

The details of the Franklin's diet are therefore not unusual, but the effect of Chaucer's description is totally different from normal gluttony satire – the nauseating enumeration of dish after dish, and the emphasis on the vomiting and excretion by which the overloaded stomach relieves itself.[32] Moreover, Gower's description of 'Delicacie' already shows up one way in which the Franklin's portrait *fuses* satire on gluttony and estates satire; Chaucer's picture of the tyrannised cook suggests not only the description of the glutton giving detailed orders for his meals, but also estates satire on the exacting demands that masters of his class make of their servants. Nicholas Bozon's Emperor Pride asks 'vavasours' to serve him in this way:

> 'Sachez, fet il, ceo est mon desir
> Ke daungerous seez a servire.
> Le quel vos serchauntz comunement
> Facent bien ou malement,
> Jeo vous pry ne enparnez
> Ke largement ne seyent blamez.'[33]

'Know' he said, 'that it is my desire that you should be pernickety about service. Whatever your servants normally do, whether badly or well, I beg you do not spare to find a lot of fault with them.'

I shall return later to the 'estates' sources of the Franklin's portrait.

The Franklin is the first pilgrim of whose complexion we are in-formed:

> Whit was his berd as is the dayesye;
> Of his complexioun he was sangwyn. (332–3)

The traditional view of the sanguine man's character undoubtedly has points of resemblance with that of the Franklin:

The sangyne by kynde... shall haue a goode stomake, good dygescion, and good delyveraunce . . . he shall be fre and lyberall.[34]

But 'good digestion' hardly suggests the snowing meat and drink of Franklin's household. Why did Chaucer link the sanguine man and the gourmet?[35] The connection between this humour and a liking for one's food is not automatic; in the *Mirour de l'Omme* it is the phlegmatic man who is tempted by gluttony, while the sanguine man is inclined to lechery, pride and gaiety (14,701–2). The clue may lie in the fact that of all humours, the sanguine is the most attractive. Chaucer uses it, that is, to persuade us of the healthy and generous nature of the Franklin's gourmandise; he associates the mountains of food, not with a diseased and queasy glutton, but with a fresh-complexioned man with an excellent stomach. The 'scientific' tradition does not dictate the *content* of the portrait, but has a subordinate role in the techniques by which Chaucer determines our attitude to the character.

Chaucer also characterises the Franklin by reference to two strangely-assorted personalities – Epicurus and St Julian.

> To lyven in delit was evere his wone,
> For he was Epicurus owene sone,
> That heeld opinioun that pleyn delit
> Was verray felicitee parfit.
> An housholdere, and that a greet, was he;
> Seint Julian he was in his contree . . .
> Was nowhere swich a worthy vavasour. (335–40, 360)

The classical philosopher appears in Latin satire as a type of good living,[36] and Gower's comment on him hardly differs – except for its critical tone – from Chaucer's:

> Trop fuist du Foldelit apris
> Uns philosophes de jadys,
> Qui Epicurus noun avoit.
> Car ce fuist cil q'a son avis
> Disoit que ly charnels delitz
> Soverain des autres biens estoit. (*MO* 9529–34)

A philosopher of olden times, called Epicurus, was too well instructed in sensuality – for it was he who said that in his opinion the pleasure of the flesh was sovereign over other goods.

Chaucer himself had already translated a passage of Boethius which says that Epicurus 'juggid and establissyde that delyt is the soverayn good',[37] and this was clearly responsible for the wording of the lines in the *Prologue*. But in the Franklin's portrait, he leaves aside the condemnatory attitude which the comparison with Epicurus usually implies. Any inclination on our part to read the Franklin's admiration for Epicurus as a sign of his selfish materialism is swiftly counteracted by the second comparison, with St Julian. The hospitality implied in this comparison is also the point of Chaucer's information that his table was always 'ready for action':

> His table dormant in his halle alway
> Stood redy covered al the longe day. (353–4)

Such delight in entertaining resembles that which Guiot de Provins laments as belonging to 'vavasours' of the past:

> Les boins vavessours voi je mors: . . .
> Ja en ont trop cruels damaiges,
> qu'il estoient herbegeor
> et liberal et doneor,
> et li prince lor redonoient
> les biaus dons, et les honoroient. (*Bible*, 197–204)

I see that worthy vassals are dead: . . . they have suffered too cruel injuries, for they used to be hospitable, liberal and generous, and the princes gave them fine gifts and honoured them on their part.

The Franklin also seems to represent in this respect an inversion of Gower's complaint about the sort of knight who

> resembler
> Ne voet au bon hospiteller
> Saint Julien ne tant ne qant,
> Dont soit les povres herbergant. (*MO* 23,849–51)

doesn't want to resemble the good host St Julian in any respect, so that he might harbour the poor.

And indeed, this complaint represents a traditional criticism of lords who feast in private, and do not share their goods.[38] But lavish hospitality also warrants criticism, when it is extended to worthless parasites, or to the rich rather than the poor.[39] A sermon writer quoted by Owst describes the man who is generous in hospitality to the rich, and how he is rewarded with the same kind of praise that Chaucer gives to the Franklin:

For he wolde be callid manly and worchypfull; and also in holdyng of grete
festes, feding riche men. And the pore man stondythe at the gate with an
empti wombe . . . And then ther schall be grete praysyng of hym – how
worchypfull an howseholder he is . . . And ʒit thei that stonde a-bowte him
wil flater hym and preyse him an hundrythe tymes more than he is worthi;
and so berithe him on honde that he is the beste man in al a cuntre.[40]

John Clanvowe concurs in this view of what the world calls
worthiness:

þe world holt hem worsshipful þat been greet werryours and fiʒteres and þat
distroyen and wynnen manye londis and waasten and ʒeuen muche good to
hem that haan ynouʒ and þat dispenden oultrageously in mete in drynke in
clooþing in buyldyng and in lyuyng in eese slouþe and many ooþere
synnes / [41]

Is Chaucer ironically adopting the view of the Franklin and his
friends on what makes a 'worthy vavasour'? We may suspect it, but
we are not allowed to know. Just as no-one is visualised as the victim
of the Merchant's possible fraud, so the beneficiaries of the Franklin's
hospitality remain shadowy and undefined. Again we are invited to
admire the means, the superlative way in which the Franklin pursues a
life-style, rather than the ends towards which it is directed.

The Franklin's portrait ends with an account of his public offices.

> At sessiouns ther was he lord and sire;
> Ful ofte tyme he was knyght of the shire . . .
> A shirreve hadde he been, and a contour. (355–9)

This list of occupations links the Franklin closely with estates satire,
where similar lists of legal and administrative jobs are a conventional
way of introducing satire on the corruption of their officers.[42] The
first appearance of such a list is, as far as I know, in the *Roman de la
Rose*: Faus Semblant reveals that

> baillif, bedel, prevost, maieur:
> tuit vivent pres que de rapine. (II 11,510–11)

Bailiffs, beadles, provosts and mayors live almost entirely off extortion.

In the English translation, 'countours' have been substituted for
'maieur' (6812–13). But if Chaucer was responsible for pillorying
'contours' here, he was by no means the first satirist to do so;[43] he
was simply varying the list as other writers did. Rutebeuf repeats
Jean de Meun's list, minus the beadles,[44] but in the *Roman de Fauvel*

we find a new inclusion – the sheriff's office, which the Franklin has held: 'Viscontes, prevos et baillis' are ready to curry Fauvel (43-4). In the 'Dit des Mais' the list has grown longer:

> Baillif, prevost, viscomte, official, vicaire,
> Ont moult à escouter, et à faindre, et à taire;
> Mais si s'en scevent bel et de légier retraire
> Quant il voient les dons saillir en leur aumaire. (*NR* 1 p. 189)

Bailiffs, provosts, sherriffs, legal officials and deputies have much to listen to, to dissimulate and keep quiet about. But they know how to get out of it well and swiftly when they see gifts pouring into their lockers.

It is also significant for the Franklin's portrait that this list is preceded by mention of 'Cil qui au parlement sont pardevers les contes' ('tho se who are at parliament with the nobles'), and followed by a discussion of civil and ecclesiastical lawyers.[45] The list can also be found in English satire, where 'Iustyses, shryues, and baylyuys' are seen as oppressors of the poor.[46] 'The Simonie' advises the king not to tax the poor, but to look for wealth

> At justices, at shirreves, cheiturs and chaunceler. (*PSE* p. 338, 322)

– for they are the ones who make money out of their offices. Continuing on this theme, the author adds to his list 'baillifs and bedeles',

> And contours in benche that stonden at the barre,
> Theih wolen bigile the in thin hond, but if thu be the warre.[47]

Although the composition of these lists varies from author to author, their form is always recognisable. The estates mentioned are uniformly associated with corrupt practices and the oppression of the poor, so that no separate stereotype-traditions prevented Chaucer from selecting several of these offices and attributing them all to one figure.

But Chaucer, in line with his practice elsewhere in the *Prologue*, carefully removes any hint of corruption or extortion from his account of the Franklin's public offices. They are presented merely as evidence for his status as a 'worthy vavasour'. The Franklin *may* be oppressive; we are not to know that. What we are allowed to see is his social face, his hospitality and good 'temper'. If his love of food is a vice, it is above all a pleasant one. To secure this reaction to his portrait, Chaucer transforms what for other writers are the burdensome preparations, the loading of the stomach, the selfish guzzling, the restless search for titillating variety, into a hymn to 'pleyn delit'.

THE MILLER

The miller is another figure who is rare in estates satire. But he does appear in Langland, and as with the Summoner and the Pardoner, it seems to be the influence of *Piers Plowman* which has secured him a place in the *Prologue*.

Even in *Piers Plowman* there are only two brief references to a typical miller, but in both cases he is given the same name, and this helps to fix his image more firmly in the reader's mind. In Passus II, 'Munde the mellere' is among the signatories to Meed's marriage-document (III). The notion of the miller's dishonesty that led Langland to place him in this list may well correspond to that described by Chaucer:

> Wel koude he stelen corn and tollen thries;
> And yet he hadde a thombe of gold, pardee. (562–3)

The last line is usually explained by reference to the proverb 'An honest miller hath a golden thumb';[48] it seems that Chaucer is playing on the phrase, taking a 'thumb of gold' to mean one that brings profit to its owner. Yet it is not until the seventeenth century, according to the *Oxford English Dictionary*, that this proverb is recorded. This delay between the evidence for the existence of a popular saying, and its actual appearance in writing, suggests that the miller has a vivid history in folk-lore and popular anecdote, even if he is ignored in formal estates satire.[49] It is in just such a case that the estates stereotype, the popular image of a class, may have been used by Langland and Chaucer to 'create' new estates representatives.

The consistency with which Langland names the miller 'Munde' may be due to the demands of alliteration, but it suggests that he comes to Langland as a well-defined personality. And the cryptic nature of Langland's second allusion to him also suggests this. In the course of denouncing non-professional entertainers, Langland says that they

> conne namore mynstralcye · ne musyke, men to glade,
> Than Munde the mylnere · of *multa fecit deus*! (*PPl* x 43–4)

Although the point of the Latin tag is not clear, the passage suggests that Langland associates millers with a low kind of entertainment. This is particularly interesting since Chaucer's Miller is also a popular raconteur and a buffoon.

> He was a janglere and a goliardeys,
> And that was moost of synne and harlotries. (560–1)[50]

He is also an expert on a popular instrument:

> A baggepipe wel koude he blowe and sowne,
> And therwithal he broghte us out of towne. (565–6)[51]

It seems that the Miller, like the Summoner, has some roots in the tradition of satirising 'harlots'. There are some hints that tale-telling was traditionally connected with his estate; the strongest of them is the quotation of a proverb in the *Ancrene Wisse*:

From mulne & from cheapinge, from smiððe & from ancre hus me tidinge bringeð.[52]

The 'jangling' in which the Miller is adept can cover all types of utterance from formal story-telling to gossip.[53] 'Janglers' are frequently attacked by Langland,[54] and among his scornful references we may note one in particular. Activa-vita disassociates himself from low minstrels; for he can

> noither tabre ne trompe · ne telle none gestes,
> Farten, ne fythelen · at festes, ne harpen,
> Iape ne Iogly · ne gentlych pype,
> Ne noither sailly ne saute · ne syng with the gyterne. (*PPl* XIII 230–3)

The cruder amusements in this list remind us of the Miller's other accomplishments, which likewise seem to presuppose a crowd of admiring spectators.[55]

> The Millere was a stout carl for the nones;
> Ful byg he was of brawn and eek of bones.
> That proved wel, for over al ther he cam,
> At wrastlynge he wolde have alwey the ram.
> He was short-sholdred, brood, a thikke knarre;
> Ther was no dore that he nolde heve of harre,
> Or breke it at a rennyng with his heed. (545–51)

And indeed, in *Handlyng Synne* it is assumed that the same kind of people delight in 'iogolours' and in 'wrastlyng'.[56]

The rest of the portrait is devoted to other details of the Miller's appearance.

His berd as any sowe or fox was reed,
And therto brood, as though it were a spade.
Upon the cop right of his nose he hade
A werte, and theron stood a toft of herys,
Reed as the brustles of a sowes erys;
His nosethirles blake were and wyde.
A swerd and bokeler bar he by his syde.
His mouth as greet was as a greet forneys . . .
A whit cote and a blew hood wered he. (552-9, 564)

Curry has 'scientifically' interpreted these details in a way that is most uncomplimentary to the Miller.[57] While his examination usefully illustrates the 'reading' of these features as signs of various 'harlot'-like characteristics, it must be noted that their symbolic use is not confined to the scientific tradition. The redhead, for example, is a widespread figure of deceit and treachery.[58] Conventional descriptions of ugliness feature red hair, bristly hair, hair on the face, a huge mouth and a prominent beard, and they also make full use of the animal imagery which is so striking in the Miller's portrait.[59]

Chaucer uses material and techniques similar to those of the authors of such descriptions, in order to arouse the reader's feelings, as they do, with a sense of crudeness and brutality. Our sense of this brutality is, in Chaucer, determined by such things as the abrupt and emphatic movement of the verse, and the violence of the examples with which the Miller's strength is illustrated. The most striking aspect of the description of his face is the effect of 'close-up' that it gives; we can see the hairs on his wart, and his nostrils and mouth gape hugely at us. This is not a face observed from the distance normally observed in polite conversation; it is two or three inches away. This illusion of having a face thrust at us determines our sense of the Miller's aggressive vigour more than any interpretation we can put on his features.

Piecing together from such hints a popular image for the Miller and the stylistic origins of his portrait means that there are several striking details – the sword and buckler, the white tunic and blue hood – left unaccounted for. But we can see enough to recognise that the basis of the creation – the swaggering, story-telling, dishonest miller, who merges so easily with the outlines of the 'goliardeys', the 'ribaud' or the fox-like redhead – is a popular stereotype. And we do not need scientific manuals to tell us of his crudity; Chaucer tells us that himself in the style of the portrait, which gives us our sense of the Miller's character.[60]

THE REEVE

The Reeve is the second pilgrim to be assigned a 'complexion' by Chaucer, and part of his appearance is connected with it.

> The Reve was a sclendre colerik man.
> His berd was shave as ny as ever he kan;
> His heer was by his erys ful round yshorn;
> His top was dokked lyk a preest biforn
> Ful longe were his legges and ful lene,
> Ylyk a staf, ther was no calf ysene. (587–92)

Curry has shown that there is a traditional link between choler and thinness.[61] In the *Secreta Secretorum*, a choleric man is said to be naturally 'lene of body' (p. 220), and this is confirmed by a fifteenth-century poem which describes him as 'Sklendre and smal'.[62] Thin legs are interpreted elsewhere in the *Secreta* as a sign of lechery, and Curry therefore links them with the choleric man's liking for the company of women. Yet Curry does not quote the whole of the description of the choleric man, the total impression of which is very different from our idea of the character of the Reeve.

The colerike by kynde he sholde be lene of body, his body is hote and drye, and he shalbe Sumwhat rogh; and lyght to wrethe and lyght to Peyse; of sharp witte, wyse and of good memorie, a grette entremyttere, full-large and foole-hardy, delyuer of body, hasty of word and of answere; he louyth hasty wengeaunce; Desyrous of company of women moore than hym nedeth. he sholde haue a stomake good y-nowe, namely in colde tyme.[63]

Such an impulsive, emotional character does not resemble the Reeve very closely. What could have led Chaucer to connect this complexion with his Reeve? The link may have been made through the astuteness or fraudulence which is often attributed to the choleric man,[64] for cunning is also associated with the class of officials to which the Reeve belongs – 'sergeants', bailiffs, seneschals, stewards, reeves.[65] Gilles li Muisis' comment shows that such officials were also thought to be oppressive to those in their power.

> On fait baillius, siergans et tous officiers;
> Proumaisses et les dons ayment mieuls que pryers;
> Se dist bien li communs qu'il paient leur loyers;
> Leur conquès vaut trop plus k'en auoust li soyers. (II pp. 21–2)

Bailiffs, sergeants, and all other officials are appointed. They like promises and gifts better than requests. The people say that they pay for their salaries; their income is worth more than the harvest in August.

The lords grow poorer, while they grow richer.[66] 'Thefe is reve' is the succinct, proverbial comment of the 'Sermon of Four Wise Men',[67] and in another English poem, we hear the 'hyne' lament that

> þe bailif bockneþ us bale, & weneþ wel do.[68]

It is an example of 'great thieves' that we hear in the *Ayenbite of Inwyt* of

þe kueade / and þe ontrewe reuen.prouos. and bedeles. and seruons. þet steleþ / þe amendes. and wyþdraȝeþ þe rentes / of hire lhordes . . . þet makeþ / þe greate spendinges. and yeueþ largeliche / þe guodis of hare lhordes / wyþ-oute hare Wytende / and wyþ-oute hare wylle.[69]

These outlines of a popular stereotype are filled in by *Piers Plowman*. Along with 'Munde the mellere' as a witness to Meed's wedding, we find

> Rainalde the reue˙ of Rotland sokene. (II 110)

Langland also classes the reeve among those who over-reach themselves by being too clever:

> seruauntes that seruen lordes˙ selden falle in arrerage,
> But tho that kepen the lordes catel˙ clerkes and reues.[70]

But elsewhere he sees the reeve as the victim of the lord's greed.

> Thanne lough there a lorde˙ and 'by this liȝte' sayde,
> 'I halde it ryȝte and resoun˙ of my reue to take
> Al that myne auditour˙ or elles my stuwarde
> Conseilleth me by her acounte˙ and my clerkes wrytynge.'
> (XIX 456–61)

This is the tradition that lies behind Chaucer's presentation of the Reeve, and we hear its echoes in his references to the auditor and the 'hyne', and the Reeve's 'arrerage'.

> Ther was noon auditour koude on him wynne . . .
> [He] by his covenant yaf the rekenynge,

Syn that his lord was twenty yeer of age.
Ther koude no man brynge hym in arrerage.
Ther nas baillif, ne hierde, nor oother hyne,
That he ne knew his sleighte and his covyne;
They were adrad of hym as of the deeth . . .
He koude bettre than his lord purchace.
Ful riche he was astored pryvely:
His lorde wel koude he plesen subtilly,
To yeve and lene hym of his owene good,
And have a thank, and yet a cote and hood. (594, 600-5, 608-12)

Chaucer's Reeve is feared and hated like the rest of his class, and we feel his unpleasantness the more in viewing him through the eyes of the 'hynes' who are so afraid of him – although Chaucer removes the possibility of our seeing them as innocent victims. They are paralysed with fear because the Reeve knows about *their* malpractices; again winner and loser are united on the question of values. The question of right and wrong does not enter into their relationship; it is determined by the question of who can outwit the other.

This significant deviation from the depiction of the innocent victim alerts us to the fact that Chaucer clothes the Reeve's behaviour in the same kind of ambiguities as he has used throughout the *Prologue*. Can the auditor find no fault in the Reeve because of his scrupulous efficiency, or because he adroitly covers up his embezzlement? The same doubt attaches to the statement that no-one could claim he was liable for debt. Does the other peasants' fear of him reflect more on their dishonesty, or on his cruelty? Whose is the 'owene good' which the Reeve lends to his lord – is it the Reeve's, or the lord's own property? The *suggestion* of dishonesty runs right through the portrait, but its phraseology is constantly as ambiguous as the statement that the Reeve could please his lord 'subtilly' – cleverly or deceitfully?[71]

It seems that our impression of the Reeve's malice and harshness derives at least as much from his appearance – the thinness, the close-shaven face and cropped hair, the 'tukked' clothing, suggest a tight repressiveness that gives nothing away – as from any evidence of fraud or cruelty. One may see this portrait as similar in function to those of the Summoner and Pardoner: an experiment in showing how a person's appearance and his degree of sociability significantly affect our attitude to him.

The rest of the portrait is occupied by information of two main sorts. The first is a series of 'personal' details of different kinds.

> His wonyng was ful faire upon an heeth;
> With grene trees yshadwed was his place . . .
> In youthe he hadde lerned a good myster;
> He was a wel good wrighte, a carpenter.
> This Reve sat upon a ful good stot,
> That was al pomely grey and highte Scot.
> A long surcote of pers upon he hade,
> And by his syde he baar a rusty blade.
> Of Northfolk was this Reve of which I telle,
> Biside a toun men clepen Baldeswelle. (606–7, 613–22)

Some of these details follow naturally enough from the Reve's work – the farm-horse called by the Norfolk name of Scot is an example.[72] As for the Reve's Norfolk origins, it is interesting that a tradition of associating special characteristics with different counties envisages Norfolk people as crafty and treacherous.[73] But Chaucer is, after all, more precise than this; he mentions the town of 'Baldeswelle'. It is impossible to prove that Chaucer was *not* pointing to an individual reeve in this reference,[74] but I feel a search for 'Rainalde the reue · of Rotland sokene' might prove just as fruitful. Both Langland and Chaucer use specific names to give an illusion of concrete reality. And the other details about the Reve also contribute to this illusion.[75] But our sense of the Reve's character is more subtly produced by Chaucer's careful ambiguities, which imply a depth, an unknowable quality to the Reve's astuteness.

And against the 'personal' details, we can set the long enumeration of the Reve's daily duties:

> Wel koude he kepe a gerner and a bynne;
> Ther was noon auditour koude on him wynne.
> Wel wiste he by the droghte and by the reyn
> The yeldynge of his seed and of his greyn.
> His lordes sheep, his neet, his dayerye,
> His swyn, his hors, his stoor, and his pultrye
> Was hoolly in this Reves governynge,
> And by his covenant yaf the rekenynge,
> Syn that his lord was twenty yeer of age. (593–601)

This tells us little about the individual Reve, but a great deal about his profession. And again he has a professional past: he has kept the accounts since his lord was twenty, in his youth he was a carpenter. The time-dimension in the portrait is that of the estate. He seems to have professional loves and hates too, for he rides at the end of the cavalcade, furthest from his professional enemy the Miller.[76] However strongly we are convinced of the Reeve's *individual* existence by our fear of what might lie behind his mask of professional efficiency, Chaucer will not allow us to forget that his character is rooted in the daily work of his class.

It seems that Chaucer's use of what may be called 'scientific' traditions in these portraits does not set them apart, in material or technique, from those of the other pilgrims. Nor does it work against their function as estates representatives. The character which is 'symbolised' in the physical details must accord with what we learn of the pilgrim from the rest of the portrait (for by what other means could the scientific interpretation be shown to be relevant?). The details themselves work on an immediate as well as a symbolic level, creating their own attractive or repulsive effect. The scientific traditions therefore have an important role in Chaucer's manipulation of our *feelings* towards the pilgrims, which, as we have seen, are most often influenced by their physical appearance. But they function in the same way as the physical details derived from other sources – from rhetorical descriptions, or from satiric tradition. And the figures they animate are still recognisable estates stereotypes.

8

New Creations

Four pilgrims remain to be considered – Cook, Shipman, Yeoman, Manciple. The material of their portraits seems to be given its first literary expression in Chaucer, although we cannot be sure that thorough examination of the estates tradition in confessional manuals, for example, would not reveal resemblances with popular stereotypes. For the moment, however, these four characters appear to have the best claim to be regarded as Chaucer's 'original creations'. And yet they are hardly the pilgrims usually thought of as having most 'life'. This paradox I have emphasised in the somewhat ironic title of this chapter. Just as a rich satiric tradition facilitated Chaucer's sophisticated handling of the Friar and Monk, so in these portraits he seems rather hampered by the need for shaping his own material. But the portraits also show that when Chaucer is in need of material, it is to the work of each estate that he goes to find it.

THE COOK

The Cook's portrait is almost entirely constructed on the basis of his estate. Chaucer assures us of his professional excellence, and 'incidentally' enumerates the details of his work – different cooking techniques and different dishes in his repertory.

> A Cook they hadde with hem for the nones
> To boille the chiknes with the marybones,
> And poudre-marchant tart and galyngale ...
> He koude rooste, and sethe, and broille, and frye,
> Maken mortreux, and wel bake a pye ...
> For blankmanger, that made he with the beste. (379–87)

Similar lists of foods and cooking procedures are, as we have noticed, usual in gluttony satire,[1] and this provides one background for the Cook's portrait. The *Vox Clamantis* describes the labours of the glutton's cook by listing his activities:

Nunc cocus ecce coquit, assat, gelat atque resoluit,
  Et terit et stringit, colat et acta probat.[2]

Now see how the cook bakes, roasts, freezes and thaws, pounds and squeezes, strains, and tests his creations.

Such an incidental reference would hardly, however, have led Chaucer to include a cook in the *Prologue*; rather, we must see here also a stimulus from *Piers Plowman*. Langland's Prologue ends with a striking picture of 'Cokes and here knaues', crying

'hote pies, hote!
Gode gris and gees ' gowe dyne, gowe!' (225–6)

And later, mayors are advised to punish

Brewesteres and bakesteres' bocheres and cokes;
For thise aren men on this molde ' that moste harme worcheth
To the pore peple ' that parcel-mele buggen.[3]

Chaucer is far closer to Langland's attitude in the first of these passages; he is not concerned to show the Cook's professional mal-practices, but to show us what a cook is like. At the same time he gives the Cook's character reality by the 'knowing' nature (suggesting there is someone to know) of his reference to the Cook's fondness for drink, by the preciseness of 'London ale', and by ensuring that we have a strong emotional reaction to the portrait. This reaction is triggered by the final lines of the portrait:

But greet harm was it, as it thoughte me,
That on his shyne a mormal hadde he. (385–6)

Curry has interpreted this mormal as a sign of the Cook's personal uncleanliness and liking for women and wine.[4] As we noted in con-nection with the Summoner, the literature of the Sins uses disease as an image of moral corruption, and in a fifteenth-century Sins poem a 'lither mormale' is used as a symbol of 'luxuria'.[5] But, as with the Summoner's portrait, it is on the immediate level, where it repels us physically rather than morally, that the introduction of the Cook's mormal is most effective, especially since Chaucer juxtaposes his reference to it with a wistful mention of the Cook's excellent 'blank-manger'.[6] Such a technique for arousing feeling is something Chaucer could have learned from gluttony satire, where disease, excrement and vomit are introduced to create an aversion for the mountains of food which produce them.[7]

But Chaucer's main concern here is not to satirise gluttony, nor even the filthy habits of London cooks. He aims to condition our feelings about the Cook by introducing the mention of an unpleasant skin-disease into an account of food-preparation – and a strong reaction convinces us that there is an individual we are reacting to. But the material of the Cook's portrait is not individual; it belongs rather to his work-life, that is, to his estate.

THE SHIPMAN

The shipman plays a very minor role in estates literature. The *Chessbook* includes sailors in its section on labourers and workmen, stressing the need for 'loyalty, prudence and courage' among these classes (col. 433–4). Fidelity is especially necessary for sailors since they are entrusted with human lives, but courage is the most important quality for them. If they were to show fear in a storm, the laymen on board would despair and cease from efforts to save themselves.

Sit ergo in eis fortitudo animi, que est considerata periculorum susceptio. (col. 443–4)

Therefore let them have courage of spirit, which consists in the deliberate undertaking of dangers.

This notion seems to find an echo in Chaucer's portrait of the Shipman:

> Hardy he was and wys to undertake;
> With many a tempest hadde his berd been shake. (405–6)

It is typical of what we have noted elsewhere in the *Prologue* that the visualisation of an estates representative in an appropriate situation – the sailor in a storm – has been transformed into a 'past', an experience repeated many times, and so part of the individual's consciousness. The same sense of a working past is given by his appearance:

> The hoote somer hadde maad his hewe al broun. (394)

The detail is effective not just because it helps us to visualise the Shipman, but because it too gives him a history, and helps us to feel how it has made him what he is.

The sailor is also associated with fraud. 'Viri fratres' says curtly

Nautae maris et coloni,
Qui fuerunt quondam boni,
Sic pervertit eos dolus,
Quod vix iustus unus solus.[8]

Sailors and peasants, who used to be honest, are so corrupted by fraud that hardly
one of them is upright.

The sailor's tendency to steal is confirmed, and his tendency to murder
is also revealed, in a confessional manual in estates form called the
Memoriale Presbiterorum. It advises the priest:

Tu confessor, si contingat te audire aliquem nautam in confessione, necesse
habebis caute et studiose te habere in inquirendo; quia scire debes quod vix
sufficit calamus scribere peccata quibus inuoluuntur. Tanta est enim illorum
malicia, quod omnium hominum aliorum peccata excedunt . . . Item non
solum occidunt clericos et laicos dum sunt in terra, sed eciam quando sunt in
mari, piraticam exercent pravitatem, rapiendo bona aliorum et potissime
mercatorum mare transeuncium, et eos crudeliter interficiunt.[9]

Confessor, if it should happen to you that you hear in confession some sailor,
you will have to conduct yourself cautiously and diligently in questioning;
for you must know that pen could hardly write the sins in which they are
entangled. So great is their wickedness in fact, that they surpass the sins of all
other men . . . Also they not only kill clerks and laymen while they are on land,
but also when they are at sea, they practise wicked piracy, seizing the goods of
other people and especially of merchants as they are crossing the sea, and killing
them mercilessly.

Chaucer's Shipman is also a thief, and he too has a short way of
dealing with his enemies:

> And certainly he was a good felawe.
> Ful many a draughte of wyn had he ydrawe
> Fro Burdeux-ward, whil that the chapman sleep.
> Of nyce conscience took he no keep.
> If that he faught, and hadde the hyer hond,
> By water he sente hem hoom to every lond. (395–400)

But these typical features are presented from the point of view of the
Shipman; it is his language that Chaucer uses – for the joke about
sending his enemies home 'by water',[10] and the scorn for 'conscience'
('a sense of right and wrong', or 'sentimentality'?), surely correspond
to the Shipman's phraseology. The euphemism to express murder,
and the lack of distinction between excessive feeling and any moral
feeling at all, suggest the lack of clarity with which the Shipman

is aware of his own actions and moral assumptions. His point of view dominates his portrait. It is, for example, by the Shipman's own standards that he is judged a 'good fellow'; the proof has nothing to do with lechery, as it does in the Summoner's portrait, but is constituted by evidence of his professional skill in thieving. Behind the phrase lies the adolescent assumption that pilfering is daring and a sort of practical joke. The fact that we are adopting the Shipman's point of view also means that we do not concern ourselves with the identity or actions of his victims. The battles in which he fights may or may not have been provoked by him, and may or may not have been motivated by piracy. From the Shipman's point of view, all that matters is that he 'hadde the hyer hond'. Again, we are not allowed to evaluate his actions fully.

In this way Chaucer persuades us yet again that we are dealing with a real personality. But the characteristics he attributes to this personality are based on his estate. First of all, we have his professional knowledge and expertise.

> But of his craft to rekene wel his tydes,
> His stremes, and his daungers hym bisides,
> His herberwe, and his moone, his lodemenage,
> Ther nas noon swich from Hulle to Cartage . . .
> He knew alle the havenes, as they were,
> Fro Gootland to the cape of Fynystere,
> And every cryke in Britaigne and in Spayne. (401-4, 407-9)

Then we have the 'personal' details, which also seem to grow out of his working life; he is as unhappy on horseback as sailors traditionally are (390), and he lives in the West Country, the area traditionally inhabited by freebooters (388-9).[11] We are told the name of his ship (410), and the details of his clothing – the knee-length gown of 'faldyng',[12] and the dagger round his neck. Such details are striking, and bear out, among other things, our sense of the 'rough-and-ready' aspect of the Shipman's character. But this sense itself derives far more from the fact that Chaucer shows us the world through his eyes.

THE YEOMAN

The Yeoman's portrait is devoted almost entirely to his physical appearance, and yet he too is presented in terms of his profession. No yeoman appear in estates literature before Chaucer, but in the fifteenth century, a poem on the 'anatomy of the state' lists yeomen, 'Wiþ bent bowes and bryȝt brondes', after knights and squires.[13]

Chaucer's evident influence on this passage demonstrates the recognisability of the 'professional' aspect of the Yeoman's appearance.

> And he was clad in cote and hood of grene.
> A sheef of pecok arwes, bright and kene,
> Under his belt he bar ful thriftily, . . .
> And in his hand he baar a myghty bowe.
> A not heed hadde he, with a broun visage . . .
> Upon his arm he baar a gay bracer,
> And by his side a swerd and bokeler,
> And on that oother syde a gay daggere
> Harneised wel and sharp as point of spere;
> A Cristopher on his brest of silver sheene.
> An horn he bar, the bawdryk was of grene;
> A forster was he, soothly as I gesse. (103–17)

Every item in this passage, even to the image of St Christopher,[14] is appropriate to the Yeoman's estate; Chaucer had no need to guess that he was a forester. The picture of the estate is completed by two testimonials from Chaucer as to the Yeoman's professional competence:

> Wel koude he dresse his takel yemanly:
> His arwes drouped noght with fetheres lowe . . .
> Of wodecraft wel koude he al the usage. (106–7, 110)

How is it that we respond positively to the Yeoman,[15] when we learn nothing of his individual personality? It emerges that he is conscientious in his duties, but this is not enough to account for our positive reaction to his portrait. The answer is surely the physical attractiveness that Chaucer emphasises with such adjectives as 'bright and kene' and 'gay', with the bright colours, the gleam of polished metal, and the gaudy peacock feathers on his arrows. The positive response to an attractive appearance, which was responsible for complicating our reactions to the Monk, and was irrelevant to the portraits of Parson and Knight, is here allowed full rein. As our judgement on the Pardoner and the Summoner is determined largely by their revolting looks, so our favourable attitude to the Yeoman is produced by his colourful neatness. To show us this more clearly, the portrait is devoid of ironic touches and ambiguities. Here is an estate whose practice makes its representative pleasant to associate with.

THE MANCIPLE

The Manciple's portrait is related to the traditional satire behind the
Reeve's portrait, for the masters whom he serves are training to be
'stywardes of rent and lond'. The Manciple himself, therefore, may
be linked with the dishonesty that Langland assigns to manorial
officials, lawyers, and those who, like the Manciple, look after provisions:

> Bedelles and bailliues ˙ and brokoures of chaffare,
> Forgoeres and vitaillers ˙ and vokates of the arches. (*PPl* II 59–60)

At first it looks as if Chaucer is attributing a similar fraudulence to
the Manciple.

> A gentil Maunciple was ther of a temple,
> Of which achatours myghte take exemple
> For to be wise in byynge of vitaille;
> For wheither that he payde or took by taille,
> Algate he wayted so in his achaat
> That he was ay biforn and in good staat.
> Now is nat that of God a ful fair grace
> That swich a lewed mannes wit shal pace
> The wisdom of an heep of lerned men? (567–75)

His masters are the best lawyers in the country,

> And yet this Manciple sette hir aller cappe. (576–86)

Yet there is no certain evidence that the Manciple cooks the books,
although the statement that he outdoes his masters suggests it. The
fact that 'gentil', 'wise', 'wit', 'wisdom' and 'lernyng' seem in this
portrait to be defined in terms of financial prudence, reflects the
Manciple's own values, and we feel that it is he himself who thinks
he makes a good example for others.[16] Professional malpractice, if it
exists, is conveyed through an idiomatic expression ('sette hir aller
cappe'), which professionals, those 'in the know', could decipher,
but which must remain vague for the layman. As with the idiom
about sending one's enemies home by water in the Shipman's portrait,
the phrase reveals the euphemistic way in which the perpetrator of an
action represents it *to himself*. Such specialist, elusive idioms represent
a refusal to apply absolute values to the practices of one's profession.
    Chaucer makes us acquainted with the Manciple's consciousness,

and gives us a sense of his personality. But in the last portrait we have examined as in all the others, it is through the job, the estate, that he does so.

In these four portraits, Chaucer seems to be creating estates portraits from popular stereotypes or from his own knowledge of different occupations, rather than from a full satiric tradition. The descriptions of daily duties which are used to fill out some of the other portraits here assume a significantly prominent role. The same techniques that are used elsewhere in the *Prologue* ensure our sense that we are dealing with real individuals, but it becomes clear that when he has almost no models to work on, Chaucer turns not to real individuals, but to his notion of an estate for the framework of his portraits.

Excursus: The 'General Prologue' and the 'Descriptio' Tradition

In their authoritative *Sources and Analogues of Chaucer's Canterbury Tales*, Bryan and Dempster take the descriptive portrait of the rhetorical tradition to be the only known background for the *General Prologue* to the *Canterbury Tales* (pp. 3–5). Three pages of the introductory chapter, contributed by L. A. Haselmayer, are devoted to this tradition, and in particular to the series of portraits in the *Roman de Troie* of Benoit de Ste-Maure, but the conclusion is that

> neither in this group . . . nor in the whole range of earlier portraiture, do we find anything that could be exhibited in the present volume as a source or appropriate analogue for Chaucer's miscellaneous company of vivid and living personalities. (p. 5)

Although the fruitfulness of looking in places quite outside of the portrait tradition for 'sources or appropriate analogues' to the *Prologue* should now be clear, its connection with the *descriptio* tradition also needs clarification. In this chapter I shall discuss, first, the techniques developed in the portrait tradition which Chaucer could have used for the presentation of complex figures, and second, the links between the formal portrait and the estates tradition.

The influence of the rhetorical *descriptio personae*[1] on the *Prologue* is recognisable in the form – a series of self-contained descriptions – and in the content of these descriptions, which in certain instances shows clear affinities with the traditional content of such portraits. In considering this rhetorical figure, I make no distinction between its theoretical discussion in the medieval *artes poeticae* and its actual use in medieval literature, since the manuals themselves instruct largely by means of examples. I shall offer little in the way of new material, for the subject is an area of study in its own right and lies outside the central concern of this study, but I shall try to suggest new ways of looking at the material usually discussed in connection with Chaucer. The origin of the figure of *descriptio* in the rhetorical treatises in classical Latin, and its treatment in the manuals of the middle ages, have been described by Faral.[2] Faral also indicates some early examples of *descriptio* in Latin literature: the first elegy of Maximian, and the description of Theodoric by Sidonius Apollinaris, to which Geoffrey of Vinsauf refers in his prose work on rhetoric.[3] These references can be supplemented by Haselmayer's brief account of the early development of the figure. More recently, Claes Schaar has devoted a lengthy study to Chaucer's use of formal description and its literary background, dealing with both classical and medieval works.[4] In addition there are two articles of particular interest to students of the *Prologue*: Lumiansky's comparison of the work with the portrait-gallery in the *Roman de Troie*, and Patch's attempt to trace the origins of the *Prologue* in the descriptions found in moral treatises on the vices and virtues.[5]

Using the material and conclusions offered by these writers, an empirical classification of two different types of portrait tradition – the rhetorical and the moral/allegorical – can be made. (Later we shall add one further type – the physiological.) First, let us deal with the rhetorical type of description, 'ad laudem vel ad vituperium'.[6] The primary purpose of this type of description is affective, as Faral notes:

L'objet principal du genre oratoire que les anciens ont appelé demonstratif est l'éloge et le blâme, et le moyen par lequel on y atteint est la description . . . En apparence, l'idée est accessoire; elle est, en fait, d'importance considérable: elle explique que dans toute la littérature du moyen âge, la description ne vise que très rarement à peindre objectivement les personnes et les choses et qu'elle soit toujours dominée par une intention affective qui oscille entre la louange et la critique. (*Les Arts Poétiques*, p. 76)

This affective purpose results in portraits of a formalised, conventional nature, depicting *either* great beauty and virtue *or* extreme ugliness and moral turpitude.[7] The latter is as conventional and 'rhetorical' as the former, and cannot be taken, as it is by Haselmayer, as 'a faint strain of realism' in medieval portraiture.[8]

However, both Faral and Haselmayer over-simplify the uses to which the formal portrait is put, and over-emphasise its non-organic role in the works in which it appears.[9] The subtle use of the *descriptio* as an integral part of the purpose of a particular poem can be illustrated from instances in Haselmayer's own list. The description of a beautiful girl in Maximian's first elegy is an integral part of the speaker's lament over his old age, and the bitter contrast with his youth, when no girl was worthy to be matched with him. He describes the catalogue of perfections that such a girl would have to have had, and the young man's dream of the perfect girl he will never find merges imperceptibly into the old man's regret at the loss of love and sexual pleasure. The use of the subjunctive to indicate the hypothetical existence of the perfect girl, and of the past tense in speaking of the individual features of feminine beauty which once brought him pleasure, flavour the whole description with a mood of nostalgia and elusiveness.

> Quaerebam gracilem, sed quae non macra fuisset:
>   Carnis ad officium carnea membra placent.
> Sit quod in amplexu delectet stringere corpus,
>   Ne laedant pressum quaelibet ossa latus.
> Candida contempsi, nisi quae suffusa rubore
>   Vernarent propriis ora serena rosis . . .
> Flammea dilexi modicumque tumentia labra,
>   Quae gustata mihi basia plena darent.[10]

I sought one who was slender, but not scrawny; fleshy limbs are pleasing for the work of the flesh. Let her body be such as is a delight to crush in embrace, lest any of my bones should hurt the flank in my clasp. I scorned white faces, unless, flushed with red, they bloomed bright with their own roses . . . I loved fire-red lips, swelling gently, which, on tasting, would give me full kisses.

Another poem listed by Haselmayer is Marbod of Rennes's *Dissuasio amoris Venerei*, where the description of a beautiful girl is given rather a startling turn.

> Egregium vultum modica pinguedine fultum,
> Plus nive candentem, plusquam rosa verna rubentem,
> Sidereum visum, spondentem mollia risum,
> Flammea labrorum libamina subtumidorum,
> Dentes candentes modicos seriemque tenentes,
> Membraque cum succo, moresque bonos sine fuco
> Illa puella gerit quae se mihi jungere quaerit.
> Hanc puer insignis, cujus decor est meus ignis,
> Diligit, hanc captat, huic se placiturus adaptat.[11]

A face of surpassing beauty, filled out with a little plumpness, whiter than snow, redder than a spring rose, a starry glance, a smile promising softness, fire-red offerings of swelling lips, little white teeth in a row, plump limbs and honest ways without guile – all this has the girl who wants to unite herself to me. Her, the noble boy, whose beauty is *my* passion, loves, pursues, fits himself to her pleasure.

The description seems at first to be that of the girl the writer adores;

only with the last three lines of this passage are we deliberately surprised with the information that the writer is indifferent to the girl's love for him, and instead prefers the boy who in turn languishes hopelessly for her. Chaucer was, in fact, far from being the first writer who could skilfully adapt the rhetorical *descriptio* to an individual literary function, or make satirical play of its formal character.

Beside this evidence of sensitivity in the handling of the conventional portrait, we may also notice innovations in its content in Benoit de Ste-Maure's portrait-gallery of the heroes and heroines of the Trojan war. Benoit's use of *descriptio* before this point in the *Roman de Troie* is appropriate in conventional ways: Jason's physical beauty is described at the moment when Medea sees him for the first time, while his warlike appearance is conveyed through the description of his arming for the exploit of the Golden Fleece (1265–79, 1815–42). But the portrait-gallery achieves a far from conventional effect. Lumiansky has correctly noted that Lowes' comment on the lack of individuality in Benoit's portraits is unjust; that Benoit, like Chaucer, combines physical and temperamental traits in his portraits, and also like Chaucer, organises structural groupings of characters based on blood-relationship and contrast of personalities. Further, some of the portraits outline distinct personalities which the characters have already revealed, or are later to reveal in the course of the action.[12]

However, it seems to me that there are even more important similarities than these between the techniques of Benoit and Chaucer. This can be seen in the portrait of Hector:

> De pris toz homes sormontot,
> Mais un sol petit baubeoit.
> D'andous les ieuz borgnes esteit,
> Mais point ne li mesaveneit. (5329–32)

In worth he surpassed all men, but he had a slight stammer. He squinted in both eyes – but it didn't make him at all unattractive.

The construction of these four lines is as interesting as their content; our attitude to Hector goes through rapid modifications as we hear, first, the testimony to his worth, next, of his stammer and squint, and finally, the assurance that this did not make him unattractive. The successive modifications are marked by the word 'Mais' at the beginning of the line. This use of 'Mais', introducing features which contradict our first, or even our second, impressions, is fairly frequent in Benoit's portraits,[13] and is paralleled in Chaucer's *Prologue*, where 'But' is also used to preface modifications, drastic or subtle, to what has gone before.

> But greet harm was it, as it thoughte me,
> That on his shyne a mormal hadde he. (385-6)[14]

The last line quoted from Benoit's portrait – 'Mais point ne li mesaveneit' – is similar to places in the *Prologue* where Chaucer steps in with an assurance that seems genially to deny the implications of what he has just said:

> Housbondes at chirche dore she hadde fyve,
> Withouten oother compaignye in youthe, –
> But therof nedeth nat to speke as nowthe. (460-2)

The effect of Benoit's modifications is to ensure reactions similar to those produced by the 'complex' Canterbury pilgrims: a sense of the co-existence of attractive and unattractive features, and the impossibility of adopting any single attitude to the person described.

It is also interesting that Benoit jumbles together, in inconsequential fashion, conventional items of eulogy and gratuitous pieces of information which have no relevance to the progress of the action. Hector's stammer is one example of this, and there is another in the portrait of Priam:

> Le nes e la boche e le vis
> Ot bien estant e bien asis;
> La parole aveit auques basse,
> Soëf voiz ot e douce e quasse.
> Mout par esteit bons chevaliers,
> E matin manjot volentiers. (5297-302)

His nose, mouth and face were handsome and well set; his speech was rather low, his voice gentle, soft and weak. He was indeed a good knight, and ate heartily in the mornings.

In the same way, Chaucer offers gratuitous information, which gives the impression of accurate reporting, in an inconsequential order suggestive of an observer jotting down his impressions. In Benoit, these features are clearly the result of an attempt to create an 'historical' impression; he frequently refers to his source in Dares, and states he can go no further in describing an episode than Dares warrants.[15] At the opening of the portrait-series this 'historical' accuracy is emphasised by the explanation that Dares was able to describe the leading figures on both sides of the war because he deliberately went about observing them in times of truce.[16] Benoit's particular reasons for giving his story a historical atmosphere, or the fact that the content of Benoit's portraits is to some extent determined by his source-material, do not preclude Chaucer's learning from him.

The rhetorical tradition of *descriptio* was one line of tradition which presented Chaucer with numerous models of sophisticated and flexible usage. A second line of tradition, as Patch has indicated, is that represented in moral and allegorical treatises, which depict vices and virtues. The descriptions of the Seven Deadly Sins in the *Ancrene Wisse* are perhaps the most vivid examples of this tradition in English until *Piers Plowman*, which abounds in rich and dramatic description of representative figures. Although Patch overstates his case, we may for the moment simply note and accept his point that in this tradition also there are techniques that Chaucer uses:

there is sometimes a dramatic quality, sometimes a bit of quoted speech. It is only necessary to set them going with personal names and freer action in order to have something like the human comedy of the Canterbury Tales.[17]

The third line of tradition in *descriptio*, which has not, so far as I know, received any comment in connection with Chaucer, is that contained in physiological works. Some idea of this kind of description may be gleaned incidentally from Curry's book on *Chaucer and the Medieval Sciences*; Curry is interested in the *content* of the descriptions of the four humours, but it becomes clear from the quotations that he gives that the vehicle for this information is the *descriptio* form. This can be verified, for example, in the English version of the *Secreta Secretorum* (p. 220). An interesting and little-known example of this tradition can be found already in the twelfth century in the *Causae et Curae* of Hildegard of Bingen, which gives a series of portraits of the four humours as they determine character and appearance in both men and women.[18] As has been noted, these portraits attain integrity and authenticity by virtue of the fact that they are primarily constructed around an account of the sexual behaviour of each type.[19] A quotation from the description of choleric men will show the nature of Hildegard's treatment.

Quidam autem masculi sunt, qui viriles existunt, et hi cerebrum forte et spissum habent. Cuius exteriores venulae, quae pelliculam eius continent, aliquantum rubeae sunt. Et color faciei eorum aliquantum rubicundus velut in quibusdam imaginibus videtur, qui rubeo colore colorantur, et spissas ac fortes venas habent, quae ardentem sanguinem cerei coloris portant, et spissi circa pectus sunt atque fortia brachia tenent; sed valde pingues non sunt, quoniam fortes venae et fortis sanguis ac fortia membra carnes eorum in multa pinguedine non permittunt ... viri isti ... femineam formam tam valde amant, quod se continere non possunt, quin sanguis eorum magno ardore ardeat, cum aliquam feminam viderint vel audierint vel cum eam in cogitationibus suis ad memoriam suam duxerint, quia oculi eorum velut sagittae sunt ad amorem feminae, cum eam viderint, et auditus eorum velut validissimus ventus, cum eam audierint, et cogitationes eorum quasi procella tempestatum, quae contineri non potest, quin super terram cadat. ... Qui si coniunctionem feminarum habent, tunc sani et laeti sunt; si autem eis caruerint, tunc in semet ipsis arescunt et quasi moribundi vadunt, nisi aut ex superfluitate somniorum aut cogitationum aut perversitate alterius rei spumam seminis sui de se excutiant.[20]

There are some men who are virile and have a strong, thick brain, the veins on the outside of their heads containing the brain tissue are rather red. And the colour of their faces is reddish – as is seen in some statues which are stained with red colour – and they have thick, strong veins, which carry their hot, wax-coloured blood, and they are thick-chested and have strong arms, but they are not very fat, since the strength of their veins, blood and limbs does not permit their flesh to be very fat ... these men ... love the female form so greatly that they cannot restrain their blood from being inflamed with great passion, when they see or hear a woman, or recall one in their thoughts, because their eyes are like arrows directed at a woman's love when they see her, and their hearing is like a mighty wind, when they hear her, and their thoughts are like a tempestuous hurricane, which cannot be restrained from falling upon the earth. ... If they have intercourse with women, then they are well-balanced and happy, if however they are without them, then they dry up in themselves and go about as if dying, unless they can discharge the foam of their seed through the excesses of their dreams or of their thoughts, or through the abuse of some other thing.

It is extremely unlikely that Chaucer could have known Hildegard's work, but these descriptions are an interesting indication of the way in which yet another type of *descriptio* rapidly developed accounts drawing on physical appearance, temperamental constitution, and customary behaviour.

The influence of all three of these lines of tradition can be observed in the *Prologue*. Curry has suggested that Chaucer utilised the physiological tradition in the portraits of the Reeve and the Miller,[21] and it has not escaped notice that the Franklin is a 'sangwyn' man.[22] Other characters who seem to have connections with this tradition of description are the Pardoner and the Wife of Bath. The 'moral' descriptive tradition seems to have influenced certain features which strike us as 'grotesque' in the *Prologue*, such as the Miller's face, or the Summoner's garland and cake. As for the rhetorical tradition, it was long ago noted that the description of the courtly heroine is put to novel use in the Prioress' portrait,[23] and we have seen that it is equally true, if not so well recognised, that the rhetorical descriptions of ugliness contribute to the portraits of the Miller and Summoner. Finally, the techniques of Benoit may have suggested to Chaucer certain overall principles in the creation of the Prologue portraits.

Detailed study of the role played by particular types of *descriptio* in Chaucer's portraits has already been given in the discussion of the individual pilgrims; what remains to be examined is the nature of the *descriptio* tradition and Chaucer's development of it. So far, the guidelines for the study of the development of the figure have been idealisation *versus* realism, or, in Schaar's slightly different approach, abstract *versus* concrete description.[24] The *Prologue* portraits have thus posed a great problem to critics who have viewed them as 'realistic' descriptions arising suddenly at the end of a long tradition of artificial and idealised portraits. We can minimise this paradox, as I have been trying to show, by noting that the 'real-life' nature of Chaucer's portraits has been exaggerated, and that traditional elements of *descriptio* appear in them; that the artificial nature of earlier portraits has also been exaggerated; most important, that the *content* of Chaucer's descriptions, as this study shows, is drawn from quite other literary traditions which had developed to a point not nearly so distant from the *Prologue*. But when all these allowances have been made, it is true that if we classify the portraits in terms of idealism and realism, we have no way of suggesting how Chaucer made the shift from one to the other, other than an assumption that he suddenly began to set down his own observations of life.

The result is quite different, however, if we adopt a different means of analysis – if we return to the affective intention which Faral perceived, but which he refused to see as a serious literary purpose. The portraits in both the rhetorical and moralising traditions aim at producing a strong and *unified* emotional effect, whether of admiration or disgust. The physiological portraits do not have the same aim, and in this may lie the importance of what they could have suggested to Chaucer. However, even in the physiological tradition, the character described usually attracts or repels us in a fairly uniform way. From this point of view, the *General Prologue* portraits are still startlingly original in their manipulation of attraction and repulsion, not only within the same portrait, but as simultaneous responses to the same items of information. Yet it is at least possible to see how Chaucer could have developed the complex effects of the *General Prologue* portraits by combining the two usually separate effects of *descriptio*. Chaucer was steeped in the literary traditions of his time; he had shown no previous resentment at handling rhetorical models, and was to use them again, with no sign of frustration, in the *Canterbury Tales*. It is difficult to imagine him suddenly abandoning these traditions in favour of observations of 'real life', and simultaneously discovering exactly the means to convey that life in literary form. It is much more likely, as Manly noted long ago, that observation had always fed Chaucer's literary interests, while literature had shown him different ways to give his perceptions expression. It is therefore much easier to imagine that Chaucer saw the possibility of combining the two affective tendencies of admiration and vituperation – whose separation in other portraits gave an impression of artificiality – in such a way as to reproduce the complex response which we normally have to real people. The combination is not, of course, a matter of simple addition; its most frequent form, as we have seen, is the presentation of morally reprehensible traits in terms of enthusiastic appreciation. Chaucer further complicates our responses by the use of ambiguities which represent a development of medieval satiric irony, but could have been adopted with the same general aim of complicating the reader's emotional responses. Such an intention is more comprehensible as a development from *descriptio* when described in medieval terms 'for praise or blame' than when it is anachronistically analysed in terms of the 'artificial' and the 'real'. It only remains to note that from this point of view, Benoit's portraits, which provide a model for the production of varying responses in the reader, become even more significant than before for the *Prologue*.

In discussing the individual portraits, I have tried to show the importance of estates material as a literary background for the *General Prologue*. Was Chaucer the first writer to conceive of the possibility of combining estates material with the figure of *descriptio*? Although *descriptio* is very rare in estates literature, even a cursory glance at theoretical works on rhetoric immediately reveals *descriptiones* shaped from estates material. The *Ars Versificatoria* of Matthew of Vendôme, for example, contains a series of model descriptions, several of which aim at describing the interior person rather than the external appearance.[25] Two of these are descriptions of 'Caesar' and 'Ulysses', but they reveal no features which we would recognise as personal ones; they are, respectively, types of the good ruler and of the sage.[26] That is, they are described by office and function rather than personality. Ulysses, as the ideal *savant*, makes sure that his eloquence is joined with sense, and that his words are matched by his deeds:

> Ne sit lingua potens sensu viduata, maritat
> Se linguae sensus interioris honor . . .
> Propositum facto vicino mancipat, ori
> Concolor est mentis expositiva manus.[27]

Lest his powerful eloquence be widowed of sense, the dignity of inner meaning is married with his speech. His designs he translates into the kindred action, his hand, glossator of his mind, is in harmony with his words.

Matthew's model description of a pope has an even clearer connection with estates traditions; the outlines of his character conform with those of the ideal pastor.[28] He can be both cruel and compassionate:

> Condolet afflicto, misero miseretur, anhelat
> Ad leges, reprimit crimina, jura fovet.[29]

He feels with the afflicted, pities the pitiable, is zealous for the laws, checks crimes, protests rights.

He is described in the pastoral imagery which figures largely in the estates tradition:

> Nos proles, nos ejus oves, nos membra tuetur,
> Membra caput, genitor pignora, pastor oves.[30]

He cares for us as children, as sheep, as bodily members – as the head for the members, the father for the children, the shepherd for the sheep.

These resemblances are not accidental; elsewhere in his work Matthew uses quotations which show his familiarity with Latin satire.[31] The literature concerned with the morals of every rank of society was clearly as relevant for him as courtly narrative or Latin *comedia*.

An even clearer proof of the possible connection between estates literature and *descriptio* is furnished by a text beginning 'Debemus cunctis proponere noscere montis', mentioned but not printed by Faral (*Les Arts Poétiques*, p. 47). Fierville, who edits it in *Notices et Extraits*,[32] notes that although it is clearly an 'Art poétique' it shows an interesting difference from the usual form of such works: 'Il n'y est pas question de métrique, ni de figures de mots ou de pensées. Il

s'agit des caracteres des différents âges et des différentes positions
sociales.' The text gives a series of short model descriptions of different
types of people – woman, youth, old man, sage, and so on. Two
portraits, of 'miles' and 'villanus', may be quoted as examples.

> Sit miles parma, galea quoque tectus, et arma
> Ille severa volet, fortia bella colet.
> Sitque coloratus armis ad bella paratus,
> Ense ferire sciat, iraque conveniat.

The knight should be protected by a shield and a helmet; he will wish for harsh
weapons, and reverence stern warfare. He should be painted armed and ready
for war; let him know how to strike with the sword, and let wrath be fitting
for him.

> Villanus laudem querat, vitet quoque fraudem,
> Semper dicat idem, servet ametque fidem,
> †Semper idem reticet†, meretrices, crimina vitet;
> Ille iocos nolet; seria verba volet.
> Pulveris os atrum scabies sit, portet aratrum,
> Et clavam teneat, ruraque circueat.[33]

The peasant should seek praise, and shun deceit; his speech should be without
deviation. He should love and keep loyalty; he should be silent (?) and avoid loose
women and evil-doing. He should not like jokes, but serious conversation. Let
his face be dusty black, and let him have scurf; carrying a plough and holding
a club let him traverse the countryside.

This text shows the juxtaposition of estates types and moralised
types which we have noticed in estates works proper. It shows the
possible links between estates literature and *descriptio*. It also provides a
model for a linked series of self-contained portraits largely based on
estates material. It allows us therefore with added confidence to claim
that Chaucer chose to make the portrait-gallery only the vehicle for
his estates poem.

9

Conclusions

It is a cliché of Chaucer criticism that the Canterbury pilgrims are both individuals and types.[1] But this critical unanimity coexists with striking divergencies on what constitutes the typical or the individual.

One could begin by suggesting that the 'individual' quality is that which distinguishes one person from other people. But this cannot be a single character-trait, since financial greed, for example, is a feature of both Friar and Pardoner. Is individuality constituted by the peculiar *combination* of traits? Unfortunately, this is precisely what some critics take to be the typical. For example, Root thought that the combination of 'individualising traits' in the Prioress's portrait suggests 'that type which finds fullest realisation in the head of a young lady's school'.[2] The 'individual' is then reduced to the level of 'a local habitation and a name'; 'the Wife of Bath is typical of certain primary instincts of woman,[3] but she is given local habitation "bisyde Bathe", and is still further individualised by her partial deafness and the peculiar setting of her teeth.'

J. L. Lowes also seemed to accept that 'the typical' refers to general outlines of personality when he praises 'the delicate balance between the *character*, in the technical, Theophrastian sense of the word, and the *individual* – a balance which preserves at once the typical qualities of the one and the human idiosyncrasies of the other.'[4] However, Lowes' 'human idiosyncrasies' suggest something different from the isolated physical traits to which Root attributes the individualisation of the pilgrims; and indeed concrete details, such as the Yeoman's clothing, can help to realise an estates type.[5]

Agreement on the nature of the typical is no greater than on that of the individual. Speirs, for example, classifies the characters at times by social situation (the Squire is 'the eternal young bachelor', the Yeoman 'simply a solid English countryman', the Clerk is 'the unworldly scholar of all time', the Pardoner is 'the eternal cheapjack at the fair whose impudence and success never fail to fascinate and amaze'), and at times by moral qualities ('Gluttony underlies the Frankeleyn,

Avarice the Doctor of Physic').[6] Baldwin attempts a sort of *ad hoc* isolation of what he calls the 'radix traits' of the characters:

the Knight can be described by 'worthynesse', the Squire by 'youth', the Yeoman by 'forester', and the Prioress by 'noblesse oblige'. The Wife of Bath may be summed up by 'archwife' of disposition, eye and conversation; the Monk by 'game' . . .; the Friar by 'wantonnesse', the Merchant by 'façade', and the Parson by 'pastoral activity'.[7]

Faced with this plethora of conceptions of 'type', I have preferred not to attempt another way of defining or describing the typical and the individual, but to work on lines similar to those suggested by R. M. Lumiansky's terms: 'the expected and the unexpected'.[8] Rather than trying to decide whether a character corresponds to a credible combination of personality traits, rooted in the eternal aspects of human nature, I have tried to consider how far the information given about him accords with the expectations raised by his introduction as 'a knight' or 'a monk'. The results of this consideration have shown that the estates type was the basis for Chaucer's creation of the Canterbury pilgrims. But the accompanying analysis of the style in which Chaucer presents the estates type has also shown that the answer to the question 'are the pilgrims individuals or types?' would vary according to whether it was based on source-material or the reader's impression.

In the past, there seems to have been an assumption that the effect of the *Prologue*'s material would be identical with the source from which it was drawn: if the portraits were drawn from observations of real individuals, they would suggest these individuals to Chaucer's audience; if they were drawn from social satire, they would convey the impression of moralised types.[9] The same assumption encouraged critics to see the union of type and individual in terms of the combination of well-known features of certain social classes with invented details.[10] Thus Lumiansky goes on to say of the Knight: 'As a result of a combination of expected and unexpected traits, he assumes memorable individuality in the mind of the reader'. But our chapter on the Knight has shown that the qualities Lumiansky finds unexpected in 'a professional military man' – the fact that he is 'prudent, humble, circumspect in speech, modest in dress, and serious in religious devotion' – would not be at all unexpected in the stereotyped ideal of his estate. The preceding chapters have also shown that it is not the *concreteness* of invented or unexpected details (where we do find them) which produces individuality, for they are not essentially different from the concrete details that are a traditional part of estates satire. Moreover, invented details are used to extend the typical, just as well as the individual, aspects of a character.

A hint of the means by which Chaucer persuades us that the pilgrims *are* individuals – that they exist as independent people – is however given in Lumiansky's comment that the terminology of 'the expected and the unexpected' 'has the advantage of placing the emphasis upon the reader's reaction to the technique'. This emphasis I believe to be correct, and I have tried to show that our strong impression of the individuality of the figures in the *Prologue* is due to the fact that Chaucer encourages us to *respond* to them as individuals. Their 'individuality' lies in the techniques whereby Chaucer elicits from us a reaction, whether complicated or unequivocal, similar to the reactions aroused in us by real-life individuals.[11]

We have already seen what these techniques are. Chaucer calls forth contradictory responses – a positive emotional or sensuous response, conflicting with an expectation that moral disapproval is called for – in order to make us feel the complexity of his characters. He makes us uncertain of the 'facts' that lie behind their social or professional façades. He uses a sense of past experience, discernible from present appearance, personality or behaviour, to give us the conviction that his characters are not eternal abstractions but are affected by time. And he incorporates an awareness of their point of view – their reactions to the traditional attitudes to their existence, their terminology and standards of judgement – which also gives us a strong sense of their independent life. Chaucer forces us to feel that we are dealing with real people because we cannot apply to them the absolute responses appropriate to the abstractions of moralistic satire.

We may also make some suggestions about the different functions of the 'typical' and 'individual' aspects of the characters. This is left rather vague by some critics; Root, for example, remarked that the combination of individual and typical in the portraits makes them more effective, but did not say why, nor what they are effectively doing.[12] One reason why Chaucer is at pains to give his characters 'life' as individuals is obviously that they are to act as individuals in the drama of the *Canterbury Tales*; they talk and react to each other as individual human beings would do. The 'individual' aspect is therefore vital to the frame of the tales. The 'typical' aspect is, however, equally vital to Chaucer's purpose in the whole work. The most obvious aspect of the *Canterbury Tales*, even in its incomplete state, is its comprehensiveness. It clearly aims at universality, at taking up all the themes and styles of contemporary literature and making one glorious compendium of them. The *Prologue* in a sense constitutes a kind of sample of what is to follow by its wide range of tone and mood. The serious ideals – chivalric, religious, labouring – which operate in the portraits of Knight, Parson and Ploughman, furnish a serious tone in addition to the comic and savage ones on which Chaucer can draw in the main body of his work. But as well as this, the *Prologue* makes its own contribution to the genres included in the *Canterbury Tales*, by the clear reference to estates literature in its form and content. It is especially appropriate that estates literature should perform this introductory function, since it lays claim to a universality of its own, and since its subject-matter is the whole society, the 'raw material' from which the other genres select their own areas of interest.

The *Canterbury Tales*, however, is not a compendium of literary genres in any simple sense. The method of the work is not additive, but dialectic; the tales modify and even contradict each other, exploring subjects in a way that emphasises their different and opposed implications. Sometimes we can follow the development of one theme through various mutations; even where the unifying theme is absent, it is noteworthy that the stimulus for tale-telling is the quarrel. The overall effect of this process of exploring tensions and contradictions is to relativise our values until we reach the absolute values of the Parson, who is willing to admit of no compromise or modification – but in assigning these absolute values to a character *within* the *Tales* (and, moreover, not to the narrator) Chaucer in one sense makes these values relative too.

The same refusal to take up an absolute standpoint can be found in the *Prologue*. One important demonstration of this has emerged from a comparison with other estates material – the fact that the persons who suffer from behaviour attributed to some of the pilgrims are left out of account – what I have called 'omission of the victim'. I have already stressed the importance of not letting our awareness of these victims, an awareness for which other satiric works are responsible, lead us into supplying them in the *Prologue* for the purposes of making a moral judgement, whether on Prioress, Merchant, Lawyer or Doctor. Chaucer deliberately omits them in order to encourage us to see the behaviour of the pilgrims from their own viewpoints, and to ignore what they necessarily ignore in following their courses of action.[13] Of course, our blindness differs from theirs in being to some extent voluntary – for the pilgrims' viewpoint is not maintained everywhere in the *Prologue* – while their blindness is unconscious and a condition of their existence. The manipulation of viewpoint, and ignorance (wilful or unconscious), are traditionally taken as features of irony, and the omission of the victim is a functional part of the ironic tone of the *Prologue*. The tone, as we have noted, becomes more forthright and moves away from irony precisely at moments when we are made conscious of the victim, and in particular of the victim's attitude to the pilgrim.[14]

The omission of the victim is part of the *Prologue*'s peculiar social ethic, which extends even to the pilgrims that Chaucer presents as morally admirable. The Yeoman, for example, is certainly an honest and hard-working member of his profession. Yet fault has been found even with him, on the grounds that

no practical application of his skill is indicated . . . The description stops short at the means, the end is never indicated. The result is the impression of a peculiarly truncated consciousness.[15]

As regards the particular portrait, this interpretation is surely mistaken; there is no criticism of the Yeoman as an individual. The comment may however usefully focus attention on the small part played by social ends in the *Prologue*. This has already been indicated in discussion of the individual portraits. The *effects* of the Knight's campaigning, of the Merchant's 'chevisaunce', of the Sergeant's legal activities, even of the Doctor's medicine, are not what Chaucer has in mind when he assures us of their professional excellence. It is by ignoring effects that he can present the expertise of his rogues on the same level as the superlative qualities of his admirable figures. His ultimate purpose in this is not to convey any naive enthusiasm for people, nor comic effect, although the *Prologue* is of course rich in comedy, nor is it even a 'connoisseur's appreciation of types', although this attitude characterises the narrator's ironic pose in presenting the individual estates. The overall effect of this method is rather to sharpen our perceptions of the basis of everyday attitudes to people, of the things we take into account and of the things we willingly ignore.

We may clarify this by pointing out that the distinction between Langland and Chaucer is not just, as is usually assumed, the distinction between a religious and a secular writer, between didacticism and comedy.[16] It is true that Langland and most of the army of estates writers before him, have a continual sense of the rewards of Heaven and the punishments of Hell, which of itself provides a 'reason' for moral behaviour, and that this sense is lacking in Chaucer. But it is also true that Langland shows, in passages such as the ploughing of Piers's half-acre, the practical bases for, and effects of, specific moral injunctions, while Chaucer has no *systematic* platform for moral values, not even an implicit one, in the *Prologue*.

When we first compare Langland and Chaucer, there is a temptation to conclude as Manly did, that Chaucer's satire is convincing because

He does not argue, and there is no temptation to refute him. He does not declaim, and there is no opportunity for reply. He merely lets us see his fools and rascals in their native foolishness and rascality, and we necessarily think of them as he would have us think. (*New Light*, p. 295)

Undoubtedly it is true that Chaucer not only persuades us that fools and rascals can be very charming people, but is at the same time taking care to make us suspect that they are fools and rascals. If, however, we examine more closely what considerations determine what 'he would have us think' of the pilgrims, we find that they are not always moral ones. For example, if we compare the portraits of the Friar and the Summoner, we find that many of the faults we attribute to them are identical: fondness for drink; parade of pretended knowledge; sexual licence and the corruption of young people; the encouragement of sinners to regard money-payments as adequate for release from sin. Yet what is our attitude to them? I think it is true to say that our judgement on the Friar is less harsh than our disgust for the Summoner.[17] The reasons for this, in a worldly sense, are perfectly adequate; the Friar's 'pleasantness' is continually stressed, he makes life easy for everyone, is a charming companion, has musical talent, he has a white neck and twinkling eyes and good clothes, while the Summoner revolts the senses with his red spotted face and the reek of garlic and onions.[18] But although adequate to account for our reactions, these considerations are not in any sense moral ones.

It is sometimes said that the physical appearance of the Summoner symbolises his inner corruption; there is certainly a link between physical ugliness and spiritual ugliness in other, moralising writers. But Chaucer is as it were turning their procedure round in order to point to its origins in our irrational, instinctive reactions. The explicit moralising attitude to beauty and ugliness – that they are irrelevant beside considerations of moral worth – coexists, paradoxically, with an implicit admission of their relevance in the use of aesthetic imagery to recommend moral values. In the *Ancrene Wisse*, for example, the author associates beautiful scents, jewels and so on, with heavenly values, and stinks and ugliness with the devil; he then finds himself in the difficult position of trying to encourage an ascetic indifference to *real* bad smells.[19] Chaucer makes this tension between moral judgement and instinctive emotional reaction into a central feature of the *Prologue* partly in order to create the ambiguity and complexity of response which persuades us that the characters are complex individuals, but at the same time to show us, in the *Prologue*, what *are* the grounds for our like or dislike of our neighbours. Moral factors have a part in our judgement, but on a level with other, less 'respectable' considerations. There is no hesitation in admiring the unquestioned moral worth of the Knight or Parson, but this will not prevent us from enjoying the company of rogues with charm, or despising those who have no mitigating graces.

I shall return in a moment to the significance of this lack of systematically expressed values, after noting some other means which produce it. The first of these again emerges in contrast to estates material, and consists of the simple but vivid similes which run through some of the portraits – head shining like glass, eyes twinkling like stars – and which plays a large part in convincing us of the attractiveness of such figures as the Monk and the Friar. The constant use of this sort of comparison creates a tone which is at once relaxed, colloquial and animated – the kind of style which, as Derek Brewer has pointed out, finds its best counterpart in the English romances, and which differs strikingly from the taut, pointed style of learned satire. Another type of simile is neutral or explanatory – 'As brood as is a bokeler or a targe' – and occasional examples of this sort may be found in French or Anglo-Norman satire. But the first group, in which the stress on attractiveness runs counter to the critical effect of the satire, would destroy the intention of a moralising satirist. A writer like Langland deals in occasional vivid imagery, but its effect usually works together with the moral comment.

> And *as a leke hadde yleye ' longe in the sonne*
> So loked he with lene chekes ' lourynge foule.
>
> And *as a letheren purs ' lolled his chekes.*[20]

Occasionally the imagery works *with* the moral comment in the *General Prologue* also; we have noted that the animal imagery in the portraits of the Miller, Pardoner and Summoner persuades us that we are dealing with crude or unpleasant personalities. In both kinds of usage, the imagery does not reflect moral comment so much as create it; and the contradictory ways in which it is used means that it is also working to destroy the *systematic* application of moral judgements.

The role of the narrator and the use of irony in the *Prologue* have received abundant comments,[21] but they can in this connection take on a new light. It is the narrator who himself constantly identifies with the pilgrim's point of view – and that means the point of view of his estate – and encourages us to see the world from this angle. Even when the narrator distinguishes the pilgrim's view from his own, this also, paradoxically, makes us sharply aware of the series of insights into estates consciousness that we are given, and of the tension between their perspectives and our own which is implied in the 'his' of such phrases as 'his bargaynes'.

Moreover, the narrator acts as a representative for the rest of society in its relation to each estate. In this role, he shows us how often the rest of society is not allowed to go beyond the professional façade, to know what is the truth, or to apply any absolute values to professional behaviour. We are in a world of 'experts', where the moral views of the layman become irrelevant. The narrator assumes that each pilgrim is an expert, and presents him in his own terms, according to his own values, in his own language. All excellence becomes 'tricks of the trade' – and this applies to the Parson's virtues as well as to the Miller's thefts. In the *Prologue* we are in a world of means rather than ends.[22] A large part of the narrator's criteria for judging people then becomes their success in social relationships at a *personal* level; they are judged on pleasantness of appearance, charm of manner, social accomplishments. Their social role is reduced to a question of sociability.

These criteria are of course ironically adopted, and we must therefore ask what is the significance of Chaucer's use of irony in the *Prologue*. We can take as starting-point the definition of irony offered by the thirteenth-century rhetorician Buoncompagno de Signa:

Yronia enim est plana et demulcens verborum positio cum indignatione animi et subsannatione . . . Ceterum vix aliquis adeo fatuus reperitur qui non intelligat si de eo quod non est conlaudetur. Nam si commendares Ethyopem de albedine, latronem de custodia, luxuriosum de castitate, de facili gressu claudum, cecum de visu, pauperem de divitiis, et servum de libertate, stuperent inenarrabili dolore laudati, immo vituperati, quia nil aliud est vituperium quam alicuius malefacta per contrarium commendare vel iocose narrare.[23]

Irony is the bland and sweet use of words to convey disdain and ridicule . . .

Hardly anyone can be found who is so foolish that he does not understand if he is praised for what he is not. For if you should praise the Ethiopian for his whiteness, the thief for his guardianship, the lecher for his chastity, the lame for his agility, the blind for his sight, the pauper for his riches, and the slave for his liberty, they would be struck dumb with inexpressible grief to have been praised, but really vituperated, for it is nothing but vituperation to commend the evil deeds of someone through their opposite, or to relate them wittily. (trans. after Benton, pp. 28–9)

This definition is a useful starting-point, precisely because it does *not* fit Chaucer's habitual use of irony. For what he does so often is to commend the lecher, not for chastity, but for lechery – to enthuse, in fact, over his being the most lecherous lecher of all.

It is true that at certain moments Chaucer seems to be praising someone 'per contrarium'; we think of the 'gentil Pardoner'. But in making his definition, Buoncompagno assumes that the truth about the person ironically described is always clear to us; we know that an Ethiopian is really black. The baffling feature of the *Prologue*, as we have seen, is how often it weakens our grasp of the truth about a character, even while suggesting that it is somehow at odds with the narrator's enthusiastic praise. We begin to wonder whether the Ethiopian was not after all born of colonial parents, and white...

The same characteristics of Chaucerian irony are revealed if we analyse it in terms of a modern definition. Earle Birney suggests that the concept of irony always implies the creation of the illusion that a real incongruity or conflict does not exist, and that this illusion is so shaped that the bystander may, immediately or ultimately, see through it, and be thereby surprised into a more vivid awareness of the very conflict.[24] A large part in the creation and dispersal of the illusion in this ironic process in the *Prologue* is played by the narrator and the shifting attitudes he adopts. The shift can be sharp:

> Nowher so bisy a man as he ther nas,
> And yet he semed bisier than he was. (320–1)

or it can be more subtle, as in the case with Chaucer's constant exploitation of the different semantic values of words like 'worthy', 'gentil', 'fair'. To illustrate briefly: the adjective 'worthy' is used as the key-word of the Knight's portrait, where it has a profound and serious significance, indicating not only the Knight's social status, but also the ethical qualities appropriate to it. In the Friar's portrait, the word is ironically used to indicate the Friar's lack of these ethical qualities –

but it can also be read non-ironically, as a reference to social status:

> For unto swich a worthy man as he
> Acorded nat, as by his facultee,
> To have with sike lazars aqueyntaunce.
> It is nat honest, it may nat avaunce,
> For to deelen with no swich poraille. (243–7)

The reference to social status seems to be the only one in the portrait of the Merchant, who 'was a worthy man with alle' (283). By the time we reach the Franklin's portrait, the word is used with a vague heartiness which seems to indicate little beside the narrator's approval: 'Was nowher swich a worthy vavasour' (360).[25] This attempt to use words with something of the different emphases and connotations that they have in conversation rather than precise and consistent meaning, produces an impression of the complexity of the characters, for it too makes it difficult to pass absolute judgement on them. The shifting meaning given to the vocabulary parallels, and indeed, helps to produce, the shifting bases from which we approach the characters. And the ambivalence reflects not merely their moral ambiguity, but also our own; the shifting semantic values we give to words reveals in us relative, not absolute, standards for judging people. The characters whose own values are absolute are described in absolute terms; the others inhabit a linguistic realm which is more applicable to our everyday unthinking acceptance of different criteria.

The irony in this word-play has a more important role than to serve as a comic cloak for moral criticism. Chaucer uses it to raise some very serious questions. For example, in the Knight's portrait, the word 'curteisie' is associated with an absolute ideal to which one may devote one's whole life (46).[26] In the literary genre of the *chanson de geste*, from which the Knight seems to have stepped, this ideal provides the whole sphere of reference for action. The Squire's 'curteisie' (99), on the other hand, is linked with other characteristics, such as his devotion to love, and his courtly accomplishments, which make it seem not so much an exacting ideal, as part of a way of life for someone who occupies a particular social station.[27] The 'curteisie' in which the Prioress 'set ful muchel hir lest' (132) should be spiritual courtesy, as we have seen, but it has become in her case embarrassingly worldly; instead of striving to please a heavenly spouse by spiritual grace, she has become the female counterpart of the type represented by the Squire. At the same time as another idealistic and religious meaning of 'curteisie' is being

evoked, the concrete manifestations of 'cheere of court' (139–40) –
personal adornment and accomplished manners – are shown to be in
sharp opposition to it. We are left with a sense of the contradictory
values implied by the term. Is it a religious value or a secular one?
Is it an absolute value, or merely appropriate to a certain social class
or age-group? Is the refined behaviour involved in the conception to
be defined as consideration of others, or as ritualised manners? The
different uses of the word reflect not only our shifting attitude to the
characters, but also to the ideal itself.

This I take to be the essence of Chaucer's satire; it does not depend
on wit and verbal pyrotechnic, but on an attitude which cannot be
pinned down, which is always escaping to another view of things and
producing comedy from the disparateness between the two. In some
cases, the disparateness is indeed that between truth and illusion:

> And over al, *ther as profit sholde arise*,
> Curteis he was, and lowely of servyse. (249–50)

> For he hadde power of confessioun,
> *As seyde hymself*, moore than a curat. (228–9)

The necessity that the illusion should be seen through, should be dis-
persed, explains why we have the presentation of characters who are
by any standards truly admirable, the use of words like 'worthy' to
indicate moral as well as purely social values, and the use of unpleasant
imagery to describe characters who are also morally unpleasant.

But in other instances we are not allowed to disperse the illusion,
because we have only suspicions to set against it. What 'true' appel-
lation are we to oppose to the description of the Franklin as a 'worthy
vavasour'? Do we *know* that his feasts are selfish ones from which the
poor are excluded? Do we feel his pleasant appearance to be *belied*
by his character? And what about the Merchant – 'Ther wiste no
wight that he was in dette' – and yet we do not know either that his
prosperity is a hollow pretence. Or the Reeve – 'Ther koude no man
brynge him in arrerage' – because he was honest, or because he was
skilled at covering up his fraud?

I should say that all these ambiguities, together with the 'omission
of the victim' and the confusion of moral and emotional reactions,
add up to Chaucer's *consistent removal of the possibility of moral judgement.*
In other words, our attention is being drawn to the *illusion*; its occasional
dispersal is to demonstrate that it is an illusion, but the illusion itself is
made into the focal point of interest. A comment of Auerbach on the

irony of the *Libro de Buen Amor* of the Archpriest Juan Ruiz enables us to express this in other terms:

> What I have in mind is not so much a conscious irony of the poet, though that too is plentiful, as a kind of objective irony implicit in the candid, untroubled coexistence of the most incompatible things.[28]

The *General Prologue* leads us to discover in ourselves the coexistence of different methods of judging people, the coexistence of different semantic values, each perfectly valid in its own context, and uses this to suggest the way in which the coexistence of the people themselves is achieved. The social cohesion revealed by the *Prologue* is not the moral or religious one of Langland's ideal, but the ironic one of the 'candid, untroubled coexistence of the most incompatible things'.

It is remarkable that many of the methods through which Chaucer achieves this significance for the *Prologue* are also those through which he persuades us of the individuality of the pilgrims. Thus, important for both irony and 'characterisation' in the *Prologue* is what may be called the lack of context. In estates satire, the estates are not described in order to inform us about their work, but in order to present moral criticism; the removal of this purpose in the *Prologue* results, as Rose-mary Woolf has noted,[29] in the presentation of class failings as if they were personal idiosyncrasies, and thus gives us a sense of the individuality of the figures. Similarly the lack of narrative context, which would provide an apparent motive for mentioning many items of description by giving them storial significance,[30] creates the illusion of factual reporting in the *Prologue*, which has been convincingly related to Boccaccio's use of this technique in the *Decameron*.

> Gratuitous information ... creates wonderfully the illusion of factual reporting. What other reason could there be for volunteering such a point if not that it actually happened?[31]

And the illusion of factual reporting in turn aids the creation of irony; there is no obligation to 'place' the pilgrims on a moral scale if one is simply reporting on their existence.

Yet the fascination of the actual is not quite the same for Chaucer and Boccaccio. The aim of the *Prologue* is not to describe human beings in the same spirit as that in which Browning's Fra Lippo Lippi painted people,

> Just as they are, careless of what comes of it
> ... and count it crime
> To let a truth slip.

In order to show the distinction, the characterisation of the pilgrims may be briefly compared with Chaucer's great achievement in *Troilus and Criseyde*: the characterisation of Criseyde.

Coghill has made a useful distinction between Chaucerian characters who are presented through description, 'the selection and adding up of outward detail into the prime number that makes a human being', and those who grow out of speech and action, such as the Host.[32] This distinction can be taken further. Pandarus is a character who grows out of speech and action, but this is almost entirely observed from the outside. We do not see very far into the workings of his mind, and his inward attitude to such an apparently important matter as his own unrequited love-affair is left undefined. With Criseyde, on the other hand, we are introduced to the minute-by-minute workings of her mind, to a complex notion of her psychological processes, and to a character subject to the influence of *time*. This development begins at the moment when she is first acquainted with Troilus's love for her, and deliberates on what to do. Her plea to Pandarus to stay, when he is marching out in anger with a threat of suicide because of her first reaction of dismay, proceeds from a whole range of motives – fear, pity, concern for her reputation, the consciousness that she has responded cruelly to what is, on the surface, an innocent request.[33] The significance of the two stanzas in which these turbulent reactions are described lies in their mixed nature. Her responses are both calculating and instinctive, selfish and charitable. No single motive can be isolated as the 'true' one.

This is equally true of Criseyde's deliberations, when left alone, on whether to accept Troilus's love. Troilus's high social rank, his handsomeness, his bravery, his intelligence and virtue, his suffering on her behalf, are all admitted as influences, and conversely, fear of unpleasantness, of betrayal, of what people will say (II 659–65, 701–28, 771–805). Criseyde is alternately overwhelmed at the honour done to her and conscious that she well deserves it (735–49). She tries to determine coolly and rationally what will be the best course of action, and is then swayed by a song, a nightingale and a dream (820ff., 918ff., 925ff.). This is a situation in which the workings of Criseyde's mind tell us more about her than the actual thoughts she entertains. We have an extraordinarily realistic presentation of the complicated responses and decisions of human beings. One further touch is worth noting; in Book IV, Criseyde earnestly assures Troilus that the reason for her yielding to him was neither pleasure, his high rank, nor even his bravery, but 'moral vertu, grounded upon trouthe' (1667–73). The fact that we have seen a very different situation in Book II does not mean that Criseyde is insincere. It is a true statement with regard to the *present* – the time dimension not only alters the character and our view of her, it retrospectively validates her selection of one single aspect of a complex past. There is no single 'truth' in the sphere of human motives.

There is no ambiguity or depth of character comparable to this in the *Prologue*. The state of the Merchant's finances is knowable, although we do not know it, in a way that the state of Criseyde's mind is not knowable. There is some ambiguity of mind indicated by external devices, such as the motto on the Prioress's brooch. But comparison with the characterisation of Criseyde reveals even more clearly that the complexity of the *Prologue* portraits consists much more in our attitude to them than in their own characteristics. Bronson seems to be saying something like this in claiming that we are much more deeply involved with the narrator than with any of the characters in the *General Prologue*, 'for he is almost the only figure in his "drama" who is fully realised psychologically and who truly matters to us'.[34] The centre of interest in the *Prologue* is not in any depiction of human character, in actuality for its own sake; it is in our relationship with the actual, the way in which we perceive it and the attitudes we adopt to it, and the narrator stands here for the ambiguities and complexities that characterise this relationship.

If we draw together the results of this discussion, we find that the ethic we have in the *Prologue* is an ethic of this world. The constant shifting of viewpoints means that it is relativist; in creating our sense of this ethic the estates aspect is of fundamental importance, for it means that in each portrait we have the sense of a specialised way of life. A world of specialised skills, experience, terminology and interests confronts us; we see the world through the eyes of a lazy Monk or a successful Merchant, and simultaneously realise the latent tension between his view and our own. But the tension is latent, because the superficial agreement and approval offered in the ironic comment has this amount of reality – it really reflects the way in which we get on with our neighbours, by tacit approval of the things we really consider wrong, by admiring techniques more than the ends they work towards, by regarding unethical behaviour as amusing as long as the results are not directly unpleasant for us, by adopting, for social reasons, the viewpoint of the person with whom we are associating, and at the same time feeling that his way of life is 'not our business'.

To say that the *General Prologue* is based on an ethic of this world is not to adopt the older critical position that Chaucer is unconcerned with morality. The adoption of this ethic at this particular point does not constitute a definitive attitude but a piece of observation – and the comic irony ensures that the reader does not identify with this ethic. Chaucer's inquiry is epistemological as well as moral. This is how the world operates, and as the world, it can operate no other way. The contrast with heavenly values is made at the end of the *Canterbury Tales*, as critics have noted,[35] but it is made in such a way that it cannot affect the validity of the initial statement – the world can only operate by the world's values. One's confidence in seeing this as the movement of the *Canterbury Tales* is increased by the observation that this parallels the movement in *Troilus and Criseyde*: consistent irony throughout the poem, the coexistence of incompatible things, the sharp demonstration of their incompatibility in the Epilogue and yet the tragic consciousness that their coexistence – indeed in the case of *Troilus* their unity – is as inevitable as their incompatibility. And yet the differences between the two works are significant. The narrator in the *Troilus* is led by the conclusion of his story to reject his own – and our – experience of the beauty and nobility of what has gone before. Although we do not accept his Epilogue as the *only* valid response to the experience of the *Troilus*, this emotional rejection plays a large part in establishing the tragic finality of the work. The *Canterbury Tales* do not have the same sort of finality. The 'final statement' in the *Tales* comes not from the narrator, but from the Parson, who has not participated as we have in the worlds of the other pilgrims. In rejecting the world of the Miller, for example, he is not rejecting something for which he has felt personal enthusiasm – such as the narrator of the *Troilus* feels at the consummation of the love-affair. And *because* the final statement is given to the Parson, the narrator of the *Canterbury Tales* remains an observer who can sympathetically adapt to or report a whole range of experiences and attitudes to them. The relation between the *General Prologue* and the Parson's Tale is more subtle than a simple opposition between *cupiditas* and *caritas*.[36]

The *Prologue* presents the world in terms of worldly values, which are largely concerned with an assessment of façades, made in the light of half-knowledge, and on the basis of subjective criteria. Subjectivity characterises both the pilgrims' attitude to the world, and the world's (or the reader's) attitude to the pilgrims. But at least in their case, it must be repeated that their views on the world are not individual ones, but are attached to their callings – in medieval terms, their estates.

The *Prologue* proves to be a poem about work. The society it evokes is not a collection of individuals or types with an eternal or universal significance, but particularly a society in which work as a social experience conditions personality and the standpoint from which an individual views the world. In the *Prologue*, as in history, it is specialised work which ushers in a world where relativised values and the individual consciousness are dominant.

Appendix A List of the order in which the estates are presented in some representative poems

Digressive references to estates are given in brackets

Rather of Verona: Praeloquia

I Christians: knights: craftsmen: doctors: merchants: advocates: judges: witnesses: public ministers: nobles: hired employees and vassals: counsellors: lords: serfs: teachers: pupils: the rich: people of moderate income: beggars.

II men: women: husbands: wives: celibates: mothers and fathers: sons and daughters: widows: virgins: children: boys: adolescents: old men.

III king.

Speculum Stultorum 2495ff.

Court of Rome: kings: spiritual pastors: abbots and priors: laity.

Chessbook

King: queen: judges: knights: vicars and legates of the king: peasants: smiths and mariners: notaries and cloth makers: merchants and changers: physicians, spicers and apothecaries: taverners, inn-keepers and victuallers: keepers of towns, customs men and toll-gatherers: ribalds, dice-players, messengers and couriers.

Apocalipsis Goliae

Bishops (pope: bishop: archdeacon: deacon): archdeacon: deacon: officials of ecclesiastical courts: priests: clergy: abbots and monks.

'Frequenter cogitans'

Bishops: (usurers): merchants: knights: peasants: bishops, priests, presbyters: monks, abbots.

'Viri fratres, servi Dei'

Pope: cardinals: bishops: priests: canons regular: monks and nuns:

friars: emperor: kings: counts, earls, barons, knights: citizens, nobles: commons: sailors and landholders: merchants.

'Totum regit saeculum'
Pope: cardinals: king: bishops: abbots: monks: friars: knights: rectors and priests: clerks: burgesses: merchants: peasants: beggars.

Sermones nulli parcentes
Pope: cardinals: patriarchs: bishops: prelates generally: monks: crusaders: lay-brothers: wandering monks: secular priests: lawyers and physicians: scholars: wanderers: nuns: emperor: kings: princes and counts: knights: nobles: squires: citizens: merchants: tradesmen: messengers, usurers, hucksters, gamblers, thieves and pimps: peasants: women: friars.

Vox Clamantis
III Prelates: priests, clergy generally: pope: curates: clerks.
IV Monks: nuns: friars.
V Knights: women: ploughmen and peasants: hired workers: burgesses – merchants, artisans.
VI Lawyers: sheriffs, jurors, bailiffs: king.

'Heu! quia per crebras humus est vitiata tenebras'
Court of Rome: monks: priests: rulers: nobles: knights and soldiers: lawyers: merchants: the commons: peasants.

Étienne de Fougères: Livre des Manières
Kings: clergy (priest, archdeacon and dean): bishop (judges, witnesses, advocates): archbishop: cardinals: knights (peasants): citizens and bourgeois: workmen and merchants: women (ladies and maids, countesses and queens, rich ladies).

Guiot de Provins: Bible
Secular clergy (bishops and archbishops, priests and canons): Benedictines: Cistercians: Carthusians: Grandimontanes: Premonstratensians: regular canons: Templars: Hospitallers: Hospitallers of St Anthony: nuns and lay sisters: masters of theology: lawyers: doctors.

Li Dis des Estas dou Monde, Jean de Condé
Clergy: knights: prince: justices: squires and 'sergeants': burgesses: merchants: minstrels: labourers: married people: women.

L'État du Monde, Rutebeuf
Monks: friars: secular canons: advocates: bailliffs, provosts and mayors: merchants: tradesmen: knights.

'Nous lisons une istoire, ou fable'
Clergy: merchant: labourer: knight: advocate: married man.

'La Lettre de L'Empéreur Orgueil', Nicholas Bozon
Court of Rome: kings: judges: sheriffs: bailliffs: prelates: bachelors: vavasours: squires: noble ladies: religious: secular clergy: peasants: matrons: court servants.

'Le Dit des Patenostres'
Pope: cardinals: prelates: clergy: officials, advocates, procurators, notaries, curates: students: masters of court of requests, advocates, judges: chancery: physicians and surgeons: religious – monks, friars, Hospitallers: king, dukes, counts: barony: knighthood: duchesses, countesses, princesses: béguines, nuns, widows, married women: young girls: Flemings: bakers: tradesmen, craftsmen, marshals: apothecaries: brokers: provosts: bailliffs: mayors: slanderers: peasants: drunkards: the sick: lovers: working people: merchants: cowards: lunatics: servants: pilgrims: beggars: Jacobins: pilgrims again.

'Mult est diables curteis'
Clergy: knights: villeins: pope (archbishop: bishop: archdeacon: dean): priests: secular canons: Templars: Hospitallers.

Matheolus's Lamentations IV 283ff.
Pastors (bishop, officials, deans): court of Rome: religious: knights: judges: advocates: physicians: bourgeois (merchants): labourers.

Mirour de l'Omme
Court of Rome: cardinals: bishops: archdeacons, officials and deans: curates: annuellers: clerks: monks: friars: emperors: kings: lords: knights and men of arms: lawyers: judges: sheriffs, reeves and jurors: merchants: trades-people and craftsmen (doctors): victuallers: labourers.

'The Simonie'
Court of Rome: archbishop: bishop: archdeacon: priests: abbots,

priors, monks, friars: officials and deans: doctors: earls, barons, knights and squires: justices, sheriffs, mayors, bailiffs: lawyers: merchants.

General Prologue
Knight: Squire: Yeoman: Prioress: Second Nun and three(?) Priests: Monk: Friar: Merchant: Clerk: Sergeant of Law: Franklin: Guilds- men – Haberdasher, Carpenter, Weaver, Dyer, Tapicer: Cook: Shipman: Doctor of Physic: Wife of Bath: Parson: Ploughman: Miller: Manciple: Reeve: Summoner: Pardoner.

Appendix B Chaucer, Langland and Gower

Three major writers of the fourteenth century made use of estates material in their works – Gower, Langland and Chaucer. Inevitably we must ask: did they do so independently, or were they acquainted with, and influenced by, each other's work?

The probability that Chaucer had read both Gower and Langland seems, on the face of it, strong. All three poets had connections with London; Gower and Chaucer were personal friends; *Piers Plowman* was a work sufficiently well-known for its terminology to be used in John Ball's famous letter to the peasants of Essex.[1] The satiric tradition was a rich one before ever these writers put pen to paper, but if Chaucer was thinking of writing an estates piece, it is surely likely that he would have consulted *Piers Plowman*, the *Vox Clamantis* and the *Mirour de l'Omme* to see how their authors handled estates material. In the preceding chapters, features in Chaucer's portraits have often been paralleled in Gower and Langland. I shall now briefly attempt to isolate these parallels, and to consider other evidence of his debt to them.

CHAUCER AND GOWER

Many of the parallels between the *Prologue* and the *Mirour de l'Omme* were pointed out long ago by Flügel, and more recently, John Fisher has argued strongly for the influence of Gower on Chaucer.[2] In view of Fisher's detailed and convincing argument, although he does not include all the parallels I have noted between Gower and Chaucer, I shall only briefly distinguish between what Chaucer probably took from the *Mirour de l'Omme*, and what is attributable to the *Vox Clamantis*.

Almost all the characters in the *Prologue* before the Ploughman, appear in the *Vox* or the *Mirour* or both. With a few exceptions (Yeoman, Cook, Shipman), it almost looks as if Chaucer was following a typical estates scheme, such as Gower uses, up to this point, and then concluded with four figures from *Piers Plowman*, plus one addition (the Manciple). The difficulty would be in suggesting why Chaucer prefers these Langlandian figures over the many artisans treated at the close of the *Mirour*; on the other hand, the shift to a new source of stimulus might explain the introduction of the last five figures in a group. However, the resemblances in the selection of estates are never so close as to suggest that Chaucer was slavishly following either Gower or Langland, and his scheme probably owes more to the haphazard workings of memory than to the conscious adherence to another writer's framework.

If we look at the material associated with the estates in Gower's two works, the *Mirour* seems to assume the greater importance. Again and again, detailed resemblances or verbal echoes refer us to this work: the monk's fur, his ornament of precious metal, his 'outriding' like a lord, his greyhounds and love of hunting; the friar who can wheedle a ha'penny out of a woman who has nothing, and is worse when he is a 'limitour'; the merchant who talks of his profits, whom we suspect to be in debt, and dabbles in exchanges, usury and chevisance; the clerk who ought to set an example in edifying conversation, the sergeant of law who makes 'fals pourchas' of lands; the doctor who collaborates profitably with apothecaries who mix up syrups and electuaries. Besides this, a jumble of reminiscences: gluttony associated with pike, partridges, sauces, cooks, sops in wine, Epicurus; a hospitable knight compared with St Julian; drunkenness which makes the laity talk Latin; short and sexually provocative tunics; archdeacons and their officers thinking that a man's soul is in his purse; and the curative powers of gold, which in Gower's case causes deaf and dumb lawyers to speak. And yet the portrait of the Parson accords more with the treatment of priests in the *Vox Clamantis*, the monk who scorns St Bernard and St Maurus appears there, and many other features are shared by the two works. I conclude therefore that Chaucer knew and used both works, but that the case is clearer for the *Mirour*.

CHAUCER AND LANGLAND

Almost all the *Prologue* figures, as we have seen, had already appeared in *Piers Plowman*, and Langland alone seems to have been responsible for Chaucer's inclusion of certain estates representatives (although not always for the material he attaches to them). There are also significant parallels in material and treatment between the two works, which have been noted in the preceding chapters. I should now like to point to some of Langland's stylistic characteristics which I believe to be equally important for the conception and execution of the *Prologue*.

It is usual practice to compare the material of the social satire in Chaucer and Langland, and to contrast their approaches to it. Langland is didactic, Chaucer is comic. The degree of evident truth to be found in this has barred the way to any deeper consideration of approaches, methods and interests common to both authors.

One might, for example, comment on the role of the narrator in *Piers Plowman*. The *Prologue* introduces the narrator as a character in his own work, who falls asleep beside a stream and dreams of 'A faire felde ful of folke'. In this capacity, the narrator is a simple observer recording without comment what he sees; this is the 'I' of 'I seigh' (14, 50), 'fonde I' (17, 58). There is however another 'I', who represents Langland as the omniscient creator of his poem, and the provider of comment on the vision. Thus he says of honest minstrels that they earn money 'synneles, I leue' (34), or interjects, à propos of 'iapers and iangelers', 'That Poule precheth of hem˙I nel nought preue it here.' (35–8). That is to say that Langland's narrator is sometimes a figure inside the poem and sometimes outside of it, as Chaucer's narrator is sometimes the immediate observer, and sometimes the omniscient author. Chaucer's method, unlike Langland's, is an ironic one; his two 'I's hold contradictory attitudes. It is precisely the alteration of function and context, however, that has obscured the similarities that do exist between the two writers. When Langland says,

> The Kyng called a clerke ˙ can I nouȝt his name. (III 3)

the anonymity barely arouses interest; any clerk would clearly serve the purpose. When Chaucer says,

> But sooth to say, I noot how men hym calle. (284)

the context of the description, an apparent piece of reportage, means that this ignorance appears as a guarantee of the real existence of the figure. A creator knows everything about his creations, a reporter is necessarily ignorant on some points.[3]

The exploitation of the narrator by both writers is of incidental interest; more important by far is the fact that Langland, above all other estates writers, is fascinated by the multifarious activities of mankind. His *explicit* purpose is indeed moralising comment on the way in which these activities make for social harmony or social chaos, but he is also capable of a non-moralising delight in human variety.

There is nothing in Gower which is comparable to the interest in different pursuits, interlocking and clashing, presented as a matter for wonder as well as comment and criticism, in the *Prologue* to Piers Plowman.

> Barones an burgeis · and bonde-men als
> I sei3 in this assemble · as 3e shul here after.
> Baxsteres and brewesteres · and bocheres manye,
> Wollwebsteres · and weueres of lynnen,
> Taillours and tynkeres · and tolleres in marketes,
> Masons and mynours · and many other craftes.
> Of alkin libbyng laboreres · lopen forth somme,
> As dykers and delueres · that doth here dedes ille,
> And dryuen forth the longe day · with '*Dieu vous saue, Dame Emme!*'
> Cokes and here knaues · crieden, 'hote pies, hote!
> Gode gris and gees · gowe dyne, gowe!'
> Tauerners vn-til hem · tolde the same,
> 'White wyn of Oseye · and red wyn of Gascoigne,
> Of the Ryne and of the Rochel · the roste to defye.'
> All this sei3 I slepyng · and seuene sythes more. (216–30)

This is the way Langland's *Prologue* ends, and it means that we are left with a sense of exuberance and richness rather than a grim didacticism. The presence of Heaven and Hell at right and left of Langland's stage undoubtedly means a greater concern to *evaluate* human activity than we find in Chaucer, but it also means a larger perspective than we find in Gower.

Langland and Chaucer share this fascination with human variety, and also an interest in different viewpoints. Gower, in contrast, deals with many different trades in the *Mirour de l'Omme*, but views them all from the point of view of the disgruntled customer. Langland sometimes adopts this attitude, but on other occasions he presents things from the point of view of the practitioner of the trade. Thus, in the passage quoted above, when we picture the cooks calling their wares, we briefly visualise their interests and motives; we look at the rest of the world through their eyes, in which other people figure only as potential customers. At the same time, we realise the difference between this viewpoint and the larger perspective that Langland has established; *as outsiders*, we savour the occupation of cooks. This is just the sort of process we have observed in the *Prologue*: we are given a strong sense of a specialised way of life, and the viewpoint of the person practising it, along with the feeling that this is 'not our business'.

Without attempting documentation, I think it is clear that there is a strong sense, especially in the early Passus of *Piers Plowman*, of what 'the world asketh' of different estates, and of the way in which this affects their view of the world. We may think of the descriptions of the Seven Deadly Sins conveyed in confessions – that is, from their point of view – or the self-interested approach of Meed to the sin of lechery:

> It is frelete of flesh · ʒe fynde it in bokes,
> And a course of kynde · wher-of we komen alle. (III 35–6)

Thus, we also find in *Piers Plowman* a sense of different viewpoints, and the sense of an ethic of the world, developed alongside the sense of eternal values.[4] What Chaucer has done is to reverse the importance that the two sets of values had in Langland.

Other features of *Piers Plowman* can be related to the *Prologue* – the consistent use of representative individuals as the medium for Langland's estates satire, his use of the figure of *descriptio*.[5] But their contribution to Chaucer's satiric style could have been made by other works also, and is for that reason less important. One feature, however, comes into a special category. It was of course possible for Chaucer to be familiar with the idea of human life as a pilgrimage from other sources.[6] It is even possible that he knew the *Novelle* of Giovanni Sercambi, in which the author presents himself telling tales to a band of fellow-pilgrims.[7] But it is at least equally possible that he had read the following:

> Pilgrymes and palmeres · pliʒted hem togidere
> To seke seynt Iames · and seyntes in Rome.
> Thei went forth in here way · with many wise tales,
> And hadden leue to lye · al here lyf after. (*PPl* Prol. 46–9)

Here we have the pilgrims themselves telling tales, the situation which Harry Bailly presents as expected (*General Prologue*, 771–4). In the Parson's Prologue, the pilgrimage has become metaphorical, directed to 'Jerusalem celestial', and this allegorical application we also find in Langland, not only in the journeys constantly being initiated to find Truth, or Piers himself, but also in the explicit statement that 'pylgrymes are we alle' (XI 234). Is it not likely that although pilgrimages, both literal and allegorical, had been put to literary use elsewhere, it is Langland's picture of the roads of England thronged with minstrels, beggars, hermits and pilgrims travelling to Walsingham or London, Spain or Italy, and enjoying the journey more than the arrival, that stimulated the ride to Canterbury?[8]

John Fisher has suggested that we should see Gower's influence on Chaucer not as a matter of verbal echo but as 'stimulus diffusion'.[9] While agreeing whole-heartedly with his estimate of Gower's importance for Chaucer, I should qualify his statement that 'only the parallels between [Chaucer's] work and Gower's have not hitherto received full consideration'. The parallels between Chaucer and Langland have received even less attention. Coghill has pointed to some resemblances, and Professor Bennett has published an article indicating others;[10] both stress the probability that Chaucer knew Langland's work. Fisher's notion of 'stimulus diffusion' is in this instance even more relevant than with Gower. If we confine ourselves to looking for verbal echoes and exact parallels, we shall miss opportunities for understanding both writers better. If we take a broader view, we shall realise the importance of Langland's function in making the topic of human work, and the 'worship of this worlde' the central interest of the *General Prologue* to the *Canterbury Tales*.

Notes

CHAPTER I

1. As by G. L. Kittredge, *Chaucer's Poetry*, Chapters 5 and 6.
2. As by J. M. Manly, *Some New Light on Chaucer*.
3. As by D. W. Robertson, *A Preface to Chaucer: Studies in Medieval Perspectives*, pp. 242–8, and W. C. Curry, *Chaucer and the Mediæval Sciences*, Chapters 1–5.
4. In a brief article ('The Plan of the *Canterbury Tales*', *MP* 13 (May 1915), 45–8), H. S. V. Jones claimed the importance of estates literature for the *Prologue*, but did not substantiate his claim at length, or consider its further implications. The more usual critical approach can be illustrated from F. N. Robinson (ed.) *The Works of Geoffrey Chaucer*, p. 3, introductory notes to the *General Prologue*:

> Whole works ... were devoted to the description of the various orders of society, and others to the classification of men and women by physical and temperamental characteristics. With this lore of the physiognomists and social philosophers Chaucer was doubtless familiar. But in none of his predecessors has there been found a gallery of portraits like that in the *Prologue*.

In considering the 'portrait-gallery' aspect of the *Prologue* as its fundamental one, and in treating estates literature and studies in physiognomy as *equal* contributors to its material, Robinson immediately begs several questions of criticism and source-study which I should like to examine in detail.

The low status accorded to the role of estates literature can also be seen from the fact that Bryan and Dempster's *Sources and Analogues of Chaucer's Canterbury Tales* does not mention this genre in connection with the *Prologue*.

5. This is, for example, the approach of Muriel Bowden's *Commentary on the General Prologue to the Canterbury Tales*, and also seems to lie behind E. Flügel's article on 'Gower's Mirour de l'Omme und Chaucer's Prolog' (*Anglia*, 24 (1901), 437–508). For Flügel, a collection of literary parallels with Chaucer 'zeigt, wie genau Chaucer nach dem Leben schildert' (p. 452). Flügel's article lists parallels with many other estates poems besides Gower's, most of which I shall discuss, but he draws no general conclusions

for the *Prologue* and is uninterested in analysing literary style. I shall not specifically signal a literary parallel which has already been brought to attention by Flügel or Bowden, unless I would have failed to notice it otherwise, and I make here the acknowledgement of a general debt to these scholars (and those whose articles lie behind Bowden's book) for their explanation of historical detail.

6. Originally published in 1926.

7. He specifies the five Guildsmen, the Squire, Yeoman, Manciple and Ploughman (*New Light*, p. 253).

8. Manly implies (*New Light*, pp. 294–5) that Chaucer's satire had a moral purpose, but he does not try to show how the selection and treatment of the pilgrims is determined by any particular or consistent moral standpoint.

9. *The Three Estates in Medieval and Renaissance Literature*, pp. 6–7.

10. And it is this word which is picked up in Lydgate's reference to the Canterbury pilgrims:

> The tyme in soth / whan Canterbury talys
> Complet and told / at many sondry stage
> Of estatis // in the pilgrimage,
> Everich man / lik to his degrè,
> Some of desport / some of moralitè,
> Some of knyghthode / love and gentillesse . . .

(*Siege of Thebes* ed. A. Erdmann, EETS e.s. 108 (London, 1911), p. 2, 18–23.)

11. 'Chaucer's Pilgrims' reprinted in Wagenknecht, p. 23. Cf. Clawson, 'The Framework of the Canterbury Tales', reprinted in Wagenknecht, p. 13, 'Chaucer's group of pilgrims is not schematically representative of English society, but covers well enough the main social elements', and H. R. Patch, *On Rereading Chaucer*, pp. 176–7. Baum takes exception to Hulbert's statements on the grounds that 'society is too complex to be generalised so easily' (*Chaucer, A Critical Appreciation*, p. 68) – to which it might be replied that society itself is complex but people's schematic ideas of it are far simpler.

12. *In Search of Chaucer*, p. 60.

13. Langland is as always the exception; he incidentally portrays female retailers, brewers, and so on (*PPl* v, 215–27). Estates literature sometimes classifies women further according to marital status – maid, wife, widow – but the attributes, as opposed to the duties, of each group are very similar.

14. *Chaucer and the French Tradition*, p. 170. Muscatine is referring to the portrait-gallery form.

15. See, for example, W. W. Lawrence, *Chaucer and the Canterbury Tales*, pp. 55–7, who says that the *Prologue* 'does not follow the favourite procedure of classifying mankind according to feudal principles and setting forth the distinctive marks of each class, as in the estates of the world literature'.

16. *The Mind and Art of Chaucer*, p. 92.
17. Kemp Malone says that Chaucer is not 'so negligent of rank as he pretends to be. His descriptions of the pilgrims begin with the knight, the ranking member of the company ... The sequence of the first three descriptions is one of rank.' The Prioress and the Monk, he thinks, outrank everyone except the Knight. For these and other comments on the ranking of the pilgrims, see *Chapters on Chaucer*, pp. 155–6.
    Cf. also R. Baldwin, *The Unity of the Canterbury Tales*, p. 35; J. Swart, 'The Construction of Chaucer's *General Prologue*', *Neophilologus*, 38 (1954), 131; H. F. Brooks, *Chaucer's Pilgrims: The Artistic Order of the Portraits in the Prologue*, p. 31, and R. K. Root, *The Poetry of Chaucer*, p. 231.
18. One interesting piece of evidence on this point is the scale for the graduated poll tax of 1379, which indicates the assumed income and social status of each group in fixing the amount of tax that each had to pay (R. B. Dobson, *The Peasants' Revolt of 1381* (London, 1970), pp. 105ff.). This scheme, like that of estates literature, divides the clergy from the laity and works from top to bottom in each group.
19. Chaucer's use of the word 'degree' does not invalidate this argument, since it can mean much more than 'social rank' (*MED* 4) in Middle English; like 'estaat', it also means 'condition, state' in a very general sense (*MED* 6; cf. *CT* I(A)1841, IX(H)146), and a subordinate sense of its use in this way is 'order, position' (*MED* 6d), which could well be the meaning here.
20. Cf., for example, the article by Ruth Nevo, 'Chaucer: Motive and Mask in the "General Prologue"', *MLR* 58 (1963), 1–9, which sees in the *Prologue* 'a classification of society based upon the various sources of income'.
21. Clawson, 'Framework of the Canterbury Tales', Wagenknecht, p. 14. Northrop Frye's general comment on satire has relevance here:

> The romantic fixation which revolves around the beauty of perfect form, in art or elsewhere, is ... a logical target for satire. The word satire is said to come from *satura*, or hash, and a kind of parody of form seems to run all through its tradition ... A deliberate rambling digressiveness ... is endemic in the narrative technique of satire ... An extraordinary number of great satires are fragmentary, unfinished, or anonymous (*Anatomy of Criticism*, pp. 233–4).

22. For social stereotypes, see Krech, Crutchfield and Ballachey, *Individual in Society* (New York, 1962), pp. 30ff.
23. It is an estates tradition to protest that one is simply writing down what everyone else says; Gower, for example, does this in the *Vox Clamantis*, and Gilles li Muisis throughout his works. C. S. Lewis has commented on Skelton's exploitation of this tradition in *Colin Clout* and *Why Come Ye Not to Court?* (*English Literature in the Sixteenth Century* (Oxford, 1954), p. 139.)

For the two-way exchange between aristocratic and popular cultures, see G. Duby, 'The Diffusion of Cultural Patterns in Feudal Society', *Past and Present*, 39 (1968), 3–10. I am grateful to Derek Brewer for this reference.

24. An excellent example of this can be found in W. A. Pantin, *The English Church in the Fourteenth Century*, p. 159, in an account of a bill of complaints against the friars presented at the Convocation of Canterbury in May 1356. (Pantin's appendix of the Latin text gives the date as November 1355.) It complains that they squander money on splendid horses and equipment, frequent the courts of magnates and public places, slander the secular clergy, flatter magnates and act as their confessors, conduct secular business, act as mediators of marriages and as business agents, take for themselves payments offered as penance for sins, are bloated with luxuries, have ruddy cheeks or fat bellies, and so on. The close correspondence between this description and the stereotype that we shall see was built up over two centuries and in different countries, makes it very difficult to decide whether the clergy of the province of Canterbury had really observed everything they describe.

Another interesting example of the relationship between stereotype and observation occurs in Ruotger's biography of Bishop Bruno of Cologne, a tenth-century work discussed by Auerbach (*Literary Language and its Public in Late Latin Antiquity and in the Middle Ages*, pp. 159ff.). Ruotger says of Bruno that he always set a good example, and 'Apud mites et humiles nemo humilior, contra improbos et elatos nemo vehementior fuit' – 'No one was more humble toward the meek and humble, and no one more terrible against evil and presumptuous men' (trans. Auerbach, *ibid.*, p. 162). Auerbach's comment is that the second half of this sentence 'takes us rather by surprise' and such unexpected elements convince him that 'the account comes close to the truth' (p. 163). The description may well be true of Bruno, but the chapter on the Parson will show how conventional it is for testimonies of humility to be accompanied by the assurance that it is matched by rigour toward sinners. The observation and description of a historical person is determined by the balanced formulae of convention.

25. All quotations from Chaucer's works are taken from the second edition of F. N. Robinson.

26. Manly notes that 'the battles in which the knight had been engaged were all battles against the infidels' ('A Knight Ther Was', reprinted in Wagenknecht, p. 47).

27. The passages I have in mind at this point are *General Prologue* 94–6, 106–7, 110, 278, 282, 318–20, 323–8, 355–6, 359–60, 380–1, 383–4, 387, 401–4, 406–9, 412–20, 429–34, 447–8, 593–9, 692–3. These represent only the most easily isolable passages on the work-lives of the pilgrims, yet together with the lines quoted from the Knight's portrait they amount to over seventy lines, or a good tenth of the space given to the descriptions. This will give

us an idea of the importance of plain, non-satirical, information about the professions in the *Prologue*.

28. For the general idea that Chaucer's individual style, 'lively, conversational, emphatic, dramatic, stuffed with doublets and alternatives, asseverations that are mild oaths, expletives and parentheses', derives from the Middle English rhyming romances, see pp. 2ff. of D. S. Brewer's article, 'The Relationship of Chaucer to the English and European Traditions', in Brewer (ed.), *Chaucer and Chaucerians*.

29. E.g., R. W. V. Elliott, *Chaucer's Prologue to the Canterbury Tales*, p. 49, and R. M. Lumiansky, *Of Sondry Folk: The Dramatic Principle in the Canterbury Tales*, p. 20.

30. E.g., R. Woolf, 'Chaucer as a Satirist in the *General Prologue* to *the Canterbury Tales*', *Critical Quarterly*, I (1959), 152.

31. Malone, *Chapters on Chaucer*, p. 167.

32. In an attempt to discover whether the Merchant belonged to the Staplers or Adventurers, for example (Bowden, *Commentary*, p. 147). Manly tried to relate the places to Chaucer's experience (*New Light*, p. 198).

33. There can be different stereotypes for a social class besides the 'ideal' and the 'normal'. For example, a knight's role can be conceived as part of a national system of justice, or part of aggressive religious proselytisation abroad.

34. This has been recognised by R. Preston, *Chaucer*, p. 168, and by J. Speirs, who writes of the presentation of the ecclesiastics:

> The art is in seeing exactly what each is in relation to what each ought to be ... That the criticism is implied itself implies an audience which shared the same social and moral standards as the poet. The art is as much in what is left unsaid as in what is said; and what is said consists in the simple juxtaposition of statements which it is left to the audience to know how to relate (*Chaucer the Maker*, pp. 103–4).

35. 'Chaucer's Pilgrims', Wagenknecht, p. 23. Similarly, Baldwin recognises the role of the stereotype ('the recognised status of class') in the portraits – 'One had only to mention knight, friar, miller, reeve, for instance, for a compendium of traits to be invoked by the very name' – but he thinks that an equally important role was played by 'nuclear personal characterisation within that class' (*Unity of the Canterbury Tales*, pp. 42 and 50).

36. See, for example, *Renart le Contrefait*, II, p. 41, 26,355ff.; the section devoted to 'ceaux qui vivont du mestier et d'artifice' in the *Mirour de l'Omme* (25,501ff.) and the confession of Avarice in *Piers Plowman* (V 200ff.).

37. Cf. Robertson, *Preface to Chaucer*, p. 248: '[Chaucer's] interest was not in the "surface reality" but in the reality of the idea.'

CHAPTER 2

1. For a wide selection of contemporary generalisations about the medieval religious orders, see Coulton, *Five Centuries of Religion*, II, appendices 34 and 36.

2. 881–2. The speed with which monks run to their meals had been noted in Nigel's source, the *Ysengrimus* (ed. E. Voigt (Halle a.S., 1884), p. 31, I 433–4). Gower reproduces the comparison (*VC* IV 79–82). It seems to have been a commonplace; Owst quotes one of Robert Rypon's sermons to the effect that some clerics 'run swifter to the cookhouse than to mass' (*Lit. and Pulp.*, p. 272).

3. 'Dum pater abbas filiam', *Map Poems*, pp. 184ff.

4. p. 33, st. 90–9; see also *MO* 20,893–904, which has strong resemblances to the Latin poem.

5. 'Nuper ductu serio plagam ad australem', *Map Poems*, pp. 243ff. Cf. also the debate 'Dum Saturno conjuge partus parit Rhea', where gluttony plays a minor role in the changes brought by the White Monk (*ibid.*, p. 242, 147), but the debate itself is so heated because *both* monks are 'vino crapulati' (*ibid.*, p. 238, 43).

6. *MO* 20,877–80; *VC* IV 57–8, 65–6. A contrast can also be made between past asceticism and present degenerateness; cf. *Roman de Carité*, p. 78 CXLVI 8ff., and *MO* 20,857–65, 20,869–70.

7. 2087–8 (the Black Monks eat meats and fats), 2129–32 (the Cistercians debate whether the prohibition of quadrupeds includes birds), 2259–60 (the Augustinian Canons eat fat meats). See also 969–72, where Burnellus proposes to punish the monks who have insulted him, by restricting their diet to raw vegetables, and forbidding wine.

8. 'L'Ordre de Bel Ayse', ed. Aspin, p. 134, 95–100. See also 56–8, 61–70, 79–94.

9. *Apocalipsis Goliae*, p. 33, st. 88; *VC* IV 131–2, 141–2.

10. The use of spices is also incorporated into the descriptions of elaborate cooking methods, for which see 'Nuper ductu serio', *Map Poems*, p. 248, 161–8; *Magister Golyas de quodam abbate, ibid.*, pp. xlii–iii; *VC* IV 69–70 (Stockton – *Major Latin Works of John Gower*, p. 414 – compares this passage with the Pardoner's Tale, VI (C)538); *MO* 20,871–6, where the elaborate cooking preparations become part of the monk's defence of his gluttony: meat chopped and pounded 'isn't really meat'. Cf. Langland's Doctor of Divinity, who will 'prove' that 'blancmangere' and 'mortrewes' are 'noither fisshe ne flesshe' but 'fode for a penaunte' (*PPl* XIII 89–92. Unless otherwise assigned, quotations from *Piers Plowman* are from the B text).

11. See 'Nuper ductu serio', *Map Poems*, p. 247, 134, 145–8 ('panes cum potibus dulce pigmentatis . . . | Placentas, artocreas, et cornutas micas, | crispas,

fabas mysticas, pastillos et picas' – 'Bread with sweetly-spiced drinks . . .
Cakes, meat pies, croissants, pastries, sacred beans, rolls, pies . . . '. Beans
were sacred to the Pythagoreans: see Pauly's *Real-Encyclopädie*, ed. G.
Wissowa, vol. 3 (Stuttgart, 1899) col. 619, and cf. the proverb cited by
Kervyn de Lettenhove in his edition of Gilles li Muisis, II p. 329, s. Fève:
'Manger febves, n'est moindre faute faire, | Que de manger la teste de son
père'. See also *Magister Golyas de quodam abbate*, ibid., pp. xlii–iii, *VC*
IV 67–8; Guiot de Provins, *Bible*, p. 49, 1267–77; *Roman de Carité*, p. 78
CXLVI 11–12.

12. See *SS* 2129–32; *Magister Golyas de quodam abbate*, *Map Poems*, p. xlii
('pavones, *cignos*, grues et anseres, gallinas et gallinaceos, id est gallos
castratos . . . Fasianos . . . perdices, et columbas' – 'Peacocks, *swans*, cranes
and geese, hens and poultry-cocks, that is castrated cocks . . . pheasants,
partridges and doves'. My italics. The 'excuse' is made:

> Abstinetne ab omni carne? Non, sed a quadrupedibus tantum.
> Comeditne volatilia pennata? Non, sed si fuerint deplumata et cocta
> tunc vescitur ipsis, quia oriuntur ab aquis.

> Does he abstain from all meat? No, only from quadrupeds. Does he
> eat winged fowl? No, but if they have been plucked and cooked, then
> he eats them because they come from the water);

MO 20,897 ('Le perdis et la pulletrie').

13. Ed. Bennett and Smithers, pp. 141–2, 102–4, 107–10.

14. See 'Nuper ductu serio' *Map Poems*, pp. 248–9, 189–92; Gilles li Muisis,
I pp. 18, 146, 148, 151, 176; *MO* 20,865–6 (where a reference to 'la crasse
pance' is followed by the mention of 'pelliçouns', thus giving us an idea of
what an easy-living monk would like) and 7927. Note also that Gilles li
Muisis associates gluttony especially with monastic officers, such as
Chaucer's Monk was (I, p. 161); the *Lamentations* of Matheolus, which were
only translated into French after Gilles wrote, had already described the
abbot who retires to his room to feast alone (p. 279, Lat. 4523ff., Fr.
393ff. For monks in general, see *ibid.* p. 278, Lat. 4497ff., Fr. 341ff.).

15. *PSE* p. 330, 151–62. For proverbs on monastic gluttony, see Walther,
Proverbia Sententiaeque 19,506–7. For monastic gluttony as a feature of
comic anecdote, see Nos LI and LIX in *Latin Stories*. For historical evidence
of this failing, see D. Knowles, *The Religious Orders in England*, pp. 100,
105, 107.

16. N.B. Knowles's remark that 'the fact that one of the *dubia* to be put to
Rome *ca.* 1275 concerned the lawfulness of eating the flesh of birds
suggests that this was not currently considered to be a breach of the Rule'
(*Religious Orders*, p. 20).

17. The comparisons appear to be deliberately chosen for this portrait; they
are not commonplace. 'Not worth a hen' is found elsewhere in Chaucer

(but not before him), but the reference to a 'pulled hen' (according to *OED*, chicken in a rich white sauce) is only here, and after Chaucer. The comparison with an oyster is found only here. (See *OED*, *MED*, and *Chaucer Concordance*.)

18. For the bald head I have found no parallel. The gleaming eyes may, as McPeek suggested with reference to the friar (*Speculum* 26 (1951), 334), derive from such a description as that of the abbot terrifying his assembled monks with his 'eyes rolling to and fro like a wandering planet' ('oculos huc illuc devagantes quasi planeta erratiens'), in the *Magister Golyas de quodam abbate* (*Map Poems*, p. xli).

19. SS 2089–90. See also 2137–8, 2228, 2259, which refer to the luxurious clothing of different monastic orders. Walter of Châtillon inverts the topic and asks who now imitates the camel-hair garments and simple food of John the Baptist (No v v. 15). The feature is so firmly linked with monks that even though in the *De Nugis Curialium* Walter Map is attacking Cistercian miserliness, he still hints at a forbidden diet and a plurality of tunics (dist. I, cap. XXXIII, p. 37, 14–20, and cap. XXV, p. 44, 20). See also 'Dum Saturno conjuge', *Map Poems*, p. 241, 137–8, p. 242, 148.

20. 'Nuper ductu serio', *Map Poems*, p. 244, 37–8. See also the opening of the attack (pp. 244–5, 17–24) where Zoilus comments on the fine tunic visible beneath Maurus' robe.

21. 20,866–8. 'Mole leine' is also used as an example of luxury: see 5312–16.
    Gilles li Muisis frequently complains of monastic luxuries in dress, and is occasionally quite specific in describing the new 'curieuses viestures':

> Viestirs vieus est buriaus, noble viestirs brunette...
> Tissus, tasces d'argent noblement clawetées,
> Doivent yestre de nos moines portées? (I pp. 203–4)

The old robe was frieze, burnet is a luxury dress. Woven cloths, purses with locks – should our monks wear such things?
(See also I pp. 146, 147, 150, 152, 170.)

22. See, however, 'La Vie du Monde', Rutebeuf (I p. 397, 69–70) which complains that the wealth of the Church is being spent 'en joiaux et en vair et en gris'.

23. *Magister Golyas de quodam abbate*, *Map Poems*, p. xli.

24. p. 74 CXXXIX 6ff. The whole passage goes from p. 71 CXXXIII to p. 75 CXLI.
    Cf. the thirteenth-century Latin criticism of an abbot quoted by Bowden (*Commentary*, p. 114 and n. 30): 'He wore boots so smoothly stretched without crease, it was as if he had been born with them' ('Ocreas habebat in cruribus quasi innatae essent sine plica porrectas'). Since the Monk's boots are supple, we may assume they are also tight; supple leather would follow the ankle more closely. But it is not important to prove this, only

to show that footwear was one of the items traditionally 'read' as an indication of monastic strictness or laxity. See also the chapter on the Prioress, and the Wife of Bath. Fine shoes are also provided for in the Order of Fair-Ease. Although 'well-fitting shoes and leg coverings' together with 'becoming robes' and 'fat, gently ambling palfreys' ('Soudlers & chauses bien seantz'; 'robes bien avenauntz'; 'gros palefrois bien amblantz') are there associated with Hospitallers, who are not monks but knights, the inclusion of the knightly orders in the list of those that furnish rules for the Order of Fair-Ease may well mean that the features were readily attributed to monks also. In particular it is tempting to see in Chaucer's line – 'His bootes souple, his hors in greet estaat' – an echo of this poem in which the line on the fine shoes is immediately followed by the reference to 'gros palefrois' (ed. Aspin, p. 134, 73–5).

25. *PSE* p. 330, 145–50.

26. 'Du Mercier' (Inc: 'Moult a çi bele compagnie'), ed. F. W. Fairholt, *Satirical Songs and Poems on Costume*, p. 11. Fairholt ascribes the poem to the thirteenth century.

27. 'Purfil', fur trimming, is a favourite sign of vanity in Langland (though not specifically associated with monks): see *PPl* IV 116 and V 26.

28. I pp. 157–9.

   The *Lamentations* of Matheolus also mention riding 'fat horses' among reproaches of clerical luxury (p. 176, 618ff., Lat. 2571ff.), and Thomas Wimbledon complains of clerical spending on 'fatte palfreies . . . houndes . . . hawkes' (*Medieval Studies* 28 (1966), p. 182).

   Fine horses are also included in the 'ideal' monastic orders of Burnellus the Ass (*SS* 2057ff.) and of Fair-Ease ('L'Ordre de Bel Ayse', ed. Aspin, p. 134, 75), although they are derived from the knightly orders of the Templars and Hospitallers, where they are more appropriate.

29. E.g., *SS* 2789ff.; *PPl* IV 124–5 (prelate): 'Totum regit saeculum', *Map Poems*, p. 232, 122–3 (rector): *VC* III 1487ff.; *Roman de Carité*, p. 42, st. LXXVIII 10ff.; Matheolus' *Lamentations*, p. 174, Fr. 541; *MO* 20,314–16; 'The Simonie', *PSE* p. 327, 73–7; *PPl* V 422–6 (parson): the thirteenth to fourteenth-century poem 'In vere virencia' (ed. Dronke, *Medieval Latin and the Rise of European Love-Lyric* (Oxford, 1968), II, pp. 400ff.); *Handlyng Synne*, p. 108, 3085ff. (clerk).

   For sermon uses of the topic, see Owst, *Lit. and Pulp.*, pp. 260, 264, 270, 279.

   For historical evidence on hunting monks and the keeping of hawks and hounds, see Knowles, *Religious Orders*, pp. 88, 100, 102, 103, 108.

   Gilles li Muisis's treatment of hunting deserves special mention. In an account of the customs of St Martin – that is, in describing his own experiences – he mentions that it was a custom for the prior,

   si li plaisoit, qu'il avoit se quinsaine pour chevaucher ou aler en riviere et esbannyer là il li plaisoit, et on li livroit chevaus et son despense. (1 p. 132)

if he wanted, he should have a fortnight to ride out or go hunting by the water and enjoy himself where he wanted, and he was given horses and his expenses.

Gilles does not criticise this practice; it is just part of 'the good old days'. But when he is writing moral satire, he criticises the abbot who loves to ride about (1 p. 153), and warns that the cellarer must not have 'brakes, ne faukenier' (1 p. 165). He also complains that livings are not awarded to 'les boins clers' but to

> les gentieus gens qui vont cachier à bisses;
> Si laiscent les moustiers et quèrent leurs delisces. (1 p. 107)

the fine ones who go hunting does – leaving their monasteries and seeking their pleasures.

This inconsistency colours much of his satire; he laments the decay of the monasteries, not as centres of ascetic life, but as 'great houses' with large incomes.

30. 'In vere virencia', ed. Dronke, *Medieval Latin*, II p. 401, 30; *VC* III 1495–6; *PPl* v 422–6.

31. See Hoffman, *Ovid and the Canterbury Tales*, pp. 32–3, and P. F. Baum 'Chaucer's Puns', *PMLA* 71 (1956), 242 and 243. The Host assumes that the Monk is a man of sexual prowess (VII 1945 [B² 3135]).

32. For the general treatment of the lechery of monks, see *CB* 1 No 39 v. 7, 5–8; *De Nugis Curialium*, p. 39, dist. 1 cap. XXIII 7–20 (homosexuality) and p. 49, cap. XXV 1–31; *Apocalipsis Goliae*, p. 35 st. 102, 2; 'Sompno et silentio plusquam satis usa', *Map Poems*, pp. 56–7, 49–52; 'Dum Saturno conjuge partus parit Rhea', *ibid.*, p. 241, 139–44; *VC* IV 329–30, 431ff.; 'L'Ordre de Bel Ayse', ed. Aspin, p. 133, 31–52; *MO* 21,050 and 21,145ff.; 'The Land of Cokaygne', ed. Bennett and Smithers, pp. 142–3, 133ff. The monk of the Shipman's Tale is also an 'outridere' who makes the most of his opportunities for sexual satisfaction.

33. See *VC* III 1515ff.; 'The Simonie', *PSE* p. 327, 73–6.

34. Ed. Dronke, *Medieval Latin*, II p. 401, 30.

35. 6583–94 (my italics). In the French, these lines are an interpolation, and appear in only a few MSS. (See Robinson's note.)

36. 20,885–90. For the use of the proper name Robin in contexts of idle amusement and self-indulgence, see *Romaunt of the Rose* (Eng. version) 6337 and 7453; *PPl* VI 75; *Troilus and Criseyde* v 1174.

37. 1 pp. 142, 152, 157–8, 244.

38. 1 pp. 177–8.

39.1 No 39 v. 7 1–2. This comment was proverbial: see Walther (ed.), *Proverbia Sententiaeque Latinitatis Medii Aevi*, Nos 19,504–5.

40. 'Nuper ductu serio', *Map Poems*, p. 245, 69–70.

41.1 pp. 18, 150, 188.

42. 961; see also 967–8. Cf. 2637–8: if 'munera' were abolished, monks would no longer leave their cloisters to work in royal palaces.

43. 'Frequenter cogitans de factis hominum', *Poésies Pop. Lat.*, p. 134.

44.1 pp. 147, 182; II p. 146.

45. For the whole passage see IV 277–304.

46. *PPl* x 292ff. Langland first introduces the topic in Reason's sermon (IV 120–1) and recurs to it in the speech of Ymaginatif (XII 36ff.). Note that most of these passages from Gower and Langland contain the names of saints and church fathers as authority, and cf. the 'placing' of the Monk's contempt for claustration as part of his general contempt for 'seint Maure or seint Beneit' and 'Austyn'.

47. Walter Map had already described the brazen self-defence of Cistercians:

> Si de singulis queras inposturis, racio tam probabiliter est, ut arguere possit evangelium falsi. (*De Nugis Curialium*, dist. 1 cap XXV p. 42, 8–9)

> Inquire into any one of their frauds, and an answer is ready so plausible that he who sees it might accuse the very gospel of error. (trans. James p. 46)

48. p. 78, CXLVI, 1–7.

Guiot de Provins also ironically identifies himself with the more 'genteel' order of regular canons:

> L'ordre des chanoines rigleiz
> poroie je soffrir asseiz,
> qu'il sont molt natement vestu,
> et bien chauciet et bien päu.
> Il sont dou siecle plainnement,
> il vont per tout a lor talant.
> Ic'est l'ordre saint Augustin
> qui fut cortois, per Saint Martin,
> plus que ne fut Sainz Beneois,
> se m'est avis, et plus adrois.
>
> (*Bible*, p. 61, 1641–50; cf. also 1689–94)

I could well tolerate the order of regular canons, for they are very decently clothed, and well shod and well fed. They are wholly of the world, going everywhere they wish. This is the order of St Augustine, who, by St Martin! was more refined than St Benedict, as I think, and shrewder as well.

49. 7921–5. Cf. 21,080–2: 'Chascuns s'en fuyt de la penance . . . Sanz garder la viele observance' – 'Everyone runs away from hardship . . . Without observing the old rule.'

50. 'Cum sint plures ordines', *Map Poems*, p. 45, 21ff. Cf. the passage from Matheolus's *Lamentations* cited above (p. 279, Lat. 4523ff., Fr. 393ff.).

The meaning of the phrase 'keepere of the celle' (a subordinate monastery) is not a precise one, but, taken together with line 167, it clearly enables us to associate the Monk with comments on abbots, priors, etc.

51. 'Noctis crepusculo brumali tempore', *Map Poems*, pp. 188–9, 43–9.

52. I p. 145. Cf. I pp. 18, 149, 185 – all of which refer to the monk's desire to have monastic office, which will make life easier for him.

53. Chaucer's acquaintance with the tradition of proud and self-indulgent monastic officers can be demonstrated from the Host's later address to the Monk:

> It is a gentil pasture ther thow goost.
> Thou art not lyk a penant or a goost:
> Upon my feith, thou art som officer,
> Som worthy sexteyn, or som celerer,
> For by my fader soule, as to my doom,
> Thou art a maister whan thou art at hoom;
> No povre cloysterer, ne no novys,
> But a governour, wily and wys,
> And therwithal of brawnes and of bones,
> A wel farynge persone for the nones.
>
> (VII 1933–42 [B² 3123–32])

Cf. also the monk in the Shipman's Tale (VII 62–7 [B² 1252–7]).

54. Owst, *Lit. and Pulp.*, p. 45.

55. p. 174, Fr. 542.

56. *PSE* p. 329, 121–3. My italics.

57. p. 108, 3085ff.

58. pp. 78–9, CXLVI–CXLVII.

59. Ed. Aspin, p. 132, 16–17.

60. I pp. 158, 165, 178, 198 etc. See also Guiot de Provins, *Bible*, p. 45, 1125, and Rutebeuf, I p. 398, 90.

61. See the examples given in Godefroy and Tobler-Lommatzsch, s.v.

62. There are two characteristics associated with monks which Chaucer omits from his portrait; both are features which are not 'attractive' sins, although it would have been possible for Chaucer to transform them into testimonies of 'professional skill'. For association of monks with greed and avarice see: *SS* 959–61; *CB* I No 11, p. 15, 4; Walter of Châtillon No V p. 76, v. 13, 3–4; *De Nugis Curialium*, dist. I cap. XVI pp. 25–6, cap. XXV p. 41, 19ff., and p. 46, 6–9; 'Sompno et silentio plusquam satis usa', *Map Poems*, p. 55, 29–34; *VC* IV 231–2; *Latin Stories*, p. 30 No XXVIII; 'L'État du

Monde', Rutebeuf, I p. 384, 20ff., and 'La Vie du Monde' *ibid.*, p. 398, 85ff.; *PPl* III 131–2, XV 407–18.

For association of monks with envy and quarrelsomeness see: *SS* 1011–12; *Apocalipsis Goliae*, p. 35 st. 97–9; 'Frequenter cogitans' *Poésies Pop. Lat.*, pp. 133–4; *VC* IV 175–8; *MO* 3194ff., 20,913ff., 21,077ff. Langland (sarcastically?) represents the cloister as free from strife (*PPl* X 302–3, V 169).

63. Speirs comments on the Monk: 'In what sense is he 'a fair prelat'? . . . in the worldly, the corporal, not spiritual sense.' (*Chaucer the Maker*, p. 110). Speirs sees Chaucer's irony as a way of making traditional criticism of the Monk; in my view, the irony operates at the expense of the reader, who is used to judging by worldly standards, as well as at the expense of the Monk.

64. *Bible*, p. 43, 1086–8.

65. The following are the aspects of the friar's stereotype whose use in traditional satire we shall explore: the exercise of persuasive eloquence, which may be a means of deception; a sense of self-importance, usually based on learning; lechery; skill and practice in secular business; fine clothing; the Friar's musical skill; strong mercenary motives; venality in hearing confessions; the mendicant quarrel with the secular clergy; a preference for the company of the rich and powerful.

66. See, for example, 'Totum regit saeculum' which ironically approves of this deception: 'quid culpantur dum sic per figmenta lucrantur?' – 'how are they to be blamed when their tall stories make them so much money?' (*Map Poems*, p. 232, 92); 'Viri fratres, servi Dei': 'Fere omnes sunt trufantes' – 'they are almost all tricksters' (*AH* XXXIII, p. 270, 110); *Sermones nulli parcentes*, which implies the cunning eloquence of the friars in the exhortation: 'sit in ore non vel ita | lingua semper stabilita.' – 'Let your words be yea or nay [after Matt. 5: 37] and your tongue always held in check.' (p. 44, 1069–70); 'Ecce dolet Anglia': 'fratrum dolositas jungit caput caude' – 'the friars' cunning joins head to tail' (*PPS* I, p. 281).

For vernacular literature, see Boccaccio, who, like Langland, often makes friars his 'villains', and will turn aside from a story to describe 'quanta e quale sia la ipocresia de' religiosi' – 'how great and of what kind is the hypocrisy of the religious' (*Decameron*, Second Story, Fourth Day, p. 479, 5). Cf. 'Le Dit des Patenostres': 'Dire souvent le bien aucun font a rebours' – 'some of them often get the truth the wrong way round in their talk' (*NR* I p. 241). For Langland, 'faitour' or 'cheat' is the idea associated with 'frere' (*PPl* II 182, VI 74, C X 208). In Meed's wedding procession, friars are in the 'longe carte' of Liar (II 181–2), and when the procession breaks up, 'Falsenesse' flees to the friars for protection (210). Cf. also V 136–8, XX 237–8. See also *Mum and the Sothsegger*, p. 67, 1402–4.

For late sermon evidence, see Owst, *Lit. and Pulp.*, pp. 95–6 (Hypocrisy is wedded to the friars).

67. *SS* Appendix A, p. 183.

68. *AH* XXXIII, p. 270, 125–6. See the quotation below.

69. IV 1065–8. See also 1069ff., and 1035ff., where Gower describes a representative figure.

70. Eng. version 6210. Fr. version, II 11044. Although the figure of Faus Semblant is not meant exclusively as a representation of friars, he has such clear connections with this branch of the 'fals religious' that Jean de Meun's treatment of him exercised a strong influence on later antimendicant satire. Note that the English version of the *Roman* has 'Abit ne makith neithir monk *ne frere*' (6192) where the French only has 'la robe ne fet pas le moine' (11,028).

71. I p. 257. Cf. I p. 269.

72. I p. 280. See also *Renart le Contrefait*, I p. 5, 359ff.

73. 21,240ff., 21,249ff.

74. 21,233–6; 21,582–5. The biblical reference is to Rom. 16: 17, 18.

75. 'Preste, ne monke, ne ʒit chanoun', *PPS* I p. 268. (This poem is printed by Wright from MS Cotton Cleopatra B II, fol. 26 v, which contains another poem that can be dated 1382 from internal evidence. Thus our poem is probably late fourteenth century. See *PPS* I p. 253.)

76. *PPl* XV 75–7.

77. See *PPl* Prol. 58–61, X 71–5, and the description of the sophistical arguments of the Doctor of Divinity, who is, according to the C text, 'a man ylike a frere' (C XVI 30). Langland also clearly has friars in mind when speaking of the advent of 'fals prophetes fele˙ flatereres and gloseres' who will rule the affairs of kings and earls (XIX 216–17). Cf. also Gilles li Muisis, II p. 124; *Mum and the Sothsegger*, p. 38, 388–9. Chaucer's acquaintance with this tradition is demonstrated by his use of it in the Summoner's Tale (III (D) 1788ff. and 1919ff.).

78. p. 3, 51. The specific reference here is to the Carmelites, but the Ploughman later applies the remark to friars in general (p. 29, 767).

79. 'Daliaunce' could mean 'Serious, edifying or spiritual conversation; communication' according to *MED* (2); in this sense, according to *OED*, it is used in the fifteenth century of Martha and Christ (s.v.1). However, *MED* classes *GP* 211 under the meaning 'Polite, leisurely, intimate conversation or entertainment…chatting, small talk, gossip' (1). What we know of the Friar might suggest yet another meaning – 'Amorous talk or to-do; flirting, coquetry; sexual union' (*MED* 3). Dictionary definitions are, of course, almost bound to ignore the ironic undercurrents of a word, and I think Chaucer is deliberately keeping all three meanings in view. Contrast the following passage from Wycliff, where the *context* firmly excludes any ambiguity from the word: 'freris…chesen to ete

wiþ riche men where þei may fare lustfulliche, & haue heere daliaunce wiþ wymmen for here leccherose lyues' (ed. Matthew, p. 309).

80. For mendicant pride in general, see *SS* Appendix A, p. 184 (a contrast between the Minorites's name and their desire for self-aggrandisement); *RR* II 11,007–9 (Eng. version 6171–3); Gilles li Muisis, I pp. 250ff.; *PPl* XV 75–7; *PPl Crede* 75–6, 250–7, 354–81, 546–84. (Some of these passages include a treatment of pride in learning and intellect.)

For pride in learning, see 'Totum regit saeculum', 90 (*Map Poems*, p. 231) – the line echoes Walter of Châtillon's satire on intellectual pride (No VI, p. 85, v. 13, 1); Gilles li Muisis, I pp. 113, 258–60, II pp. 40, 149.

For the association of 'hiegh clergye' with friars, see, besides the references above and those in n. 101, Gilles li Muisis, I pp. 109, 190, 257–8, 268–9.

81. Matt. 23: 1–10.

82. See D. Wiesen, *St Jerome as a Satirist*, pp. 80–1.

83. See the appendix to 'Missus sum in vineam' (Walter of Châtillon, No VI, p. 87, vv. 18 a–b). These six stanzas are possibly not by Walter; see Strecker's introduction to the poem, p. 81.

84. *Collationes Monasticae*, PL VI, col. xix. Francis is referring to Christ's words in the passage from Matthew.

85. 6917–19. The whole passage (6889–922; Fr. II 11,575–602) is based on Matt. 23.

86. See *VC* IV 813ff.; Gilles li Muisis, I p. 270; *MO* 21,493ff.; *PPl Crede* 497–500, 550–84.

87. III(D) 1300 and 1337.

88. *Ibid.*, 1781 and 2185–8. As with the Monk and the proverb about the fish out of water, Chaucer gains a new 'realistic' slant by making the cleric aware of anti-clerical satire.

89. Equally elusive is the hint given in Chaucer's description of the Friar as 'a ful solempne man' (209). If we follow *OED* in seeing 'of great dignity or importance' (46) as the meaning here, we can derive the suggestion that the Friar is as status-conscious as the rest of his class. But the preceding adjectives, 'wantowne' and 'merye', suggest the meaning 'festive, merry' as another possibility. (This sense is not recognised in *OED*, but is given in the glossaries of the editions of Chaucer of Skeat and Robinson, s.v. The *Chaucer Concordance* shows that Chaucer uses the word and its associates 'solemnity' and 'solemnly' most often in connection with feasts and celebrations. See, for example, IV(E) 1125, I(A) 870, IV(E) 1709, II(B[1]) 691.)

90. 'Chaucer and the Friars', reprinted in Schoeck and Taylor, p. 80. Williams's article shows how Chaucer's portrait is influenced by the traditional anti-mendicant satire originated by William of St Amour's attacks on the friars, and continued by Archbishop FitzRalph of Armagh. While Williams uses much of the same material as this chapter, he is not concerned with the

literary implications of Chaucer's use of anti-mendicant satire, but rather to prove that Chaucer reflects the attitude of the secular clergy, who 'must have dominated the thinking of the upper-class, governmental circles in which Chaucer moved' (p. 81).

On the question of spiritual, as opposed to bodily seduction, it should be noticed how often satire describes the corruption of church and society in sexual images – prostitution, homosexuality, and so on. See Walter of Châtillon, No I p. 7, v. 13, 4, No IV p. 70, v. 27, No VIII p. 102, v. 11, No XIII p. 124, v. 7, and Philip the Chancellor's 'Bulla fulminante' (*AH* XXI p. 126), where the story of Danäe's seduction symbolises pecuniary corruption. This is a range of analogies exploited in the twentieth century by Burroughs' *Naked Lunch*.

91. See, for example, 'Totum regit saeculum', *Map Poems*, p. 231, 83 (sarcastically) 'In them purity flourishes'; Matheolus' *Lamentations*, p. 92, Lat. 1263ff. (Beghines have affairs with friars); *Sermones nulli parcentes*, 1073–80 (friars are exhorted to flee the company of women, but apparently recognising this to be impossible, the author despairingly adds that at least they should refrain from touching them); *SS* Appendix A p. 185 (Minorites wear no breeches so as to be constantly ready for love-making), and p. 187 (the letters 'me' in the Carmelites's name refer to their fornication – 'mechus habetur'); *Decameron*, Seventh Story, Third Day, p. 389, 38 (friars attack lust in others, so that when they give it up, the friars can have the women all to their own use); *Roman de Fauvel*, p. 35, 858–63; 'Preste, ne monke, ne ȝit chanoun', *PPS* I pp. 265–6 (were the author head of a household, no friar would enter unless he were gelded,

> For may he til a woman wynne,
> In priveyté, he wyl not blynne,
> Er he a child put hir withinne,
> And perchaunce two at ones.);

PPl Crede 44, 82–5, 766–7; *Mum and the Sothsegger*, p. 42, 511–12. Chaucer satirises this aspect of the ubiquitous 'lymytour' in the Wife of Bath's Tale (III(D) 865–81).

92. *Decameron* Seventh Story, Third Day, p. 388, 35. For other occasions on which friars' confessions or preaching are described as directed at women, see *MO* 21,301–10 and 21,249–64; *PPl* III 35ff.; *PPl Crede* 48–52, 59–63, 77–9.

93. *VC* IV 835–6, 863–4. 'Titivil' was originally the name of a devil employed to collect words missed or mumbled in divine service, and to carry them off to be registered against the offender. Hence the name was applied to devils in the mystery plays, and thus to scoundrels in general. (P. Harvey, *The Oxford Companion to English Literature*, 4th ed. rev. D. Beagle (Oxford 1967), s.v.)

94. The meaning involved is *OED* 3, 'To behave wantonly or riotously; to take one's pleasure; to play', which can be interpreted more or less innocently according to the context. Most of the early uses quoted by *OED* seem to occur in a sexual context.

95. 'Wantowne' can mean both 'jovial . . . waggish' (*OED* 3*a*) or 'lascivious, unchaste, lewd' (*OED* 2); *OED* assigns the former meaning to this quotation, but the suggestion of the latter cannot be excluded.

96. 'Totum regit saeculum', *Map Poems*, p. 232, 91–6. This view of the friar is connected with the satire on their close association with the great, and the influence over their actions which could be exerted in confession. For this, see, in addition to the references given below in discussion of the venality of mendicant confessions, Gilles li Muisis, I p. 25 and II p. 41; *PPl Crede*, p. 29, 770–4; *Mum and the Sothsegger*, p. 40, 461–5. For historical evidence that Dominicans, at least, were royal confessors, see Knowles, *Religious Orders*, p. 167.

97. *RR* II 11,649–53 (Eng. version 6971–8).

98. See *VC* IV 831–4; *Roman de Fauvel*, pp. 35–6, 879ff.; 'Le Dit des Mais' *NR* I p. 185; *MO* 21,385–96; *PPl Crede*, p. 14, 358.

99. See K. Young, 'A Note on Chaucer's Friar', *MLN* 50 (1935), 83–5.

100. See J. W. Spargo, 'Chaucer's Love-Days', *Speculum* 15 (1940), 36–56.

101. *PPl* V 427–8, X 307, 19–22. The features described in the last passage suggest that Langland is talking about friars, although he does not explicitly name them.

   Wycliff (ed. Matthew, pp. 234 and 242) and Gower (*MO* 23,683ff.) mention love-days in connection with lords and knights. Wycliff also connects them with priests (*ibid.*, p. 172).

102. *PPl* Prol., 64–5.

103. 'Preste, ne monke, ne ȝit chanoun', *PPS* I p. 265.

104. *SS* Appendix A, p. 184. See also p. 185 on the comfort of Franciscan dress.

105. 'Preste, ne monke, ne ȝit chanoun', *PPS* I p. 267.

106. *Decameron*, Seventh Story, Third Day, p. 388, 34.

107. *Ibid.*, Third Story, Seventh Day, p. 219, 12. See also Second Story, Fourth Day, p. 479, 5–7; First Story, Seventh Day, p. 202, 6.

108. *PPl* Prol. 61, xx 57.

109. p. 9, 227–30. My italics. For more description of rich mendicant clothing, see p. 28, 734–41, and p. 21, 550–3. The latter passage elaborates the biblical criticism of the scribes and the Pharisees making broad their phylacteries and enlarging the borders of their garments (Matt. 23), which Boccaccio had already used in the same way (see the quotation on p. 40).

   For further reference to friars' rich clothing, see 'Le Dit des Patenostres', *NR* I p. 241: 'Les grans chaperons ont par villes et par bours' – 'They wear their wide copes in cities and towns'; Gilles li Muisis, I p. 362.

110. Third Story, Seventh Day, p. 217, 7.

111. Ed. Matthew, p. 8. The passage comes from *Of the Leaven of the Pharisees*, which according to Matthew was written *ca.* 1383 (*ibid.*, p. 1).

112. This was suggested to me by Peter Dronke.

113. The expression 'viellatores Dei' comes from a thirteenth-century Latin sermon. For this, and the whole subject of religious 'jongleurs', see Menéndez Pidal, *Poesía Juglaresca y Origenes de las Literaturas Romanicas*, p. 8, n. 3 and pp. 71ff.

114. *SS* Appendix A, p. 183. For other references to the avarice of friars, see *RR* 6963–4:

> We ben the folk, without lesyng,
> That all thing have without havyng.

(Fr. II 11,647–8). This parody of 2 Cor. 6: 10 is repeated by Gilles li Muisis, I p. 201, and Gower, *MO* 21,193–204; see also 21,217–22. See also 'L'État du Monde', Rutebeuf, I p. 384, 40–6; 'Le Dit des Mais', *NR* I pp. 184–5; 'The Simonie', *PSE* p. 331, 165–7; *Winner and Waster*, 161–2; *PPl* Prol. 59.

115. *NR* I p. 241.

116. *RR* II 11,535–6 (Eng. version 6837–8).

117. See *Wakefield Pageants*, ed. Cawley, p. 82, 160–2, where it is applied to the 'prelate' Caiaphas. For the interpretation of the expression, and evidence for its proverbial nature, see E. A. Greenlaw, 'A Note on Chaucer's Prologue', *MLN* 23 (1908), 142–4, and a letter from G. L. Kittredge, *ibid.*, p. 200; also a letter from J. D. Bruce, *MLN* 24 (1919), 118–19.

118. I p. 191. See also I p. 257, and 269: 'Leur pourchac pour leur ordènes vallent une contet' – 'Their earnings are worth an earldom to their orders.' The verbal resemblances between Gilles and Chaucer are probably due to the influence of the *Roman de la Rose* on both, but they serve to demonstrate that Chaucer's Friar belongs to a *literary* tradition.

119. Second Story, Fourth Day, pp. 480–1, 9–10. My italics.

120. *MO* 21,277ff. See also *VC* IV 757–62, and Gilles li Muisis, II p. 148.

121. 'Preste, ne monke, ne ȝit chanoun', *PPS* I p. 266.

122. 'Of thes frer mynours me thenkes moch wonder', *PPS* I p. 270. This poem also comes from MS Cotton Cleopatra B II (fol. 64 v), for the dating of which, see above.

123. *PPl* III 38–40.

124. *Ibid.*, xx 361ff. See also *PPl Crede*, where each friar in turn offers to absolve the narrator from his ignorance of the creed – for a fee – and the Ploughman comments explicitly on this characteristic (468, 634–6, 711–16).

125. 'Viri fratres, servi Dei', *AH* XXXIII p. 270, 117–18.

126. 'Preste, ne monke, ne ȝit chanoun', *PPS* I p. 267.

127. *PPl* V 141–5. See also 418 (Sloth sleeps until service is over and then goes to the friars for confession). Langland introduces the topic into his first mention of the friars (Prol. 66–7).

For other references to the conflict of interest, see Matheolus' *Lamentations*, p. 92, Lat. 1281ff. (not in French); *VC* IV 889–936; Gilles li Muisis, I p. 191; *MO* 21,469ff.; *Mum and the Sothsegger*, p. 39, 408–14. The friar in the Summoner's Tale claims to be more skilled in confession than a secular cleric (III(D) 1816–18).

128. Ed. Aspin, p. 137, 211–18.

129. *RR* II 12,309–21 (Eng. version 7677ff.). See also 11,557–68 (Eng. version 6869ff.).

130. There is, of course, a subtler irony of situation here, since the 'moralist' who discovers with horror that Faus Semblant does not fear God (II 11,497–8, Eng. version 6799–800) is the God of Love. Jean de Meun's irony is not achieved in the same way that Chaucer's is, but it has a complexity I am aware of having to ignore in concentrating on Chaucer.

131. See *SS* Appendix A pp. 183, 186, 187; *RR* II 11,013–16, 11,203–6, 11,527–30, 11,693–729; 'Le Dit des Mais' *NR* I pp. 184–5; *Inferno*, Canto XXVII 92–3; *Decameron* Third Story, Seventh Day, p. 218, 10–11; *Winner and Waster*, 175; *PPl* C X 207–8; *PPS* I pp. 264, 270; *PPl Crede* 53–4, 72–3, 92–3, 221–6, 762–5. (Some of these references are primarily to the corpulence which reveals gluttony.)

Chaucer gives a satiric treatment of mendicant gluttony in the Summoner's Tale (III(D) 1838–50).

132. *SS* Appendix A, p. 188.

133. 'Viri fratres, servi Dei', *AH* XXXIII p. 270, 119–32. See also 'Totum regit saeculum', *Map Poems*, p. 231, 87: 'pauperes et exules hos adhaerent tuti' – 'the poor and exiled cling to them with safety' (sarcastically meant), and p. 232, 94: 'divitis familiam totam gubernabit' – 'he will rule the whole family of the rich man'; *SS* Appendix A p. 184 (Burnellus, a dumb animal, is tempted to become a friar because they are mute in face of the sins of the rich); *PPl* XI 54–7, XV 78–9, 82–6, XX 231–4 (cf. XV 335–6, of all religious): *PPl Crede* 364–9, 770–4; *Mum and the Sothsegger*, p. 38, 386, p. 41, 474ff.

134. See *VC* IV 735–40; *RR* II 11,211–30; 'La Vie du Monde' Rutebeuf, I p. 398, 103–4; 'Le Dit des Patenostres', *NR* I p. 241; *MO* 21,469–76; 'The Simonie', *PSE* pp. 331–2, 181–92; *PPl* XI 63ff., XIII 7–10; *PPl Crede* 469–70.

135. 'Le Dit des Mais', *NR* I p. 185 (see also ff.). See also *RR*, where Faus Semblant boasts of living with those who

> gon and gadren gret pitaunces,
> And purchace hem the acqueyntaunces
> Of men that myghty lyf may leden;
> And feyne hem pore, and hemsilf feden
> With gode morcels delicious,
> And drinken good wyn precious.

(6175–80; Fr. II 11,011ff.). See also *MO* 21,356–60, a description of 'Ipocresie', mollified by a good dinner, excusing the sins of his hosts.

136. Ed. Aspin, pp. 136–7, 178–92.

137. *RR* II 11,542–6 (Eng. version, which does not use the same vocabulary, 6852–7).

138. The 'moral' sense of the word 'worthy' is *OED* 2: 'Distinguished by good qualities, entitled to honour or respect on this account; estimable.' Sense 3 shows how 'estimable' shades into merely 'respectable': 'Holding a prominent place in the community; of rank or standing.'

139. Only two features commonly mentioned in connection with friars are omitted by Chaucer. The first is their quarrelsomeness, a trait also omitted from the Monk's portrait. The Friar later gives dramatic proof of this characteristic in his quarrel with the Summoner, and the Summoner's Tale provides a good example of an angry friar (III(D) 2152–69). For this feature, see 'Totum regit saeculum', *Map Poems*, p. 231, 88 (sarcastic); *SS* Appendix A, p. 187; *VC* IV 1037–8; *PPl* V 136ff.; *PPl Crede* 525–7, 631–3, 645–9.

The splendour of friars' buildings is also traditionally satirised. This topic also appears in the Summoner's Tale, where the friar claims that he only wants the dying man's money 'for to buylden cristes owene chirche' (III(D) 1977). See also *VC* IV 1149–52; *RR* II 11,285–6, 11,526, 11,675–7; Gilles li Muisis, I p. 252; *MO* 21,403–4; *Winner and Waster*, 299; *PPl* V 48–50; 'Of thes frer mynours me thinkes moch wonder', *PPS* I p. 270; *PPl Crede* 118–20, 160ff.

For estimation of the historical accuracy of these comments, see Knowles, *Religious Orders*, pp. 142 and 187, where it is suggested that although Franciscan buildings were probably unassuming until at least 1270, thereafter there is construction of large convents and churches without a comparable increase in the numbers of friars.

The influence of Gower and Langland on this portrait can be discerned in so apparently trivial a detail as the fact that the Friar is a 'limitour', or beggar within assigned limits. Both Gower and Langland mention 'limitoures' with disgust (*MO* 21,654–8; *PPl* V 138, XX 344). For a discussion of the meaning of the word 'limitour', see an article by A. Williams in *SP* 57 (1960), 463–78.

140. The most apparently 'individualising' detail of Chaucer's Friar – his being given the name of Huberd (269) – may have character connotations which make it appropriate for his estate. E. Reiss tries to establish an association between the 'man in the moon', the name Huberd, and friars (*JEGP* 62 (1963), 481–5) – an attempt which I find less convincing than Muscatine's article relating the name to 'Hubert l'escoufle', the kite who hears the confession of Renart the fox (*MLN* 70 (1955), 169–72).

141. Later I shall develop the theme of the 'double standards' discernible in the

Prologue, but I should say at once that I am not trying to prove that Chaucer was a sort of fourteenth-century anarchist; it makes all the difference that the tone of the *Prologue* is comic, not cynical or tragic. The tensions between different versions of an ideal, or between different ideals operating within the same social context, are 'accepted' – perhaps because Chaucer assumed them to be an inevitable consequence of human fallibility – in the adoption of the comic mode to describe them. And Chaucer is not prepared to abandon or diminish the appeal of the traditional medieval ideals, as we shall see in the next chapter.

CHAPTER 3

1. D. S. Brewer, *Chaucer*, p. 135. For medieval expression of this ideology, see, for example, *Chessbook* col. 395–6:

    Sic enim sunt artes disposite, ut nulle sibi sufficiant, sed sua aliis communicando prevaleant.

    For skills are distributed in such a way that they are not sufficient for themselves, but thrive by passing on their own commodities to others.

2. Satirists make little alteration in their treatment of the different ranks of the clergy; in this chapter, therefore, material taken from discussion of the duties and failings of bishops will sometimes be used alongside that drawn from the treatment of parish priests.

3. From John 10: 1–16.

4. See also 496, 504, 506, 507ff.

5. 2681–2; see also 2673–708 as a whole.

6. *PPS* I pp. 279–80. For other examples of this traditional metaphor in discussions of the clergy's role, see Walter of Châtillon, No I, p. 5, v. 8; 'Frequenter cogitans', *Poésies Pop. Lat.*, p. 129; 'Cum declinent homines'; *Map Poems*, p. 166, 105; *CB* I No 36, p. 58, v. 3a; *ibid.*, No 39, p. 62, v. I, 5–6; *ibid.*, No 43 p. 84, v. 3; *ibid.*, No 91, v. 8; *Apocalipsis Goliae*, p. 22, vv. 34, 36; 'Viri venerabiles', Hauréau, *NE* VI pp. 14–15, *passim*; 'A legis doctoribus', *Map Poems*, p. 43, 21–2; 'Cum sint plures ordines', *ibid.*, p. 44, 17–20; *VC* III 20, 81–2, 175ff.; Guiot de Provins, *Bible*, p. 35, 813ff.; *Roman de Carité*, p. 35 LXIV–LXV, p. 37 LXVIII; 'La Vie du Monde', Rutebeuf, I p. 397, 60; *Roman de Fauvel*, p. 25, 609ff., p. 29, 695ff.; 'Le Dit des Mais' *NR* I p. 183; Gilles li Muisis, I pp. 344–5, 348, 349, 374, 377; Matheolus' *Lamentations*, p. 276, 288ff. (Lat. 4455ff.); *MO* 19,484ff.; *Handlyng Synne*, p. 160, 4819ff., p. 337, 10,881ff. For sermon references, see Owst, *Lit. and Pulp.*, pp. 241, 244, etc.

7. 'Cum sint plures ordines', *Map Poems*, p. 44, 17–20.

8. p. 65 CXXII 1–4. For conventional uses of the image of sickness, see pp. 63–8, *passim*.

Wycliff also gives a 'realistic' turn to the image, (*De Officio Pastorali*, ed. Matthew, p. 439):

> þe þridde offiss þat falliþ to persouns is to greese þer scabbid sheep & to telle hem medicyn of goddis lawe wherby þat þey may be hool; & ʒif þes herdis faylen in þes þre, þey ben hirid hynes or woluys.

9. I p. 108. Is there also a pun on sheep noises in *a* and *b*?

Chaucer's description of how his 'lerned' Parson stays at home and teaches his parishioners inverts such complaints about the ignorance of the substitutes appointed by absentee parsons.

10. p. 31 v. 76:

> Ecce vicario persona primitus
> committit animas et iura spiritus
> sibique retinet causas et reditus,
> quas audax devorat et inperterritus.

See, the parson hands over to the vicar the souls and spiritual rights, retaining for himself the properties and rents, which, bold and undaunted, he devours.

11. *Lamentations*, p. 174, 535ff. (Lat. 2539ff.); *VC* III 1353-4; *MO* 20,245ff.

12. *PPl* Prol. 83-6. Later he refers to the secular posts taken on by the clergy (92-6). Cf. *Mum and the Sothsegger*, p. 66, 1353-7 – also a reference to the attraction of the courts. For sermons, see Owst, *Lit. and Pulp.*, pp. 247, 261, 271.

13. *Map Poems*, p. 233, 125-6.

14. For treatment of clerical avarice and simony, see Walter of Châtillon, No I pp. 5-6, vv. 8-9; *ibid.*, No IV especially pp. 64-8, vv. 6-21; *ibid.*, No VIII especially pp. 101-2, vv. 6-9; *ibid.*, No XVI p. 144 v. 23, 2; No XVII p. 151 v. 6, 10; *SS* 104-5; 'Cum declinent homines', *Map Poems*, p. 166, 109-24; *CB* I No 33, p. 55, v. 3, 4-7; *ibid.*, No 91, v. 8; *Apocalipsis Goliae*, p. 29 v. 65; 'Viri venerabiles', Hauréau, *NE* VI p. 15; 'Rumor novus', *Map Poems*, p. 180, 3: 'Hora nona sabbati' *NE* 32, I, p. 292; *Sermones nulli parcentes*, p. 27, 409-11; *VC* III almost *passim*; 'Ecce dolet Anglia' *PPS* I p. 280, 37-40; Étienne de Fougères, *Livre des Manières*, p. 122, 213ff.; Guiot de Provins, *Bible*, p. 39, 960ff.; *Roman de Carité*, p. 46 LXXV 1-7; *Roman de Fauvel*, p. 29, 695ff.; 'Le Dit des Patenostres' *NR* I p. 240: Matheolus' *Lamentations*, pp. 177-8, 626ff. (Lat. 2574ff.); *MO* 20,281-2; *PPl* Prol. 86, I 188-9, XI 274-7, XIII 11, XV 122-7, XX 219. For sermon references see Owst, *Lit. and Pulp.*, pp. 241, 244, 245, 248, 258, 276-7. The wealth of material is due to the obsession of medieval satirists with financial corruption, which itself seems due to the difficulties, both ideological and practical, caused by the shift to a monetary economy. See J. A. Yunck, *The Lineage of Lady Meed: the development of medieval venality satire* (Notre Dame, Indiana, 1963).

15. 'The Simonie', *PSE* p. 327, 79, 85.
16. Ed. Matthew, pp. 145 and 245. See also pp. 36, 150, 160, 453.
17. *Handlyng Synne*, p. 337, 10,881–4.
18. Earlier sermon writers had, however, described at length how diligent priests were in exacting their tithes; see Owst, *Lit. and Pulp.*, pp. 249, 253 (n. 6), 260–1. See also in the fifteenth century, Myrc's *Instructions* (p. 11, 356ff.):

> I holde hyt but an ydul þynge
> To speke myche of teythynge,
> For þaȝ a preste be but a fonne,
> Aske hys teyþynge wel he conne.

See also *Mum and the Sothsegger*, p. 45, 597ff.

19. *CB* I No 33 p. 55, v. 3.
20. *Map Poems*, p. 232, 118.
21. *Ibid.*, p. 49, 32, p. 51, 122–5. (The last verse is not in the *Carmina Burana* MS, but ends the poem in the fourteenth-century English MS, BM Cotton Vespasian A xix.) For other references to the priest's duty to care for the poor (sometimes conveyed through complaints that he is not performing it), see Walter of Châtillon, No viii p. 101, v. 5, 1, p. 102, v. 12, 2; *SS* 1738–9; *CB* I No 36 p. 58, v. 26, 3–4; 'Viri fratres, servi Dei' *AH* xxxiii p. 269, 73–4; *VC* iii 1491–2, 1499–504; Étienne de Fougères, *Livre des Manières*, p. 125, 349ff.; *Roman de Carité*, p. 30 lvi 1–3; Gilles li Muisis, i p. 371; Matheolus' *Lamentations*, p. 175, 553–4 (Lat. 2545–6), p. 179, 706 (Lat. 2611); *MO* 19,352–3; *PPl* Prol. 90, iv 119. See also a 'Punctuation Poem' in *Secular Lyrics* ed. Robbins, No 110, p. 101, which, read uncharitably, says 'Wher nede is gevyng neyther rewarde ne ffee | . . . Thus lyve prestys parde.'
22. My italics. The simple phrase 'Upon his feet' assumes a wealth of meaning if read as an inversion of the satire on the fine horses of the clergy; see, for example, 'Hora nona sabbati', *NE* 32, 1, p. 293, and Langland's reference to 'bisschopes baiardes', *PPl* iv 124.
23. *Map Poems*, p. 232, 119.
24. *NR* I p. 240. I have tried to indicate in my translation the *double entendre* in 'crevace', whose secondary meaning is 'con' (see Tobler–Lommatzsch, s.v.).
25. *CB* I No 33, p. 55 v. 3, 3.
26. Hauréau, *NE* vi p. 15.
27. *VC* iii 1153–4. For similar references to this dual role of the clergy, see 'Nulli beneficium' *CB* I No 36, p. 58 v. 2*b*, 9–10; Étienne de Fougères, *Livre des Manières*, p. 127 465–8; *Roman de Carité*, p. 30 lvi 4–5.
28. *Handlyng Synne*, p. 338, 10,907–8.
29. See 'Frequenter cogitans' *Poésies Pop. Lat.*, pp. 129–30; 'Tempus acceptabile' *AH* xxxiii p. 293, v. 13, 1–4; *VC* iii 189–92, 1149–50; Étienne de Fougères,

Livre des Manières, p. 124, 325ff.; 'La Vie du Monde', Rutebeuf, I p. 397, 57; Gilles li Muisis, I pp. 108, 358; *MO* 19,085–6, 19,093–8, 19,468–71; *Handlyng Synne*, p. 160, 4819ff.; *Mum and the Sothsegger*, p. 49, 746ff.

30. 2 Tim. 4: 2. See also Gilles li Muisis, I p. 358, and Thomas Wimbledon's sermon of 1388 (*Medieval Studies*, 28 (1966), 180), where this text is quoted in connection with priests.

31. *MO* 19,097; see also 19,085ff., 19,468–71. For sermon references to clerical toleration of the sins of the rich, see Owst, *Lit. and Pulp.*, pp. 246, 253, 261, 274–5. See also the Punctuation Poem, *Secular Lyrics*, ed. Robbins, No 110, p. 101: 'Who is most riche · with them þey wyl be sewer'.

32. *CB* I No 33 p. 54 v. 2, 1–3.

33. Hauréau, *NE* VI p. 15. A shorter list appears in Flacius Illyricus's version of 'Tempus acceptabile': priests should be 'merciful, generous, humble, worthy' – 'pios, largos, humiles, dignos'. (*Map Poems*, p. 54, 65–8. This stanza is not in the version printed in *AH* XXXIII pp. 292ff.) See also *Mum and the Sothsegger*, p. 48, 702ff., whose language seems to be influenced by both Chaucer and Langland:

> For prestz been not perillous but pacient of þaire werkes,
> And eeke þe plantz of pees and ful of pitie euer,
> And chief of al charite y-chose a-fore other.

(Cf. *PPl* I 150.)

34. Cf. 2 Tim. 2: 24–5, 4: 5; Tit. 2: 12; Pet. 3: 8–9, 5: 8.

35. Cf. also 2 Cor. 8: 9; Rev. 2: 9.

36. No VIII p. 101, v. 4. The last line is based on Ps. 66: 5.

37. No XVII p. 150 v. 4, 4–8.

38. For the clergy's example as a light to the laity, see *VC* III 1071–80; 'Heu! quia per crebras', Gower, p. 355, 16–21; Gilles li Muisis, I p. 343. For the clergy as a mirror to the laity, see *SS* 2709–10; *Roman de Carité*, p. 33 IX; *Roman de Fauvel*, p. 28, 670–1.

39. The image of the blind leading the blind comes from Matt. 15: 14; for its use see *VC* III 1064; *Roman de Fauvel*, p. 33, 824; Myrc's *Instructions*, p. 1, 1–6. For 'sicut populus, sic sacerdos', see Hosea, 4: 9, and *PPl* XV, between 115 and 116. Walter of Châtillon uses both quotations in one line (No IV p. 70 v. 27, 2).

40. 'Defluit in subditos vitiorum macula' – 'The stain of their vices flows into their inferiors' (No IV p. 64 v. 5, 4).

41. p. 34 LXII 10, and p. 38 LXXI 9–11. See G. L. Kittredge, 'Chaucer and the *Roman de Carité*', *MLN* 12 (1897), col. 113–15. Kittredge suggests the origin of the gold image in Gregory's *Pastoral Care*, and gives further references to Hrabanus Maurus, Alanus de Insulis, and others. Kittredge notes that the similes occur in the same order in Chaucer and the *Roman*, but although he says it is not impossible for Chaucer to have known the *Roman*, he prefers

to suppose a common source for both. This seems to me to be complicating matters unnecessarily; as Flügel notes, Chaucer's acquaintance with the *Roman* is not to be established on a single passage (*Anglia*, 26 (1901), 500), but in the course of this study other striking parallels with the *Roman* are noted. (See, for example, the chapter on the Monk.)

42. Owst, *Lit. and Pulp.*, p. 241. For other sermon references, see *ibid.*, pp. 267, 271, 273–4. For estates treatments, besides those given above, see *SS* 1735ff.; 'Frequenter cogitans' *Poésies Pop. Lat.*, p. 133; 'Quam sit lata scelerum' *PSE* p. 33; 'Viri fratres, servi Dei' *AH* xxxiii p. 269, 75–8; *VC* iii 1751–2, 1893–4; Guiot de Provins, *Bible*, p. 35, 830; *Roman de Carité*, p. 32 lviiiff. (a whole series of images on this theme); 'Mult est diables curteis', ed. Aspin, p. 119, 17–18; Gilles li Muisis, i pp. 83, 108, 110, 347, 367, 369, 370, 372, 384, ii p. 8; *MO* 19,069ff., 19,339ff., 20,447ff., 20,629ff., 20,746; *PPl* xv 90ff., 385, 426–9.

43. See *SS* 2667–8; *CB* i No 33, p. 55, v. 6; *VC* iii 209–18; Étienne de Fougères, *Livre des Manières*, p. 125, lxxxiv; *Roman de Carité*, p. 32 lviii 9; Gilles li Muisis, i pp. 350, 381, ii p. 15; *MO* 19,350–1, 21,697–708; *PPl* iv 122, v 42–5, 266–71, xiii 115–17.

The idea is biblical; see Matt. 4: 23 and 5: 19. It can of course be applied to any class in authority: see *SS* 2333–4 (on secular canons); 'Viri fratres, servi Dei' *AH* xxxiii p. 270 113–14 (on friars); *Chessbook*, col. 285–6 (on knights); *Sermones nulli parcentes*, p. 44, 1045–56; *Decameron* Seventh Story, Third Day, p. 390, 43; *RR* ii 11,581–8; *PPl* xiii 79 (all on friars); *Mum and the Sothsegger*, p. 78, 1747–8 (on bishops). The topic was not, therefore, exclusively linked with priests, but its occurrence in any treatment of priests was well-nigh inevitable.

44. 'Viri venerabiles, sacerdotes Dei', Hauréau, *NE* vi p. 14.

45. *PPl* xv 106–8. See also Gower's similar linking of the two ideas; *VC* iii 689–90, 1037–40; *MO* 19,069–80.

46. See 'Totum regit saeculum', *Map Poems*, p. 232, 117–18; 'Viri venerabiles', Hauréau, *NE* vi p. 14 ('gentium doctores' – 'teachers of the people') and p. 15 ('subditos docentes' – 'teaching their inferiors'); 'Ecce dolet Anglia' *PPS* i p. 279; Étienne de Fougères, *Livre des Manières*, p. 124, 321ff., p. 125, 329ff.; Gilles li Muisis, i pp. 108, 380; Matheolus' *Lamentations*, p. 179, 705 (Lat. 2611), p. 180, 758ff. (Lat. 2631ff.).

47. The only example I have found is Gilles li Muisis, i p. 368.

48. 'Tempus acceptabile' *AH* xxxiii p. 293, v. 14, 1–4. Cf. for the links between learning and teaching, *Roman de Fauvel*, p. 33, 808–9; Gilles li Muisis, i pp. 370–1.

49. E.g., 'The Simonie' *PSE* p. 328, 97–108.

50. *PPl* v 422–8. See also Owst, *Lit. and Pulp.*, pp. 269, 279, and Gower's comments on the futility of being a 'lerned man' if one does not teach or set a good example:

Cil q'ad science et point ne cure
De nous precher, et en ordure
Sa vie meine nequedent,
Au fume que noz oils oscure
Resemble, qant nous fait lesure
De son malvois essamplement. (*MO* 21,733–8)

He who is learned and makes no effort to preach to us, and at the same time leads his life in filth, is like the smoke that blurs our vision, when he harms us by his bad example.

On the failure of the clergy to teach as they ought, see *VC* III 1067–9, 1491.

51. *NE* 32, 1, p. 290.
52. Two satiric topics do not seem to find an echo in Chaucer's portrait: the lechery of the clergy, and their indulgence in fine food, dress, houses, and so on. Chaucer's statement that the Parson 'koude in litel thyng have suffisaunce' may be the briefest of allusions to the description of clerical luxury; cf. the Summoner's Tale (III (D) 1843) where the friar's idea of a 'hoomly suffisaunce' is ironically different from the Parson's.

For clerical luxury, or injunctions to abstemiousness, see *SS* 2717–44; *Apocalipsis Goliae*, p. 29, vv. 66–7, p. 31, vv. 78–9; 'Totum regit saeculum', *Map Poems*, p. 233, 137–40; 'Hora nona sabbati' *NE* 32, 1, p. 294; *Sermones nulli parcentes*, p. 27, 413; *VC* III 85ff., 1329; 'Ecce dolet Anglia' *PPS* I p. 280, 42; 'Heu!quia per crebras', Gower, p. 355, 19–20; Étienne de Fougéres, *Livre des Manières*, p. 122, 197–200, p. 125, 349–52; Guiot de Provins, *Bible*, p. 40, 979ff.; Gilles li Muisis, I pp. 110, 371, 376; Matheolus' *Lamentations*, p. 174, 540ff. (Lat. 2541ff.); 'Nous lisons une istoire', ed. Montaiglon and Raynaud, II p. 264; *MO* 20,449ff., 20,515ff., 20,653ff.; *PPl* xv 101, 116–21, xx 217–22; Myrc's *Instructions*, pp. 2ff. Also see Owst, *Lit and Pulp.*, pp. 242–83, almost *passim*.

For clerical lechery, adultery, concubinage, etc., see Walter of Châtillon, No v p. 77, v. 17; *ibid.*, No VIII p. 102, vv. 10–11; *SS* 1260–1; 'Cum declinent homines', *Map Poems*, p. 166, 107–8; 'Quam sit lata scelerum' *PSE* p. 33; *Apocalipsis Goliae.* p. 29, vv. 69–72; 'Cum sint plures ordines', *Map Poems*, pp. 48ff. (almost *passim*); 'Hora nona sabbati' *NE* 32, 1, pp. 295ff; 'Prisciani regula', *Map Poems*, pp. 171ff. (almost *passim*); 'Clerus et presbyteri', *ibid.*, pp. 174ff. (almost *passim*); *Sermones nulli parcentes*, p. 28, 447–56; *VC* III 89–96, 209–14, 1330, 1403ff., 1515, etc.; 'Heu! quia per crebras', Gower, p. 355, 19; *Latin Stories*, p. 37; Étienne de Fougères, *Livre des Manières*, p. 122, 193, 201ff.; *RR* II 11,704; Gilles li Muisis, I p. 372; Matheolus' *Lamentations*, p. 174, 539 (Lat. 2541); *MO* 20,329ff., 20,458ff., 20,485ff., 20,713ff.; *Handlyng Synne*, p. 252, 7935–6;

'The Simonie' *PSE* p. 327, 70, 82, 91–3; *PPl* III 148–51, XV 129–30. For sermons, see Owst, *Lit and Pulp.*, pp. 244ff.

53. 'Two Notes on *Piers Plowman*: II. Chaucer's Debt to Langland', *Medium Aevum*, 4 (1935), 89–94. For discussion of Chaucer's more general indebtedness to Langland, see my Appendix B.

Coghill points out that the similarities between the two ploughmen have a special importance, since other resemblances between the two authors may be due to independent observation of 'fraudulent pardoners, friars, chantry-seeking priests and the like' ('Two Notes', pp. 90–1), whereas virtuous ploughmen were not such an everyday phenomenon.

54. See 'Frequenter cogitans', *Poésies Pop. Lat.*, p. 132; *Sermones nulli parcentes*, pp. 41 and 42, cap. XXV and XXVI; *VC* V 579, 615, etc.

55. See 'Viri fratres, servi Dei' *AH* XXXIII p. 270, 173; *VC* V 593.

56. See *Chessbook*, col. 377–8ff.; 'Totum regit saeculum', *Map Poems*, p. 235, 193ff. 'Cultor' and 'laborarius' were also possible terms in Latin; see, for example, *VC* V 629, and the chapter heading to V, chapter X.

57. See Étienne de Fougères, *Livre des Manières*, p. 131, 676; 'Li Mariages des Filles au Diable' *NR* I p. 286.

58. See Étienne de Fougères, *Livre des Manières*, p. 131, 678; 'Nous lisons une istoire', ed. Montaiglon and Raynaud, II p. 265; 'Des Vilains', *Anecdota Literaria*, ed. Wright, pp. 53ff. (This poem, which begins 'Or escoutez un autre conte | A toz les vilains doint Dex honte', is printed by Wright from MS Berne 354 fol. 57v. – a large fourteenth-century MS. See H. Hagen, *Catalogus Codicum Bernensium* (Berne, 1875), p. 340.)

59. See *Roman de Carité*, p. 81 CLI 4; *Roman de Fauvel*, p. 45, 1139; 'Le Dit des Mais' *NR* I p. 192; 'Le Dit des Planètes', *ibid.*, p. 378.

60. See *OED*, s.v.

61. Luke 9: 62. The earliest reference to Christ as a ploughman is probably that found in the Byzantine Greek Hymnos-Akathistos, which hails the Virgin Mary as 'γεωργὸν γεωργοῦσα φιλάνθρωπον' – 'nourisher of the loving ploughman'. (The ninth-century Latin version translates this as 'agricolam agricolans humanum'.) See G. G. Meersseman, *Der Hymnos Akathistos im Abendland* (Freiburg, 1958), pp. 108–9. I am grateful to Peter Dronke for this reference.

62. *PPl* V 630–1. The link between these three virtues may ultimately be due to the influential passage on Charity in 1 Cor. 13.

63. *PPl* V 568–73.

64. Ed. Arnold, III, 207, quoted by E. Flügel, 'Gower's Mirour de l'Omme und Chaucer's Prolog', *Anglia*, 24 (1901), 504.

65. See 'Totum regit saeculum', *Map Poems*, p. 235, 197–200. For the tradition of exalting agricultural labour, see Flügel, 'Chaucer's Prolog', p. 504, notes 1–4.

66. For the traditional abuse of peasants, see F. Novati, *Carmina Medii Aevi* (Florence, 1883), pp. 25ff.

67. The sense of 'true' involved here is *OED* 2: 'Honest, honourable, upright, virtuous, trustworthy'. Flügel (Chaucer's Prolog', p. 504) aptly compares with Chaucer Wycliff's statement that no life is as pleasing to God as that of a 'trewe plow man' (ed. Matthew, p. 321).

   For Langland's connection of 'treuthe' and 'lewte' with ploughmen, see *PPl* I 119–22, C text 144–6. (These passages are not noted by Coghill, whose suggested parallels for *GP* 531 are not very convincing.) 'Treuthe' is especially important in Passus I. For a discussion of 'lewte' and its meaning for Langland, see E. T. Donaldson, *Piers Plowman: The C-Text and its Poet* (2nd edition, London, 1966), pp. 65ff.

68. *NE* 31, 1, p. 134, 46. For details of this poem, see p. 288 n. 32.

69. Col. 393–4.

70. *Livre des Manières*, p. 131, 708.

71. 'Dis des Estas dou Monde', p. 183, 214.

72. p. 45, 1139. See also Matheolus' *Lamentations*, p. 288, 663 (not in Latin): labourers living off their '*loial* labour' are worthy of praise. In the thirteenth-century German poem *Meier Helmbrecht*, Helmbrecht's peasant father claims to be 'getriuwe, gewære' – 'honest, upright' (p. 11, 253). Thomas Wimbledon's sermon of 1388 urges the 'laborer or crafti man' to work 'trewli' (*Medieval Studies*, 27 (1966), p. 179).

73. Col. 329–40, 381–2.

74. Ed. Aspin, p. 119 v. 5. See also Étienne de Fougères, *Livre des Manières*, p. 131, 676–81; Matheolus' *Lamentations*, p. 288, 661–3 (Lat. 4677–8); and the stress on the virtue of labour in *PPl Crede* p. 29, 785ff.

75. See *VC* v 577–88; 'Le Dit des Mais', *NR* I p. 193; 'Le Dit des Planètes', *ibid.*, pp. 378–9; *MO* 26,434.

76. *Livre des Manières*, p. 131, CLXX–CLXXII.

77. *PPl* IV 147–8. See the interesting parallel in *Meier Helmbrecht*, p. 12, 266–7; 'ich sol ouch dir ûf dînen wagen | nimmer mist gevazzen' – 'Never more shall I load dung on to your cart for you'. The other tasks of the peasant which are listed in *Meier Helmbrecht* are carrying sacks (264), driving oxen (269), sowing oats (270), threshing (315), driving stakes (318), hedging (323).

78. *PPl* v 552–3. This and the previous parallel with Langland were noted by Coghill, 'Two Notes'.

79. See *MED*, s.v., sense 1.

80. See 'Frequenter cogitans', *Poésies Pop. Lat.*, p. 132; Matheolus' *Lamentations*, p. 288, 670ff., (Lat. 4681ff.). Cf. *Meier Helmbrecht*, p. 12, 257–8; 'ich han gelebet mîne zit | âne haz und âne nît' – 'I have lived all my life without hatred or envy.'

81. See 'Li Mariages des Filles au Diable' *NR* I p. 287; 'Le Dit des Planètes', *ibid.*, p. 379; Matheolus' *Lamentations*, p. 289, 684ff. (Lat. 4689–90).

82. See *Chessbook*, col. 403-4; *Sermones nulli parcentes*, p. 42, 969-72. See also E. Lommatzsch, *Gautier de Coincy als Satiriker* (Halle a.S., 1913), p. 72. Note that the complaints that the peasant never works more than he has to, and the complaints that he won't stop working for religious holidays, exist side by side; social stereotypes were no more self-consistent in the Middle Ages than they are today.

83. Rather of Verona gives tithing honestly, and working hard, as general Christian duties (*PL* 136, *Praeloquia*, 1 col. 149). This illustrates the meagre development of differentiated treatments of the third estate before the fourteenth century; specialised features and duties were attached much earlier to the different orders of the clergy.

84. *Livre des Manières*, p. 132, 733ff. See also Lommatzsch, *Gautier de Coincy*, p. 72.

85. See the *Wakefield Pageants*, ed. Cawley, pp. 3ff.; the surviving plays are, however, too late to be used as sources for Chaucer.

86. *PPl* VI 93-5. This parallel is noted by Coghill, 'Two Notes', p. 94.

87. For further illustration, see *Roman de Carité*, p. 105, CXCVIII 3-4; 'Li Mariages des Filles au Diable' *NR* 1 p. 287; Matheolus' *Lamentations*, p. 288, 664-5 (Lat. 4678-80). For sermons, see Owst, *Lit. and Pulp.*, pp. 365-6.

88. See Matt. 22: 40.

89. See 'Frequenter cogitans', *Poésies Pop. Lat.*, p. 132; *VC* v 577ff.; *Roman de Carité*, p. 105 CXCVIII 1-4; 'Le Dit des Planètes' *NR* 1 p. 379; 'Des Vilains', *Anecdota Literaria*, ed. Wright, p. 53; *MO* 26,434.

90. *PPl* VII 504. This parallel is noted by Coghill ('Two Notes', p. 93), who also compares *GP* 538 ('Withouten hire, if it lay in his myght') and *PPl* 565-7, where Piers refuses payment from the pilgrims. The similarity is however slight, since the payment is there offered for Piers' services as guide to Treuthe, not for his labour.

91. *PPl* VI 204-39. This passage is not noted by Coghill, but is in my view an important influence on the Ploughman's portrait, because of the combined emphasis on 'swynk', on 'dykynge and deluynge' (250), and on charity to the poor. For this combination, note also v 548, where Piers says he has promised to serve Treuthe 'the while I swynke myghte', three lines before talking about 'dykyng and delvyng'.

92. As early as the eleventh-century romance, *Ruodlieb*, we find a portrayal of an idealised peasant who distributes food to the needy of his village, in a scene whose 'sacramental quality' has been noted by Peter Dronke. (Ed. H. Zeydel, VII 1ff.; *Poetic Individuality in the Middle Ages* (Oxford, 1970), p. 51.)

93. Bowden, *Commentary*, p. 242.

94. See *OED* s.v., I.

95. See *MO* 26,514-15. Meier Helmbrecht's culpable desire to rise above his

station is conveyed by the long description of his resplendent clothing at the beginning of the poem (p. 1, 26ff.).

96. See 'Totum regit saeculum', *Map Poems*, p. 235, 201-2; Étienne de Fougères, *Livre des Manières*, p. 131, 681-712; 'Mult est diables curteis', ed. Aspin, p. 119, v. 5, 30; 'Nous lisons une istoire', ed. Montaiglon and Raynaud, II p. 265; *Renart le Contrefait*, II pp. 47-8, 27,031-65; 'Lay des Douze Estas du Monde', Deschamps, II p. 228, 55-60; 'Ich herde men vpo molde', ed. Böddekker, pp. 102ff.; *PPl Crede*, p. 16, 421ff. Cf. Lommatzsch, *Gautier de Coincy*, pp. 70ff.

Several writers sympathise with the peasant's lot even while regarding it as right and proper that his lord should enjoy the fruits of his labour: see, for example, the *Chessbook*, col. 395-6 ('Sepe enim fit, ut agricola cibetur grossioribus, ut domino suo subtiliora apportet' – 'Often it happens that the peasant is fed with coarser things, so that he may take the finer produce to his lord'), and Étienne de Fougères, *loc. cit.* Gautier de Coincy, however, sees the peasant's labour as punishment for his treacherousness (Lommatzsch, *Gautier de Coincy*, pp. 75-6).

97. See the famous passage on 'oure neigheboures', *PPl* C x 71ff., for Langland's ability to present the sufferings of the poor in a way that makes them seem Christ-like, and xIV 215ff., where he describes how rich men are more susceptible to sin than poor men.

98. See Walter of Châtillon, No XI, p. 115, vv. 13-14; *CB* I No 6 pp. 7-8, 1-20; *VC* III 2065-6; *PPl* xv 366-79.

99. *NE* 32, 1, p. 290.

100. *NR* I p. 184. The translation represents the best sense I can make of the last line of the first stanza quoted; I take 'bouclers ot motez (motets)' to be the object of 'miex aimment', in apposition to the noun phrase 'oublier leur loez'. See also a similar complaint about priests, Owst, *Lit. and Pulp.*, p. 269.

101. See *CB* I No 6 p. 8, 21-2; 'Totum regit saeculum', *Map Poems*, p. 233, 156; *Sermones nulli parcentes*, p. 29, 509-20; *VC* III 2132; *PPl* x 163-4; *Mum and the Sothsegger*, p. 46, 645-7. Absalon in the Miller's Tale is a tavern-haunter (I (A) 3334-6).

102. See *CB* I No 6 p. 8, 35-6; 'Hora nona sabbati' *NE* 32, I p. 295; *Sermones nulli parcentes*, p. 29, 505-8; *VC* III 2132; *PPl* x 161-2.

103. See 'Totum regit saeculum', *Map Poems*, p. 233, 153-4. Absalon also acts in plays (I (A) 3383-5).

104. *SS* 1189; *VC* III 2069.

105. See, for example, the ecclesiastical prohibitions against clerks singing and playing musical instruments, printed by Helen Waddell in Appendix E to *The Wandering Scholars* (6th edition), especially those for 1227, *ca.* 1245, 1279 and 1332; and Pidal, *Poesía Juglaresca*, pp. 28-31.

NOTES TO PAGES 75-8

106. Nicholas plays the 'sautrie' (I (A) 3213ff.) and Absalon plays the 'rubible' and the 'giterne' (I (A) 3331-3).

107. 20,801-20. See also Étienne de Fougères, *Livre des Manières*, p. 124, 317ff., where the bishop is advised to ordain clerks who are 'sage' and 'de bones mors' ('wise' and 'of virtuous character').

108. Another anticipation has been noticed in John of Salisbury's *Policraticus* by J. Fleming (*ELN* 2 (1964), 5-6).

109. Cf. *PPl* XII 99-114, where Langland says that 'letterure' is the key to salvation.

110. *CB* I No 6 p. 8, 33.

111. *SS* 1190-1.

112. *Map Poems*, p. 233, 145. Cf. an article by H. E. Ussery citing a passage from William of Wheatley which says a clerk ought to be like 'a virgin newly-espoused' (*Tulane Studies in English*, 15 (1967), 1-18). The same metaphor can be discerned behind the description of Ruodlieb's nephew, who, has 'so tender and maidenly ('virginea') a face', that no-one can tell whether he is clerk, woman or schoolboy (*Ruodlieb*, p. 118, XIII, 4). This metaphor appears in Chaucer in the Prologue to the Clerk's Tale:

> 'Sire Clerk of Oxenford', oure Hooste sayde,
> 'Ye ryde as coy and stille as dooth a mayde
> Were newe spoused, sittynge at the bord.' (IV (E) 1-3)

Chaucer makes the image more concrete and in so doing gives it a comic touch, but the Latin poem shows that the metaphor was, originally, neither his nor comic. The phrase is given another twist altogether in the description of Nicholas in the Miller's Tale, who is 'lyk a mayden meke for to see' (I (A) 3202).

113. *NE* 32, I p. 293.

114. For the clerk's pride in his learning, see Walter of Châtillon, No VI, p. 86, v. 18; *SS* 1205-6, 1999-2003; *De Planctu Naturae, Anglo-Latin Satirical Poets*, II prose VII, p. 494; *Sermones nulli parcentes*, p. 30, 529-30; *VC* III 2130, 2137-8; *Renart le Contrefait*, II p. 29, 25,193-210; Gilles li Muisis, I p. 263; *MO* 1447-52; *Handlyng Synne*, p. 108, 3078-82.

115. The phrase is from 'Meum est propositum', ed. Strecker, *Studi Medievali*, n.s. I (1928), p. 387, v. 9, 4.

116. Appendix to 'Missus sum in vineam', No VI p. 87, vv. 18bff. For comment on the authorship, see *ibid.*, p. 81. This passage provides a background against which the Host's words to the Clerk have precise relevance:

> Youre termes, youre colours, and youre figures,
> Keepe hem in stoor til so be that ye endite
> Heigh style, as whan that men to kynges write.
> Spekketh so pleyn at this tyme, we yow preye,
> That we may understonde what ye seye. (*CT* IV (E) 16-20)

117. *MO* 20,818–20. See also on this topic *Mum and the Sothsegger*, p. 37, 340–5. The idea probably derives from Prov. 10: 19: 'In multiloquio non deerit peccatum.' Brevity and simplicity of speech are also recommended to priests (see *CB* I No 33, p. 55, v. 6, 2; 'Viri venerabiles', Hauréau, *NE* VI p. 15, Gilles li Muisis, I p. 393). They are also generally recommended: see *Ancrene Wisse*, p. 39, fol. 18*a*, 11ff.; Gilles li Muisis, II p. 74.

118. 'Vix nodosum valeo', ed. P. Leyser, *Historia Poetarum et Poematum medii aevi* (1721), p. 1096, v. 27, 4. The *Roman de Fauvel* also takes it for granted that clerks are 'povres' and 'sans rente' (p. 6, 73). See also *PPl* X 159–60:

> ryde forth by Ricchesse ‘ ac rest thow nau3t therinne,
> For if thow couplest the ther-with ’ to Clergye comestow neuere.

The poor clerk is a stock figure in medieval stories; see the 'Gospel according to the Mark of Silver' *CB* I No 44 p. 86, and *Latin Stories*, No LXXXII, p. 73.

119. See Owst, *Lit. and Pulp.*, p. 571. Note also the picture of Poverty in Robert Holcot's commentary on the Twelve Prophets: 'quasi una domina, vulta letata, *philosophis maritata*'. Thomas Ringstead follows Hugh of St Victor in listing six requirements for serious study: humility, inquiry, silence, poverty and a foreign land. Ringstead's idea of study is also that it is a means to salvation: 'Secunda clavis apperiens est assiduitas studii inquirendo, dum modo tamen ad Christum per opera fructuosa ipsa studii aviditas referatur.' – 'The second unlocking key is diligent intellectual inquiry, so long as such eagerness in study is related to Christ through its fruit in action.' (This information is derived from B. Smalley, *English Friars and Antiquity in the Early Fourteenth Century* (Oxford, 1960), pp. 178, 216).

120. No XI p. 113, v. 3, 4.

121. *NE* 32, I, p. 293.

122. See especially Walter of Châtillon, No VI p. 86 v. 16, 4: 'nam sine divitiis vita est quasi mortis imago' – 'for life without riches is as an image of death'. (The line is adapted from the Proverbs of Dionysius Cato where it reads 'sine *doctrina* vita'.)

123. See 'Hora nona sabbati' *NE* 32 I, *passim*; 'Nous lisons une istoire', ed. Montaiglon and Raynaud, II p. 264 (where the young man looking for a profession is first attracted by the 'trés aisiés, trés delicieux' ('very comfortable, very sumptuous') life of the clergy, but then repelled by the hardships he would have to undergo when training for this life as a student. The 'clericus' of the twelfth-century debate poem 'Anni parte florida', who enjoys every luxury, is clearly a member of the beneficed clergy, not a student. (*CB* I No 92; for a discussion of the poem see Raby, *Secular Latin Poetry*, II pp. 291ff.)

124. No III p. 45, v. 20, 4.

125. 'Meum est propositum', ed. Strecker, *Studi Medievali*, n.s. I p. 387 v. 8, 1–2, pp. 390–1, vv. 21–2. See also the whole poem.
126.1 pp. 111 and 262ff. See also Thomas Wimbledon's sermon of 1388: men 'putteþ . . . here sones raþere to lawe syuyle and to þe kyngis court to writen lettres or writis þan to philosophie oþer deuinitie' (*Medieval Studies*, 28 (1966), p. 181).
127. For the two senses of the word, see *OED* s.v., 1a and 3. For Chaucer's uses of it, see the *Chaucer Concordance*, s.v.; it is especially frequent in the *Melibeus*, the Tales of the Parson and the Prioress, and the Clerk's Tale. Note also the Sergeant's own introduction to his Tale:

> If thou be povre, farwel thy reverence! (II (B¹) 116)

Other uses of the word in the *General Prologue* also bring out the disparity between moral and social status; see 141 and 525.
128. Ed. Strecker, *Studi Medievali*, n.s. I p. 387, v. 5.
129. *NE* 32, I, pp. 290, 292. See also complaints that modern scholars fuss about their appearance: *VC* III 2131; *Mum and the Sothsegger*, p. 46, 642–3.
130. *SS* 1185; Walter of Châtillon, No VI p. 85, v. 11, 4; 'Hora nona sabbati' *NE* 32, I, p. 294.
131. See 'Meum est propositum', ed. Strecker, *Studi Medievali* n.s. I, p. 388, v. 12, 4; 'Hora nona sabbati' *NE* 32, I, p. 293; and a complaint that modern scholars ride about unlike the poor students of old, *Mum and the Sothsegger*, p. 46, 643.
132. 'Dis des Estas dou Monde', p. 178, 39–40.
133.1 pp. 106, 278.
134. *Handlyng Synne*, p. 44, 1209–10. The obligation to pray for benefactors applied to all recipients of alms: see Owst, *Lit. and Pulp.*, p. 561.
135. Nicholas in the Miller's Tale also lives off his obliging friends (I (A) 3220).
136. *Map Poems*, p. 234, 157. Cf. however 149–50, where the author seems to regard a secular administrative post as inevitable for clerks, and exhorts them to perform their duties honestly and obediently.
137. *PPl* x 469–70. See also *Mum and the Sothsegger*, p. 46, 644ff. Involvement in secular business is also imputed to other educated classes, such as friars (see Chapter 2) and priests (see, for example, *PPl* Prol. 92–6).
138. See Walter of Châtillon, No IV p. 65, vv. 9 and 15; *ibid.*, No VI p. 83, v. 6; *ibid.*, No IX p. 106, vv. 6–7 ('non est, qui pro paupere spondeat scolari' – 'there is no one to sponsor the poor student'); *CB* I No 5 p. 5, v. 3; 'Ecce dolet Anglia', *PPS* I p. 280 ('Favor non scientia promovet rectores' – 'influence, not learning, wins promotion to rector'); *Roman de Fauvel*, p. 6, 73, p. 33, 805ff.; 'Le Dit des Mais' *NR* I pp. 181–2; 'Dis des Estas dou Monde', Jean de Condé, p. 178, 56–8; Gilles li Muisis, I pp. 107, 363; *MO* 16,081ff.; 'The Simonie', *PSE* p. 326, 55–60. On the scholar who studies only for the sake of a rich living, see *VC* III 2107–10.

139. *Livre des Manières*, p. 123 LXVI 261–4.
140. See Pantin, *The English Church in the Fourteenth Century*, pp. 107ff.
141. *Anglia*, 24 (1901), pp. 480–2.
142. See the complaints cited by Helen Waddell (*The Wandering Scholars*, 6th edition, pp. 104ff.) about the length of time which scholars devote to studying 'logyk' and secular authors, when they should have mastered theology and gone out into the parishes.
143. Ed. Matthew, p. 250:

> ȝif siche curatis ben stired to gone lerne goddis lawe & teche here parischenys þe gospel, comynly þei schullen gete no leue of bischopis but for gold; & whanne þei schullen most profite in here lernynge þan schulle þei be clepid hom at þe prelatis wille.

(This passage is quoted by Flügel, 'Chaucer's Prolog'.)
144. *Ibid.*, pp. 251–2.
145. The supremacy of theology is stressed by Gilles li Muisis (I pp. 113, 263–4).
146. See 'Hora nona sabbati', *NE* 32, I, p. 291, where the clerk is attacked for studying Socrates, not God, and asked what fruit will come of such study. In the twelfth century, Hugh Primas had praised the city of Rheims (since he himself was a teacher of rhetoric, probably with his tongue in his cheek) for neglecting secular studies in favour of theology:

> Non est scola vanitatis,
> Sed doctrina veritatis;
> Ibi nomen non Socratis,
> Sed eterne trinitatis.

It is not the teaching of vanity, but the doctrine of truth; Socrates is not named there, but the eternal Trinity.

(ed. K. Langosch, *Hymnen und Vagantenlieder* (Darmstadt, 1961), p. 150.) Distrust of the pagan authors goes back to Jerome, who sneers at heretics as 'Platonici et Aristotelici' (Wiesen, *St Jerome as a Satirist*, p. 180).
147. *Bible*, pp. 80–1, 2282–310. Guiot goes on to say that he does not criticise the study of pagan authors, provided that they help towards salvation (*ibid.*, pp. 81–2, 2314–16).
148. A contrasting attitude, can be found, for example, in Thomas Wimbledon's sermon of 1388, where 'philosophie' *and* 'deuinitie' are named as honourable disciplines, which are being neglected for law and 'business studies' (*Medieval Studies*, 28 (1966), p. 181).
149. 'Hora nona sabbati', *NE* 32, I, p. 291.
150. Two features of the traditional conception of the scholar's life that Chaucer does not refer to in his portrait are: (1) the cold he endures: see Walter of Châtillon, No VI p. 85, v. 12; 'Hora nona sabbati', *NE* 32, I, p. 294. (2)

study through the hours of darkness: see Walter of Châtillon, No VI
p. 85, v. 12; *SS* 1181.

CHAPTER 4

1. It is a feature not confined to this group of portraits, but is the most
   interesting aspect to emerge from comparison between them and the
   traditional satire of their estates.
2. The outlines of the lawyer's stereotype remain the same whether he is
   judge or simple apprentice, ecclesiastical or civil lawyer. This is well
   illustrated by the ease with which Langland moves from one group to
   another in satirising legal corruption:

   > Men of lawe lest pardoun hadde˙that pleteden for mede,
   > For the sauter saueth hem nou3t˙such as taketh 3iftes,
   > And namelich of innocentz˙that none yuel ne kunneth;...
   > Pledoures shulde peynen hem˙to plede for such, an helpe,...
   > Ac many a Iustice an Iurore˙wolde for Iohan do more,
   > Than *pro dei pietate*˙leue thow none other! (*PPl* VII 39–45).

3. 'The Parvys' is usually taken to be the porch of St Paul's, but it may be
   the court or colonnade at Westminster (see Robinson's note, and Sir John
   Fortescue, *De laudibus legum Anglie*, ed. S. B. Chrimes (Cambridge, 1942),
   p. 205); the reference *may* be to hearing the disputations of students, but it
   is much more likely that it is to consultations with clients. G. L. Frost
   ('Chaucer's Man of Law at the Parvis', *MLN* 44 (1929), 496–501) explains
   the comment as a reference to investiture ceremonies for new sergeants.
   This is an entirely hypothetical meaning for the phrase, and I think it is
   better to take it as a reference to the scene of the Sergeant's regular working
   activities, and as an under-statement: thus it would mean no more than
   'He (of course) knew the Parvis inside out.' For a similar presentation of the
   prosaic daily activities of a pilgrim, see the Ploughman's portrait, 'He hadde
   ylad of dong ful many a fother.' There is nothing extraordinary about this,
   and I think there is probably nothing extraordinary about the Sergeant's
   having often been at the Parvis.
4. See *OED* s.v., 6a. From this order the Common Law judges were chosen.
5. The 'patente' would be an open letter of authorisation from the king, and
   the 'pleyn commissioun' would give him jurisdiction in all kinds of cases.
   (See Bowden, *Commentary*, p. 167.)
6. 'Fee simple' was perpetual tenure of land without limitation to any particular
   class of heirs.
7. 'In termes' is explained by *OED* as 'in express words, expressly, plainly,
   "in so many words"' (s.v. Term, 14*b*). This does not fit the context very
   well, and I prefer to accept R. C. Goffin's interpretation of the phrase as a

reference to legal jargon: 'the plural use in Chaucer always suggests clerkly jargon of some sort'. ('Notes on Chaucer' *MLR* 18 (1923), 336–7). For confirmation of Goffin's statement, see *Chaucer Concordance*, s.v.

8. This poem, printed in *PSE* pp. 224ff., is found in several manuscripts, two of them English and at least two of them thirteenth-century. It belongs to the school of Walter of Châtillon (Strecker, *ZfDA* 64 (1927), 188).

9. *VC* VI 357–8. Cf. also 343–4.

10. *PSE* p. 338, 327. The reference is to 'justices...shirreves, cheiturs, and chaunceler' (322). See also a sermon reference to judges 'buying lands, building mansions, and laying up a fortune' (Owst, *Lit. and Pulp.*, p. 346). For historical evidence of the land-buying of a fourteenth-century lawyer, see M. Eliason, 'The Peasant and the Lawyer', *SP* 48 (1951), 523–4.

11. *OED* classes 'purchasour' in this passage under sense 1, 'One who acquires or aims at acquiring possessions; one who "feathers his nest"', although 'many explain *purchasour* as "conveyancer", which is possible' – in which case it would presumably have sense 2: 'One who acquires land or property in any way other than by inheritance'. 'Purchas' (noun and verb) and 'purchasyng' are used by Chaucer in neutral or honourable situations, but they also, significantly, recur in sinister contexts: see *GP* 256, 608, Friar's Tale III (D) 1449, 1451, 1530. See also Parson's Tale X (I) 740–5, 1065–70. (*Chaucer Concordance* s.v.) The uses seem to be particularly suspect when the object of the 'purchas' is not indicated.

12. *Handlyng Synne*, p. 196, 6049–50.

13. See *MO* 6220–2, 2415–16, 24,745–7; *Winner and Waster*, 149–52 (the enlistment of lawyers in Winner's army); *PPl* XIV 286–7. Most often the rich lawyer is linked with the rich doctor, as we saw in discussion of the Clerk; see Walter of Châtillon, No III p. 45 v. 20; 'Meum est propositum' ed. Strecker, *Studi Medievali* n.s. 1 (1928), p. 391, v. 22; *Sermones nulli parcentes*, p. 28, 465–70; 'Crux est denarii potens in saeculo', *Map Poems*, p. 225, 61–4; *VC* VI 121–4; *RR* I 5061–4; Gilles li Muisis, I p. 111; *MO* 24,289–312.

14. See Walter of Châtillon, No III, p. 45, v. 22, 2; *VC* VI 391–2; Matheolus' *Lamentations*, p. 285, 567ff. (Lat. 4614ff.), and Lommatzsch, *Gautier de Coincy*, p. 58 and n. 1.

15. *PPl* III 293–4. See also XX 137–8, where Coueityse corrupts civil law, and arranges divorces for 'a mantel of menyuere'.

16. For 'medlee', see *OED* s.v. I, 'Of a mixed colour; variegated, motley', and M. C. Linthicum ' "Faldyng" and "Medlee" ', *JEGP* 34 (1935), 40–1. Sir John Fortescue (*De laudibus legum Anglie*, ed. S. B. Chrimes, Chapter 51), writing in the fifteenth century, says that sergeants wear 'stragulata vestis' – 'a striped gown' which is laid aside by justices. (See Flügel, 'Chaucer's Prolog', p. 492. See also J. H. Fisher, *John Gower: Moral Philosopher and*

Friend of Chaucer (London, 1965), pp. 55–6.) 'Medlee' is not necessarily striped material, but see Bowden, *Commentary*, p. 171.

The Sergeant's belt with its thin bars has a parallel in Nicholas Bozon's description of 'Joye du pecché', who has a similar belt with a purse attached (like Chaucer's Franklin). But the difference is that Bozon gives each item an allegorical significance which characterises the sin (*Le Char d'Orgueil*, p. 23, CIV 413–16). Chaucer's originality shows not in his inclusion of these concrete details, but in the way he sets them free from moralising associations.

17. Cf. Wycliff's reference to bribes of 'money & fees & robis' (ed. Matthew, p. 234).

18. See *CB* I No 5, p. 6, v. 16; *ibid.*, No 39, p. 62, v. 3; 'Quam sit lata scelerum', *PSE* p. 31; 'Tempus acceptabile' *AH* XXXIII p. 293, vv. 8–10; *CB* I, No 1, p. 1; 'Beati qui esuriunt' *PSE* pp. 224ff.; 'Crux est denarii potens in saeculo', *Map Poems*, p. 225, 29ff., 62ff.; *VC* VI Chapters I–IV; 'Heu! quia per crebras', Gower, p. 356, 55–62; Guiot de Provins, *Bible*, p. 85, 2440ff.; *RR* I 5061ff., 8201–3; 'L'État du Monde', Rutebeuf I, p. 386, 87–8; 'La Vie du Monde', *ibid.*, p. 397, 61–4; 'Le Dit des Patenostres' *NR* I, p. 240; 'Le Dit des Mais', *ibid.*, p. 189; 'Dis des Estas dou Monde', Jean de Condé, p. 181, 143–56; *Renart le Contrefait*, II pp. 27–8, 25,026–75; Gilles li Muisis, I p. 112, II p. 155; Matheolus' *Lamentations*, p. 282, 480ff. (Lat. 4559ff.); 'The Simonie' *PSE* p. 339; *PPl* II 60, III 157, IV 152–3, VII 39–45, XX 131–8; Thomas Wimbledon's sermon, *Medieval Studies*, 28 (1966), 184; 'Syngyn y wolde', *PPS* I pp. 272–3. For sermons, see Owst, *Lit. and Pulp.*, pp. 339–49. See also Lommatzsch, *Gautier de Coincy*, pp. 56–7.

19. See *VC* VI 249–52; *MO* 6220ff., 24,378ff.; *PPl* Prol. 210–15, III 293–4.

20. pp. 28–9, 471–6. See also, for example, *CB* I No 1, p. 1, v. 2, 3–4, v. 3, 5–6, v. 5, 6–7; *ibid.*, No 39 v. 3; Gilles li Muisis, II p. 155.

21. The adjective 'busy' seems to have had a wider range of connotations than in modern English; as well as implying industriousness or diligence, it could also be used to suggest fussing about worldly affairs, or thoughtless activity – the opposite of virtuous contemplation. See *MED* s.v. 1, especially the quotations from the *Ancrene Wisse* and the *Ayenbite of Inwyt*, its use (sense 2) in re-tellings of the biblical story of Martha and Mary, and in Wycliff, 'men shulden not be bisi to þe morowe'. Cf. Chaucer's Parson's Tale (X (I) 473–4):

> Certes, the commendacioun of the people is somtyme ful fals and ful brotel for to triste; this day they preyse, tomorwe they blame./God woot, desir to have commendacioun eek of the peple hath caused deeth to many a bisy man.

and, for another ambiguous use, the reference in the Summoner's Tale (III (D) 1940) to the 'chaste bisy freres'. The suggestion of a cultivated 'front of importance is also present in Skelton's irritated repetition 'Busy,

busy, busy' (followed by the comment 'too wise is no virtue') in *Speke Parrot*.

22. *PPl* xv 5-9. See also Matheolus' *Lamentations*, p. 285, 569-70: 'Et de nobles robes se parent, | Affin que plus sages apparent.' - 'And they dress in fine gowns so as to appear wiser.' (Lat. 4614-15); *MO* 24,377-8: 'pour son pris | Le noun voet porter de sergant' - 'for the sake of his prestige he wants to bear the name of sergeant'; Thomas Wimbledon's sermon of 1388 (*Medieval Studies*, 28 (1966), 183): 'þey þenkeþ not þat þey beþ pore mennys breþeryn, but þey weneþ to passe hem in kynde as þey passeþ in worldly worschipe' (of kings, princes, mayors, sheriffs, justices).

23. This pair of adjectives is interpreted by W. Héraucourt (*Chaucers Wertwelt* (Heidelberg, 1939), p. 93, quoted by Bowden, *Commentary*, p. 166) as less complimentary than the pair 'worthy and wys'. However, 'war and wys' are found in perfectly respectable contexts, such as an elegy on the death of Edward I (*PSE* p. 246, v. 2) where the king is described as 'in werre war ant wys'. See also *Handlyng Synne*, p. 256, 8084. In *Mum and the Sothsegger*, p. 77, 1716, the phrase seems to indicate the self-interested prudence of Chaucer's Sergeant.

24. In view of this link, it is rather surprising that the Doctor's portrait does not immediately follow the Sergeant's, but for the traditional connection that likewise exists between the Sergeant's estate and the Franklin's, see Chapter 7, p. 159, n. 45.

25. See, for example, *SS* 105-18; Guiot de Provins, *Bible*, p. 89, 2547ff.; 'Le Dit des Patenostres' *NR* I p. 241; 'Le Dit des Mais', *ibid.*, p. 191; *Renart le Contrefait*, II p. 28, 25,125ff., p. 44, 26,647ff.; Matheolus' *Lamentations*, p. 286, 619ff. (Lat. 4648ff.); 'The Simonie' *PSE* p. 333, 211ff.; *PPl* II 223-4, VI 275-6, XX 171-8. For sermons, see Owst, *Lit. and Pulp.*, pp. 349-50. See also Lommatzsch, *Gautier de Coincy*, p. 61.

26. For identification of these authorities and their works, see Bowden, *Commentary*, pp. 200ff.

27. See *RR* II 15,929-31 ('Ypocras...Galian...Rasi, Constantin, Avicenne'); *Renart le Contrefait*, II p. 11, 23,388-97 ('Ypocras...Galien...Ruffin, Constantin, Tholomée [Ptolemy], Alixandres [of Tralles], Avisain, Platon, Ancises [Alkindi?], et Jasaine, [Aboul Hassan], Senecque, Galien, Constantin.' According to Raynaud and Lemaître, Aboul Hassan was author of a treatise on astronomy. For the scientific works of Seneca and Ptolemy, see L. Thorndike, *History of Magic and Experimental Science* (London, 1923-), vol. I, Chapter 3; for Plato, see *ibid.*, pp. 25-6; for Alexander of Tralles pp. 566ff., and for Alkindi, pp. 642-9. For the other medical authorities, see Bowden, *Commentary*.

28. p. 287, 623-31 (Lat. 4652-5). I have not been able to decide on a satisfactory meaning for 'temps' in this passage; it might be a reference to administering medicine when the astrological influences are favourable, or it might be

a reference to the different stages of a disease which require different methods of treatment. For the argument that the second of these is what Chaucer also means by 'houres', see P. Aiken, 'Vincent of Beauvais and the "Houres" of Chaucer's Physician', *SP* 53 (1956), 22–4. For 'Isaac', see M. Neuburger and J. Pagel, *Handbuch der Geschichte der Medizin*, vol. 1 (Jena, 1902), p. 128.

29. *Renart le Contrefait*, II p. 28, 25,078–86.

30. A 'Liber de membris' went under the name of Aesculapius, and is cited by Bartholomaeus Anglicus and Albertus Magnus (Thorndike, *History of Magic*, vol. 2, pp. 431–2; see also p. 496), but the article by Robbins cited in the next note shows that Chaucer is very unusual in citing Aesculapius as a medical authority.

31. For differing estimates of Chaucer's acquaintance with the works of these and other medical authorities, see J. L. Lowes, 'The Loveres Maladye of Hereos', *MP* 2 (April 1914), 1–56; A. G. Nicholls, 'Medicine in Chaucer's Day', *Dalhousie Review* 12 (1932), 218–30; Curry, *Chaucer and the Medieval Sciences*, pp. xxi–ii, and the articles by P. Aiken on Chaucer and Vincent of Beauvais in *Speculum* 10 (1935), 281–7; *PMLA* 51 (1936), 316–19, and *SP* 33 (1936), 40–4. R. H. Robbins refutes Aiken's statement (repeated by Robinson and Bowden) that the *Speculum Naturale* of Vincent of Beauvais contains all the Doctor's authorities; several of them post-date Vincent, and so could not have been mentioned by him. After an examination of the authorities cited in medical manuscripts, Robbins concludes that Chaucer's list represents what an educated doctor of the period would have cited, with the exception of Rufus of Ephesus, who is virtually unknown in English MSS. ('The Physician's Authorities', *Studies in Language and Literature in Honour of Margaret Schlauch* (Warsaw, 1966), pp. 335–41; Robbins' comparative tables show that Chaucer is also exceptional in citing Aesculapius, though he does not comment on this).

32. For a commentary on these processes of medieval medicine, see Curry, *Chaucer and the Mediæval Sciences*, Chapter 1.

33. Avicenna, for example, mentions medical astrology only to dismiss it along with other supernatural processes (O. C. Gruner, *A Treatise on the Canon of Medicine of Avicenna, incorporating a translation of the First Book* (London, 1930), p. 149). Rather of Verona, in his *Praeloquia*, prescribes knowledge of 'potions, herbs and animals' for doctors; 'auguries, enchantments and superstitions' belong to the realm of 'mathematici' (*PL* 136 col. 152). For the varying positions on medical astrology in the Middle Ages, see T. O. Wedel, *The Medieval Attitude Toward Astrology* (*Yale Studies in English* 50 (1920, repr. 1968), pp. 54, 65–7, 73, 88).

34. *Renart le Contrefait*, II p. 28, 25,091–101, 25,111–22. See also p. 44, 26,719ff.: to take a medicine unnecessarily injures health,

Car toutes choses, che sçavons,
Ont temps par mois et par saisons,
Telle chose est cest an nuisable,
Qui encor sera profitable
Selon la constellacion
Et selon la complexion.

For all things, as we know, have their time, their month or season. A thing may be harmful now, and profitable at some other time, according to the stars and the humours.

35. *Ibid.*, p. 43, 26,458ff.
36. *Bible*, p. 91, 2614ff.
37. *Renart le Contrefait*, II p. 28, 25,127–31.
38. *MO* 25,645–63. The apothecary sometimes appears by himself in estates satire, as he does in 'Le Dit des Patenostres' (*NR* I p. 245): 'aposticaires | Qui vendent les cyrops et les bons laituaires' – 'apothecaries who sell syrups and good electuaries'. But doctors and apothecaries were closely linked as a rule: the *Chessbook* deals with physicians, spicers and apothecaries in the same section (col. 589ff.); 'Le Dit des Mais' deals with 'apoticaires' immediately after 'phisiciens', and in similar terms (*NR* I p. 191). In *Piers Plowman*, an account of Liar's sojourn with 'leches' is followed by his removal to 'spicereres' (II 223–6). Gower's satire on physicians is stimulated by his discussion of dishonesty among spicers (*MO* 25,621ff.). 'The Simonie', on the other hand attributes the fraudulent practice with drugs to the doctor himself (*PSE* p. 332, 223ff.).
39. *Bible*, pp. 91–2, 2610–36.
40. *Renart le Contrefait*, II p. 28, 25,087–9. See also p. 44, 26,729ff., where he also opts for 'chauldes sausses et confis' ('hot sauces and preserves') instead of medicine.
41. The actual vocabulary of *GP* 435–7 seems to be drawn from Gower's treatment of gluttony in *MO*. The fourth daughter of 'Gule', called 'Superfluité', gobbles down food and

Sanz digester, sanz avaler
Laist sa viande a realer,
Par ou entra par la revait.
D'ice pecche par dueté
Le noun est *Superflueté*,
Q'est l'anemye de *mesure*. (8338–43; my italics)

without digesting, without swallowing, lets her meat come back again – it returns the way it entered. The right name of this sin is Superfluity, who is the enemy of moderation.

See also the description of 'Mesure', whose first daughter is 'Diete':

Le ventre vit en grant quiete

Qui se governe par Diete.
Et vit solonc bonne attemprance
De sa pitance consüete;
Car qui se paist au droite mete,
Son corps du sante bien avance. (16,249–54; my italics)

The stomach that is ruled by Diet lives in great peace. And it lives, in accordance with self-control, on the food it is accustomed to. For whoever feeds on the right food, increases the health of his body.

The third daughter of 'Mesure' is 'Norreture', who combats 'Superfluite' (16,369–74). The Parson's Tale also opposes Gluttony to Measure (x (I) 817, 829), and interestingly adds,

Agayns Glotonye is the remedie abstinence, as seith Galien; but that holde I nat meritorie, if he do it oonly for the heele of his body. (x (I) 831)

This suggests very strongly that the Doctor's abstemiousness is not a personal virtue, but a piece of professional wisdom.

42. See Walter of Châtillon, No III p. 45, v. 20, 4; 'Meum est propositum', ed. Strecker, *Studi Medievali* n.s. 1 (1928), p. 391, v. 22, 4 (this line also appears in other works, and independently; see *loc. cit.*).
43. VI 271–2. See also XX 175.
44. See *CB* I No 11, p. 16, 28; *Sermones nulli parcentes*, p. 28, 465–96; 'Crux est denarii' *Map Poems*, p. 225, 61–6; *RR* I 5061ff.; 'Le Dit des Mais' *NR* I p. 191; Gilles li Muisis, I p. 112; *PPl* XX 170. See also Lommatzsch, *Gautier de Coincy*, pp. 60–1.
45. *Lamentations*, p. 286, 602–6 (Lat. 4634ff.).
46. *MO* 24,289–91. See also *VC* VI 121–2.
47. *CB* I No 44, p. 86, 20–1. The biblical passages parodied are Philipp. 2: 27 and John 5: 9. For another 'gold-joke', see *MO* 24,421–6.
48. See Bowden, *Commentary*, pp. 207–8.
49. See Rather of Verona, *Praeloquia*, *PL* 136, col. 159; 'Frequenter cogitans', *Poésies Pop. Lat.*, p. 131; 'Viri fratres' *AH* XXXIII pp. 270–1, 177–98; 'Totum regit saeculum', *Map Poems*, p. 234, 185–92; *Sermones nulli parcentes*, p. 40, 893ff.; *VC* V Chapters XII–XIV; 'Heu! quia per crebras', Gower, p. 356, 63ff.; Étienne de Fougères, *Livre des Manières*, p. 133, 813ff., p. 135, 889ff.; 'L'État du Monde', Rutebeuf, I p. 387, 125–9; Nicholas Bozon, *Le Char d'Orgueil*, p. 13, LV, 217–20; 'Li Mariages des Filles au Diable' *NR* I p. 286; *Roman de Fauvel*, p. 45, 1138; 'Dis des Estas dou Monde', Jean de Condé, p. 182, 177–81; 'Le Dit des Mais' *NR* I p. 191; 'Le Dit des Planètes', *ibid.*, p. 378; *Renart le Contrefait*, II p. 45, 27,007–10; Gilles li Muisis, II pp. 57–8, 156; Matheolus' *Lamentations*, p. 287, 633ff. (Lat. 4658ff.); *MO* 6505–13; *Handlyng Synne*, p. 193, 5945–50; 'The Simonie' *PSE* p. 339, 356; *PPl* II 211–14, V 201–27, VII 21–2; Thomas Wimbledon's sermon of

1388, *Medieval Studies* 28 (1966), 179. For sermon references, see Owst, *Lit. and Pulp.*, pp. 353–61.

50. Anti-mercantile satire is extended by describing at length the different kinds of dishonesty practised with different kinds of merchandise, rather than by describing different traits of the merchant's stereotype. See Étienne de Fougères, *Livre des Manières*, p. 134, 817ff.; *Renart le Contrefait*, II p. 45, 26,851ff.; *MO* 25,237ff.; *PPl* v 201–27.

51. *VC* v 706; see also Rather of Verona, *Praeloquia, PL* 136 col. 159; 'Frequenter cogitans', *Poésies Pop. Lat.*, p. 131; *Chessbook*, col. 529–50; *Sermones nulli parcentes*, pp. 38–40, 845–92; *VC* v Chapter XII; 'Le Dit des Mais' *NR* I p. 191; *MO* 6505–16; *Handlyng Synne*, p. 193, 5945ff.; *Winner and Waster*, 190; *PPl* v 200ff.

52. *VC* v 703ff. See, for other references to usury, 'Viri fratres' *AH* XXXIII p. 270, 170–2, p. 271, 199–200; 'Heu! quia per crebras', Gower, p. 356, 65–6; Étienne de Fougères, *Livre des Manières*, p. 132, 807–8, p. 134, 825–8, p.135, 880ff.; 'Li Mariages des Filles au Diable' *NR* I p. 286; 'L'État du Monde', Rutebeuf, I p. 387, 130–4; 'La Vie du Monde', *ibid.*, p. 400, 9–10; Matheolus' *Lamentations*, p. 287, 641ff. (Lat. 4660ff.); *PPl* XIX 346–7. For sermons, see Owst, *Lit. and Pulp.*, pp. 300, 353, 360.

53. 'Ecce dolet Anglia', *PPS* I p. 279. See also p. 281.

54. Flügel quoted a statute of 1350 to show that money exchange by private individuals was illegal ('Chaucer's Prolog', p. 474); a new examination of the evidence by B. A. Park ('The Character of Chaucer's Merchant', *ELN* I (1964), 167–75) shows that the Merchant was probably within the law in *selling* French écus. But even Park admits that there were opportunities for sharp practice in the business of money exchange.

55. *PPl* v 249; see also XIII 392–4.

56. *Renart le Contrefait*, II p. 41, 26,362.

57. II pp. 65, 72. The *Chessbook* takes it for granted that merchants should be money-exchangers ('pecuniarum commutatores', col. 529–30).

58. 'Le Dit des Planètes' *NR* I p. 378.

59. Gower gives a rather obscure explanation of the practice, *MO* 7237–48. For the two senses of the word, see *MED* s.v., sense 3, 'The act of acquiring something, or what one acquires; acquisition, gain, profit...', and 6(*a*), 'The borrowing of money, esp. on security or/and at interest...(*b*) the lending of money at interest, esp. also at high interest; usury'. Cf. also its use to indicate the technicalities of the merchant's business in the Shipman's Tale (VII 325–48 [B² 1515–38]), and by Wycliff, who says that merchants steal 'bi usure, under colour of treuþe þat þei clepyn chevysaunce, to blynde wiþ þe puple' (ed. Arnold, III p. 88).

60. For the traditional presentation of merchants as solemn and self-conscious of manner in French fabliaux, see G. Stillwell, 'Chaucer's "Sad" Merchant', *RES* 20 (1944), 1–18. The merchant stereotype in estates literature was

certainly influenced by his role in fabliau, for some satirists dwell on the likelihood of his being cuckolded while abroad on business. (See Étienne de Fougères, *Livre des Manières*, p. 134, 841ff.; *Sermones nulli parcentes*, p. 38, 845ff.)

61. See *VC* v 679–80:

> Non sapit ille deum qui totus inheret habendum
> Has pompas mundi, nomen vt addat ei.

He does not know God who clings to the possession of worldly vanities in order to gain reputation.

and 765–8:

> Sicque per ypocrisim ciuis perquirit honorem,
> Quo genuflexa procul plebs valedicat ei.
> Accidit inde sibi quasi furtim maior vt ipse
> Astat in vrbe sua, qui minor omnibus est.

Thus through hypocrisy the citizen acquires honour, whence the common people will bow their way out of his presence. So it happens to him that as if stealthily he grows greater in his town – he who is inferior to everyone.

See also *Winner and Waster*, 375–7 ('Prowde marchandes of pris'), and Owst, *Lit. and Pulp.*, p. 352.

62. *MO* 25,362–3. Since Chaucer's Merchant is so concerned about Middelburgh, where the wool staple was situated, we may assume him to be a wool-merchant too.

63. Sermon of 1388, *Medieval Studies*, 28 (1966), 182; cf. Owst, *Lit. and Pulp.*, p. 352.

64. See O. E. Johnson, 'Was Chaucer's Merchant in Debt?: A Study in Chaucerian Syntax and Rhetoric', *JEGP* 52 (1953), 50–7, and the article by G. Stillwell cited below.

65. *MO* 25,813–30. The *Chessbook* had warned merchants against contracting debts they were unable to pay (col. 549–52).

66. In stressing this I concur with G. Stillwell ('Chaucer's Merchant: No Debts?' *JEGP* 57 (1958), 192–6), who points out that Chaucer directs our attention 'not so much to the Merchant's actual financial status as to his *manner* of giving a certain impression of his status' (p. 194). Stillwell compares him in this respect with 'those other ironically described middle-class figures of the *Prologue*, the Lawyer, the Five Guildsmen, and the Physician'. I am very glad of this confirmation of my selection of this as a unifying feature of these particular portraits – a selection which was made before I read Stillwell's article. However, I would disagree with Stillwell's opinion that Chaucer is hostile to the Lawyer and Merchant, and is attacking their façade; this is still to read the portraits in terms of *individual* moral criticism.

67. For a suggestion that the Merchant's concern over a free sea-route hints at possible embezzlement, piracy and manipulation of his financial interest, see J. K. Crane, 'An Honest Merchant?', *ELN* 4 (1966), 81–5.

68. A. S. Walker, 'Note on Chaucer's *Prologue*', *MLN* 38 (1923), 314. The plague of pirates was 'at its height' between 1385 and 1386.

69. See Bowden, *Commentary*, pp. 150–1, and pp. 53–4 above on fine shoes as a sign of wealth. For the association of the merchant with foreign travel, see Étienne de Fougères, *Livre des Manières*, p. 133, 809–16; Gilles li Muisis, II p. 57; *MO* 25,244ff.; *PPl* XIII 392–3.

70. One other feature with which the merchant is sometimes associated is ungodliness – blaspheming and neglecting the Sabbath. See 'Viri fratres' *AH* XXXIII p. 271, 181; Étienne de Fougères, *Livre des Manières*, p. 135, 873–84; 'Le Dit des Planètes', *NR* I p. 387; Matheolus' *Lamentations*, p. 287, 635–6.

71. Although there are references to 'draperes' and 'weueres' in *PPl* (Prol. 219, V 209–18).

72. For attempts to identify the fraternity, see the articles by A. B. Fullerton, *MLN* 61 (1946), 515–23; J. W. McCutchan, *PMLA* 74 (1959), 313–17; T. J. Garbáty, *JEGP* 59 (1960), 691–709. The difficulty in establishing even what kind of fraternity the Guildsmen belonged to – craft guild or parish association – makes it at least worth considering that Chaucer did not intend it to be precisely identified.

73. For an attempt to find meaning in the list, see E. P. Kuhl, *Trans. of the Wisconsin Acad. of Sciences, Arts and Letters* 18 (1916), 652–75, and for objections to Kuhl's argument, see Fullerton, *MLN* 61 (1946), 515–23.

74. See 'Viri fratres' *AH* XXXIII p. 270, 167–73; 'Totum regit saeculum', *Map Poems*, p. 234, 161–76; *VC* v, Chapters XI–XVI; Étienne de Fougères, *Livre des Manières*, p. 133, 801ff.; 'Li Mariages des Filles au Diable' *NR* I p. 286.

75. *Sermones nulli parcentes*, p. 38, 825–34, and ff.

76. *VC* v Chapters XIII–XIV; *MO* 25,501ff. Cf. 'L'État du Monde', Rutebeuf I p. 387, 135–46; *PPl* v 200ff.

77. See the passages from estates works already cited in the notes to this section.

78. Cf. P. Lisca ('Chaucer's Guildsmen and their Cook', *MLN* 70 (1955), 321–4): 'It is certainly doubtful that Chaucer considered property and a socially ambitious wife sufficient qualifications for a lawgiver, or that these really constitute "wisdom".' Lisca notes the frequency of this use of a 'modifying context' in the *Prologue*.

79. See Étienne de Fougères, *Livre des Manières*, p. 138, 1073ff., where the rich lady hopes to meet her lover at the vigil. The Wife of Bath shows off her fine clothes at 'vigilies' (III (D) 555–9).

80. They may be compared with Gower's lines on 'Vaine gloire', who is a

worldly lady who exerts herself 'Pour estre appellé cheventeine' – 'to be called mistress' (*MO* 1201–9).

81. Skeat, in his edition, notes that the ordinary tradesman or craftsman was forbidden to wear a knife ornamented with a precious metal, and that the Guildsmen must therefore be of a superior estate; alternatively, as Bowden suggests (*Commentary*, p. 183), they are doing something they shouldn't. Significantly, we can't be *sure* which interpretation is correct.

82. Langland criticises priests who wear daggers and 'a gerdel of syluer' (*PPl* XV 120–1). See also Owst, *Lit. and Pulp.*, p. 369.

CHAPTER 5

1. For an important recent study of medieval knighthood, see J. Bumke, *Studien zum Ritterbegriff im 12. und 13. Jahrhundert* (*Beihefte zum Euphorion* I, (Heidelberg, 1964)).

2. The meaning of 'worthy' here is *OED* 2: 'Distinguished by good qualities, entitled to honour or respect on this account; estimable'. 'Worthy' is often applied to knights by Chaucer; see *Chaucer Concordance*, s.v.

3. See *VC* 475–96; *MO* 23,653ff.

4. *Dits*, ed. Scheler, p. 44, 30–3. Watriquet flourished in the early part of the fourteenth century (*ibid.*, pp. viii, xii). For circumstances that make it possible that Chaucer would have been interested in Watriquet's writings, see Bowden, *Commentary*, pp. 46–7. However, the *Dit du Conestable* survives in only one mid-fourteenth-century MS (Scheler, p. xvii), and Bowden allows that both writers may have been using the 'same common medieval conception of an ideal' (p. 49). For her discussion of Chaucer's list in relation to Watriquet's, see pp. 47–9. The similarities between the two passages were first pointed out by W. H. Schofield (*Chivalry in English Literature* (Cambridge, Mass., 1912), pp. 30–3).

Watriquet's 'Prouesce' can correspond to Chaucer's 'chivalrie'; see *MED* s.v., 4 and 5. The phrase 'to love chivalry' seems to be used by Chaucer in contexts where the exercise of arms is involved (see Knight's Tale I (A) 2106, 2184). Similarly, 'loiauté' stands for Chaucer's 'trouthe' (*OED* 1, 'faithfulness, fidelity, loyalty'), and 'largesce' for 'fredom' (*MED* 2, 'generosity, liberality'). Chaucer uses such lists of virtues to characterise other knightly heroes; in *Troilus and Criseyde*, Hector is said to possess 'alle trouth and alle gentilesse, | Wisdom, honour, fredom and worthinesse' (II 160–1), and in the Knight's Tale, Arcite praises Palamon for all the proper qualifications of a knightly lover – 'trouthe, honour, knyghthede, | Wysdom, humblesse, estaat, and heigh kynrede, | Fredom' (I (A) 2789–91).

5. The most important group is 'Proesce', 'Largesce', 'Courtoisie' and 'Loiaute', who were 'engendered' by him on 'Honour', and are now 'orphaned' (ed. Scheler, pp. 53–4) but Gautier is also praised for being

'courtois, humbles, douz et frans' (p. 50, 213), and 'Largesce, Courtoisie, Honneurs' and 'Noblesce' are said to have lost their names with his death (p. 50, 222–3).

6. Col. 225–6.

7. *MO* 24,085–7. For other estates passages that mention traditional chivalric virtues, see Étienne de Fougères, *Livre des Manières*, p. 129, 593ff.; 'Dis des Estas dou Monde', Jean de Condé, p. 179, 86–9; Gilles li Muisis, II p. 54. See also the French version of Ramón Lull's work on chivalry, *Lordre de chevalerie* (printed in P. Allut, *Étude sur Symphorien Champier* (Lyons, 1859)), pp. 281 and 293. Lull wrote the *Libre de l'orde de cavalleria* in 1275 or 1276; it was an influential work and was translated into French, probably by way of a lost Latin version, in the fourteenth century. (See M. De Riquer, *Història de la Literatura Catalana, Part Antiga* (Barcelona, 1964), vol. I, pp. 256–63). The French version was known in England; one of the three surviving fourteenth-century MSS is English in origin. (For a list of the MSS, see M. Ruffini, 'Un ignoto MS della traduzione francese del "Libre de Cavalleria" di Raimondo Lullo', *Estudios Lulianos*, 2 (1958), p. 77.) Lull's text was expanded in the French version, which was on the whole very accurately translated by Caxton (see Byles's edition, pp. xlviff.). I quote Caxton's translation after quotations of the French version.

8. The implied opposition between the two qualities leads Bowden to translate 'worthy' here as 'brave' (*Commentary*, p. 49; she also cites Roland and Oliver as illustrations of the need to combine the two virtues). This is perhaps too narrow; Chaucer frequently uses these adjectives together in knightly contexts, with apparently little consciousness of their being opposites (see *Parlement of Foules*, 395, *Hous of Fame*, 1438, 1756, *Troilus and Criseyde*, II 180, 317, *CT* II (B^1) 579, *Romaunt of the Rose* 1197).

9. *Le Livre de Chevalerie*, ed. Kervyn de Lettenhove, in *Oeuvres de Froissart* (Brussels, 1873), vol. I part III, pp. 505–6. For the MS of the work, and the life of Geoffroi de Charny, whose death is described by Froissart, see A. Piaget, 'Le Livre Messire Geoffroi de Charny', *Romania*, 26 (1897), 394–411. The 'Livre' of which Piaget prints a part is another work of Geoffroi's on chivalry, in verse; towards the end there is a list of chivalric virtues which includes those of the Knight.

> Honneur, bonté y trouveras,
> Prouesce, vaillance y verras,
> Et courtoisie,
> Hardiesce si n'i faut mie,
> Loyauté y maine grant vie,
> Et puis largesce. (p. 410, 740ff.)

You will find in it [the exercise of war] honour, excellence; valour, courage will you see there, and courtesy. Daring is in no way lacking, and faithfulness flourishes there, and generosity too.

10. *Dits*, ed. Scheler, p. 44, 42–5.

11. *PSE* p. 335, 258–64. For the association of humility with the ideal of the knight, see *Lordre de chevalerie*, p. 290. It is possible that 'meekness' as a knightly virtue derives from St Bernard's ideal role for the Templars, which miraculously unites the 'fortitudo' or 'bravery' of the soldier with the 'mansuetudo' or 'mildness' of the monk (*PL* 182, col. 927).

For the attribution of increased 'vilanie' to contemporary knights, see *Roman de Fauvel*, p. 62, 1623–6; Gilles li Muisis, II p. 54.

12. *De Laude Novae Militiae*, *PL* 182, col. 923.

13. *Ibid.*, col. 926.

14. *Lordre de chevalerie*, p. 319; 'tout chevalier est tenu a honnorer son corps & estre bien vestu & noblement'. For analysis of the different knightly ideals of St Bernard and Ramón Lull, see A. Oliver, 'El "Llibre del Orde de Cavalleria" de Ramón Lull y el "De Laude Novae Militiae" de San Bernardo', *Estudios Lulianos*, 2 (1958), 175–86.

15. *Lordre de chevalerie*, pp. 289, 319.

16. 'Frequenter cogitans', *Poésies Pop. Lat.*, pp. 131–2. See also Gilles li Muisis, II p. 55 and Owst, *Lit. and Pulp.*, pp. 332, 334, 337.

17. In the assembly of knights to Theseus's tournament, Evandro has a shield which is rough with use ('assai rozzo per lavoro'), and is himself rust-marked with armour and sweat ('rugginoso | dell'arme e del sudor' – ed. S. Battaglia (Florence, 1938) st. 38 and 40). Sir Gawain's armour is also cleaned of rust (ed. J. R. R. Tolkien and E. V. Gordon, rev. N. Davis (Oxford, 1958), 2017–20).

18. The *Sermones nulli parcentes* go so far as to recognise crusaders as a separate estate, and attack them for worldly habits (pp. 24–5).

19. The Teutonic Order was responsible for the campaigns in Prussia, Lithuania and Russia (see Manly, 'A Knight Ther Was', repr. Wagenknecht, pp. 55ff.). A. S. Cook suggests that the Knight 'began the board' in Prussia at the Order's table of honour ('Beginning the Board in Prussia', *JEGP* 14 (1915), 375–88).

20. Skeat, in his edition, takes the phrase to refer to the Knight's service of the king.

21. *Chessbook*, col. 235–6. Cf. *Lordre de chevalerie*, pp. 280, 282. Geoffroi de Charny also gives fighting for one's lord as one of the motivating forces of chivalry (*Livre de Chevalerie*, p. 465).

22. See Manly, 'A Knight Ther Was', repr. Wagenknecht, pp. 46–59, and *New Light*, pp. 255–7, and A. S. Cook, 'The Historical Background of Chaucer's Knight', *Trans. Connecticut Acad. of Arts and Sciences*, 20 (1916), 196–237. For criticism of such attempts at identification, see Z. S. Fink, 'Another Knight Ther Was', *PQ* 7 (1938), 321–30.

For the popularity of crusading campaigns among English knights, see also D. Sandberger, *Studien über das Rittertum in England, Historische Studien,* vol. 310 (Berlin, 1937), Chapter 6.

23. *Chanson de Roland,* ed. F. Whitehead (Oxford, 1965), 2322–32.

24. Ed. M. A. Pey (Paris, 1859), p. 241, 7986–9. 'Biaulande' – 'ville, sur mer, peut-être Nice à l'origine' (Langlois). For the date of the poem, see Gröber, *Grundriss der Romanischen Philologie,* II, i, p. 798. See also *Li Charroi de Nymes,* ed. M. W. J. A. Jonckbloet, in *Guillaume d'Orange, Chansons de Geste des XIᵉ et XIIᵉ Siècles* (La Haye, 1854), vol. I, p. 104, 1175–89 (what looks like a list of campaigns is here ironically 'disguised' as the journeys of a merchant), and *La Prise d'Orenge, ibid.,* p. 113, 21–4 (both twelfth century); *Gui de Bourgogne,* ed. F. Guessard and H. Michelant, (Paris, 1859), p. 3, 62–73, and *La Chevalerie d'Ogier de Danemarche,* ed. M. Eusebi (Milan, 1963), p. 210, 4447–52 (both thirteenth century).

25. *Oeuvres,* II pp. 208–10, 1416–55.

26. *Le Confort d'Ami,* III p. 103, 2924–9; see also p. 116, 3278–86, where Machaut again talks about going to seek honour and prowess ('honneur et vasselage') abroad:

> Soit en Castelle ou en Grenade,
> Qui est une voie moult sade,
> En Alemaigne, en Rommenie
> Ou en Prusse ou en Lombardie.

whether it is in Castille or in Granada – which is a very agreeable road – in Germany, in Romagna, in Prussia or in Lombardy.

27. See Geoffroi de Charny, *Livre de Chevalerie,* p. 468; M. McKisack, *The Fourteenth Century* (Oxford, 1959), p. 248, n. 5.

28. Although we are left to infer that he has fought *for* a heathen as well, from ll. 64–6. For possible identification of the 'lord of Palatye', see the articles by Manly and Cook cited above.

29. See *Pontificale Romanum,* ed. J. Catalani (Rome, 1738), I pp. 419 and 424, and *Monumenta Liturgica, PL* 138 col. 1121. This phrase is not always included in the liturgies for the dubbing.

30. 'Mult est diables curteis', ed. Aspin, p. 119 v. 4.

31. *PSE* p. 334, 248–51. See also 'Le Dit des Patenostres', *NR* I p. 242; Gilles li Muisis, II pp. 18, 20, 53; *Lordre de chevalerie,* pp. 309–10. Fighting pagans is a duty also urged on kings and nobles; see 'Viri fratres, servi Dei', *AH* XXXIII p. 270, 153–4; *Sermones nulli parcentes,* p. 34, 668–76; 'Heu! quia per crebras', Gower, pp. 355–6, 31–4; Gilles li Muisis, I pp. 288, 314. See also Dante, *Inferno,* Canto XXVIII 85–9. For the view that the Holy Land should be re-conquered by preaching rather than fighting, see Map, *De Nugis Curialium,* p. 30, dist. I, cap. XX, 11ff. This was a view also held by Ramón Lull, in contradiction to the passage cited above, which is in his text (Oliver, 'Libre del Orde de Cavalleria', pp. 183–4).

32. 'Le Dit des Planètes', *NR* I p. 377; *MO* 23,895.

33. See *Pontificale Romanum*, and *Monumenta Liturgica*, PL 138, and Hittorp, *De Divinis Catholicis Ecclesiae Officiis* (Paris, 1624), col. 178.

Odo of Cluny (878/9–942) seems to have been the first to put forward this role for knights; see his *Vita Sancti Geraldi*, PL 133, col. 646 C. For a discussion, see W. Braun, *Studien zum Ruodlieb* (Berlin, 1962), pp. 35ff. The definition of 'Pure religion and undefiled' as compassion for orphans and widows is, of course, apostolic (James 1: 27), and is applied to an ideal king in Ælfric's life of St Edmund (G. I. Needham (ed.) *Lives of Three English Saints*, (London, 1966), p. 44, 21–2).

34. See 'Le Dit des Planètes', *NR* I p. 377; *Lordre de chevalerie*, pp. 278–9 (defending the faith against 'miscreants'), 281 (preserving justice), 282 (maintaining the land), 285 (defending widows, orphans, and the weak), 286 (guarding roads and peasants, punishing robbers and criminals), 309–10 (fighting abroad against the enemies of the cross).

35. For the contradictory notions involved in different aspects of the knightly role, see S. Painter, *French Chivalry* (Baltimore, 1940); D. Rocher, ' "Chevalerie" et Littérature "Chevaleresque" ' (I), *Études Germaniques*, 21 (1966), 167.

36. See for example, the poems which unite the ideal of knightly love with that of the crusade, discussed in Peter Dronke, *The Medieval Lyric* (London, 1968), pp. 127–8, 138–9.

37. D. Rocher, ' "Chevalerie" et Littérature "Chevaleresque" ' (II), *Études Germaniques* 23 (1968), 349–50.

38. See 'Viri fratres, servi Dei' *AH* XXXIII p. 270, 159–62; *Chessbook*, col. 273–7; *VC* v 5; Étienne de Fougères, *Livre des Manières*, p. 128, 537ff.; *Roman de Carité*, p. 22, XL 6ff., p. 27, LI, 4–8; 'Le Dit des Planètes' *NR* I p. 377; Gilles li Muisis, II p. 130; Matheolus' *Lamentations*, p. 281, 452–5 (Lat. 4539ff.); *MO* 23,593–611; *Lordre de chevalerie*, pp. 281, 282, 285, 286; *PPl* I 94–8; Thomas Wimbledon's sermon of 1388, *Medieval Studies*, 28 (1966), 179. Cf. Owst, *Lit. and Pulp.*, p. 338.

Some writers also stress the knight's duty to fight in a just war, not necessarily against the heathen: see 'Totum regit saeculum', *Map Poems*, p. 232, 97–102; *Sermones nulli parcentes*, p. 36, 755–6; *VC* v 13–14, 489–92; *MO* 23,611.

39. See Rather of Verona, *Praeloquia*, PL 136 col. 149; 'Frequenter cogitans', *Poésies Pop. Lat.*, p. 132; 'Viri fratres' *AH* XXXIII p. 270, 162–4; 'Totum regit saeculum', *Map Poems*, p. 232, 105–8; *VC* v 519–20, 543–8; Étienne de Fougères, *Livre des Manières*, p. 128, 541ff.; 'L'État du Monde', Rutebeuf, I p. 388, 154; 'Li Mariages des Filles au Diable' *NR* I pp. 285–6; *Roman de Fauvel*, p. 42, 1056–8 and ff.; 'Le Dit des Mais' *NR* I pp. 188–9; 'Dis des Estas dou Monde', Jean de Condé, p. 180, 104–9; Gilles li Muisis, II pp. 16–20, 54–5; Matheolus' *Lamentations*, p. 114, 2463–4 (Lat. 1677–8), p. 281, 476ff. (Lat. 4552–6); *MO* 23,732–48; *Lordre de chevalerie*, p. 286; *Handlyng*

Synne, p. 81, 2264–5, 2275–8; *PPl* VI 39–45; Owst, *Lit. and Pulp.*, pp. 95–6, 337–8.

40. If this was a real historical aim of the crusading knights, it was not very satisfactorily fulfilled; Walsingham's account of the taking of Vilna reports that there were 4000 dead and 8 converts to the Christian faith (Cook, 'Chaucer's Knight', p. 199).

41. See St Bernard, *De Laude Novae Militiae*, PL 182, col. 924–5.

42. This can well be consistent with the presentation of the Knight as an ideal representative of chivalry; Daniel Rocher ('Chevalerie' (II), especially pp. 354–7) has noted that the different aspects of chivalry as it is treated in literature represent attempts to tie it to different *functions*, and that such attempts are possible precisely because adventure, or fighting itself, is the only essential feature of chivalry. This attitude certainly seems to underlie the *Livre de Chevalerie* of Geoffroi de Charny; having listed many causes which will lead knights to prowess in arms – such as defence of lords or friends, desire for profit or advancement, love of a lady – he then describes those who are the best of all, who love arms and fighting for their own sake – who are, that is, what might be called 'academic enthusiasts' (*Oeuvres de Froissart*, I part III, pp. 472ff.).

43. In an interesting article ('The Worthiness of Chaucer's Knight', *MLQ* 25 (1964), 66–75), Charles Mitchell argues that the Knight is not on the same plane of virtue as the Parson, and brings out the 'amoral' tendency of Chaucer's praise of him. While much of what I argue agrees with Mitchell's approach, he does not apply the concept of function to the pilgrims, nor does he develop the implications of his observation that the meanings of 'worthy, virtuous, good' overlap with one another.

44. See *Roman de Fauvel*, p. 9, 149–52; Gilles li Muisis, II p. 130.

45. The *Chessbook* implies the relative ages of the two in stressing the need for the knight to undergo a long period of training before he is dubbed (col. 229–30). The squire was not *necessarily* a young man: from the twelfth to the thirteenth century on, there was a growing reluctance to be knighted, because of the expense of arms (F. L. Ganshof, 'Qu'est-ce que la chevalerie?', *Revue Générale Belge* 25 (November 1947), 80–1).

46. Jean de Condé ('Dis des Estas dou Monde', pp. 181–2, 167–9) also exhorts 'Escuijers et siergans':

> Soies courtois sans vilenie
> Deboinnaires sans felenie
> Si siers haus et bas liement.

Be considerate, free from bad manners, affable, without malice, and serve high and low cheerfully.

47. The meaning of 'lusty' here is 'healthy, strong, vigorous' (*OED* 5a). 'Lusty bacheler' or 'lusty knight' are frequent in Chaucer: see *CT* I (A)

2111; IX (H) 107; *Anelida and Arcite* 86; *Troilus and Criseyde*, I 165, IV 1485. However, Chaucer sometimes uses the word in contexts where it can take on sexual overtones (see the Wife of Bath's Prologue, III (D) 605, and her Tale, 883); thus, it may be that lines 97–8 of the *Prologue* suggest what kind of 'vigour' characterises the Squire.

48. For comment on the Squire's campaigns – against the French, rather than the heathen – see Bowden, *Commentary*, pp. 83–4.

49. See Geoffroi de Charny, *Livre de Chevalerie*, *Oeuvres de Froissart*, I part III, p. 469.

50. 'Totum regit saeculum', *Map Poems*, p. 232, 100.

51. *PPS* I p. 276. The lines can be paraphrased as follows:

> When men take rest, refreshed in sleep at night, such fellows stay up, ready to perform wicked acts. Often they burn in frigid (heartless?) love; if I kiss their sweethearts, [I find that] their nose runs.

52. *Livre de Chevalerie*, p. 464.

53. p. 297. Caxton's translation (p. 63) reads:

> A man lame / or ouer fatte / or that hath any other evyl disposycion in his body / For whiche he may not vse thoffyce of chyualrye is not suffysaunt to be a kny3t.

54. p. 294. Caxton's translation (p. 57) reads:

> If by beaute of facion / or by a body fayr grete or wel aourned / or by fayr here / by regard / or for to holde the myrrour in the hand / and by the other Iolytees / shold a squyer be adoubed knyght of vylayns...

> – you might as well make peasants knights.

55. II p. 154. Cf. Nicholas Bozon, *La Lettre de l'Empéreur Orgueil*, p. 68, 215–18; Pride sends these orders to chaplains:

> 'Gardez', fet il 'la chevelure,
> Et mettez la coyfe par desure,
> Fetis tailler la vesture
> A fur de esquier a mesure.'

> 'Look after your hair', he said, 'and perch your coif on top; have your clothing cut just like a squire's.'

56. 'The Simonie', *PSE* p. 335, 271–2, p. 336, 283–5. Line 284 is difficult to interpret; Wright glosses 'raye' as 'cloth, garment' and 'overthuert' as 'crosswise', but does not explain the whole. Ross glosses 'ray' as 'banner' in his edition (*Anglia*, 85 (1957), 183), without giving his reasons. I suggest that the writer is complaining about short gowns, and that 'ray' has its usual meaning of 'striped cloth' (*OED* sb.[4], 1). In a long gown, the garment might well be cut so that the weft, and the stripe, would run from top to bottom; a short gown could be cut so that the warp ran from top to bottom, and the

8 -->

stripe would then run crosswise, or 'overthuert'. For squires and fine clothing, see also Owst, *Lit. and Pulp.*, p. 337.

57. *De Laude Novae Militiae*, PL 182, col. 923.

58. *Le Char d'Orgueil*, p. 26, CXVIII 469–72.

59. See *De Planctu Naturae*, *Anglo-Latin Satirical Poets* II p. 495; 'Anglia faex hominum' (a poem from the fourteenth-century MS Cotton Titus A xx), *PPS* I p. 92. Part of Meier Helmbrecht's splendid and 'upper-class' appearance is due to his curly hair (p. 1, 11).

60. See 'L'en puet fere et defere', *PSE* p. 255, ('pride hath sleve'); *Mum and the Sothsegger*, p. 17, 152, p. 18, 196, p. 19, 234; Owst, *Lit. and Pulp.*, pp. 409–10, and especially p. 369: a 'wrecchid cnave' must have a 'costli gowne with bagges hangyng to his kne...and gaili hosid and schood as thouȝ it were a squyer of a cuntre'. Bag-sleeves, which have their fullness caught in at the wrist, differ from the older fashion for loose-flowing sleeves, which are probably what the Squire wears. (See D. C. Calthrop, *English Costume*, (London, 1906) vol. 2, pp. 46–7, 72; I. Brooke, *English Costume of the Later Middle Ages* (London, 1935), p. 38.) The satire on exaggerated sleeves is as appropriate to the one fashion as to the other.

61. See Gilles li Muisis, II pp. 46, 153 (where short gowns are associated with increasing sexual licentiousness); *MO* 20,677–9 (where the priest is asked whether he has assumed 'ce courte cote' – 'this short gown' – to impress 'Katelote'); Owst, *Lit. and Pulp.*, p. 277, n. 2, where such fashions are said to make priests look like knights. See also the Parson's Tale, which in the section on Pride criticises both 'embrowdynge' and

the horrible disordinat scantinesse of clothyng, as been thise kutted sloppes, or haynselyns, that thurgh hire shortnesse ne covere nat the shameful membres of man, to wikked entente.

x (I) 417, 421. As Robinson notes, Chaucer is much more detailed here than Peraldus.

62. 'As if they had been pressed by a curling-iron' (Bowden, *Commentary*, p. 81).

63. *Livre de Chevalerie*, p. 530. Again, Geoffroi tells us that it is right for young people to dress nicely, provided they do not carry it to excess or spend a lot of money (p. 528).

64. 'Dis des Estas dou Monde', p. 182, 170.

65. 2255–64, 2284; Fr. version I 2129–36, 2157. The last line in the French reads 'Cous tes manches, tes cheveus pigne' – 'sew your sleeves, comb your hair'.

66. p. 54, 559ff. (Lat. pp. 53–4, 749ff.).

67. 2311–28. (Fr. version I 2183–98. Chaucer leaves out Amours' advice to 'saillir' or 'leap', and adds the advice to 'make' songs.) See also Geoffroi de Charny, *Livre de Chevalerie*, p. 480 (the good knight shouldn't spend his

time playing dice or tennis, but should converse, dance and sing with ladies), and Nicholas Bozon, *La Lettre de l'Empéreur Orgueil*, p. 68, 224–6 (Pride advises chaplains to imitate squires and sing carols in their company).

68. One last aspect of these two portraits which may refer itself to traditional satire is the accompaniment of the Yeoman. It is not clear whether the Yeoman is the servant of the Squire or the Knight; the 'he' in lines 101–2 might be either:

> A Yemen hadde he and servantz namo
> At that tyme, for hym liste ride so.

But a sermon quoted by Owst, complaining about the huge entourages of knights and squires, shows why Chaucer stresses that there are 'namo servantz' with them (*Lit. and Pulp.*, p. 337).

69. For bibliography and discussion of anti-feminist literature in the Middle Ages, see A. Wulff, *Die Frauenfeindlichen Dichtungen in den Romanischen Literaturen des Mittelalters, bis zum ende des XIII Jahrhunderts, Romanistische Arbeiten IV* (Halle a.S., 1914), and, for English literature, F. L. Utley, *The Crooked Rib: An Analytical Index to the Argument about Women in English and Scots Literature to the end of the Year 1568* (Columbus, 1944).

70. This has been noted by H. S. V. Jones ('The Plan of the Canterbury Tales', *MP* 13 (May 1915), 46).

71. pp. 42–3 (nuns pp. 30–2).

72. 'Dis des Estas dou Monde', p. 183, 231ff.; cf. a poem like 'Ecce dolet Anglia', which does not list the estates, but refers to the weakness of women in exactly the same way as it does to the dishonesty of merchants and the cunning of the friars (*PPS* I p. 281). Some writers break down the class into smaller units – virgin, wife, widow, and so on (e.g. Rather of Verona's *Praeloquia*, *PL* 136, Book II, already deals separately with 'mulier', 'vidua' and 'virgo'). And women can even have an estates poem all to themselves, as is shown by a little twelfth-century poem 'Fuge cetus feminarum', which explains the drawbacks of loving each class of women in turn – virgin, wife, widow, beghine, nun (ed. W. Wattenbach, *Anzeiger für Kunde der deutschen Vorzeit*, 17 (1870), col. 10).

73. See *RR* II 12,751 and *GP* 461, *RR* I 3908 and *GP* 476. For satire on *widows*, see Matheolus' *Lamentations*, p. 8, 293ff. (Lat. 104ff.), and *Handlyng Synne*, p. 333, 10,729ff.

74. I p. 215, II p. 178.

75. *Livre des Manières*, p. 138, 1054. See also Matheolus' *Lamentations*, pp. 24–5, 775ff. (Lat. 351ff.).

76. *PPl* VI 9–14. See also V 215–18.

77. It is also interesting to note that the bawd's trade is carried on under cover of that of the seamstress in Rojas' *La Celestina*, written at the end of the fifteenth century (ed. J. Cejador (Madrid, 1913), p. 70); a girl can make the excuse that she wants to see about some sewing, and arrange to meet, or

collect a letter from, her lover. This makes it perhaps possible that the 'remedies of love' of which the Wife knows include the particular 'remedy' of the 'vetula', patching up maidenheads (Peter Dronke's suggestion).

It is also worth noting the ambiguity of the phrase 'remedies of love' itself; are they remedies *for* love, to ensure successful love-affairs, or are they remedies *against* love, in the sense of Ovid's title, to ensure that she is not so carried away as to lose her domination over a man?

78. See, for example, Gilles li Muisis, II p. 23; Matheolus' *Lamentations*, p. 113, 2437ff. (Lat. 1661ff.) St Jerome describes how a widow in particular, feeling herself uncurbed by any husband, gives vent to her pride (Wiesen, *St Jerome as a Satirist*, p. 124).

79. I p. 839 (cf. II p. 185); II p. 77.

80. *Lettre de l'Empéreur Orgueil*, p. 69, 255–64. Bozon also presents two pictures of ladies hanging back, apparently with a false parade of courtesy, to let others pass (*ibid.* 267–72, and *Le Char d'Orgueil*, p. 16, LXXII).

81. *Lamentations*, p. 82, 1431–40. This passage is not in the Latin. See also Deschamps' *Miroir de Mariage* (*Oeuvres* IX, p. 109, 3262ff.), where an old woman tries to persuade her son-in-law to let his wife go to church, where (she claims) the ladies show examples of such good behaviour that each hangs back in favour of her social inferiors. (The parallel was noted by G. L. Kittredge, 'Chauceriana', *MP* VII (1910), p. 475.)

82. See 'Frequenter cogitans', *Poésies Pop. Lat.*, p. 133 (monks are 'like women' when they quarrel); 'Sit Deo gloria', *Map Poems*, p. 79, 35–6, p. 82, 133–4 (for details of this poem, see next note); 'Totum regit saeculum', *ibid.*, p. 235, 204; Gilles li Muisis, II p. 177; Matheolus' *Lamentations*, p. 7, 251ff. (Lat. 80), p. 22, 699–700 (Lat. 313), p. 48, 41ff. (Lat. 669ff.); *MO* 4092–5, 4264–7; *Handlyng Synne*, p. 112, 3215–16, p. 347, 11,229–30. See also *Secular Lyrics* ed. Robbins, p. 36, 23–4, 29–31, and pp. 38–40, and Owst, *Lit. and Pulp.*, p. 42 and n. 10.

83. 'Sit Deo gloria, laus, benedictio!', *Map Poems*, p. 81, 98–101. This poem is early thirteenth century, and survives in about sixty MSS; for a discussion, see P. Lehmann, *Die Parodie im Mittelalter mit 24 ausgewählten parodistischen Texten* (2nd edition, Stuttgart 1963), pp. 117–18.

84. *Lamentations*, p. 73, 1004ff. (Lat. 1012ff.). The Lendi was a great church festival and annual market held at St-Denis in Paris on 11 June (see Tobler-Lommatzsch, s.v.). See also on women's fondness for pilgrimages, Deschamps' *Miroir de Mariage* (*Oeuvres* IX 807–9, 3500–15, 3729–31), cited in this connection by J. L. Lowes, 'Illustrations of Chaucer', *Romanic Review*, 2 (1911), 120–1.

85. See *OED* s.v. Wander, v., 3*b* '. . .to fall into error (moral or intellectual)', and for discussion of the possible pun here, D. S. Biggins, *NQ* n.s. 7 (1960), 129–30.

86. Manly suggested that the Wife was out of date in following this fashion

for kerchiefs (*New Light*, pp. 230ff.), but see also his edition of the *Canterbury Tales* (London, n.d.), p. 527, where he implies that the wife *is* in fashion. For disagreement with Manly's statement that the Wife is behind the times, see Bowden, *Commentary*, p. 227, n. 8, and D. E. Wretlind, *MLN* 63 (1948), 381-2. Wretlind is, however, occasionally misleading; e.g. he implies that Manly cites F. W. Fairholt, *Costume in England: a history of dress from the earliest period till the close of the 18th century* (London, 1846) in *New Light* to show that huge head-dresses were out of date, whereas the reference to Fairholt actually occurs in support of the opposite point of view in Manly's edition of the *Tales*, *loc. cit.* Wretlind also suggests that the definition 'head-dress', 'hat', for which he cites *OED*, is the appropriate meaning for 'coverchief' here; *OED* in fact gives 'head-dress', but not 'hat' for either 'coverchief' or 'kerchief'. The *Chaucer Concordance* shows that 'coverchief' is for Chaucer most often a handkerchief or piece of cloth, but that he also uses the word for the head-dresses of the court ladies before whom the knight in the Wife of Bath's Tale is arraigned, without any hint that this is an archaic touch to fit the Arthurian setting (III (D) 1017-18). I believe that the Wife's head-dresses were fashionable, and they are an example of Chaucer's *topical* illustration of long-established estates characteristics.

87. See Wulff, *Die Frauenfeindlichen Dichtungen*, p. 83.

88. See 'Sit Deo gloria', *Map Poems*, p. 83, 170-1; *RR* II 13,267-8 (La Vieille advises that the girl should wear them); Nicholas Bozon, *Le Char d'Orgueil*, p. 15, LXV 259-60; 'Li Mariages des Filles au Diable' *NR* I p. 287; 'Li evesques parisiens | Est devins et naturiens', ed. Fairholt, pp. 29ff. (a thirteenth-century poem; see *Hist. Litt. de la France*, XXIII p. 248); Gilles li Muisis, II pp. 25, 33, 166; Matheolus' *Lamentations*, p. 115, 2514ff. (Lat. 1695), p. 129, 3015 (Lat. 1900), p. 183, 877ff. (Lat. 2679) (contrasted with the simple veil of old); *Handlyng Synne*, p. 112, 3223-4. See also Owst, *Lit. and Pulp.*, pp. 96, 399ff. For an illustration of this fashion, see F. W. Fairholt, *Satirical Songs and Poems on Costume from the 13th to the 19th century*, Percy Society 27 (London, 1849), p. 30.

89. See *VC* v 345: 'Crinibus et velis tinctis caput ornat' – 'She adorns her head with false hair and dyed veils'; Nicholas Bozon, *Le Char d'Orgueil*, p. 15, LXVI 262; 'Lord that lenest us lyf', ed. C. Brown, *English Lyrics of the XIIIth Century* (Oxford, 1932), p. 134 ('a fauce filet').

However, Matheolus' *Lamentations* also complain that women want 'un nouveau cuevrechief' for each feast (p. 129, 3032).

90. *Handlyng Synne*, p. 119, 3445, p. 279, 8883. For general satire on women's head-dresses, see Nicholas Bozon, *La Lettre de l'Empéreur Orgueil*, p. 67, 166, p. 69, 268; *Secular Lyrics*, ed. Robbins, p. 36, 37-40; *PPl Crede*, p. 4, 84.

91. II 9234-5. Cf. *PPl* v 30-1.

92. *RR* II 9259-61. Cf. 9275-7, and 13,312.

93. See Gilles li Muisis, II p. 28, and Owst, *Lit. and Pulp.*, p. 401, n. 10. See also my comments on the Monk and the Prioress.

94. *Chaucer and the Medieval Sciences*, pp. 107ff.

95. Thus, according to Curry, the Wife's 'suspiciously red or florid complexion ...indicates that the woman is immodest, loquacious, and given to drunkenness' (*Chaucer and the Mediaeval Sciences*, p. 108). This description would hardly help a medieval satirist to distinguish her from the rest of her sex. They would have been similarly surprised at the notion that only women with 'gat-teeth' were 'envious, irreverent, luxurious by nature, bold, deceitful, faithless, and suspicious' (p. 109). Even the 'excessive virility' indicated by her large hips (p. 108) can be linked with the traditional image of a virago reducing men to submission ('Sit Deo gloria', *Map Poems*, p. 83, 149–50). Medieval physiognomy is clearly connected with contemporary character-analysis of other sorts, and the combination of traits which a physiognomist finds convincingly life-like clearly either reflects or establishes stereotypes which appear also outside his work. As a final demonstration we may take part of the account of the character of the woman born when 'the first face of Taurus is in the ascendent':

> She shall be lightly given to affairs of the heart, having a lover for the greater part of her life; ... She shall be inconstant, changeable, speaking (or gossiping) with fluency and volubility, now to this one, now to that. (pp. 95–6)

Despite the more 'individual' traits of which the rest of it is composed, the traditional medieval image of women has clearly influenced this description.

96. See the two descriptions of Adam de la Halle's wife Marie, seen through the eyes of the lover and the husband respectively, in the *Jeu de la Feuillée* (pp. 28–38, 81–174), and the similar double view of woman in Matheolus' *Lamentations*, p. 18, 575ff. (Lat. 241ff.). This 'dual description' goes back at least to the eleventh century, for it occurs in *Ruodlieb* (ed. Zeydel, p. 126, XV, 3ff.).

97. *MO* 17,893–901. For the ugly old woman who paints herself up, see also Matheolus' *Lamentations*, p. 70, 884ff. (Lat. 966ff.), p. 94, 1807ff. (Lat. 1362ff.), and Jerome's description of painted crones (Wiesen, *St Jerome as a Satirist*, p. 129). Gower also has a figure called La Maquerelle, who is too old to attract men and so satisfies her lust by acting as a bawd (*MO* 9440ff.).

98. See 'Dis des Estas dou Monde', Jean de Condé, p. 183, 237; Gilles li Muisis, II p. 177; Matheolus' *Lamentations*, p. 48, 41ff., and the traditional proverb quoted below, p. 129, n. 9.

CHAPTER 6

1. See J. L. Lowes, *Convention and Revolt in Poetry* (2nd edition, London, 1930), pp. 41–5.
2. For detailed comparison with descriptions of romantic beauties, see J. L. Lowes, 'Simple and Coy: A Note on Fourteenth Century Poetic Diction', *Anglia*, 32 (1910), p. 441, n. 3, and also D. S. Brewer, 'The Ideal of Feminine Beauty in Medieval Literature', *MLR* 50 (1955), 257–69. See also the similarities in Adam de la Halle's description of his wife as he used to see her (*Jeu de la Feuillée*, pp. 30–2);

> Ele avoit front bien compassé,
> Blanc, onni, large, fenestric, . . .
> Si noir oeil me sanloient vair, . . .
> A deus petis plochons jumiaus,
> Ouvrans et cloans a dangier
> En rewars simples amoureus;
> Puis se descendoit entre deus
> Li tuiaus du nés bel et droit, . . .
> Li bouke après se poursievoit,
> Graille as cors et grosse ou moilon,
> Freske et vermeille comme rose. (91–120)

She had a well-proportioned forehead, white, smooth, broad, open. . . Her black eyes seemed to me to be crystal. . . with two little twin lids opening and shutting as she pleased in innocent, alluring glances. Between them descended the ridge of her lovely straight nose. . . then came her mouth, thin at the ends and full in the middle, fresh and red as a rose.

3. For the romantic aura attached to this name, see Lowes, 'Simple and Coy' p. 440, n. 1.
4. *Ibid.*, pp. 442ff.
5. II 13,377ff.; the parallel was noted by Lowes, 'Simple and Coy', p. 441.
6. Singing divine office is the one duty of nuns which estates writers mention, although in the course of satirising them; see *SS* 2377–8; Guiot de Provins, *Bible*, p. 77, 2172–3 (nuns sing service but perform no fruitful actions).
7. The way in which the Prioress's appearance and behaviour contravenes her duties as a nun and head of a convent has been amply demonstrated by Eileen Power, *Medieval English Nunneries* (Cambridge, 1922), p. 76, and *Medieval People* (New York, 1963), Chapter 4; for a (not very convincing) attempt to defend the Prioress, see Sister Mary Madeleva, *Chaucer's Nuns and Other Essays* (Appleton, 1925). Part of my discussion will aim at showing that the Prioress's profession is not *directly* at odds with an ideal of 'curteisie'; the incongruity lies rather in the way in which she understands the term.
8. See Wulff, *Die Frauenfeindlichen Dichtungen*, p. 81.

9. *Decameron*, First Story, Third Day, p. 318, 2. See also 'Le Dit des Patenostres', *NR* I p. 243, which addresses 'Béguines... Filles-Dieu, nonnains, veuves et mariées' corporately; Gilles li Muisis analyses the duties of nuns in terms of the proverb 'Flere, loqui, nere, statuit Deus in muliere' – 'God assigned to women weeping, talking and spinning' (I p. 213).

10. The phrase is applied to the Prioress by Lowes, *Convention and Revolt in Poetry*, p. 41.

11. See *SS* 2371ff.; *VC* IV 579–94; 'L'Ordre de Bel Ayse', ed. Aspin, p. 133, 31–52; 'Le Dit des Mais', *NR* I pp. 185–6; Gilles li Muisis, I pp. 215–16; *Decameron*, First Story, Third Day, and Second Story, Ninth Day; 'The Land of Cokaygne', ed. Bennett and Smithers, pp. 143–4, 147–76; *PPl* v 160–1.

12. See *SS* 2393–4; 'Viri fratres' *AH* XXXIII p. 270, 103–5; *Sermones nulli parcentes*, p. 31, 561–4; Guiot de Provins, *Bible*, p. 75, 2098–107; Gilles li Muisis, I p. 214; *PPl* v 162–5.

13. See Guiot de Provins, *Bible*, p. 75, 2109–12.

14. See *Sermones nulli parcentes*, pp. 31–2, 581–8.

15. *Ibid.*, p. 31, 569–72.

16. See *SS* 2381–2; Gilles li Muisis, I p. 213 (he thinks the nun should make use of her feminine lacrimosity to weep for the sins of mankind) and p. 216. Cf. the Prioress's ready tears at the sight of a suffering animal (144–5).

17. See *Sermones nulli parcentes*, p. 31, 565–8; *RR* II 9915–20.

18. 'Plangit nonna fletibus', ed. Dronke, *Medieval Latin*, II p. 357, 19–27; see also his discussion.

19. p. 215, fol. 113b, 22–8, especially:

wummon seið þe apostle. schal wreon hire heaued. wrihen he seið nawt wimplin.

20. p. 103, fol. 53a, 23.

21. I pp. 212–13, 216, 217, 226–7.

22. This is the effect of nuns' finery predicted by Gilles li Muisis (I pp. 214, 215–16).

23. Ed. W. Meyer, *Nachrichten von der königlichen Gesellschaft der Wissenschaften zu Göttingen* (1914), pp. 1ff. For a discussion, see Dronke, *Medieval Latin*, I pp. 229ff.

24. See K. Bartsch, *Altfranzösische Romanzen und Pastourellen* (Leipzig, 1870), Nos 33 and 34, I pp. 28–30. A nun in a courtly love relationship also appears in the eleventh-century Latin poem, 'Suavissima nunna', ed. Dronke, *Medieval Latin*, II pp. 353ff., discussed I pp. 277ff.

For a full list of references to literary treatments of the unhappy nun in several medieval languages, see María Rosa Lida de Malkiel, 'Nuevas Notas Para la Interpretación del "Libro de Buen Amor"', *Nueva Revista de Filología Hispánica*, 13 (1959), 66, n. 56.

25. *SS* 2389–90. For the 'straight' use of this convention, see *Jeu de la Feuillée*, p. 34, 151–2.
26. 'L'Ordre de Bel Ayse', ed. Aspin, p. 132, 17.
27. p. 31, 549–56. The text then shifts into an anti-feminist mood, however; correction is said to be useless, because a woman always does what is forbidden her (see also *VC* IV 575–6; Guiot de Provins, *Bible*, p. 75, 2098ff.).
28. The similarity between the two descriptions has been noted by J. A. W. Bennett ('Chaucer's Contemporary', in Hussey (ed.), *Critical Approaches to Piers Plowman*, p. 318).
29. Robinson seems to be right in concluding that the reference to 'English French' is disparaging of the Prioress's efforts to be courtly; besides the references which he gives, see D. Legge, *Anglo-Norman Literature and its Background* (Oxford, 1963), pp. 65, 217, 236, 358. See also *De Nugis Curialium*, p. 271, for a reference to 'Marlborough French' (cited by C. H. Livingston in 'The Fabliau "Des Deux Anglois et de L'Anel" ', *PMLA* 40 (1925), 217–24, which discusses yet another joke at the expense of the French spoken by the English), and *PPl* v 238–9, for a humorous reference to French 'of the ferthest ende of Norfolke'.

It is possible that the Prioress's oath is also a sign of breeding – a very genteel way of swearing; however, I think the point of the line is not to tell us which saint the Prioress swears by, but rather that she swears at all.
30. As J. M. Steadman has noted, Chaucer uses an account of the Prioress's flouting of the rule against pets to suggest her contravention of other rules as well; unless (perhaps) the 'rosted flessh' was poultry, it should not have been on her table ('The Prioress' Dogs and Benedictine Rule', *MP* 54 (1956), 1–6).

This use of incidental suggestion is exactly what we have noted in the other *Prologue* portraits as a way of hinting at shortcomings without providing a firm basis for criticism.
31. 2797–8. See also *VC* III 1499–1502, and Owst, *Lit. and Pulp.*, p. 327.
32. *Le Char d'Orgueil*, p. 22, C 397–400.
33. *The Book of the Knight of La Tour Landry*, ed. T. Wright (EETS o.s. 33, London, 1868) pp. 28–9. (The translation of this work into English was not made until the fifteenth century, but the French original was written in 1372.)
34. The quotation is from the late fourteenth-century version of *Sir Launfal* (ed. A. J. Bliss (London, 1960), p. 80, 965); in Marie de France's *Lanval* (ed. A. Ewert (Oxford, 1965), p. 72, 574), written in the twelfth century, the fairy mistress has one greyhound.
35. See Chapter 9 for a discussion of 'curteisie' in the *Prologue*.
36. Ed. E. V. Gordon, (Oxford, 1953), p. 17, 432ff. God's love is called 'amour fine' in the *Roman de Fauvel* (p. 90, 2493), and in Gilles li Muisis (I p. 211).

Langland attributes God's care for man's food, drink and clothing to his 'curteisie' (*PPl* I 20).

37. Ed. Gollancz, 1057-68; cf. *RR* I 7689-706.

38. See the *Council of Remiremont*, *Nachrichten von der königlichen Gesellschaft der Wissenschaften zu Göttingen* (1914), p. 13, 142ff. and Bartsch, *Altfranzösische Romanzen*, No 34, 8.

39. See Dronke, *Medieval Latin*, I p. 229. Cf. *Gilles li Muisis*, I p. 222; *Ancrene Wisse*, p. 198, fol. 105a, 18ff.

40. Cf. *Gilles li Muisis*, I p. 216, complaining about the high-flown airs assumed by nuns, and admitting that ladies of birth ('Dames emparentees') have some excuse, but should not go too far.

41. See Smalley, *English Friars*, p. 41. I have been unable to check Miss Smalley's reference; all other reference works I have consulted given the date of Guibert's death as 1270. Guibert taught at Paris where, according to the *Histoire Littéraire*, he was one of the most distinguished thirteenth-century theologians (XIX p. 138). The *Sermones ad status* were written after 1261 (A. Lecoy de la Marche, *La Chaire Française au Moyen Age, Spécialement au XIIIᵉ Siècle* (Paris, 1868), p. 140).

42. See Lecoy de la Marche, *La Chaire Française*, p. 469, he lists nine MSS of the *sermones ad status*; all those that he dates are fourteenth century. They were also printed at Louvain in 1473, at Lyons in 1511, and at Paris in 1513. I cite the 1511 edition. Guibert's works were known in England; he is mentioned in the fourteenth-century Dominican Robert Holcot's commentary on the Book of Wisdom (Cap. VI, lect. 75).

43. It begins (fol. clxvff.) with Wisdom 4:1: 'Quam pulchra est casta generatio cum claritate!'

44. 'Pulchritudo genarum vel faciei signat simplicitatem vt quando facies est alba sicut lilium et rubea sicut rosa. isti enim duo colores permixti faciunt faciem pulchram quia vera simplicitas reddit animam castam et verecundam.' (fol. clxvᵥ)

Guibert then compares the nun to the turtle-dove in simplicity (as does Gautier de Coincy, ed. Nurmela, p. 165, 785; the image of the dove – but not its simplicity – is a feature of the Song of Songs).

45. Song of Songs 7:1. (fol. clxvᵥ).

46. Ed. T. Nurmela, *Annales Academiae Scientiarum Fennicae*, Ser. B XXXVIII (Helsinki, 1937). The poem was written for the nuns of Notre-Dame at Soissons between 1223 and 1227 (*ibid.*, p. 14), and survives, wholly or partially, in twenty MSS, one of which is English (London BM Harley 4401, foll. 133-40, thirteenth century).

47. See Tobler–Lommatzsch, s.v.

48. II p. 170; cf. his repeated insistence that nuns ought to be 'coyes' (I pp. 213,

216, 218, 228). Gilles also applies 'simple et coyes' to virtuous secular girls (II p. 109).

49. As Bowden observes, the best comment on this is J. L. Lowes':

> Now it is earthly love which conquers all, now heavenly; the phrase plays back and forth between the two... *Which of the two loves does 'amor' mean to the Prioress?* I do not know; but I think she thought she meant love celestial.

(*Convention and Revolt in Poetry* p. 45.) F. Manley has seen a similar ambiguity in the 'smal coral' of which the Prioress's rosary is made; coral, originally a charm against the evil eye, also served to ward off the devil, but at the same time was thought to be a love-charm (*MLN* 74 (1959), 385–8).

50. The modulations in the meaning of 'curteisie' in the portraits of Knight, Squire and Prioress, and the ambivalent nature of the concept itself, are admirably discussed by Mitchell, 'Chaucer's Knight'.

51. Moreover, Chaucer presents some of the features which might indicate the Prioress's failings as 'involuntary' in the same way that the Squire's curly hair is; as Schoeck comments, 'the Prioress could not help being beautiful' ('Chaucer's Prioress: Mercy and Tender Heart', R. J. Schoeck and J. Taylor (eds.), *Chaucer Criticism* (Notre Dame, Indiana, 1960–1) p. 247).

52. H. Morris notes that cherubin are usually blue in iconographic tradition ('Some Uses of Angel Iconography in English Literature', *Comparative Literature*, 10 (1958), 36–44).

For red faces in descriptions of ugly people, see A. M. Colby, *The Portrait in Twelfth Century French Literature* (Geneva, 1965), p. 77.

53. See Curry, *Chaucer and the Medieval Sciences*, pp. 37ff.; P. Aiken, 'The Summoner's Malady', *SP* 33 (1936), 40–4; T. J. Garbáty, 'The Summoner's Occupational Disease', *Medical History*, 7 (1963), 348–58. Garbáty's argument that the Summoner is suffering from a form of syphilis derives some support from a passage in *Handlyng Synne* where prostitutes are said to pass on 'meseles' (pp. 237–8, 7447–50).

D. Biggins (*NQ* n.s. 11 (1964), 48) quotes post-Chaucerian evidence for the view that onions, garlic and leeks are sexually arousing.

54. See R. E. Kaske, 'The Summoner's Garleek, Onyons and eek Lekes', *MLN* 84 (1959), 481–4, showing that an exegetical tradition derived from Num. 11: 5. We can bear out Kaske's interpretation with examples from moral satire; see Map, *De Nugis Curialium*, dist. I cap. I, p. 2, 16–18; *VC* III 85–6.

55. See *Handlyng Synne*, p. 317, 10,159ff. (a story of a parish priest who was allowed to see in his parishioners' faces their moral state; some are marked with 'meselrye'). Cf. p. 357, 11,465ff., where deadly sin is said to be a 'mesyl'. See also M. W. Bloomfield, *The Deadly Sins* (Michigan, 1952), pp. 177, 196.

56. 'Of rybaudz y ryme', ed. Böddeker, p. 137, 41–8. The poem is from MS Harley 2253, and was written before 1310 (Wells). The last two lines of the quotation can be translated: 'he is delousing a sycophant, and putting shoes on a rogue [i.e. himself]'.

57. It is certainly older than the twelfth century, however, for the description of the ugly old husband of a young wife in *Ruodlieb* is just such a set-piece (ed. Zeydel, p. 92, VII 98ff.).

58. Ed. Cohen, *La Comédie Latine*, I pp. 136–7, 171–4. Cf., in the *Geta*, Mercury's description of Geta to himself, especially 336: 'Eterna scabie leditur atra cutis' – 'his dark skin is afflicted with permanent scurf' (*ibid.* p. 48, 335ff.).

59. *Ars Versificatoria*, ed. E. Faral, *Les Arts Poétiques du XIIe et du XIIIe Siècle* (Paris, 1962), p. 131, 5ff. Cf. also the portrait of the married man in Matheolus' *Lamentations*, pp. 54–5, 276–308 (Lat. 753ff.).

60. For the summoner's official duties and connection with the consistory courts of the bishop and the archdeacon, see L. A. Haselmayer, 'The Apparitor and Chaucer's Summoner', *Speculum*, 12 (1937), 43–57. The best description of the kind of cases dealt with by these courts is provided by the Friar's Tale (III (D) 1301–16). The summoner's office was not introduced into England until the thirteenth century, and, given the conservative nature of estates satire, it is perhaps comprehensible that he does not figure in it much before Langland.

61. As early as the tenth century, this complex of characteristics is associated with 'procuratores' ('governors' or ministers) by Rather of Verona (*PL* 136, col. 164).

62. p. 24, vv. 44–5. See also vv. 56ff. on the 'officiales'.

63. *Map Poems*, p. 225, 73–88.

64. *Livre des Manières*, p. 123, 233ff. Line 241 presents difficulties of text and translation, but the sense of the passage as a whole is clear.

65. 'Ne mai no lewed lued libben in londe', ed. Böddeker, p. 110, 36–40. The poem is from MS Harley 2253, and is of the reign of Edward I (Wells).

66. *PSE* p. 326, 49–54, p. 332, 194–8.

67. On the sexual meaning of 'pulling finches', see the articles by G. L. Kittredge, *MP* 7 (1910), 475–7, and E. E. Ericson, *English Studies* 42 (1961), 306.

68. Summoners are consistently presented in connection with Meed: see *PPl* II 58, III 133, IV 167. For consistory court officials, see also III 141–5.

69. *PPl* II 168–76. Cf., on the consistory court in general, xv 234–6.

70. Cf. Matheolus' *Lamentations*, p. 115, 2516 (not in Lat.), where women's 'horns' are said to frighten 'enfans petis'.

71. This point is not really affected whether the 'girles' are feminine or of both sexes; on this point see M. W. Bloomfield, 'Chaucer's Summoner and the Girls of the Diocese', *PQ* 28 (1949), 503–7.

72. Ed. Lehmann, *Parodistische Texte*, p. 189, 1442–4. The piece is taken from a

larger poem written towards the end of the thirteenth century by a
Franciscan called Peter.

73. *VC* III 194–202; *MO* 20,108–9. These parallels are noted by Flügel, 'Chaucer's
Prolog', p. 505. Cf. Gilles li Muisis, II p. 65: 'Et s'auncun se meffont, en
leur bourse les pendent.' – 'And if anyone misbehaves themselves, they hang
them in their purses.' – and Matheolus' *Lamentations*, p. 282, 502–4 (not in
Latin), of judges:

> Si com le vin en la taverne
> Nous sont les jugemens vendus
> Et sont a la bourse pendus.

Verdicts are sold to us like wine in taverns, and hanging takes place in
purses.

Cf. also Owst, *Lit. and Pulp.*, pp. 43, 280.

74. See *Inferno*, XIX 69–72, noted by H. R. Patch, 'Chauceriana', *Englische
Studien*, 65 (1931), 351. But in Chaucer the equation of purse and hell
signifies the way in which the sinner, not the simoniac himself, is punished.

75. Unlike some commentators (see Robinson's note), I take line 661 as seriously
meant; however, A. C. Cawley (*Proceedings of the Leeds Philosophical and
Literary Society*, 8 (1957), 174–5) has a point when he observes that the
threat of a *significavit* is rather an anti-climax *after* the threat of eternal
damnation.

76. See Augustine, *Enarrationes in Psalmos*, 18, 2, cited by P. Brown, *Augustine
of Hippo* (London, 1967), p. 142; 'The Simonie', *PSE* p. 328, 104–9, and
Owst, *Lit. and Pulp.*, p. 27.

77. *Winner and Waster*, 26.

78. p. 34, v. 96. On the empty garrulity of birds, see also Matheolus' *Lamentations*, p. 150, 3680 (Lat. 2251), and *PPl* XII 252, where Langland says that
when the rich man cries to Christ, his 'ledne' sounds 'lyke a pyes chiteryng'.

79. See Robinson's note; *PPl* XIII 89; 'Syngyn y wolde', *PPS* I p. 277, and
Lehmann, *Die Parodie im Mittelalter*, pp. 134, 148.

80. *MO* 8149–52. Gower's reference to the laity's ignorance of French would
apply to most people outside the court and some ecclesiastical circles at this
date; see A. C. Baugh, *A History of the English Language* (2nd edition,
London, 1959), Chapter 6, esp. pp. 171ff., and Froissart's report that
Parliament, in view of the imminent war with France, decreed in the
autumn of 1337 that lords, barons, knights, and citizens should instruct
their children in the French language, so that they might be more efficient
in the campaigns (*Chronicles*, selected and translated by G. Brereton (London,
1968), Book I, p. 58).

81. On the origin of the phrase in a legal writ, see J. W. Spargo, 'Questio Quid
Iuris', *MLN* 62 (1947), 119–22.

82. Cf. Sir John Clanvowe, *The Two Ways*:

But now swiche as been synful men and wacches of þe feend been cleped of the world goode felawes | For þei þat woln waaste þe goodis þat god hath sent hem | in pryde of the world | and in lustes of here flessh and goon to þe tauerne | and to þe bordel | and pleyen at þe dees waaken loonge anyʒtes | and sweren faste and drynken | and ianglen to muche | scoornen | bakbiten iapen glosen boosten lyen fiʒten and been bandes for here felawes | And lyuen al in synne and in vanitee þei been hoolde goode felawes | .

(*Eng. Phil. Studies*, 10 (1967), 49-50). At first, Clanvowe and Chaucer seem to be making the same satiric point, but I think there is a subtle difference; in Clanvowe's text, it is essential that we adhere to his point of view, in order to be convinced of the inappropriateness of calling such people 'good fellows'. Chaucer's text allows that it is appropriate to call the Summoner a good fellow *in one sense*, though it is not a very honourable one.

CHAPTER 7

1. For the sexual *double entendre* in 'burdoun', D. Biggins, *NQ* n.s. 6 (1959), 435-6, and B. D. H. Miller, *NQ* n.s. 7 (1960), 404-6. The disclosure of the homosexual relationship prompts the question whether the Summoner's garland is a parody of that which the lover is advised to wear in the *Roman de la Rose* (I 2149-52).

2. See Curry, *Chaucer and the Mediaeval Sciences*, Chapter 3.

3. *Ibid.*, p. 58. Some 'Proverbial Verses' of the thirteenth century take a 'Liþer lok and tuinkling' to be one of the 'toknes of horelinge'; the word has a feminine ending, but doubtless the feature applied to either sex (Wright and Halliwell (eds.) *Reliquiae Antiquae*, vol. 2, p. 14).

4. See E. C. Schweitzer jr, 'Chaucer's Pardoner and the Hare', *ELN* 4 (1967), 247-50. The immediate point of the comparison is that, according to Vincent of Beauvais and Bartholomeus Anglicus, hares sleep with open eyes.

5. For early medieval treatments of sodomy, and its role as the central theme of Alanus de Insulis' *De Planctu Naturae*, see E. R. Curtius, *European Literature and the Latin Middle Ages*, (trans. W. R. Trask, New York, 1953), pp. 113-18.

6. No IV, p. 70, v. 27, 3-4, and v. 28, 3-4.

7. No XIII, pp. 124-5, v. 7, 3-4. See Strecker's commentary for the similarities between the 'Feast of the Staff' and the Feast of Fools.

8. No VIII, p. 102, v. 11, 1-2.

9. See A. L. Kellog and L. A. Haselmayer, 'Chaucer's Satire of the Pardoner', *PMLA* 66 (1951), 251-77. For a view that the relationship has personal significance and shows that Chaucer was thinking of a real pardoner who

was homosexual, see G. G. Sedgewick, 'The Progress of Chaucer's Pardoner', *MLQ* I (1940), 431-58.

10. See Alanus de Insulis, *De Planctu Naturae*, Prose VII, *Anglo-Latin Satirical Poets*, II pp. 495-6 (carefully-combed hair, plucked eyebrows, shaved faces); *Handlyng Synne*, p. 112, 3199-200 (pride in one's hair); *Mum and the Sothsegger*, p. 19, 235 (beardless fops). Cf. Wiesen, *St Jerome as a Satirist*, p. 58 (arranging one's hair, plucking hair), and 216 (the deacon Sabinianus carefully arranging the few hairs he has over his skull, plucking his hair); Owst, *Lit. and Pulp.*, p. 275 (flowing locks, like a woman's, associated with priests). For beardlessness and sexual impotence, see Hildegard of Bingen's *Causae et Curae*, p. 75, 26-8.

11. See *Winner and Waster*, 410 (women are 'nysottes of þe new gett'); *Handlyng Synne*, p. 112, 3212 (though here it is 'berded buckys' who follow 'þe newe gyse'), p. 118, 3391, 3401.

12. *PPl* V 529-31.

13. Chaucer may also have noted Dante's attack on givers of pardons in the course of his criticism of those who preach for profit (*Paradiso*, XXIX, 115ff.). The pardoners here are attached to St Anthony's hospital – the fraternity pilloried by Guiot de Provins and Boccaccio (see below).

14. See *PPl* II 108, 219-22, V 648-9. It is possible that there is yet another link between *PPl* and Chaucer's Pardoner, in Langland's scorn for 'al the pardoun' of Pampiloun and Rome' (XVII 252). Bloomfield points out that the hospital of St Mary Rouncivale at Charing Cross was a branch of the order of Nuestra Señora de Roncesvalles – which was in the diocese of Pamplona ('The Pardons of Pamplona and The Pardoner of Rounceval', *PQ* 35 (1956), 66-8).

Chaucer's choice of Rouncivale as the Pardoner's base may have been stimulated, as S. Moore has suggested, by a recent scandal over pardoners falsely claiming to represent this hospital ('Chaucer's Pardoner of Rouncival', *MP* 25 (1927), 59-66); in this case it would bear out what we have noticed of the topical situation in which Chaucer conceives of his estates stereotypes.

15. *Ibid.*, 81.

Cf. the vivid picture of 'Nummus' or 'Money' as an avaricious cleric in 'In terra summus', *CB* I No 11, p. 16, 42-5:

> Vidi cantantem Nummum,   missam celebrantem;
> Nummus cantabat,   Nummus responsa parabat;
> Vidi, quod flebat,   dum sermonem faciebat,
> Et subridebat,   populum quia decipiebat.

I saw Money singing, and celebrating mass; Money sang, and made the responses. I saw that he wept while he preached the sermon, and smiled, because he was deceiving the people.

Gilles li Muisis also describes monks singing well to attract 'pittances' (I p. 166).

16. The particular association of false relics with a pardoner does not seem to be based on historical reality; Kellogg and Haselmayer note that the evidence suggests that pardoners did not often carry relics ('Chaucer's Satire', p. 275).

17. See Lehmann, *Die Parodie im Mittelalter*, pp. 25ff.

18. This was an order of hospitallers founded in the late eleventh century to care for those suffering from 'St Anthony's fire' – a sort of epilepsy. (See *Lexikon für Theologie und Kirche*, ed. J. Höfer and K. Rahner (2nd edition, Freiburg, 1957) s.v. Antoniusorden, 6.) Such hospitals depended on alms for funds, which they obtained in the manner described by Guiot, and later by Boccaccio (see below). But the 'selling' of pardons was another way in which it was possible to raise money; this is what the Pardoner is (supposedly) doing for St Mary's hospital, and what Dante had criticised the brothers of St Anthony for doing. The satire of the hospitallers of St Anthony therefore provides a background for the Pardoner's portrait.

19. *Bible*, p. 72, 1994–2006.

20. *Les Miracles de Notre Dame de Soissons versifiés par Gautier de Coincy*, ed. L. Lindgren, *Annales Academiae Scientiarum Fennicae*, Ser. B. CXXIX. Gautier's original was a Latin story (for which see Lindgren, p. 16) written by Hugues Farsit in the twelfth century. Gautier's *Miracles* were fairly popular; Lindgren used six MSS for his edition.

21. Tenth Story, Sixth Day, p. 183, 45.

22. For sermon references to pardoners, see G. R. Owst, *Preaching in Medieval England* (Cambridge, 1926), pp. 109ff. (on pardoners carrying false relics), and *Lit. and Pulp.*, p. 372, and n. 3. The description of pardoners in the second of these references bears an interesting resemblance to the stereotype of friars; in fact Owst's first quotation on p. 373, describing 'ronners over contreys', seems to me equally likely to refer to friars (unless pardoners are named in a passage he does not quote). Cf. *PPl Crede*, p. 4, 82, on friars: 'þey ouer lond strakeþ'. But the 'lepers over londe' in Owst's next quotation are explicitly pardoners. The stereotypes of the two classes develop from the same basis; thus Chaucer's Pardoner, like his Friar, owes something to Faus Semblant (see D. S. Fansler, *Chaucer and the Roman de la Rose* (New York, 1914), pp. 162ff.).

23. They are barely mentioned in *PPl* (XIX 39), and appear in an estates list in *Mum and the Sothsegger*, p. 50, 788; also p. 54, 945–6, where a franklin's fine house is described. Late evidence such as this seems to confirm the correspondences between Chaucer's portrait and the popular view of franklins (although it may of course be reflecting Chaucer's influence). Cf. the mid-fifteenth century 'Fest for a Franklen' in John Russell's *Boke of Nurture*, ed. Furnivall (*EETS* o.s. 32, London, 1868), pp. 170–1.

24. For a discussion, see G. H. Gerould, 'The Social Status of Chaucer's Franklin', *PMLA* 41 (1926), 262–79.

25. The 'sop in wyn' varied in the luxuriousness of its ingredients; E. Birney thinks that the Franklin's sop was fairly spartan, and was intended to settle his stomach after the excesses of the night before (*NQ* n.s. 6 (1959), 345–7). But although the Franklin might *need* his sop in such a case, would he be quite so enthusiastic about it? See also the quotation from Gower on 'sops', below.

26. To discuss the Franklin's connection with gluttony satire does not contradict the assumption of an estates framework for the *Prologue*. The sample lists of estates which are given in Appendix A show that writers felt no embarrassment at shifting from professional types to sins-types, and back again; the term 'estate' can cover all aspects of the situation in which a man finds himself – marital, moral, professional. Frederick Tupper, the strongest proponent of the theory that the *CT* are based on the Sins tradition, has noted that this tradition is inextricably involved with that of estates satire ('The Quarrels of the Canterbury Pilgrims', *JEGP* 14 (1915), 256). For the argument that sins-literature is the basis of the *CT*, see F. Tupper, *PMLA* 29 (1914), 93–128; *JEGP* 13 (1914), 553–65, 15 (1916), 56–106, and, for a refutation, J. L. Lowes, *PMLA* 30 (1915), 237–71.

27. *De Planctu Naturae*, Prose VI, *Anglo-Latin Satirical Poets*, II p. 487. Cf. *CB* I No 11, p. 16, 29–30 ('Money' eats peppered fish and drinks French wines): *RR* II 11710–21 (friars can be bribed by numerous foods, including pike). The greedy Pope described by Gower, like the Franklin, provides for his table from his own estate (*VC* III 833–5).

28. *Winner and Waster*, 335. See also the rest of the passage for other delicacies.

29. *Bible*, p. 57, 1536–7 (the Grandimontanes eat garlicky fish, strong sauces and hot pepper dressings), p. 92, 2634–5 (Guiot rejects medicine in favour of good food, good wines and 'fors sauces' (strong sauces); *Renart le Contrefait*, II p. 44, 26,737 (hot sauces and preserves are better than medicine). 'Sauce' can mean 'condiment' or spice as well as 'sauce' in both Latin and English (see Du Cange, s.v. Salsa, and *OED* s.v. Sauce, 1). Highly-spiced or salted foods and sauces are said by satirists of gluttony to be used to increase the appetite: see John of Hauteville *Architrenius* (written in 1184), *Anglo-Latin Satirical Poets*, I pp. 265–6; Alanus de Insulis, *De Planctu Naturae*, Prose VI, *ibid.*, II p. 488; *MO* 7957–62. Nearly all Chaucer's uses of the word 'sauce' seem to occur in a context of gluttony satire: *CT* VI (C) 545; VII 2834 (B²* 4024); 'The Former Age' 16.

30. It has been suggested that the Franklin's change of diet according to the season is based on the requirements of health in the humours (J. A. Bryant jr, 'The Diet of Chaucer's Franklin', *MLN* 63 (1948), 318–25). But Gower's reference to the gourmet's liking for variety seems to provide a better motivation for the Franklin. Cf. the gourmets in the *Architrenius*, who also

like variety – here in the course of the meal (*Anglo-Latin Satirical Poets*, p. 264).

31. *MO* 7907–8. Cf. Gilles li Muisis's complaint that children are now spoilt by being given a sop for breakfast ('au matinet le soupe', II p. 26).

32. See *De Planctu Naturae*, Prose VI, *Anglo-Latin Satirical Poets*, I pp. 485–7; *MO* 7783–4, 8105–6, 8333–40, 8349–50, 8521–32, 8588–604; *PPl* v 346–51.

33. *Lettre de l'Empéreur Orgueil*, p. 66, 145–50. See also *Handlyng Synne*, p. 232, 7244–58, (criticising rich men who tyrannise their cooks). For another reference to the glutton's toiling cook, see *VC* IV 69–70.

34. *Secreta Secretorum*, pp. 219–20.

35. Perhaps the association was unconsciously made through the fact that both traditionally had red faces, although the red and white of the sanguine man is more pleasant than the bright red of the glutton. See Hildegard of Bingen, *Causae et Curae*, p. 72, 8–11; *Secreta Secretorum*, p. 222, and a late fifteenth-century poem on the humours, ed. Robbins, *Secular Lyrics*, No 77, p. 72, 3 (for the sanguine man), and 'Totum regit saeculum', *Map Poems*, p. 235, 206; *PPl* XIII 99 (for the glutton).

36. See *CB* I No 8 p. 10, v. 8, 3; *ibid.*, No 5, p. 6, v. 11; *ibid.*, No 92 p. 95, v. 15, 4; 'Hora nona sabbati', *NE* 32, 1, p. 294.

37. III Prose 2, 77–82.

38. See Nicholas Bozon, *Le Char d'Orgueil*, p. 25, CXV, 459; *Renart le Contrefait*, II p. 148, 36,765–6; *Handlyng Synne*, p. 214, 6635ff., especially 6751–2; *Winner and Waster*, 329–30, 375–83; *PPl* X 94–100.

39. See *VC* III 107–10, 113–14; *MO* 8401–508.

40. *Lit. and Pulp.*, pp. 311–12. The parallel with the Franklin is noted by Owst.

41. *The Two Ways*, *Eng. Phil. Studies*, 10 (1967), 47, 457ff. This treatise, which was probably written in 1391, survives in only one MS, University College Oxford 97. (See pp. 33–4.)

42. On the existence of numerous men in late-fourteenth-century England who had held the posts mentioned in the Franklin's portrait, see K. L. Wood-Legh, 'The Franklin', *RES* 4 (1928), 145–51. According to Tout, the parliament of November 1372 passed a law forbidding lawyers and sheriffs to be returned as knights of the shire, because they acted for private interests (*Chapters in the Administrative History of Medieval England* (6 vols., Manchester, 1920–33), vol. 3, p. 282). A critic with a 'historical' viewpoint might use this as evidence for the Franklin's behaviour in office; I should prefer to point to Chaucer's significant silence on such a matter.

43. See Étienne de Fougères, *Livre des Manières*, p. 124, 308 (Christ will damn false witnesses and false 'conteors'). 'Contour' can mean either 'An accountant; esp., an official who oversees the collecting and auditing of taxes for a shire . . . etc.' (*MED* 1a), or 'a pleader in court, a lawyer' (1c). Despite the fact that some Chaucer MSS have the form 'accomptour' at this point (see the

Manly–Rickert edition) in the *Prologue*, I think there is a strong probability that the word has its legal meaning, since this is clearly how it is used by Étienne and by the author of 'The Simonie' in the passage quoted below.

44. 'L'État du Monde', 1 p. 386, 93ff.

45. This connection of the legal and administrative offices seems to lie behind the Franklin's friendship with the Sergeant of Law (*GP* 331). See also Thomas Wimbledon's sermon of 1388, *Medieval Studies*, 28 (1966) 183, where 'maires, and schyreuys, and justices' are grouped together. Similarly, in MS Lambeth 179, the poem on legal corruption, 'Beati qui esuriunt' (fol. 136*b*), is followed by a poem 'De vicecomitibus' (Inc. 'Quam duri sunt pauperibus quis potest enarrare'; see M. R. James, *Descriptive Catalogue of the Manuscripts in the Library of Lambeth Palace* (Cambridge, 1930).)

46. *Handlyng Synne*, p. 218, 6793.

47. *PSE* p. 339, 343. Gower also lists together sheriffs, bailliffs, and jurors at the assizes (*VC* VI, heading of Chapter VI; *MO* 248).

48. See *OED* s.v. Miller, 1*b*. For other proverbs incorporating the notion of the miller's dishonesty, see M. P. Tilley, *A Dictionary of the Proverbs in England* (Ann Arbor, 1950), M954–9, B. J. Whiting, *Proverbs, Sentences and Proverbial Phrases* (Cambridge, Mass., 1969), M560–1, and H. Bächtold-Stäubli, *Handwörterbuch des deutschen Aberglaubens* (10 vols., Berlin, 1927–42), s.v. Müller, esp. 4*a*, n. 15.

If the miller's habit of tolling more than once was not proverbial before Chaucer, it certainly became so after him (Whiting, M561).

49. For a discussion of Chaucer's Miller in relation to the popular image of his class (illustrated mostly from fifteenth-century German texts), see G. F. Jones, 'Chaucer and the Medieval Miller', *MLQ* 16 (1955), 3–15.

50. *MED* gives 'buffoon' as the meaning of 'goliardeys', and explains this use of 'ianglere' as 'a raconteur, teller of dirty stories; ?also a professional entertainer' (d). The word 'goliardeys' is apparently used elsewhere in Middle English only by Mannyng (*Handlyng Synne*, p. 156, 4701), and Langland (*PPl* Prol. 139).

51. For evidence that bagpipes were thought of as a 'low', peasant's, instrument in the Middle Ages, see G. F. Jones, 'Wittenweiler's *Becki* and the Medieval Bagpipe', *JEGP* 48 (1949), 209–28. For the suggestion that they are a symbol of gluttony and lechery, see E. A. Block, 'Chaucer's Millers and their Bagpipes', *Speculum* 29 (1954), 239–43, and K. L. Scott, 'Sow-and-Bagpipe Imagery in the Miller's Portrait', *RES* 18 (1967), 287–90, especially 289, and n. 1.

Scott points out a connection between sows and bagpipes, which she attributes to the similarity in the noises they make. (It surely derives also from the appearance of a swollen-teated sow.) This association may give rise, as Scott thinks, to the sow-imagery in the Miller's portrait, but the association of 'ribauds' with pigs is easily made; Langland says gluttons and 'iangeleres' breed like 'burgh-swyn' (*PPl* II 92–8).

52. p. 48, fol. 23*a*, 18–19. In Apuleius's *Golden Ass*, it is at the millhouse that tales are told.

This mill itself is used as an image for a wagging tongue by Chaucer and other writers; see *CT* IV (E) 1200, X (I) 406; E. Lommatzsch, *Gautier de Coincy*, p. 60 (on the Last Day, advocates' tongues will become a 'clapete de moulin a vent' – 'clapper [of the hopper?; see Tobler–Lommatzsch, s.v. Clapete] of a windmill'; *Ayenbite of Inwyt*, ed. Morris, p. 58 (tongues full of idle words are like 'þe cleper of þe melle'), and p. 255 (unchecked speech is like the water pouring through a mill without a sluice).

(The autograph copy of the *Ayenbite* (MS BM Arundel 57) tells us that it was finished in 1340.)

53. For its use with reference to gossip, see *Handlyng Synne*, p. 182, 5591, pp. 291–2, 9261ff.; *PPl* II 94. For the meaning 'entertainer', see *PPl* X 30–44, a piece of invective against 'Harlotes...Iaperes...Iogeloures...and Iangelers of gestes'; significantly, Langland's second reference to the miller occurs at the end of this passage.

54. Besides the above, see *PPl* Prol. 35–6, XX 142–3, 296–7. See also the reference to 'Robyn the rybaudoure' and his 'rusty wordes' (VI 75); is it coincidental that the Miller's name is Robin? (*CT* I (A) 3129). For satiric criticism of 'ianglers', see 'Dis des Estas dou Monde', Jean de Condé, p. 182, 190–205:

> Ne te faices teil appieller
> C'on die, tu soies gengleres...
> Et ne te laisses pas lacier
> D'ordure ne de ribaudie.

Don't earn yourself such a name that anyone should say you are a jangler...And don't let yourself get drawn into filth or ribaldry.

55. For reports of people from the fourth to the nineteenth century who provided entertainment by breaking down doors with their heads, see the articles by B. J. Whiting in *MLN* 52 (1937), 417–19, and 69 (1954), 309–10, by A. N. Wiley, *MLN* 53 (1938), 505–7, and F. L. Utley, *MLN* 56 (1941), 534–6.

56. p. 126, 3685–7. The Anglo-Norman version (see *ibid.*) mentions 'iugelurs... ribauz...luturs': Mannyng has mis-translated the last word as 'fighters' instead of 'lute-players'.

57. *Chaucer and the Mediaeval Sciences*, pp. 79ff. Curry suggests, among other things, that the Miller is 'shameless, immodest, loquacious, irascible, a glutton, a swaggerer and an impious fornicator' – a character well suited to a 'jangler'.

58. E.g. the swaggering traitor in *Ruodlieb*, V 585ff. (noted by G. F. Jones

Mediaeval Miller', n. 3), and Matthew of Vendôme's picture of his detractor Rufinus (Arnulf of Orléans), especially his lechery and 'sterile and barren garrulity' (*Ars Versificatoria*, ed. Faral, *Les Arts Poétiques*, pp. 109–10, and p. 2, n. 3).

59. See Colby, *The Portrait in Twelfth Century French Literature*, pp. 73–81.

60. The miller of the Reeve's Tale resembles the Miller of the *Prologue* very closely; both wrestle, wear swords and are spoiling for a fight, have flat noses (if we interpret the pilgrim's wide nostrils in this way), and are thieves (I (A) 3925–41). Is this because the Reeve is maliciously describing the individual pilgrim, or because both are typical millers?

61. *Chaucer and the Mediaeval Sciences*, p. 72. He also says (without giving evidence) that the cropped hair and close-shaven face indicate a man of low estate, and especially an obedient and humble servant.

62. 'Off yiftes large, in love hath grete delite', ed. Robbins, *Secular Lyrics*, No 77, p. 72, 11. The choleric man is not always described as thin: Hildegard of Bingen mentions his red face, thick chest, and strong arms (*Causae et Curae*, p. 70, 15–22).

63. p. 226. On p. 135, however, 'smale leggis' are interpreted as a sign of 'vnconyngnesse'; their significance was obviously not fixed, although the evidence brought by Curry might suggest the strength of the lechery interpretation (*Chaucer and the Mediaeval Sciences*, p. 75).

64. *Secreta Secretorum*, p. 226, ('of sharp witte'), and cf. a fourteenth-century poem on the humours which describes the choleric man as 'ffraudulent & suttyll' ('Sluggy & slowe, in spetynge muiche', ed. Robbins, *Secular Lyrics*, No 76, p. 72, 11).

65. As Robinson notes, the reeve (the servile representative of the peasants) was theoretically subordinate to the bailiff (the lord's appointee), but in fact many manors did not have a full hierarchy of officers, and reeves fulfilled several offices. See H. S. Bennett, 'The Reeve and the Manor in the Fourteenth Century', *EHR* 41 (1926), 358–65. Bennett shows that 'bailiff' was a term applied to several manorial offices (p. 359); this would explain why a 'bailiff' is classed with 'herdes' and 'hynes' in *GP* 603. Because of his intimate knowledge of local affairs, the reeve would in any case effectively wield greater power than the bailiff, who was an outsider.

66. The historical situation was probably very different; peasants were extremely reluctant to take on the office of reeve because they had to make good themselves any deficits in their accounts at the end of the year (Bennett, 'The Reeve').

67. 'L'en puet fere et defere', *PSE* p. 255. For other versions of the 'sayings of the four philosophers', and the diffusion of the proverb, see S. J. H. Herrtage, *Gesta Romanorum* (*EETS* e.s. 33, London, 1879), pp. 497–9, and G. Holmstedt, *Speculum Christiani* (*EETS* o.s. 182, London, 1933) pp. clxxxiii–cxc.

68. 'Ich herde men vpo molde', ed. Böddeker, p. 103, 16. See also *Handlyng Synne*, p. 177, 5407ff. (on lords' counsellors, 'wykked legystrys . . . fals a-countours . . . stywardes').

69. p. 37, see also p. 39.

70. x 469-70. The way in which Langland classes clerks and reeves together in this quotation is interesting in view of the fact that Chaucer twice compares the Reeve with a cleric. He is 'tukked as a frere' and 'dokked lyk a preest'; is Chaucer hinting at the pretensions of his class to 'clergy'? Bennett ('The Reeve') says that reeves were unlettered, and gives parallels for the oral rendering of accounts by illiterate men, but perhaps Chaucer's Reeve wanted people to think he could understand the book-work for which he was responsible.

71. See *OED* s.v. Subtly, 1 and 3. The ambiguity of Chaucer's phrasing is reflected in different estimates of the Reeve among critics; Manly saw him as a 'rascal' and 'sly' (*New Light*, pp. 92, 94), while G. B. Powley thought he was merely 'the competent but worldly servant of a manor' (*TLS* (14 July 1932), 516).

72. See Skeat's note on the line, and G. E. Evans, *Where Beards Wag All* (London, 1970), p. 162.

73. Two sets of verses on the *Characteristics of Counties* describe Norfolk as 'full of giles' and 'ful of wyles' (Wright and Halliwell (eds.), *Reliquiae Antiquae*, vol. 1, p. 269 and vol. 2, p. 41). Both these pieces are fairly late; the first is from MS BM Harley 7371, whose contents seem to belong to the seventeenth century, the second was printed by Thomas Hearne in his introduction to the fifth volume of Leland's *Itinerary*. A much earlier Latin poem describes the inhabitants of Norfolk as the worst of any people: 'gens vilissima, | Plena versutiis, fallax et invida' – 'the basest of people, full of tricks, deceitful and malicious'. ('Exiit edictum quondam a Caesare', ed. Wright, *Early Mysteries and Other Latin Poems* (London, 1838), pp. 93ff. This poem exists in several MSS, including one of the thirteenth and two of the fourteenth centuries. See Walther's *Initia*, 6074, and *Hist. litt. de la France*, vol. 12, p. 145.)

74. For suggestions as to the manor concerned and Chaucer's way of knowing about it, see Manly, *New Light*, pp. 84ff., G. B. Powley, *TLS* (14 July 1932), 516, and L. J. Redstone, *TLS* (27 October 1932), 789.

75. For an attempt to interpret some of these details as symbolic of the Reeve's old age, see B. Forehand 'Old Age and Chaucer's Reeve', *PMLA* 69 (1954), 984-9. The details might be taken as appropriate if we *knew* the Reeve was old, but they do not seem to suggest it strongly by themselves.

76. See Tupper, 'Canterbury Pilgrims', pp. 265ff. Tupper claims that the enmity between the Reeve and the Miller is 'thoroughly traditional', but

his evidence shows only that a clash of interests was likely, not that it was proverbial.

CHAPTER 8

1. See above, pp. 153–5.
2. IV 69–70. See also the Pardoner's Tale (VI (C) 538–9), where a similar list is 'put back' into a context of gluttony satire.
3. III 79–81. Cf. with these passages the Host's words in the Cook's Prologue, I (A) 4346–52.
4. *Chaucer and the Mediaeval Sciences*, pp. 48ff. However, the medical authorities quoted by Curry attribute mormals to generally intemperate or unclean habits, such as one might still today connect with skin disease, rather than any specific pattern of behaviour. For evidence that the mormal would smell strongly, see A. S. Cook, *MLN* 33 (1918), 379, and for the argument that it is a running, not a dry sore, see H. Braddy 'The Cook's Mormal and its Cure', *MLQ* 7 (1946), 265–7.
5. 'As I walked vppone a day', ed. C. Brown, *Religious Lyrics of the XVth Century* (Oxford, 1939), No 178, p. 276, 109.
6. The effect has been commented on by J. Swart, 'The Construction of Chaucer's *General Prologue*', *Neophilologus*, 38 (1954), 127–36.
7. See above, p. 155 n. 32. Alanus de Insulis says that gluttonous habits produce diseases ('morbos pariunt', *De Planctu Naturae* Prose VI, *Anglo-Latin Satirical Poets*, II p. 487).
8. *AH* XXXIII p. 270, 173–6.
9. Quoted, with slight corrections from the Cambridge MS, from Pantin, *English Church in the Fourteenth Century*, Appendix I, p. 273. The treatise instructs the priest to question people according to their estate, and so provides a useful list of the sins that each estate is prone to. It is dated 1344, and was apparently written for an English audience (see p. 205). It survives in two MSS: BM Harley 3120, and Corpus Christi College, Cambridge 148.
10. 'He drowned his prisoners' (Robinson's note).
11. See Bowden, *Commentary*, p. 193.
12. See Linthicum, ' "Faldyng" and "Medlee" ', *JEGP* 34 (1935), 39–41.
13. 'The descryuing of mannes membres', ed. J. Kail, *Twenty-Six Political and Other Poems* (EETS o.s. 124, London, 1904), Part I, p. 65.
14. He was the patron saint of foresters (see Robinson's note).
15. Bowden calls him 'likable' (*Commentary*, p. 88).
16. E. Birney has suggested that the joke about 'God's grace' is the Manciple's, and that elsewhere it is the Manciple's view on the world that Chaucer is presenting ('Chaucer's "Gentil" Manciple and his "Gentil" Tale', *Neuphilologische Mitteilungen*, 61 (1960), 257–67).

EXCURSUS

1. The term 'descriptio', which I use in preference to 'effictio' and 'notatio' (the terms used in, for example, the *Rhetorica ad Herennium*), is the one adopted by both Matthew of Vendôme (*Ars Versificatoria*, ed. Faral, *Les Arts Poétiques*, p. 118, 38), and Geoffrey of Vinsauf (*Poetria Nova*, ibid., p. 214, 554).

2. *Les Arts Poétiques*, pp. 75ff. For correction of some of Faral's statements about the organisation of the portraits in literature, see Colby, *The Portrait in Twelfth Century French Literature*, pp. 5–7.

3. *Les Arts Poétiques*, p. 80.

4. *The Golden Mirror: Studies in Chaucer's Descriptive Technique and its Literary Background* (Lund, 1955). For the discussion of descriptions of people, see pp. 167ff.

5. R. M. Lumiansky, 'Benoit's Portraits and Chaucer's General Prologue', *JEGP* 55 (1956), 431–8, and H. R. Patch, 'Characters in Medieval Literature', *MLN* 40 (1925), 1–14.

6. Matthew of Vendôme, *Ars Versificatoria*, p. 135, 74.

7. A list of representative examples of the first sort is given by Haselmayer, *SA* p. 4, n. 3. See also his article, 'The Portraits in Troilus and Criseyde' *PQ* 17 (1938), 220–3. For portraits of ugly people, see *SA*, p. 5, n. 4, and Schaar's additions in *The Golden Mirror*, pp. 306ff.

8. *SA*, p. 5, n. 4. The distinction between the two kinds of 'realism' is pointed out by Schaar, *The Golden Mirror*, p. 306.

9. 'En fait, dans les exemples qu'en offre la littérature, [la description] est souvent oiseuse; chez beaucoup d'auteurs... elle fait plus d'une fois hors-d'oeuvre et n'a d'autre raison d'être que l'observance d'une tradition routinière... Le but de la description est de mettre en lumière les caracteristiques... de la personne dont on parle... La formule empêche la vie de se manifester, et, en fin de compte, c'est contre la vérité même que se tournent les préceptes des anciens qui avaient été la proclamation de ses droits.' (*Les Arts Poétiques*, pp. 77–9.)

'The traditional motive in medieval verse and rhetorical manuals for using the portrait was the creation of an elaborate poetic amplification. Even though it was a non-organic artistic entity, poets never employed it in unexpected places. Descriptions of men and women were given when they first appeared in the action of a story, or when an account of their beauty could explain the attraction of one character for another. Although purely artificial in effect, the verse portrait was used with a certain dramatic and psychological propriety.' (*PQ* 17, p. 220) Cf. Haselmayer's article in *RES* 14 (1938), 310–14, 'The Portraits in Chaucer's Fabliaux': 'The portrait or *effictio* was a device of medieval rhetoric and was employed universally by poets in a variety of art forms in order to produce a *surface impression of elaborate and decorative brilliance* ... Artificial in representation, it did not attain any elasticity of form or freedom of diction in the many centuries of its poetic use.' (My italics.)

Even in antiquity, the figure was put to more interesting uses than these writers suggest. The *Rhetorica ad Herennium* has a brief, but vivid and distinctive example of *effictio* (the portrayal of appearance) and a brilliant example of *notatio* (character delineation), depicting the behaviour of a man who wishes to be thought rich (ed. Caplan, IV 50ff.). The development of the figure in this way shows how its possibilities had always been realised, but this particular example cannot strictly be cited as a precedent for the techniques of the *Prologue*, since the conception which dominates the portrait is a man's 'studium', or ruling passion, rather than his work and social status. It is interesting to note that, in this work, the list of types that can be described refers almost entirely to outlines of innate character – 'the envious or pompus man', etc. (IV 51, 65ff.), wheras a similar list in Matthew of Vendôme classifies entirely by external situation – cleric or emperor, girl or old woman, etc. (*Les Arts Poétiques*, p. 120, 46).

10. Ed. A. Baehrens, *Poetae Latini Minores*, V (Teubner, Leipzig, 1888), pp. 320–1, 85–98. For evidence of Chaucer's acquaintance with this elegy, see G. L. Kittredge, 'Chaucer and Maximian', *Am. Jour. Phil.* 9 (1888), 84–5.

11. *PL* CLXXI, col. 1655. I have corrected the punctuation slightly. The poem goes on to marvel at the paradox that vice (homosexual love) can make one virtuous (chaste with regard to women). (For the translation of 'membra cum succo', see Donatus' *Commentary on Terence*, ed. P. Wessner (Teubner, Leipzig, 1902), vol. I, p. 339, *ad Eun* II 3, 27: '*suci plenum* est interior pinguedo membrorum' (318). I am grateful to Dr Michael Lapidge for this reference.)

12. *JEGP* 55, pp. 431–6.

13. I, p. 268, 5178; p. 269, 5184, 5195; p. 270, 5206, 5210; p. 271, 5223, 5231; p. 273, 5260; p. 274, 5279; p. 275, 5286.

14. Cf. *General Prologue* 446, 659, and a whole series in the Pardoner's portrait. Chaucer also uses 'But' in a different way in the *Prologue*, for conversational liveliness, suggesting a contrast or opposition which the material does not really warrant (see 142, 182, 284, 401, 692).

15. In fact, although he is often simply elaborating Dares, at some points, such as the Jason–Medea episode, he is introducing new material. Cf. Dares' *De Excidio Troiae Historia*, ed. F. Meister (Teubner, Leipzig, 1873), translated, together with Dictys Cretensis, by R. M. Frazer, *The Trojan War*, (Bloomington and London, 1966).

16. I, pp. 263–4, 5093–106. This statement is taken from Dares.

17. *MLN* 40, p. 11.

18. pp. 70–6 (men), and pp. 87–9 (women).

19. R. Klibansky, E. Panofsky and F. Saxl, *Saturn and Melancholy* (London, 1964), pp. 110ff.

20. pp. 70–1. For cases where Chaucer's portraits show particular affinities with the tradition represented by Hildegard, see the chapters on the Franklin and the Pardoner.

21. *Chaucer and the Mediaeval Sciences*, Chapter 4.

22. Bowden, *Commentary*, pp. 174ff.

23. Lowes, *Convention and Revolt in Poetry*, pp. 41–5.

24. See the quotations from Faral and Haselmayer above, and *The Golden Mirror*, pp. 325ff.

25. Later, Matthew lists eleven attributes by means of which a person can be described: 'nomen, natura, convictus, fortuna, habitus, studium, affectio, consilium, casus, facta, orationes' (*Les Arts Poétiques*, p. 136, 77). This list is derived from Cicero's *De Inventione*, I 24–5 (*Opera Rhetorica*, vol. I, ed. G. Friedrich (Teubner, Leipzig, 1884), and as Cicero himself says, some of these aspects of a person are only with difficulty defined, or distinguished from each other (p. 140, 16–22). Matthew illustrates each aspect by one- or two-line quotations from classical authors, rather than by lengthy portraits. Despite the fact that this analysis seems to invite a 'realistic' approach to portraiture, it does not seem likely that it would have influenced Chaucer so much as the fully-developed examples of literary portraiture.

26. *Les Arts Poétiques*, pp. 122–5, 51–2. Matthew himself discusses the way in which the individual names in these portraits stand for types (p. 132, 60).

27. pp. 123–4, 52, 9–42. See my discussion of the Clerk and Friar for this tradition in connection with scholars.

28. Matthew himself, echoing *Aeneid*, VI 853, comments that the role of a priest is 'Parcere subjectis et debellare superbos' (p. 133, 65). See also the section on the Parson.

29. *Les Arts Poétiques*, p. 121, 50, 11–12.

30. *Ibid.*, 17–18.

31. E.g. as an example of description *a patria* Matthew gives:

> Aurum Roma sitit, dantes amat, absque datore
> Accusativis Roma favere negat. (*ibid.*, p. 137, 82)

32. 31, 1, pp. 132ff. The MS in which it is found is No 115 of St-Omer (fols. 97ff.), a large and important thirteenth-century collection of Latin verse, from the abbey of Clairmarais, near St-Omer, where it was probably written (*ibid.*, p. 50). There is no evidence of this poem being known or copied anywhere else, but this is unimportant; I am not trying to establish that Chaucer was influenced by it, simply that the union between formal description and estates material could be made by a writer as easily as the union between formal description and the Seven Deadly Sins.

33. *Ibid.*, p. 134, 33–50. I have re-punctuated slightly.

CHAPTER 9

1. E.g., G. L. Kittredge says Chaucer endows each pilgrim 'with an individuality that goes much beyond the typical', although he adds, 'If we had only the Prologue, we might, perhaps, regard the Pilgrims as types' (*Chaucer and his Poetry*, p. 154). R. K. Root's statement that 'It is by their successful blending of the individual with the typical that the portraits of Chaucer's *Prologue* attain so high a degree of effectiveness' (*Poetry of Chaucer*, p. 161), is quoted approvingly by J. R. Hulbert ('Chaucer's Pilgrims', repr. Wagenknecht, p. 24). W. H. Clawson comments: 'Each of the pilgrims . . . is revealed in such sharp and clear detail that we feel personally acquainted with him or her as an individual, and at the same time we recognise him as representative, not only of a social class, but of a type of character which may be recognised in any country and in any age.' ('Framework of the Canterbury Tales', repr. Wagenknecht, pp. 13–14). R. Baldwin says that Chaucer sensed, 'as did none of his contemporaries, the person as an artistic compromise between the extremes of type and individual' (*Unity of the Tales*, p. 43). P. F. Baum repeats, 'Each figure is in its way a type and also an individual' (*Chaucer*, p. 67).

2. *Poetry of Chaucer*, p. 161.

3. *Pace* Root, she is not, but is typical of commonplace traits in a medieval (and, apparently, modern) stereotype of woman.

4. *Geoffrey Chaucer*, p. 163.

5. Root side-steps this difficulty by saying that 'The details enumerated nearly always *suggest* at once the individual and the type' (*Poetry of Chaucer*, p. 161).

6. *Chaucer the Maker*, pp. 103–20.

7. *Unity of the Canterbury Tales*, p. 49.

8. *Of Sondry Folk*, p. 22.

9. See for example, G. H. Cowling, *Chaucer* (London, 1927), p. 153: 'other portraits are so realistic that they must have been drawn from life'.

10. Writers who assume that individualisation consists in the addition of details to a generalised outline include Patch, 'Characters in Medieval Literature', p. 13: 'The man of the fourteenth century would have recognised many an old friend here, with, however, just the proper touch – a peire of bedes, a garment, or a feature – to combine the individual with the typical.'; Hulbert, 'Chaucer's Pilgrims', repr. Wagenknecht, pp. 25 and 27; 'When one considers that the Monk is a man of wealth (the references to the cost of his hunting and his expensive dress), keeper of a cell, lover of hare-hunting, and likely to become an abbot, one recognises elements which are not generally typical.'; Baum, *Chaucer*, p. 67: 'Each figure is . . . an individual in that each is given particular marks: the Cook's ulcer, the Franklin's colouring, the Shipman's barge, the Reeve's identification with Norfolk, the Pardoner's with Rouncival, and so on'; Fisher, *John Gower*, p. 293, talks of

the 'brilliant individualising strokes (*juxta Bathon*, deafness, weaving, spurs)' in the Wife's portrait.

Benjamin Boyce recognises that 'Chaucer chose his pilgrims first on a basis of social and professional, not moral, classification', and seems to imply that the professional type is basic to the portraits, and the moral and astrological or physiological classifications subsidiary – but he too thinks that Chaucer 'vitalised the types', in Kittredge's phrase, 'by using concrete details': 'why else the Summoner's "Questio quid iuris," the Wife's deafness, the Prioress' brooch, and, worst of all, that shocking mormal on the Cook's shin?' (*The Theophrastan Character in England to 1642* (London, 1967), pp. 58–62.)

D. W. Robertson offers an exception to this critical consensus; he comments on 'the use of iconographic details as a means of calling attention to an underlying abstract reality' (*Preface to Chaucer*, p. 247). He does not, however, consider the estates type in his discussion of this underlying abstract reality, nor does he suggest how our impression of the individuality of the characters is produced.

11. Rosemary Woolf has made a similar critical point with special reference to the role of the narrator, whose 'obtuse innocence' causes him to accept the immoral premises from which the pilgrims speak. The narrator relates general facts about the classes 'as though they were both inoffensive and idiosyncratic, and in this way both the satiric point and *the illusion of individuality* are achieved.' (My italics.) Again, she comments, 'to search for historical prototypes of the characters is to be deceived by the brilliant accuracy of Chaucer's sleight-of-hand, whereby he suggests an individuality which is not there' ('Chaucer as a Satirist', p. 152). (I am much indebted to Miss Woolf's article, although I should like to modify some of its statements.) D. S. Brewer also implies that our 'sense of individuality' in the pilgrims derives more from techniques such as 'including snatches of conversation, and . . . describing in many cases the opinion, usual activities, or dwelling place of a person' than from concrete details (*Chaucer*, p. 134). E. T. Donaldson also calls our sense of the reality of the *Prologue* figures an 'illusion' but declines to suggest how it is produced (*Chaucer's Poetry: an anthology for the modern reader* (New York, 1958), p. 874).

12. *Poetry of Chaucer*, p. 161.

13. For observations on the way in which a growing sense of individual motives and points of view in the twelfth century is connected with the growing importance of the estates concept in the same period, see J. Le Goff, 'Métier et profession d'après les manuels de confesseurs au Moyen Âge', in *Beiträge zum Berufsbewusstsein des Mittelalterlichen Menschen*, ed. P. Wilpert, *Miscellanea Medievalia*, vol. 3 (Berlin, 1964), pp. 44–60.

14. An exception might seem to be the presence of the victim in the Friar's portrait, in the form of the 'sike lazars' he neglects; we come very close

to abandoning the Friar's viewpoint here, but do not quite do so because the whole passage is clothed in the Friar's own terminology, not the narrator's, and we see the lepers from the Friar's point of view, not *vice versa*. In the Reeve's portrait, the situation is reversed; we do see the Reeve from the point of view of the 'hynes'.

15. M. F. Bovill, 'The Decameron and the Canterbury Tales: a comparative study' (unpublished, Oxford B. Litt. thesis, 1966), p. 60.

16. This is the distinction usually drawn; see, for example, Baum, *Chaucer*, p. 70, who says we are struck by the 'earnestness of the one and the detachment of the other . . . Langland is not amused. His sense of humour is as keen as Chaucer's, but unlike Chaucer's it is often bitter and barbed; it does not titillate. It exposes the comic and ridiculous without smile or laughter.' Cf. also Woolf, 'Chaucer as a Satirist', pp. 154–5.

17. The lack of correlation between the moral status of the pilgrims and our response to them, seems to be implied in Patch's statement that Chaucer 'didn't necessarily like best' his ideal characters (*On Rereading Chaucer*, p. 155).

18. Other comparisons could be made. Are we prepared to accept, for example, that Chaucer thinks it morally worse for the Pardoner to be a homosexual than for the Shipman to be a murderer? Is it worse for the Reeve to terrify his underlings than for the Wife of Bath to be sexually promiscuous? The impossibility of answering these questions indicates that there is no systematic moral scale determining our likes and dislikes in the *General Prologue*; attempts to find the *moral* grounds on which, for example, the Pardoner can be shown to be the worst of the pilgrims as well as the most disgusting, are strained and unconvincing (see G. Ethel, 'Chaucer's Worste Shrewe: the Pardoner', *MLQ* 20 (1959), 211–27).

19. This paradoxical situation characterises the whole work: see especially p. 45 fol. 21*b*, 26ff., and p. 55, fol. 27*b*, 11ff.

20. *PPl* v 82–3 and 192. Even with Langland, this is not always true; the Doctor of Divinity who is as 'rody as a rose' is a case in point (XIII 99).

21. See especially E. T. Donaldson's article, 'Chaucer the Pilgrim', reprinted in *Speaking of Chaucer* (London, 1970), pp. 1–12.

22. The concentration on means rather than ends has been held by sociologists to be characteristic of the social ethic of societies dominated by economic markets, and particularly of capitalism. See Max Weber, *Economy and Society* (trans. G. Roth and C. Wittich, 3 vols., New York, 1968), especially vol. 3, p. 1188: 'under capitalism . . . a person can practice *caritas* and brotherhood only outside his vocational life'. The ideology of capitalism has taken as its starting-point the division of labour, and implicitly assumed that the sum of each group's activities will be the social good. Therefore it has not considered it necessary to analyse the nature of this good or the way in which it was to be achieved. This raises the question of whether

Chaucer felt the need to alter estates literature in order to express his consciousness that market relationships were assuming a new importance in his society, although the ironic tone which characterises the *Prologue* suggests that Chaucer is not *encouraging* the adoption of a capitalist ethic. Similar social characteristics have been especially associated with the city in a classic article by Louis Wirth (*American Journal of Sociology*, 34 (1938), 1–24):

> Our acquaintances [in the city] tend to stand in a relationship of utility to us in the sense that the role which each one plays in our life is overwhelmingly regarded as a means for the achievement of our own ends... The segmental character and utilitarian accent of interpersonal relations in the city find their institutional expression in the proliferation of specialized tasks which we see in their most developed form in the professions. The operations of the pecuniary nexus lead to predatory relationships, which tend to obstruct the efficient functioning of the social order unless checked by professional codes and occupational etiquette.

Some further comments of Wirth's on the city also have striking resemblances with the world conjured up by the *General Prologue*:

> The city... tends to resemble a mosaic of social worlds in which the transition from one to the other is abrupt. The juxtaposition of divergent personalities and modes of life tends to produce a relativistic perspective and a sense of toleration of difference.

Chaucer may equally well, therefore, be recording a response to the kind of social relationships which were increasingly dominating the growing city of London. In some ways, the ethic of city life and the market ethic are indistinguishable – but the attempt to distinguish which of them is likely to have had most influence on Chaucer, and what contemporary events might most clearly have focussed for him a change in social consciousness, are questions I should like to pursue elsewhere.

23. Quoted by J. F. Benton, 'Clio and Venus: An Historical View of Medieval Love' in F. X. Newman (ed.), *The Meaning of Courtly Love* (New York, 1968), p. 37. The quotation is taken from Buoncompagno's *Rhetorica Antiqua* which was written about 1215.

24. 'English Irony Before Chaucer', *UTQ* 6 (1937), 538–57.

25. For these senses see *OED* 2: 'Of persons: Distinguished by good qualities, entitled to honour or respect on this account; estimable', and 3: 'Of persons: Holding a prominent place in the community; of rank or standing'.

26. *MED* (2) – (perhaps too narrow a definition): 'Refinement of manners; gentlemanly or courteous conduct; courtesy, politeness, etiquette'. A. C. Cawley's gloss, 'gracious and considerate conduct' is better (see his edition of the *Canterbury Tales*, p. 2, n. to line 46).

27. 'Curteys' in this passage is glossed as 'Respectful, deferential, meek' by *MED* (3). It is important that the Squire 'proves' his 'curteisie' through his dexterous carving; this is an action which still has connotations of service to others, but to call this 'curteis' is half-way to applying the word to the refined table-manners of the Prioress.

28. *Literary Language*, trans. R. Manheim, p. 322.

29. 'Chaucer as a Satirist', p. 152.

30. I owe this comment to Dr L. P. Johnson of Pembroke College, Cambridge. In *Troilus and Criseyde*, Chaucer skilfully incorporates descriptions of both hero and heroine at moments when they will have storial significance; Troilus is described as he rides past Criseyde's window (II 624ff.), and his appearance strongly affects Criseyde's deliberations on her feelings towards his love. Criseyde herself is described at the moment when the affair is consummated (III 1247ff.), as an indication of the 'heaven' in which Troilus is delighting.

31. Bovill, 'The Decameron and the Canterbury Tales', p. 48. See also pp. 55ff. on Chaucer.

32. *The Poet Chaucer* (2nd edition, London, 1967), pp. 89–90.

33. II 449–62:

> Criseyde, which that wel neigh starf for feere,
> So as she was the ferfulleste wight
> That myghte be, and herde ek with hire ere
> And saugh the sorwful ernest of the knyght,
> And in his preier ek saugh noon unryght,
> And for the harm that myghte ek fallen moore,
> She gan to rewe, and dredde hire wonder soore,
>
> And thoughte thus: 'Unhappes fallen thikke
> Alday for love, and in swych manere cas
> As men ben cruel in hemself and wikke;
> And if this man sle here hymself, allas!
> In my presence, it wol be no solas.
> What men wolde of hit deme I kan nat seye:
> It nedeth me ful sleighly for to pleye.'

34. *In Search of Chaucer*, p. 67.

35. See Baldwin, *Unity of the Canterbury Tales*, Chapters 5–7, and A. W. Hoffman, 'Chaucer's Prologue to Pilgrimage: The Two Voices' repr. Wagenknecht, pp. 30–45.

36. These are Hoffman's terms. Hoffman's conception of the opposition between worldly and religious values is limited to the sphere of love. It seems to me that this is due to an interpretation of the spring-opening itself as particularly appropriate to love-poetry. It may therefore be worth noting that a spring-opening is found in all sorts of medieval poems:

estates works, battle-poems and satires all begin this way. See, for example, 'Quant vei lo temps renovellar' *PSE* p. 3, and 'Serpserat Angligenam rabies quadrangula gentem', *ibid.*, p. 19, a poem on the taking of Lincoln which beings with a lyrical spring description tending to the conclusion that in spring a Frenchman's fancy lightly turns to thoughts of war. Among satiric works, see the *Apocalipsis Goliae*, the *Metamorphosis Goliae* (ed. Huygens, *Studi medievali*, Ser. 3, III (1962), p. 765), the debates 'Dum Saturno conjuge' (*Map Poems*, pp. 237ff.) and 'Hora nona sabbati' (*NE* 32, I pp. 289ff.), the *Vox Clamantis* and *Piers Plowman*. One might even ask whether the opening of the *Metamorphosis Goliae* – 'Sole post Arietem Taurum subintrante' – is echoed in Chaucer's opening in the season when the sun 'Hath in the Ram his halve cors yronne'. The spring description is sometimes burlesqued in satire, but not necessarily for its associations with love: see *SS* 449ff., and 'Or vint la tens de May, que ce ros panirra', *PSE* pp. 63ff. (R. Baldwin discusses the tradition of the spring-opening (*Unity of the Canterbury Tales*, pp. 21ff.), and comments that 'even the satirist' uses it, but does not follow up this remark.)

APPENDIX B

1. Printed in K. Sisam (ed.), *Fourteenth-Century Verse and Prose* (Oxford 1921), pp. 160–1.
2. Flügel, 'Chaucer's Prolog', and Fisher, *John Gower*, Chapter 5. For line references of the detailed correspondence between the two writers, see these works, supplemented by my discussion of the *Prologue* portraits.
3. Chaucer had already used this technique to good effect in *Troilus and Criseyde* (I 132–3, V 826).
4. Langland's concern with the world is later expressed in a different way when the pilgrimage to Truth is delayed for the ploughing of Piers's half-acre (VI 3ff.).
5. See, besides the portraits of the Seven Deadly Sins in Passus V, the description of Hawkin, XIII 224ff., especially 300ff.
6. The original notion seems to derive from New Testament passages; see Matt. 7: 13–14, and Heb. 11: 13–16. It is, of course, the basis of Deguileville's *Pélerinage de la Vie Humaine* and is found incidentally in other authors (e.g., Gilles li Muisis, II p. 67 – one of many instances).
7. For a discussion of Sercambi's possible influence on the *Canterbury Tales*, see *SA* pp. 20–81.
8. Professor Bennett makes this suggestion in the article cited below.
9. *John Gower*, pp. 204, 301.
10. Respectively, in 'Two Notes', pp. 89–94, and 'Chaucer's Contemporary', in Hussey (ed.), *Piers Plowman*, pp. 310–24.

Selected Bibliography and List of Works Cited

The bibliography is in three parts. Part I lists the main sources of evidence used in Chapters 2–8. They are dealt with separately according to language. Within each section, major works are discussed in chronological order. Short poems or prose pieces are listed alphabetically by the *incipit* or title that is used to identify them in the course of this study; cross-reference to Appendix A will show if they are written on a strict estates pattern – that is, in the form of a list of social classes. Details of modern editions are given in Part II of the bibliography, while Part III contains secondary works.

Part I does not pretend to be a complete bibliography of medieval estates literature; for further references, see the works by Alter, Langlois, Lenient and Mohl cited in Part III (b) below. Unless otherwise indicated, the information in Part I is derived from the editions cited or from standard works of reference such as the *Tusculum Lexikon*, the *Dictionnaire des Lettres Françaises*, and Wells's *Manual of the Writings in Middle English 1050–1400* (see Part III (a) below). For manuscripts, see the relevant catalogues in P. O. Kristeller, *Latin Manuscript Books Before 1600*.

I

LATIN

The earliest estates work used in this study is the *Praeloquia* of *Rather, Bishop of Verona* from 931 onwards (*PL* 136). After holding his bishopric for a few years, Rather was deposed for his supposed implication in an attempt by a Bavarian Duke to seize the kingdom of Italy, and imprisoned in Pavia, where he composed the *Praeloquia*, a moral treatise which is also a self-justification. For a discussion of Rather and this work, see Auerbach, *Literary Language and its Public*, pp. 133ff. Auerbach judges that Rather was 'by far the most interesting and important Latin writer of his time' (p. 152), and it may well be that his original mind devised the question-and-answer form by which he introduces the duties of each estate, rather in the manner of the later *sermones ad status*.

The next important group of texts all belong to the great flowering of Latin secular literature in the twelfth century. *Walter of Châtillon* (ed. Strecker), 'one of the most important figures among the secular poets of the Middle Ages', was also one of the most influential (Raby, *Secular Latin Poetry*, vol. 2, pp. 190–204; see also K. Strecker, 'Walter von Chatillon, der Dichter der Lieder von St Omer', *ZfDA* 61 (1924), 197–222). The surviving MSS attest the steady popularity of Walter's writing: of those listed and dated by Strecker, ten are of the thirteenth century, one of the thirteenth to the fourteenth century, and five of the fourteenth century. Nine of the twenty-three manuscripts listed by Strecker are English. Not all of these MSS contain a complete collection of Walter's poems, and poems No VIII ('Dilatatur inpii regnum Pharaonis'), and No XVII ('Versa est in luctum') do not occur in any English MS. Poems No I ('Tanto viro locuturi'), II ('Propter Sion non tacebo'), III ('In domino confido'), IV ('Stulti cum prudentibus'), V ('Multiformis hominum'), VI ('Missus sum in vineam') and XVIII ('Dum Galterus egrotaret') seem, from the surviving MSS, to have had the widest circulation in England.

Walter had a large number of imitators, and several of the other poems used in this study belong to his school. They are all discussed by Strecker in 'Walter von Châtillon und seine Schule', *ZfDA* 64 (1927), 97–125 and 161–89.

The *Speculum Stultorum* (ed. Mozley and Raymo) was written by an Englishman, *Nigel of Longchamps*, in 1179–80, and was from the outset a favourite source of quotation and anecdote for medieval authors (see Mozley and Raymo's edition, pp. 2 and 8). It reached the height of its popularity in the late fourteenth and early fifteenth centuries, to which period all but one of the many extant manuscripts belong. Boccaccio, Gower and Chaucer all knew and used the work (see Mozley and Raymo, *loc. cit.*, and *CT* VII 3312–16). The interpolation on the friars (Mozley and Raymo, Appendix A) was of course inserted later, and is extant in one fourteenth-century manuscript and three fifteenth-century ones (*ibid.*, p. 8).

The *De Planctu Naturae* of *Alanus de Insulis* (ed. Wright, *Anglo-Latin Satirical Poets*) is another twelfth-century Latin work known to Chaucer who refers to it by name in the *Parlement of Foules* (316–17; see also Kittredge, 'Chaucer and Alanus de Insulis', p. 483). Although Alanus' work is moral satire rather than estates satire, it has close links with some of the material and techniques of estates writers, and therefore provides useful supplementary evidence at points.

Much of the twelfth-century satire in Latin is attributed by later periods to *Walter Map*; although these attributions are unlikely to be true, we have one authentic work of his, the *De Nugis Curialium* (ed. James), written between 1181 and 1193 (see James, p. xxviii). This work exists in only one late fourteenth-century manuscript, and was apparently neglected by other authors until the seventeenth century. However, the MS (Bodley 851: SC 3041) is a large and important one, which also contains several Goliardic poems, including the *Apocalipsis Goliae*, the *Speculum Stultorum*, the *Geta* and a large part of *Piers Plowman* (see Skeat's edition, Introduction, p. lxxi).

Numerous twelfth- and early thirteenth-century Latin satires are collected in the *Carmina Burana* (ed. Hilka and Schumann), the famous MS now Munich Clm 4660, which is of the first third of the thirteenth century (see B. Bischoff, *Faksimile-Ausgabe der Handschrift der Carmina Burana und der Fragmenta Burana* (2 vols., Munich, 1967), vol. 2, pp. 27–8).

Individual items from the *Carmina Burana* collection which appear in my discussion are the following:

No. 1. 'Manus ferens munera'
Also *Map Poems*, pp. 226ff. In numerous MSS. The pages of the *Carmina Burana* MS were disordered when found, and the first page lost; Wilhelm Meyer identified the last strophe, which was all that remained of the first poem in the collection, with v. 4 of the poem printed by Wright (*Nachrichten von der Gesellschaft der Wissenschaft zu Göttingen*, phil./hist. klasse (1908), p. 189). Strecker thought at one stage that the poem was by Walter of Châtillon, but later re-assigned it to his 'school'. (*ZfDA* 61 (1924), p. 214 and 64 (1927), p. 188.)

No 5. 'Flete perhorrete lugete pavete dolete'
This poem exists in several twelfth-century MSS (see the *Carmina Burana* edition). Most of it is identical with a part of the *Vita sancti Bertini metrica* of the abbé Simon, composed 1136–48. See F. Morand, *Collection de Documents Inédits sur l'Histoire de France* (Paris, 1873), vol. I, pp. 30ff., and B. Hauréau, *Des Poèmes Latins Attribués à Saint Bernard* (Paris, 1890), pp. 35–7. Hauréau assumed that the *Vita* was the source of the lines; Hilka and Schumann show that they are a separate entity, and must have been inserted into the *Vita* (*CB* II p. 7).

No 6. 'Florebat olim studium'

No 8. 'Licet eger cum egrotis'
A poem by Walter of Châtillon.

No 11. 'In terra summus rex est hoc tempore Nummus'
Appears in very many MSS, sometimes with slight differences in the first line (see Walther's *Initia*, and add to Hilka and Schumann's list of MSS another described by Lehmann, *Historische Vierteljahrsschrift*, 30 (1935–6), 37).

No 33. 'Non te lusisse pudeat'
Found in several MSS besides that of the *Carmina Burana*, the earliest being twelfth-century.

No 36. 'Nulli beneficium/iuste penitudinis'
In two MSS besides that of the *Carmina Burana*.

No 39. 'In huius mundi patria regnat idolatria'
Mid-twelfth-century (see *CB* II p. 68).

No 43. 'Roma, tue mentis oblita sanitate'

No 44. Gospel According to the Mark of Silver
A prose piece of enormous popularity in the Middle Ages, which was
expanded and altered by several later writers. It consists of a cento of
biblical quotations, satirising the Roman curia. See Lehmann, *Die
Parodie im Mittelalter*, pp. 32ff., and the three versions printed by him,
pp. 183ff.

No 91. 'Sacerdotes mementote/nihil majus sacerdote'
Also in *Map Poems* pp. 48ff. There are many MSS of this poem, dating
from the twelfth to the fifteenth century.

To the thirteenth century belongs the *Chessbook* (*Solacium ludi scacorum
sive Liber de moribus hominum*) of *Jacobus de Cessolis* (ed. Vetter). This
work is, as its name indicates, a moralised explanation of chess, and is
organised on formal estates principles, each piece standing for a different
social class. It was composed *ca.* 1275, enjoyed enormous popularity
in the Middle Ages, and was translated into many languages. An
English version was not produced before Caxton's fifteenth-century
translation, but there were two French translations in the fourteenth
century. A. van der Linde's list of the manuscripts of all the different
versions mentions almost eighty Latin MSS. (*Geschichte und Literatur
des Schachspiels* (2 vols., Berlin, 1874) vol. 1, *Beilagen*, pp. 19ff.)
   Van der Linde's list seems to have been drawn from catalogues, and
is rather confusingly presented. The MSS of the French versions are
given on pp. 114ff. Vetter's text, which is printed below the fuller
German version of Kunrat von Ammenhausen, is based mainly on one
MS, with several others used for comparison (see Vetter's edition,
col. 25-6). Most of the MSS of the Latin version of the *Chessbook*
prove, on checking with the catalogues, to be fifteenth-century;
however, there is at least one fourteenth-century MS in an English
library which van der Linde has missed (London BM Royal 12 E XXI).
It seems at any rate very likely that a work of such extensive popularity
would have been available to Chaucer in either its Latin or its French
form.
   At the other extreme, as far as diffusion is concerned, are the
Sermones nulli parcentes (ed. Karajan), which we know from only one
fourteenth-century MS (Berlin, oct. germ. 138, foll. 17ff.), where they
are accompanied by a German version. The *Sermones* are also organised

on a formal estates basis, with one chapter for each class. Karajan thought that the Latin poem was thirteenth-century, although the German translation is probably a century later (*ZfDA* 2 (1842), 9).

Finally, we have the major Latin estates work of *John Gower*, the *Vox Clamantis* (ed. Macaulay), composed around 1374–85 (see Fisher, *John Gower*, Chronology of the Writings of Gower and Chaucer). This is a work which Chaucer, from his friendship with Gower, almost certainly knew well, but as we have seen, it is not the only piece of Latin estates writing that he knew or was likely to have known.

'A legis doctoribus lex evacuatur'
'Sermo Goliae ad Praelatos', *Map Poems*, pp. 43ff. Wright's text is taken from Flacius Illyricus (*Varia...de corrupto Ecclesiae statu poemata* (Basle, 1557), p. 152), which was the only source for the poem until H. Walther found it incorporated as the central section in a longer poem, 'Pastores ecclesie, principes inferni', and printed it in this version. Walther dates the poem to the twelfth to thirteenth centuries (*Historische Vierteljahrsschrift*, 28 (1933), 522–34).

Apocalipsis Goliae
Inc: 'A tauro torrida lampade Cinthii', ed. Strecker. This poem was one of the most popular Latin satires of the Middle Ages; it survives in almost seventy MSS. By far the largest number of these MSS originate in England, and it is quite probable that the author was English. There is no way of dating the poem precisely, but style and content assign it to 'the era of Alanus, Walter of Châtillon and Walter Map' (Strecker, p. 8).

'Clerus et presbyteri nuper consedere'
'Consultatio Sacerdotum', *Map Poems*, pp. 174ff. Probably English, about 1200. (See Lehmann, *Die Parodie im Mittelalter*, pp. 112ff, and Walther, *Streitgedicht*, pp. 143ff.)

'Crux est denarii potens in saeculo'
'De Cruce Denarii', *Map Poems*, pp. 223ff.
In two sixteenth-century MSS, but must, as Wells suggests, be much earlier than this (*Manual*, 1 p. 239).

'Cum declinent homines a tenore veri'
'De Avaritia et Luxuria Mundi', *Map Poems*, pp. 163ff.

Belongs to the school of Walter of Châtillon, and may well be by Walter himself. (See Strecker, *ZfDA* 64 (1927), 169ff.)

'Cum sint plures ordines atque dignitates'
'Goliae Versus de Praelatis', *Map Poems*, pp. 44ff.
Like 'Crux est denarii', this poem must be older than the MS in which it survives, which appears from the contents to be sixteenth-century (London BM Cotton Vespasian A xix fol. 55v.).

'Dum pater abbas filiam/suam proponit visere'
'De Visitatione Abbatis', *Map Poems*, pp. 184ff.
In one thirteenth-century MS, London BM Arundel 139 fol. 39.

'Dum Saturno conjuge partus parit Rhea'
'De Clarivallensibus et Cluniacensibus', *Map Poems*, pp. 237ff.
Found in only one MS, London BM Sloane 1580 fol. 24v. Walther dates the poem as thirteenth-century, and earlier than 'Nuper ductu serio', because in the latter poem the Cistercian concedes that his order is declining from its original high standards – not a very convincing reason (*Streitgedicht*, p. 164).

'Ecce dolet Anglia luctibus imbuta'
'On the Pestilence', *PPS* I pp. 279ff. Also *PSE*, Appendix, pp. 400ff.
Found in one fourteenth-century MS (Cambridge UL Ee vi 29 fol. 27r), and dated around 1391 by Wright, who interprets its complaint about the 'pestilence' killing men and beasts as a reference to the great plague of that year. However, as Wright notes, the versification is that of a much earlier period, and it seems to me that the reference to a plague may well be the reason for it being copied, rather than composed, in the late fourteenth century.

'Filia, si vox tua'
Ed. J. Feifalik, *Sitzungsberichte der kaiserlichen Akademie der Wissenschaften in Wien*, phil./hist. klasse, 36 (1861), 169–70.
An estates poem not cited in my discussion, in which a mother proposes as husband for her daughter a knight, monk, peasant, cleric, in turn, and has all of them rejected in favour of a student. The poem was printed by Feifalik from a fifteenth-century MS written in Prague, and also survives in another from Czechoslovakia (see Dronke, *Medieval Latin*, vol. 2, p. 580).

'Frequenter cogitans de factis hominum'
'Des diverses classes d'hommes', *Poésies Pop. Lat.*, ed. du Méril, pp. 128ff.; from MS Notre Dame 133, now Paris BN 17656 (twelfth-century). Also printed by du Méril from MS Douai 702 (now 751) in *Poésies inédites du Moyen Age* (Paris, 1854), pp. 313ff., and by W. Stubbs from MS Phillipps 11604 in his introduction to William of Malmesbury's *De Gestis Regum Anglorum* (2 vols., Rolls series 90, London, 1887–9), vol. I, pp. cviiiff.; the Phillipps MS formerly belonged to the church of St Martin at Tournai. The poem is also found in two twelfth-century MSS: BN nouv. acq. lat. 264, and BM Add. 39646 (see the British Museum catalogue under this MS for a discussion of some of these MSS and their relationships), and a thirteenth-century MS, BN 8865.

'Heu! quia per crebras humus est vitiata tenebras'
John Gower, 'De Lucis Scrutinio', ed. Macaulay, pp. 355ff. In several MSS; Macaulay dates the poem in the late 1390s (p. lvii).

'Hora nona sabati tempore florenti'
NE 32, 1, pp. 289ff. (also in *Map Poems*, pp. 251ff.)
In several MSS, at least two of them thirteenth-century.

Magister Golyas de quodam abbate
Map Poems, pp. xlff.
From MS Digby 53 fol. 27 v. (SC 1654), a late twelfth-century MS written at Bridlington (see Ker, *Medieval Libraries of Great Britain*). For a discussion see Lehmann, *Die Parodie im Mittelalter*, pp. 137ff.

Metamorphosis Goliae
Inc.: 'Sole post Arietem Taurum subintrante', ed. Huygens, *Studi medievali* ser. 3, III (1962), pp. 764ff. (also in *Map Poems*, pp. 21ff.).
Survives in two MSS, one English, of the thirteenth-century (BM Harley 978), and the other fourteenth-century and French (St-Omer 710).

'Meum est propositum gentis imperite'
Ed. Strecker, *Studi medievali*, n.s. I (1928), 386ff. (also in *PSE*, pp. 206ff.).
There are three MSS, all of them English. The poem cannot be later than the end of the thirteenth century, the date of the earliest MSS,

and although its subject is 'timeless', Strecker believes it to be earlier than 1250 (*op. cit.*, p. 383) and to belong to the school of Walter of Châtillon (*ZfDA* 64 (1927), p. 180).

'*Noctis crepusculo brumali tempore*'
'De Malis Monachorum', *Map Poems*, pp. 187ff.
There are five MSS, the earliest being thirteenth-century.

'*Nuper ductu serio plagam ad australem*'
'De Mauro et Zoilo', *Map Poems*, pp. 243ff.
The poem is found in one thirteenth century MS, and is dated at the end of this period by Walther (*Streitgedicht*, p. 161).

'*Prisciani regula penitus cassatur*'
'De Concubinis Sacerdotum', *Map Poems*, pp. 171ff.
There are several MSS of this poem, which was written about 1200 (see Lehmann, *Die Parodie im Mittelalter*, pp. 112ff.).

'*Quam sit lata scelerum et quam longa tela*'
'Song on the Corruptions of the Times', *PSE* pp. 27ff.
Belongs to the school of Walter of Châtillon. There are two thirteenth-century MSS; the poem itself is probably twelfth-century (see *ZfDA* 64 (1927), 178ff., and C. L. Kingsford, *EHR* 5 (1890), 311ff.).

'*Rumor novus Angliae partes pergiravit*'
'De Convocatione Sacerdotum', *Map Poems*, pp. 180ff.
An English poem, written *ca.* 1200 (see Lehmann, *Die Parodie im Mittelalter*, pp. 112ff.). It survives in two MSS (one of the thirteenth and one of the fourteenth century).

'*Sompno et silentio plusquam satis usa*'
'Discipulus Goliae de Grisis Monachis', *Map Poems*, pp. 54ff.
The poem is found in one MS, and is assigned to the thirteenth century by Walther (*Streitgedicht*, p. 165).

'*Tempus acceptabile, tempus est salutis*'
AH XXXIII pp. 292ff. (also in *Map Poems*, pp. 52ff.).
This poem is found in a large number of MSS from the thirteenth to the fifteenth centuries.

'*Totum regit saeculum papa potestate*'
'De Diversis Ordinibus Hominum', *Map Poems*, pp. 229ff.

This poem survives in two MSS, BM Cotton Titus A xx fol. 159v. (a fourteenth-century collection of Latin *comediae* and Goliardic verse, including the *Speculum Stultorum* and the *Apocalipsis Goliae*) and Oxford Rawlinson B 214 fol. 173v. (a large fifteenth-century MS, containing several satiric pieces). A sixteenth-century hand in the Cottonian MS ascribes the poem to Robert Baston, a poet who flourished under Edward I and II. Mohl (*The Three Estates*, p. 25) places the poem in a group written during the reigns of Henry II, Henry III and Edward III; it cannot however be earlier than the thirteenth century, since it includes friars in its list of estates.

'*Viri venerabiles, sacerdotes Dei*'
Hauréau, *NE* vi pp. 13ff. (also in *Map Poems*, pp. 45ff.).

There are many MSS of this poem, a large proportion of them English. They date from the thirteenth to the sixteenth centuries, and Hauréau assigns the poem to the twelfth to thirteenth centuries (*NE* vi p. 13).

'*Viri fratres, servi Dei*'
AH xxxiii pp. 269ff. (also in *Poésies Pop. Lat.*, ed. du Méril, pp. 136ff.; see also the references to Roth and Wattenbach below).

This poem is found in a large number of fifteenth-century MSS. However it also appears in at least two MSS of the fourteenth century: Cod. Palat. Vindobon. 883, and a Darmstadt MS from which it was printed by F. W. E. Roth (*Romanische Forschungen*, 6 (1891), 8–16). Wattenbach, who also printed the poem from a fifteenth-century MS compiled by a Hungarian monk in a Prussian monastery, considered it characteristic of an earlier period – probably thirteenth century (*Monumenta Lubensia*, Breslau 1861, p. 20).

FRENCH

The earliest French estates work discussed in this study is the *Livre des Manières*. It was probably written by *Étienne de Fougères*, bishop of Rennes, formerly chaplain of the English king, Henry II (see Langlois, *La Vie en France*, pp. 1–2). The work, which was written in the 1170s (*ibid.*, p. 7), survives in only one MS (see Kremer, p. 76). There is, however, evidence that it had some influence on at least one later

French satirist (see A. Långfors, 'Étienne de Fougères et Gautier de Coinci', *Neuphilologische Mitteilungen*, 46 (1945), 113–22).

In the early thirteenth century (between 1204 and 1209), *Guiot de Provins* wrote his *Bible* (ed. Orr). Our knowledge of Guiot, and of the date when he was writing, are derived solely from his works; he appears to have been a monk, but, as Langlois says (*La Vie en France*, p. 31), a very odd one. His *Bible* is lively and literate, and he adopts a humorous personality which is far from the conventional idea of the moral satirist. Although we have only two MSS of the work, we know also of the former existence of five others.

The *Roman de Carité* of the *Renclus de Moilliens* (ed. van Hamel) was dated by its editor as late twelfth century (Introduction, pp. clxxxiff.), but was more probably composed *ca.* 1226 (see Langlois, *La Vie en France*, p. 116, and Gröber, *Grundriss der Romanischen Philologie*, II p. 697). The *Roman*, and the *Miserere*, also by the Renclus de Moilliens, were extremely popular. Twenty-five MSS of the *Roman de Carité* survive, not counting fragments, and van Hamel shows that this is probably just a fraction of what once existed (p. vi). For the probability that Chaucer himself knew this work, see G. L. Kittredge, 'Chaucer and the Roman de Carité', *MLN* 12 (1897), col. 113–15.

A work which Chaucer certainly knew, since he had translated it (see *Legend of Good Women*, F 329/G 255), is the *Roman de la Rose* (ed. Lecoy). It is not, of course, an estates work, but it contains much incidental satire on the estates, particularly on women and friars. Part I of the *Roman* (up to line 4028) was written *ca.* 1225–30 by Guillaume de Lorris, and Part II was added by Jean de Meun about forty years later (see Lecoy, I pp. vi–viii).

The writings of *Gautier de Coincy* (1177/8–1236: see Nurmela, *Annales Academiae Scientiarum Fennicae*, Ser. B, XXXVIII pp. 5–6) are rich in incidental satire on the estates, but I have been unable to consult the Abbé Poquet's edition of Gautier's *Miracles de la Sainte Vierge* (Soissons, 1857). Since this is in any case an unreliable edition, I have used E. Lommatzsch's summary of Gautier's social satire, *Gautier de Coincy als Satiriker*, for supplementary evidence to statements made in my discussion. I have also made use of two individual works of Gautier, which have been re-edited in recent times: *La Chastée as Nonnains*, ed. Nurmela, *Annales Academiae*, and *Les Miracles de Notre Dame de Soissons*, ed. Lindgren, *Annales Academiae Scientiarum Fennicae*, Ser. B, CXXIX. For a bibliography, description of manuscripts, and discussion of Gautier's life and work, see A. P. Ducrot-Granderye, 'Études sur les

Miracles Nostre Dame de Gautier de Coinci', *Annales Academiae Scientiarum Fennicae*, Ser. B, xxv.

Another work which provides useful evidence of estates stereotypes, although not itself written on an estates basis, is the *Jeu de la Feuillée* of *Adam de la Halle* (ed. Rony). It was probably written about 1277 (*ibid.*, p. 6).

Another famous thirteenth-century French writer, *Rutebeuf* (ed. Faral and Bastin), has left two estates poems, 'L'État du Monde' (written a little before 1265), and 'La Vie du Monde' (1285) – see Faral and Bastin, pp. 383 and 389.

In the late thirteenth or early fourteenth century, the Anglo-Norman writer Nicholas Bozon composed two works containing social satire. The *Char d'Orgueil* has only incidental satire on social classes, but the *Lettre de l'Empéreur Orgueil* is a poem constructed on estates principles, satirising the domination of Pride in all classes. (Both are edited by Vising, *Göteborgs Högskolas Årsskrift* xxv, 1919.) The *Lettre* was probably written between 1291 and 1310 (see Vising, p. ix), and survives in two MSS (*ibid.*, p. xxi).

In the fourteenth century, we have the *Roman de Fauvel* of *Gervais du Bus* (ed. Långfors), a popular work surviving in twelve MSS (not all complete). Gervais himself tells us that the first part of the *Roman* was completed in 1310, and the second part in 1314. For the success of the work abroad, and its influence on *Renart le Contrefait*, see Långfors, pp. cixff.

In the first half of the fourteenth century, Jean de Condé composed a 'Dis des Estas dou Monde' (ed. Tobler; for the date see *Dictionnaire des Lettres Françaises*, vol. I, p. 410). The MS from which Tobler prints the work is fourteenth-century, and also contains the *Roman de la Rose*.

Renart le Contrefait (ed. Raynaud and Lemaître), the last important version of the *Roman de Renart*, was composed between 1319 and 1342. Besides incidental satire on the estates, it contains two important pieces of formal estates satire (Fourth Branch, II pp. 27ff., and pp. 41ff.), in which Renart first looks back on the professions he had practised, and then surveys the occupations that he might henceforth pursue. The work exists in only two MSS, representing two versions of the poem; version A was written 1319–22, version B (which is published by Raynaud and Lemaître) was written 1328–42.

Renart le Contrefait is an original and sophisticated satire; the same cannot be said of the estates poems of *Gilles li Muisis* (ed. Kervyn de Lettenhove), the perusal of which Langlois understandably found 'écoeurant' (*La Vie en France*, p. 308). Gilles, who was abbot of the monastery of St Martin at Tournai, began writing when struck blind at the age of nearly eighty in 1350, and ceased again when he recovered his sight about eighteen months later. He tells us himself that he had read and admired the *Roman de la Rose*, and the works of the Renclus de Moilliens.

Around 1370, the *Lamentations of Matheolus* (ed. van Hamel) were translated into French by Jean le Fèvre. The work is mainly devoted to anti-feminist satire, but it concludes with a long piece of satire on the estates (Book IV, 283ff.). The Latin text, which the French expands, had been composed *ca.* 1290, but it was not very well known, although Deschamps read it (see van Hamel, II pp. clvff.). The French version was more popular; van Hamel refers to ten MSS. There is evidence that Chaucer was acquainted with this work; see A. K. Moore, 'Chaucer and Matheolus', *NQ* 190 (1946), 245–8.

Finally, in England, around 1374–85, Gower wrote his French estates work, the *Mirour de l'Omme*, which almost certainly influenced Chaucer (see Fisher, *John Gower*, Chronology of the writings of Gower and Chaucer, and Chapter 5).

'Le Dit des Mais'

Inc.: 'Rome du mont est chief, ainsi est apelee' [Jubinal: 'Royne du mont ch'ier ainsi est apelée'], ed. Jubinal, *NR* I pp. 181ff.

The poet himself tells us that the date of this poem is 1324. It is contained in MS BN fr. 24,432, a large collection of fabliaux and poems.

'Le Dit des Patenostres'

Inc.: 'Dites vos patenostres pour toute sainte Eglise', ed. Jubinal, *NR* I pp. 238ff.

From the same MS as the above; the date of composition is given in the poem as 1320.

'Le Dit des Planètes'

Inc.: 'Pour ce que je voi grant partie', ed. Jubinal, *NR* I pp. 372ff.

From the same fourteenth-century MS as the two preceding poems.

'L'en puet fere et defere'

'On the King's Breaking his Confirmation of Magna Charta', *PSE* pp. 253ff. After the first stanza, this poem is completely written in English.

This poem is contained in two MSS, one of which is the Auchinleck MS (early fourteenth century), which Chaucer probably knew (see L. H. Loomis, 'Chaucer and the Auchinleck MS', in *Essays and Studies in Honour of Carleton Brown*, pp. 111–28).

'Li Mariages des Filles au Diable'
Inc.: 'Seignour, cis siecles ne vaut rien', ed. Jubinal, *NR* 1 pp. 283ff.
A thirteenth-century poem (see *Hist. litt. de la France*, XXIII, p. 118) contained in two thirteenth-century MSS, one of which (Paris, Arsenal 3142) also includes the *Roman de Carité*.

'L'Ordre de Bel Ayse'
Inc.: 'Qui vodra a moi entendre', ed. Aspin, pp. 130ff.
This poem is dated *ca.* 1300 by Aspin, who also thinks that the author was English. It is found only in MS Harley 2253.
Aspin thinks it would be difficult to prove the existence of direct links between the several satiric treatments of an 'ideal' monastic order.

'Mult est diables curteis'
'Sur Les États du Monde', ed. Aspin, pp. 116ff.
From MS Gonville and Caius College Cambridge 435, and probably, like the MS, of the first half of the thirteenth century (Aspin, *loc. cit.*).

'Nous lisons une istoire, ou fable'
'Des Estats du Siècle', ed. Montaiglon and Raynaud, II pp. 264ff.
I have not been able to date this poem precisely; it is contained in one MS, Bibl. de Genève man. fr. 179 foll. 37–8.

ENGLISH

The first work in English to concern us is the *Ancrene Wisse* (ed. Tolkien). The rule which is the basis of this work was first written *ca.* 1200, and the version that we now have can be dated *ca.* 1225–35 (see G. Shepherd, *Ancrene Wisse*, *Parts 6 and 7* (London, 1959), pp. xxiii–iv). There are several English MSS of this work, and versions of it in French and Latin. For its popularity, and some evidence of its influence, see H. E. Allen, 'Some Fourteenth Century Borrowings from "Ancren Riwle" ', *MLR* 18 (1923), 1–8, partially corrected in *MLR* 19 (1924), 95. The *Ancrene Wisse* is, however, only of incidental use to us since moral satire is only a part of it.

Moral satire looms larger in *Robert Mannyng*'s translation of the Anglo-Norman *Manuel des Péchés*, *Handlyng Synne* (ed. Furnivall). Mannyng gives the date of his translation as 1303. The work survives in two fourteenth-century MSS. It is not based on an estates framework, but it contains a good deal of incidental satire on social classes.

'The Simonie', on the other hand, has an estates framework (*Inc.*: 'Whi werre and wrake in londe and manslauht is i-come', *PSE* pp. 323ff.). There is good reason for thinking that Chaucer knew this poem; not only is its general popularity attested by the fact that it survives in three versions (for the other two, see H. C. Hardwick, *A Poem on the Times of Edward II* (Percy Soc. XXVIII, London, 1849) – from MS Peterhouse, Cambridge, 104, and T. W. Ross, 'On the Evil Times of Edward II: A New Version from MS Bodley 48', *Anglia*, 75 (1957), 173–93), but one of them is contained in the Auchinleck MS (Nat. Lib. Scotland 19. 2. 1), which Chaucer very probably knew (see L. H. Loomis, 'Chaucer and the Auchinleck MS', in *Essays and Studies in Honour of Carleton Brown*, pp. 111–28). Ross dates the poem itself during the middle or last years of Edward II ('Edward II', p. 174).

Winner and Waster (ed. Gollancz), which is dated 1352 from internal evidence, contains incidental satire on the estates.

Of major importance, though not based on a formal estates framework, is *Piers Plowman* (ed. Skeat). The B text, which is the version generally cited in my discussion, was written in the 1370s. Langland's own knowledge of Goliardic satire is apparent from his writing, and the list of estates that he includes is of unparalleled richness. For the tentative suggestion that this fullness of detail is due to the influence of the sermon tradition, see Owst, *Lit. and Pulp.*, pp. 586ff.

In 1388, we have the sermon that *Thomas Wimbledon* preached at St Paul's Cross, which was obviously influenced in part by an estates form (ed. Owen, *Medieval Studies*, 38 (1966), 176ff.). This sermon survives in numerous fifteenth-century MSS; on its popularity, and the identity of its author, see Owen, *Medieval Studies*, 24 (1962), 377–81.

Pierce the Ploughmans Crede (ed. Skeat), a work mainly devoted to satire of the friars, was written about 1394. It is therefore too late for evidence of what influenced Chaucer, but perhaps gives an indication of popular stereotypes relatively free from Chaucer's influence (see however the chapter on the Friar, p. 44).

The same applies to *Mum and the Sothsegger* (ed. Day and Steele), which was written 1403–6. Where these works reveal the influence of Langland and Chaucer, they provide evidence that later writers interpreted *Piers Plowman* and the *General Prologue* as part of a tradition that could still be carried on.

'*Ich herde men vpo molde make muche mon*'
'Klage des Landmanns', ed. Böddeker, *Altenglische Dichtungen*, pp. 102ff. (also in *PSE* pp. 149ff.).
The poem is from MS Harley 2253, and was probably written at the end of the thirteenth or the beginning of the fourteenth century (Wells, *Manual*, vol. 1, p. 229).

'*Land of Cokaygne*'
Inc.: 'Fur in see bi west Spayngne', ed. Bennett and Smithers, pp. 138ff.
Of Irish origin, and written in the thirteenth century (*ibid.*, p. 138). Only in one MS (BM Harley 913).

'*Syngyn y wolde, but, alas!*'
'On the Times', *PPS* I pp. 270ff.
In four MSS; appears from internal evidence to have been written in 1389 (see G. Matthew, *The Court of Richard II* (London, 1968), p. 26).

OTHER WORKS

I have cited two major Italian works, the *Divine Comedy* and Boccaccio's *Decameron*. For Chaucer's knowledge of Dante, see J. L. Lowes 'Chaucer and Dante', *MP* 14 (1916–17), 705ff. His acquaintance with the *Decameron* is disputed. H. M. Cummings thought it unlikely (*The Indebtedness of Chaucer's Works to the Italian Works of Boccaccio*, Univ. of Cincinnati Studies, x (1916), Chapter 9), as did Mario Praz (a paper reported in *English Studies*, 9 (1927), 81–2). On the late arrival of the *Decameron* at popularity in England, see W. Farnham, 'England's Discovery of the *Decameron*', *PMLA* 39 (1924), 123–39. For the view that Chaucer did know the *Decameron*, see T. H. McNeal, 'Chaucer and the *Decameron*', *MLN* 52 (1938), 257–8, and M. F. Bovill, 'The Decameron and the Canterbury Tales' (unpublished Oxford B. Litt. thesis, 1966).

Two important scientific works used in the discussion are the *Causae et Curae* of *Hildegard of Bingen* (ed. Kaiser), and the *Secreta Secretorum*. Hildegard's twelfth-century work survives in only one MS, and its usefulness therefore lies in its illustration of the diversity of the scientific tradition, and the development of a portrait form based on scientific material. The earliest English translation of the *Secreta* (MS Lambeth 501) was written shortly after 1400, but the translation made by James Yonge in 1422 (both ed. Steele), which is the one cited in my discussion, is in large part a direct translation of a thirteenth-century French version. For details of this and other versions of the *Secreta* that Chaucer might have known, see R. Tuve, *Seasons and Months: Studies in a Tradition of Middle English Poetry* (Paris, 1933), pp. 48–50.

I have also cited two major works written in medieval Germany. The first of these, the romance *Ruodlieb* (ed. Zeydel) is in Latin and was written in the eleventh century; it survives only in fragments. For the most recent critical discussion of the poem, see Peter Dronke, *Poetic Individuality in the Middle Ages* (Oxford, 1970), Chapter 2. The second, *Meier Helmbrecht* (ed. Gough), is in German, and was written in the thirteenth century. There is of course no reason for supposing that Chaucer knew either; they do, however, illustrate vividly the diffusion of certain stereotyped ideas and literary topics.

Estates material can also be found in abundance in sermons and confessional manuals. I have made full use of Owst, *Literature and Pulpit in Medieval England*, but there still remains to be covered a great deal of material with an estates framework. For references to *sermones ad status*, see Lecoy de la Marche, *La Chaire Française*, p. 253, and for references to confessional manuals organised on estates principles, see H. C. Lea, *A History of Auricular Confession and Indulgences* (London, 1896), vol. 1, p. 371, and D. W. Robertson jr, 'The Cultural Tradition of *Handlyng Synne*', *Speculum*, 22 (1947), 162–85, especially pp. 183ff.

Adam de la Halle *Le Jeu de la Feuillée*, ed. J. Rony, Paris, 1969.

Ancrene Wisse ed. J. R. R. Tolkien, EETS o.s. 249, London, 1962.

Apocalipsis Goliae, Die Apokalypse des Golias, ed. K. Strecker, Rome, 1928.

Aspin, I. S. T. (ed.) *Anglo-Norman Political Songs*, Anglo-Norman Text Society, XI, Oxford, 1953.

Ayenbite of Inwyt ed. R. Morris, EETS o.s. 23, London, 1886.

Baehrens, A. (ed.) *Poetae Latini Minores*, Teubner, 5 vols., Leipzig, 1879–88.

Bennett, J. A. W. and Smithers, G. V. (eds.) *Early Middle English Verse and Prose*, 2nd edition, Oxford, 1968.

Benoit de Ste-Maure *Le Roman de Troie*, ed. L. Constans, SATF, 6 vols., Paris, 1904–12.

Boccaccio, Giovanni *Teseida*, ed. S. Battaglia, Florence, 1938.

Decamerone, ed. V. Branca, 2nd edition, 2 vols., Florence, 1960.

Böddeker, K. (ed.) *Altenglische Dichtungen des MS. Harl. 2253*, Berlin, 1878.

Bozon, Nicholas *Deux Poèmes de Nicholas Bozon: Le Char d'Orgueil, La Lettre de l'Empéreur Orgueil, Göteborgs Högskolas Årsskrift*, 25 (1919).

Cawley, A. C. (ed.) *The Wakefield Pageants in the Towneley Cycle*, Manchester, 1958.

Chessbook, Das Schachzelbuch Kunrats von Ammenhausen nebst den Schachbüchern des Jakob von Cessole und des Jakob Mennel, ed. F. Vetter, Frauenfeld, 1892.

Game and Playe of the Chesse, trans. W. Caxton, 1474 (A Verbatim Reprint of the First Edition with an Introduction by W. E. A. Axon . . .), British Chess Magazine Reprints, n.d.

Clanvowe, John '*The Two Ways*: An Unpublished Religious Treatise by Sir John Clanvowe', ed. V. J. Scattergood, *English Philological Studies*, 10 (1967), 33–56.

Dante Alighieri *The Divine Comedy*, with translation and comment by J. D. Sinclair, rev. edition, 3 vols., London, 1958.

De Nugis Curialium – see Map.

Deschamps, Eustace *Oeuvres Complètes*, ed. G. Raynaud and Le Marquis de Queux de St-Hilaire, SATF, 11 vols., Paris, 1878–1903.

Dreves, G. M., Blume, C., and Bannister, H. M. (eds.) *Analecta Hymnica*, 56 vols., Leipzig, 1886–1922 (for satire, especially vols. 15, 21, 33) du Méril, E. (ed.) *Poésies Populaires Latines du Moyen Âge*, Paris, 1847.

Étienne de Fougères *Livre des Manières*, ed. J. Kremer, *Ausgaben und Abhandlungen aus dem Gebiete der Romanischen Philologie*, 39, Marburg, 1887.

Fairholt, F. W. (ed.) *Satirical Songs and Poems on Costume from the 13th to the 19th century*, Percy Society 27, London, 1849.

Flacius Illyricus, M. (ed.) *Varia doctorum piorumque virorum De corrupto Ecclesiae statu poemata*, Basle, 1557.

Gautier de Coincy *La Chastée as Nonains de Gautier de Coinci*, ed. T. Nurmela, *Annales Acadaemiae Scientiarum Fennicae*, ser. B, xxxviii, Helsinki, 1937.

Les Miracles de Notre Dame de Soissons versifiés par Gautier de Coinci, ed. L. Lindgren, *Annales Acadaemiae Scientiarum Fennicae* ser. B, cxxix, Helsinki, 1963.

Geoffroi de Charny *Le Livre de Chevalerie*, ed. J. B. M. C. Kervyn de Lettenhove, in *Oeuvres de Froissart*, vol. 1, part iii, Brussels, 1873, pp. 462–533.

'Le Livre Messire Geoffroi de Charny', ed. A. Piaget, *Romania*, 26 (1897), 394–311.

Gilles li Muisis *Poésies*, ed. J. B. M. C. Kervyn de Lettenhove, 2 vols., Louvain, 1882.

Gower, John *Complete Works*, ed. G. C. Macaulay, 4 vols., Oxford, 1899–1902.

The Major Latin Works of John Gower, trans. E. W. Stockton, Seattle, 1962.

Guibertus Tornacensis *Sermones ad status*, printed 'per magistrum Johannem de Uingle', 1511.

Guiot de Provins *Oeuvres*, ed. J. Orr, Manchester, 1915.

Handlyng Synne – see Mannyng.

Hardwick, H. C. *A Poem on the Times of Edward II* ['The Simonie'], Percy Society 28, London, 1849.

Hildegard of Bingen *Causae et Curae*, ed. P. Kaiser, Teubner, Leipzig, 1903.

Hilka, A., and Schumann, O. (eds.) *Carmina Burana*, 2 vols., Heidelberg, 1930–41; vol. 3, ed. B. Bischoff, Heidelberg, 1971.

Huygens, R. B. C. (ed.) 'Metamorphosis Goliae', *Studi medievali* ser. 3, iii (1962), 764–72.

Jean de Condé *Gedichte von Jehan de Condet nach der Casanatensischen Handschrift*, Bibliothek des Litterarischen Vereins in Stuttgart, liv, Stuttgart, 1860.

Jubinal, A. (ed.) *Nouveau Recueil de Contes, Dits, Fabliaux, et Autres Pièces Inédites des XIIIe, XIVe et XVe Siècles . . . d'Après les MSS. de la Bibliothèque du Roi*, 2 vols., Paris, 1839–42.

Langosch, K. (ed.) *Hymnen und Vagantenlieder*, Darmstadt, 1961.

Lordre de chevalerie ed. P. Allut, in *Étude . . . sur Symphorien Champier*, Lyons, 1859.

The Book of the Ordre of Chyualry translated by W. Caxton, ed. A. T. P. Byles, EETS o.s. 168, London, 1926.

Machaut, Guillaume *Oeuvres*, ed. E. Hoepffner, SATF, 3 vols., Paris, 1908–21.

Mannyng, Robert *Robert of Brunne's Handlyng Synne with those parts of the*

Anglo-French treatise on which it was founded . . ., ed. F. J. Furnivall, 2nd edition, EETS o.s. 119 and 123, London, 1901–3.

Map, Walter *De Nugis Curialium*, ed. M. R. James, Anecdota Oxoniensa, med. amd mod. ser., xiv, Oxford, 1914.

Walter Map's De Nugis Curialium, trans. M. R. James, ed. E. S. Hartland, London, 1923.

Matheolus *Les Lamentations de Matheolus et le Livre de Leesce de Jehan le Fevre*, Bibliothèque de l'École des Hautes Études 95–6, 2 vols., Paris, 1892–1905 (*Lamentations* in vol. 1).

Meier Helmbrecht: a poem by Wernher der Gartenaere, ed. C. E. Gough, Oxford, 1942.

Peasant Life in Old German Epics: Meier Helmbrecht and Der Arme Heinrich, trans. C. H. Bell, New York, 1965.

Migne, J. P. (ed.) *Patrologiae Cursus Completus*, series latina, 217 vols., Paris, 1844–

Montaiglon, A. de and Raynaud, G. (eds.) *Recueil Général et Complet des Fabliaux des XIIIe et XIVe Siecles*, 6 vols., Paris, 1872–90.

Mum and the Sothsegger ed. M. Day and R. Steele, EETS o.s. 199, London, 1936.

Myrc, John *Instructions for Parish Priests*, ed. E. Peacock, EETS o.s. 31, London, 1868.

Nigel de Longchamps *Speculum Stultorum*, ed. J. H. Mozley and R. R. Raymo, Berkeley and Los Angeles, 1960.

The Book of Daun Burnel the Ass: Nigellus Wireker's Speculum Stultorum, trans. G. W. Regenos, Austin, Texas, 1959.

A Mirror for Fools or the Book of Burnel the Ass, by Nigel Longchamp, trans. J. H. Mozley, Oxford, 1961.

Pierce the Ploughmans Crede ed. W. W. Skeat, EETS o.s. 30, London, 1867.

Piers Plowman ed. W. W. Skeat, 2 vols., London, 1886, reprinted with added bibliography, 1961.

Rather of Verona *Praeloquiorum Libri Sex*, PL 136.

Renart le Contrefait, Le Roman de Renart le Contrefait, ed. G. Raynaud and H. Lemaître, 2 vols., Paris, 1914.

Robbins, R. H. (ed.) *Secular Lyrics of the XIVth and XVth Centuries*, 2nd edition, Oxford, 1955.

Roman de Carité, Li Romans de Carité et Miserere du Renclus de Moilliens, ed. A. G. van Hamel, Bibliothèque de l'École des Hautes Études 61–2, 2 vols., Paris, 1885. [*Roman de Carité* in vol. 1.]

Roman de Fauvel, Le Roman de Fauvel par Gervais du Bus, ed. A. Långfors, SATF, Paris, 1914–19.

Roman de la Rose Guillaume de Lorris et Jean de Meun, *Le Roman de la Rose*, ed. F. Lecoy, 3 vols., CFMA, Paris, 1965–70.

Ross, T. W. (ed.) 'On the Evil Times of Edward II: A New Version from MS. Bodley 48', *Anglia*, 75 (1957), 173–93.

Ruodlieb: the Earliest Courtly Novel, ed. E. H. Zeydel, Chapel Hill, North Carolina, n.d.

Rutebeuf *Oeuvres Complètes*, ed. E. Faral and J. Bastin, 2 vols., Paris, 1959–60.

Secreta Secretorum, Three Prose Versions of the 'Secreta Secretorum', ed. R. R. Steele, EETS e.s. 74, London, 1898.

Sermones nulli parcentes 'Buch der Rügen', *ZfDA* 2 (1842), 6–92 (Lat. text pp. 14–45).

Speculum Stultorum – see Nigel of Longchamps.

Strecker, K. (ed.) 'Quid dant artes nisi luctum!' [edition of 'Meum est propositum'], *Studi medievali* n.s. 1 (1928), 380–91.

Tarbé, P. (ed.) *Poètes de Champagne Antérieurs au Siècle de François 1er*, 22 vols., Reims, 1847–63.

Walter of Châtillon *Moralisch-Satirische Gedichte Walters von Chatillon*, ed. K. Strecker, Heidelberg, 1929.

Watriquet de Couvin *Dits*, ed. A. Scheler, Brussels, 1868.

Wattenbach, W. (ed.) 'De fugiendo cetum feminarum rigmus', *Anzeiger für kunde der deutschen Vorzeit*, 17 (1870), col. 10.

Wimbledon, Thomas 'Thomas Wimbledon's Sermon: "Redde racionem villicacionis tue" ', ed. N. H. Owen, *Medieval Studies*, 28 (1966), 176–97.

Winner and Waster ed. I. Gollancz, 2nd edition, London, 1930.

Wright, T. (ed.) *The Political Songs of England from the Reign of John to that of Edward II*, Camden Society 6, London, 1839.

The Latin Poems Commonly Attributed to Walter Mapes, Camden Society 16, London, 1841.

A Selection of Latin Stories from Manuscripts of the Thirteenth and Fourteenth Centuries, Percy Society VIII, London, 1842.

Anecdota Literaria: a collection of short poems in English, Latin and French, illustrative of the literature and history of England in the thirteenth century, London, 1844.

Political Poems and Songs, Rolls series 14, 2 vols., London, 1859–61.

The Anglo-Latin Satirical Poets and Epigrammatists of the Twelfth Century, [contains Alanus de Insulis: *De Planctu Naturae*], Rolls series 59, 2 vols., London, 1872.

Alanus de Insulis: The Complaint of Nature (trans. D. M. Moffat), Yale Studies in English, vol. 36, New York, 1908.

Wright, T. and Halliwell, J. O. (eds.) *Reliquiae Antiquae: scraps from ancient manuscripts, illustrating chiefly early English literature and the English language*, 2 vols., London, 1845.

Wycliff, John *Select English Works of John Wyclif*, ed. T. Arnold, 3 vols., Oxford, 1869–71.

The English Works of Wyclif Hitherto Unprinted, ed. F. Matthew, EETS o.s. 74, London, 1880.

III

(A) WORKS OF REFERENCE AND EDITIONS OF CHAUCER

Bischoff, B. *Faksimile-Ausgabe der Handschrift der Carmina Burana und der Fragmenta Burana*, 2 vols., Munich, 1967.

Bossuat, R. *Manuel Bibliographique de la Littérature Française du Moyen Age*, Melun, 1951, with 2 supplements, 1955-61.

Brown, C. and Robbins, R. H. *The Index of Middle English Verse*, New York, 1943.

Bryan, W. F. and Dempster, G. *Sources and Analogues of Chaucer's Canterbury Tales*, New York, 1941.

Burke Severs, J. *A Manual of the Writings in Middle English 1050-1500*, 2 vols. so far, New Haven, Connecticut 1967-

Cawley, A. C. (ed.) Chaucer: *Canterbury Tales*, rev. edition, London and New York, 1958.

Crawford, W. R. *Bibliography of Chaucer 1954-63*, Seattle and London, 1967.

Dictionnaire des Lettres Françaises, vol. I, ed. R. Bossuat, L. Pichard, G. R. de Lage, Paris, 1964.

Griffith, D. D. *Bibliography of Chaucer 1908-1953*, Seattle, 1955.

Hammond, E. P. *Chaucer: a bibliographical manual*, New York, 1908.

Hauréau, B. (ed.) *Notices et Extraits de Quelques Manuscrits Latins de la Bibliothèque Nationale*, 6 vols., Paris, 1890-3.

Histoire Littéraire de la France par les religieux bénédictins de la congrégation de Saint-Maur, Paris, 1733-

Ker, N. R. *Medieval Libraries of Great Britain: a list of Surviving Books*, 2nd edition, London, 1964.

Kristeller, P. O. *Latin Manuscript Books Before 1600*, 3rd edition, New York, 1967-8.

Långfors, A. *Les Incipit des Poèmes Français Antérieurs au XVIe Siècle*, Paris, 1917.

Langlois, E. *Table des Noms Propres . . . dans les Chansons de Geste*, Paris, 1904.

Langosch, K. *et al. Geschichte der Textüberlieferung der antiken und mittelalterlichen Literatur*, vol. 2, Zurich, 1964.

Levy, R. *Chronologie Approximative de la Littérature Française du Moyen Âge*, Tübingen, 1957.

Manly, J. M. and Rickert, E. (eds.) *The Text of the Canterbury Tales*, 8 vols., Chicago, 1940.

Notices et Extraits des manuscrits de la Bibliothèque Nationale, et autres bibliothèques, Paris, 1787–

Robinson, F. N. (ed.) *The Works of Geoffrey Chaucer*, 2nd edition, London, 1957.

Skeat, W. W. (ed.) *Chaucer: Complete Works*, 7 vols., Oxford, 1894–7.

Tatlock, J. S. P. and Kennedy, A. G. *A Concordance to the Complete Works of Geoffrey Chaucer and to the Romaunt of the Rose*, Washington, 1927.

Tusculum Lexikon Grieschischer und Lateinischen Autoren des Altertums und des Mittelalters, rev. by W. Buchwald, A. Hohlweg, O. Prinz, Munich, 1963.

Walther, H. *Initia Carminum ac versuum Medii Aevi Posterioris Latinorum*, Göttingen, 1959.

Walther, H. (ed.) *Proverbia Sententiaeque Latinitatis Medii Aevi*, 5 vols. and index, Göttingen, 1963–7.

Wells, J. E. *A Manual of the Writings in Middle English 1050–1400*, New Haven, 1916, with 9 supplements, 1919–51.

(B) SECONDARY WORKS

Adams, G. R. 'Chaucer's *General Prologue*: A Study in Tradition and the Individual Talent', Ph.D. thesis, University of Oklahoma, 1962. *DA* 22, 2382.

Alter, J. V. *Les Origines de la Satire Anti-Bourgeoise en France: Moyen Âge – XVIᵉ Siècle*, Geneva, 1966.

Auerbach, E. *Literary Language and its Public in Late Latin Antiquity and in the Middle Ages*, trans. R. Manheim, London, 1965.

Baldwin, R. *The Unity of the Canterbury Tales*, *Anglistica* series, v, Copenhagen, 1955.

Baum, P. F. *Chaucer, A Critical Appreciation*, Durham, N.C., 1958.

'Chaucer's Puns', *PMLA* 71 (March 1956), 225–46.

'Chaucer's Puns: A Supplementary List', *PMLA* 73 (March 1958), 167–70.

Bennett, H. S. 'The Reeve and the Manor in the 14th Century', *EHR* 41 (1926), 358–65.

Biggar, R. G. 'Langland and Chaucer's Treatment of Monks, Friars, Priests', Ph.D. thesis, University of Wisconsin, 1961. *DA* 22, 1992.

Birney, E. 'Is Chaucer's Irony a Modern Discovery?' *JEGP* 41 (1942), 303–19.

Bloomfield, M. W. *The Seven Deadly Sins*, Michigan, 1952.

Borst, A. 'Das Rittertum im Hochmittelalter: Idee und Wirklichkeit', *Saeculum*, 10 (1959), 213–31 (translated in *Lordship and Community in Medieval Europe*, ed. F. L. Cheyette, New York, 1968).

Bovill, M. F. 'The Decameron and the Canterbury Tales: a comparative study', B.Litt. thesis, Oxford University, 1966.

Bowden, M. *A Commentary on the General Prologue to the Canterbury Tales*, 2nd edition, New York and London, 1967.

Boyce, B. *The Theophrastan Character in England to 1642*, London, 1967.

Brewer, D. S. *Chaucer*, 2nd edition, London, 1960.

Brewer, D. S. (ed.) *Chaucer and Chaucerians*, London and Edinburgh, 1966.

Bronson, B. H. *In Search of Chaucer*, Toronto, 1960.

Brooks, H. F. *Chaucer's Pilgrims: The Artistic Order of the Portraits in the Prologue*, London, 1962.

Chute, M. *Geoffrey Chaucer of England*, London, 1951.

Clawson, W. H. 'The Framework of the Canterbury Tales', *UTQ* 20 (1951), 137–54, repr. Wagenknecht, pp. 3–22.

Coghill, N. 'Two Notes on Piers Plowman', *Medium Aevum*, 4 (1935), 83–94. *The Poet Chaucer*, 2nd edition, London, 1967.

Colby, A. M. *The Portrait in Twelfth Century French Literature*, Geneva, 1965.

Coulton, G. G. *Five Centuries of Religion*, 4 vols., Cambridge, 1923–50.

Curry, W. C. *Chaucer and the Medieval Sciences*, 2nd edition, London, 1960.

De Riquer, M. *Història de la Literatura Catalana, Part Antiga*, 3 vols., Barcelona, 1964.

Dobiache-Rojdestvensky, O. *Les Poésies des Goliards*, Paris, 1931.

Donaldson, E. T. (ed.) *Chaucer's Poetry: an anthology for the modern reader*, New York, 1958.

Donaldson, E. T. *Piers Plowman: The C-Text and its Poet*, 2nd edition, London, 1966.

Dronke, P. *Medieval Latin and the Rise of European Love-Lyric*, 2nd edition, 2 vols., Oxford, 1968.

Elliott, R. W. V. *Chaucer's Prologue to the Canterbury Tales*, Oxford, 1960.

Fansler, D. S. *Chaucer and the Roman de la Rose*, New York, 1914.

Fisher, J. H. *John Gower: Moral Philosopher and Friend of Chaucer*, London, 1965.

Flügel, E. 'Some Notes on Chaucer's Prologue', *JEGP* 1 (1897), 118–35. 'Gower's Mirour de l'Omme und Chaucer's Prolog', *Anglia*, 24 (1901), 437–508.

Hoffman, A. W. 'Chaucer's Prologue to Pilgrimage: The Two Voices', *ELH* 21 (1954), 1–16, repr. Wagenknecht, pp. 30–45.

Hoffman, R. L. *Ovid and the Canterbury Tales*, University of Pa., 1966.

Hulbert, J. R. 'Chaucer's Pilgrims', *PMLA* 64 (1949), 823–8, repr. Wagenknecht, pp. 23–9.

Jones, H. S. V. 'The Plan of the *Canterbury Tales*', *MP* 13 (May 1915), 45–8.

Jordan, R. M. *Chaucer and the Shape of Creation*, Cambridge, Mass., 1967.

Kellogg, A. L. and Haselmayer, L. A. 'Chaucer's Satire of the Pardoner', *PMLA* 66 (March 1951), 251–77.

Kittredge, G. L. 'Chaucer and the *Roman de Carité*', *MLN* 12 (1897), col. 113–15. 'Chaucer and Alanus de Insulis', *MP* 7 (1910), 483. *Chaucer and his Poetry*, Cambridge, Mass., 1927.

Knowles, D. *The Religious Orders in England*, vol. 1, Cambridge, 1948.

Krog, F. *Studien zu Chaucer und Langland, Anglistische Forschungen*, vol. 65, Heidelberg, 1928.

Labande-Mailfert, Y. 'L'Iconographie des Laïcs dans la Société Religieuse aux XIe et XIIIe Siècles', *Atti della terza Settimana internazionale di studio Mendola 21–27 agosto 1965*, Milan.

Langlois, Ch.-V. *La Vie en France au Moyen Âge D'Après Quelques Moralistes du Temps* (Paris, 1908).

Lawlor, J. *Chaucer*, London, 1968.

Lawrence, W. W. *Chaucer and the Canterbury Tales*, New York and London, 1950.

Lea, H. C. *A History of Auricular Confession*, 3 vols., Philadelphia, 1896.

Lecoy de la Marche, A. *La Chaire Française au Moyen Age, Spécialement au XIIIe Siècle*, Paris, 1868.

Legge, M. D. *Anglo-Norman Literature and its Background*, Oxford, 1963.

Le Goff, J. 'Métier et Profession d'Après les Manuels de Confesseurs au Moyen Âge', *Beiträge zum Berufsbewusstsein des Mittelalterlichen Menschen*, ed. P. Wilpert, *Miscellanea Medievalia*, vol. 3, Berlin, 1964.

Lehmann, P. *Die Parodie im Mittelalter mit 24 ausgewählten parodistischen Texten*, 2nd edition, Stuttgart, 1963.

Lenient, C. *La Satire en France au Moyen Âge*, 2nd edition, Paris, 1883.

Lommatzsch, E. *Gautier de Coincy als Satiriker*, Halle a.S., 1913.

Loomis, L. H. 'Chaucer and the Auchinleck MS: "Thopas" and "Guy of Warwick" ', *Essays and Studies in Honour of Carleton Brown*, New York, 1940, pp. 111–28.

'Chaucer and the Breton Lays of the Auchinleck MS', *SP* 38 (1941), 14–33.

Lowes, J. L.

'Simple and Coy: A Note on Fourteenth Century Poetic Diction', *Anglia*, 33 (1910), 440–51.

Convention and Revolt in Poetry, 2nd edition, London, 1930.

Geoffrey Chaucer, Bloomington, 1958.

Lumiansky, R. M. *Of Sondry Folk: the Dramatic Principle in the Canterbury Tales*, Austin, 1955.

'Benoit's Portraits and Chaucer's General Prologue', *JEGP* 55 (1956), 431–8.

McPeek, J. A. S. 'Chaucer and the Goliards', *Speculum*, 26 (1951), 332–6.

Maeterlinck, L. *Le Genre Satirique dans la Peinture Flamande*, Brussels, 1907.

Malone, K. *Chapters on Chaucer*, Baltimore, 1951.

Manly, J. M. 'A Knight Ther Was', *Trans. Am. Phil. Assoc.*, 38 (1907), 89–107, repr. Wagenknecht, pp. 46–59.

Some New Light on Chaucer, London, 1926, repr. Gloucester, Mass., 1959.

Mathew, G. *The Court of Richard II*, London, 1968.

Menéndez Pidal, R. *Poesía Juglaresca y Orígenes de las Literaturas Romanicas*, 6th edition, Madrid, 1957.

Mohl, R. *The Three Estates in Medieval and Renaissance Literature*, New York, 1933.

Moore, A. K. 'Chaucer and Matheolus', *NQ* 190 (1946), 245–8.

Muscatine, C. *Chaucer and the French Tradition*, Berkeley and Los Angeles, 1964.

Neubert, F. *Die volkstümlichen Anschauungen über Physiognomik, Romanische Forschungen* 29 (1911), 557–679.

Owst, G. R. *Literature and Pulpit in Medieval England*, 2nd edition, Oxford, 1961.

Painter, S. *French Chivalry: Chivalric Ideas and Practices in Medieval France*, Baltimore, 1940.

Pantin, W. A. *The English Church in the Fourteenth Century*, Cambridge, 1955.

Patch, H. R. 'Characters in Medieval Literature', *MLN* 40 (1925), 1–14.

On Rereading Chaucer, Cambridge, Mass., 1959.

Peter, J. *Complaint and Satire in early English Literature*, Oxford, 1956.

Preston, R. *Chaucer*, London and New York, 1952.

Raby, F. J. E. *A History of Secular Latin Poetry*, 2 vols., 2nd edition, Oxford, 1957.

Robertson, D. W. jr 'The Cultural Tradition of *Handlyng Synne*', *Speculum*, 22 (1947), 162–85.

'Frequency of Preaching in 13th Century England', *Speculum*, 24 (1949), 376–88.

A Preface to Chaucer: Studies in Medieval Perspectives, Princeton, 1963.

Chaucer's London, New York, London, etc., 1968.

Rocher, D. ' "Chevalerie" et Littérature "Chevaleresque" ', (I) *Études Germaniques*, 21 (1966), 165–79; (II) *Études Germaniques*, 23 (1968), 345–57.

Root, R. K. *The Poetry of Chaucer*, London, 1906.

Ruggiers, P. G. *The Art of the Canterbury Tales*, Madison and Milwaukee, 1965.

Schaar, C. *The Golden Mirror: Studies in Chaucer's Descriptive Technique and its Literary Background*, Lund, 1955.

Schoeck, R. J. and Taylor, J. (eds.) *Chaucer Criticism*, 2 vols., Notre Dame, Indiana, 1960–1.

Speirs, J. *Chaucer the Maker*, London, 1964.

Strecker, K. 'Walter von Chatillon und seine Schule', *ZfDA* 64 (1927), 97–125 and 161–89.

Swart, J. 'The Construction of Chaucer's *General Prologue*', *Neophilologus*, 38 (1954), 127–36.

Tatlock, J. S. P. 'Chaucer and Wyclif', *MP* 14 (1916), 257–68.

The Mind and Art of Chaucer, Syracuse, 1950.

Thorndike, L. *A History of Magic and Experimental Science*, 8 vols., London, 1923–

Tristram, E. W. '*Piers Plowman* in English Wall-Painting', *Burlington Magazine*, 31 (1917), 135–40.

Tupper, F. *Types of Society in Medieval Literature*, New York, 1926.

'Twelfth-Century Scholarship and Satire', *Essays and Studies in Honour of Carleton Brown*, New York, 1940, pp. 46–61.

Utley, F. L. *The Crooked Rib: An Analytical Index to the Argument about Women in English and Scots Literature to the end of the Year 1568*, Columbus, 1944.

Wagenknecht, E. (ed.) *Chaucer: Modern Essays in Criticism*, New York, 1959.

Walther, H. *Das Streitgedicht in der Lateinischen Literatur des Mittelalters*, Munich, 1920.

Wiesen, D. *St Jerome as a Satirist*, Ithaca, New York, 1964.

Wirth, L. 'Urbanism as a Way of Life', *American Journal of Sociology*, 44 (1938).

Woolf, R. 'Chaucer as a Satirist in the *General Prologue* to the *Canterbury Tales*', *Critical Quarterly*, 1 (1959), 150–7.

Wulff, A. *Die Frauenfeindlichen Dichtungen in den Romanischen Literaturen des Mittelalters bis zum ende des XIII Jahrhunderts*, Romanistische Arbeiten, IV, Halle a.S., 1914.

Yunck, J. A. *The Lineage of Lady Meed: the development of medieval venality satire*, Notre Dame, Indiana, 1963.

Index

The index contains the names of the medieval authors and literary works, and of the modern critics and scholars, discussed or referred to on points of importance. On the whole the list of contents is taken to be a sufficient guide to the material covered by the book, but some analysis of references to medieval ideas about different social classes has been included, as have a few references to key literary techniques and to Middle English words whose usage is especially interesting.

The references will be found to take slightly differing forms, due to the separation of text and notes. If a work or writer is identified within the text, the page-number of the text alone is given. If a work or writer is discussed or quoted in the text, but only identified by the note, the page-number of the text and the number of the identifying note are given. If a work or author is merely cited in a note to support or clarify a general statement in the text, the page-number on which the note appears, and the number of the note, are given.

For medieval estates works, the index should be supplemented by reference to Part I of the bibliography.

Roman de la Rose—cont.
officials, 158; on pleasing one's
lover, 119, 120, 129, 133, 276 n. 1;
on gluttony, 279 n. 27; on lists of
medical authorities, 250 n. 27;
on table manners, 129; use of name
Robin in, 222 n. 36; verbal
resemblances in, to Chaucer, 38,
121, 230 n. 118, to Gilles li Muisis,
230 n. 118; influence on stereotype
of pardoner as well as friar, 278
n. 22
romance traditions, medieval, 12, 109,
128-9, 131, 133-5, 193
Romaunt of the Rose – see Roman de la
Rose
Root, R. K., 187, 189, 215 n. 17, 289
n. 1, n. 5
Ruodlieb, 241 n. 92, 243 n. 112, 268
n. 96, 274 n. 57, 282 n. 58
Rutebeuf, 159, 205, 220 n. 22, 224 n. 60,
224-5 n. 62, 230 n. 114, 231 n. 134,
233 n. 6, 236 n. 29, 249 n. 18,
253 n. 49, 254 n. 52, 256 n. 76, 261
n. 39

sailors – *see* shipmen
St Bernard, 108-9, 118, 259 n. 11, n. 14
St Francis, 39, 45
St Jerome, 39, 246 n. 146, 266 n. 78,
268 n. 97, 277 n. 10
sanguine man, the character of the, 156
Schaar, C., 177, 286 nn. 7-8
Secreta Secretorum, 156 n. 34, 163, 181,
280 n. 35, 283 n. 64
Secular Lyrics, 235 n. 21, 236 n. 31,
266 n. 82, 267 n. 90, 280 n. 35,
283 n. 62, n. 64
Sermones nulli parcentes: estates structure
of, 204; on friars, 225 n. 66, 228
n. 91, 237 n. 43; on priests, 234
n. 14, 238 n. 52 (*bis*); on peasants,
69, 71, 72, 229 n. 54, 241 n. 82;
on clerks and scholars, 75, 76, 81,
242 nn. 101-2, 243 n. 114; on
lawyers, 90, 248 n. 13; on doctors,
248 n. 13, 253 n. 44; on merchants,
253 n. 49, 254 n. 51, 255 n. 60; on
the bourgeoisie, 104 n. 75; on
knights, 261 n. 38; on crusaders,
259 n. 18, 260 n. 31; on women,
121; on nuns, 131, 270 n. 12, nn. 14-
15, n. 17
sermons, 8; on monks, 218 n. 2; on
friars, 226 n. 66; on priests, 64,
233 n. 6, 234 n. 12, n. 14, 235 n. 18,
236 n. 31, 237 n. 50, 238-9 n. 52
(*bis*), 242 n. 100, 264 n. 61; on
hunting clerics, 221 n. 29; on
peasants, 241 n. 87; on clerks, 244

n. 119; on lawyers, 248 n. 10,
249 n. 18; on doctors, 250 n. 25;
on merchants, 254 n. 49, n. 52, 255
n. 61, n. 63; on knights, 259 n. 16,
261 n. 38, 262 n. 39, 265 n. 68;
on squires, 264 n. 56, 265 n. 68; on
women, 266 n. 82, 267 n. 88; on
pardoners, 278 n. 22; on fops,
264 nn. 60-1, 277 n. 10; on
hospitality, 157-8; on 'punishing
purses', 275 n. 73; on beggars,
245 n. 134; on daggers, 257 n. 82;
on tight shoes, 268 n. 93; on feeling
for animals, 271 n. 31; on
chattering birds, 275 n. 76;
'manliness' in, 33, 158; 'worchyp' in,
157-8; *see also* Wimbledon, Thomas
sheriffs, 158-9
shipmen, fidelity and courage necessary
for, 170; associated with fraud and
murder, 170-1
'Simonie, The': estates structure of,
205-6; on monks, 19, 23, 34; on
friars, 230 n. 114, 231 n. 134; on
priests, 59 n. 15, 237 n. 49, 238-9
n. 52; on hunting parsons, 221
n. 29, 222 n. 33; on clerks, 245
n. 138; on lawyers, 88, 159, 249
n. 18; on doctors, 250 n. 25, 252
n. 38; on merchants, 253 n. 49;
on knights, 108, 109, 114; on
squires, 118 n. 56, 148; on
sheriffs and administrative officials,
159; on 'contours', 281 n. 43; on
consistory court officials, 140; on
fops, 148; on chattering birds,
275 n. 76
Sir Gawain and the Green Knight, 109
Sir Launfal, 133
Sit Deo gloria, 123 n. 83, 266 n. 82, 267
n. 88, 268 n. 95
Skelton, John, 215 n. 23, 249-50 n. 21
social stereotypes in estates literature,
the role of, 8-10; inconsistency of,
241 n. 82
Sompno et silentio, 222 n. 32, 224 n. 62
Speculum Stultorum: estates structure of,
203; on monks, 18 (*bis*), 21 n. 19,
29, 219 n. 12, 221 n. 28, 224 n. 62;
on secular canons, 237 n. 43; on
friars, 37 n. 67, 43 n. 104, 46 n. 114,
50 n. 132, 227 n. 80, 228 n. 91,
231 n. 131, n. 133, 232 n. 139; on
hunting bishops, 26, 132, 221 n. 29;
on priests, 56, 234 n. 14, 235 n. 21,
237 nn. 42-3, 238 n. 52 (*bis*); on
peasants, 67; on clerks and scholars,
76 n. 111, 81 and n. 130, 242 n. 104,
243 n. 114, 247 n. 150; on doctors,
250 n. 25; on merchants, 99; on

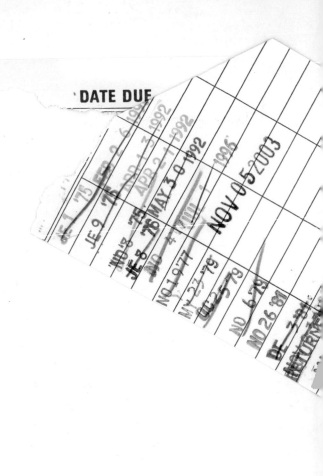